# STATE AUTONOMY OR CLASS DOMINANCE?

## SOCIAL INSTITUTIONS AND SOCIAL CHANGE
*An Aldine de Gruyter Series of Texts and Monographs*
EDITED BY
James D. Wright

# STATE AUTONOMY OR CLASS DOMINANCE?
## Case Studies on Policy Making in America

G. WILLIAM DOMHOFF

ALDINE DE GRUYTER
New York

## About the Author

G. William Domhoff is Professor of Psychology and Sociology at the University of California, Santa Cruz. Dr. Domhoff has authored or edited sixteen books, beginning with *Who Rules America?* (1969), and inclusive of this title. A complete list of the authors' books may be found on page viii.

ALDINE DE GRUYTER
A division of Walter de Gruyter, Inc.
200 Saw Mill River Road
Hawthorne, New York 10532

This publication is printed on acid free paper ∞

Library of Congress Cataloging-in-Publication Data

Domhoff, G. William.
    State autonomy or class dominance? : case studies on policy making
in America / G. William Domhoff.
        p. cm.
    Includes bibliographical references and index.
    ISBN 0-202-30511-2 (cloth : alk. paper) 0-202-30512-0 (paper : alk. paper)
    1. Elite (Social sciences)—United States.   2. Political
consultants—United States.   3. Business and politics—United
States.   4. Progressivism (United States politics)   5. United
States—Politics and government—1933–1945.   I. Title.
HN90.E4D6515   1996
305.5'2'0973—dc20                                                    95-42077
                                                                     CIP

Manufactured in the United States of America

10 9 8 7 6 5 4 3 2 1

# Contents

# Preface

The argument inspiring this book can be put very simply: who has more power in the United States, the federal government or the owners and managers of large income-producing property? I say the big property owners dominate the government, even on seemingly liberal issues like the Social Security Act of 1935, which gave Americans their pension system and welfare benefits. My designated opponents, the state autonomy theorists, say elected politicians and appointed officials run the show, with a little bit of help from liberal reformers and academic experts. I counter that the experts and politicians matter to some extent, but are secondary to the corporate rich, and I cite chapter and verse. Sometimes experts and government officials have a little room to maneuver, but most experts are less independent than state autonomy theorists imagine, and most elected officials are dependent on help from the corporate rich to win and stay in office. That goes for many Democrats as well as virtually all Republicans.

The terrain of disagreement will be the New Deal and the Progressive Era, when reformers and liberals probably had their greatest impact in American history. State autonomy theorists have based most of their claims on those eras, so that is where I have to engage them. The issues will be such important policy decisions as the origins of subsidy payments through the Agricultural Adjustment Act of 1933, the decline and fall of the National Recovery Administration between 1933 and 1935, the origins of the Social Security Act of 1935, and the importance of the military in shaping the industrial mobilization for World War II. The wide range of social legislation that was proposed during the Progressive Era also will be analyzed in an attempt to understand why some bills passed and some did not. Following the case studies, the final chapter will present an explanation for the great acclaim that was accorded to one state autonomy book on the Progressive Era by mainstream social scientists who are not of the state autonomy persuasion.

It would be ideal if I could base all of my critiques of case studies by state autonomy theorists on new empirical findings of my own doing. Although my previous books are grounded in network analysis, content analysis, archival digging, and interviews, I am not able to do original research as fast as state autonomy theorists can turn out their interpretative histories based on secondary sources. Thus, my original research for this book is primarily confined to my new analysis of the Social Security Act. However, I also present some new archival findings on the origins of the Agricultural Adjustment Act that contradict the claim by some state autonomy theorists that it was created by government economists who were working in the public interest. Moreover, we are not entirely at a loss for "new" information for the chapters where I could not do original research because there are sources that the state autonomy theorists overlooked as well as new studies since they wrote the claims I will critique.

Chapters 1, 2, 4, 5, and 8 are completely new efforts that were written especially for this book. Chapters 3 and 6 are extensively revised versions of earlier papers. Chapter 7 builds on a short book review–essay by adding much new material and extending it greatly. Due to the revisions and extensions of the three chapters that are based in previous work, the book is a seamless whole with a clear thesis and progression. This seamlessness was not difficult to accomplish because I envisioned this book when I was writing the earlier essays.

My deepest thanks to Harvey Molotch and an anonymous reader for Aldine de Gruyter for helpful comments that greatly shaped the tone of the book and sharpened my argument. I am also extremely grateful to Jeff Manza for very useful general discussions of many of the issues analyzed in this book and for his valuable reading of the final three chapters. Walter Goldfrank gave me very helpful commentary on the two final chapters, and Richard Hamilton was equally helpful on Chapters 6 and 7. I derived exceptional benefit from Gwendolyn Mink's extensive help on Chapter 7, for which I am deeply grateful. I thank the late Grant McConnell, Richard Kirkendall, Bill Friedland, and Michael Goldfield for their many useful substantive comments on an earlier version of Chapter 3, and Jordon Schwarz, Frank Kofsky, and Val Burris for their excellent suggestions on an earlier version of Chapter 6. I am grateful to Craig Reinarman for his invaluable comments on tone and substance in a very early version of what became this manuscript. The mistakes that remain are mine, but I hope the collective help of these fine colleagues and scholars has made the mistakes fewer and less glaring.

Setting the Stage

## INTRODUCTION

The 1980s saw the rise of a new school of thought on an issue of long-standing contention in the social sciences: the location and concentration of social power in the United States. Theorists in this school claimed that the American government (called "the state," as in European theorizing) is more independent ("autonomous") than previous analysts had realized. The old arguments about the relative power of corporate owners, unions, various interest groups, and politicians supposedly missed the point. Theorists who discussed such issues were dismissed as society-centric, which certainly sounds ominous enough. The state has interests and goals of its own, carried out by elected and appointed officials (sometimes called *state managers* or *state elites*). *State autonomy* and *state-centric* were the names chosen for themselves by these theorists in the 1980s, but the label later was changed to *structured polity approach,* and then to *historical institutionalism,* for reasons that will become apparent as the book unfolds.

Formally speaking, state autonomy theorists define the state as "any set of relatively differentiated organizations that claims sovereignty and coercive control over a territory and its population, defending and perhaps extending that claim in competition with other states" (Skocpol 1992:43). The "core organizations" of the state are said to be "the administrative, judicial, and policing organizations," although some states have "institutions of representative decision-making linked to their core organizations" (ibid.). Despite this emphasis on bureaucracies and coercion, it is said that the United States has been unusual because its state did not have much of a bureaucracy or army until recently, and its legislature has been more important than legislatures usually are. So too for its courts.

Whatever organizations are important in any given state, the important point to remember is that "politicians and administrators must be taken seriously" as "actors in their own right" because states are "sites of autonomous action, not reducible to the demands or preferences of any social group" (pp., 41–42). Anyone who does not accept this emphasis on the independent role of politicians and administrators in the case of the United States is trapped in the false cultural belief that America is a "stateless" society: "the American people and their social analysts lack a sense of the state" (pp. 42–43). By means of this claim about American culture, rival analysts are defeated before they put their data on the table by a subtle ad hominem argument: they cannot be taken seriously because they have not transcended their culture like the state-centric theorists have.

The idea of state autonomy is closely linked to that of *state capacity*, which is defined as "the extent to which state goals, however determined, can actually be carried out" (Finegold and Skocpol 1995:52). State capacity is in part determined by "organizational resources," which include the size of the budget and the educational level of employees, but it also includes the ability to manage such resources (p. 53).

When it comes to the United States, state-centric theorists also put strong emphasis on political parties as organizations for obtaining power that are closely related to the state system. The competition for votes between the two major parties gives ordinary citizens some leverage and leads to shifting coalitions of voters that are called *party alignments*. Party alignments are in turn closely related to *political strategies*, which are the political visions and appeals used by a party (pp. 40–41). Just as autonomy and capacity are the key variables in understanding the state, so too are alignments and strategies the key issues in understanding parties (pp. 23–24).

In making their pitch, the state autonomy theorists were reacting against a new school of Marxists who briefly climbed to the top of the theoretical hill in the 1970s, dispatching the previous combatants with a dialectical snap of the fingers. Quickly stipulating that, of course, capitalists inexorably and inevitably dominate the state for deep structural reasons having to do with the means of production and the nature of capitalism, these "structural Marxists" disparaged empirical research on the details of the power relationship between capital and the state. Instead, they debated the reasons for the "relative autonomy" of the state from the capitalists, arguing over the varying importance of systemic needs, the contradictions of capitalism, divisions within the capitalist class, and the potential power of the organized working class in creating this relative autonomy. But the structural Marxists and state autonomy theorists did agree on one issue: anyone who disagreed with them was blinded by their cultural beliefs.

Coming of age in this kind of atmosphere, state autonomy theorists stressed the "potential autonomy" of the state to distinguish themselves from all types of Marxists, thereby signaling that they did not see the state as an entity created to protect private property from slaves, serfs, peasants, or proletarians. They pointed to other times and places, like eighteenth-century France or nineteenth-century Russia, where states allegedly displayed considerable autonomy (e.g., Skocpol 1979). Then they set about reading existing accounts of nineteenth- and twentieth-century American, Canadian, and British history in search of "autonomous administrative organs," indepen-

dent bureaucracies, and other evidence of state autonomy in these countries. The claims they make about one of these countries, the United States,
will be my sole focus in this book.

The state autonomy theorists, led by sociologist Theda Skocpol and her
students, but soon drawing in other social scientists, came away from their
reading convinced they had found what they were looking for. In the process, they heaped scorn and doubt on the value of any empirical evidence
supporting corporate or class dominance, calling it misleading or superficial
(e.g., Skocpol 1980:162–63; 1986/1987). Since I collected some of that
evidence, and synthesized the rest of it into several books, I must protest
(e.g., Domhoff 1967, 1970, 1979, 1983, 1990). Nay, I must counterattack.

Well, the structural Marxists were gone by the late 1980s, many of them
abandoning Marxism altogether, and the state autonomy theorists were disappearing as a distinctive focus by the early 1990s. The idea of the American state having any significant degree of autonomy from the owners and
managers of banks, corporations, and agribusinesses is a theoretical mistake
based in empirical inaccuracies. In this book I will demonstrate this assertion with new findings and telling counterarguments.


## THE COUNTERATTACK

State-centric theorists make three main empirical assertions. First, the
federal government has a considerable degree of independence from social
classes and interest groups. Second, independent experts are important in
providing the state with policy advice and administrative capacity. Third,
the competition between the two parties leads them to be responsive to
voters, and in the process generates new political strategies and party alignments. In response to these claims, I will point to the three findings that most
clearly refute them:

First, the idea of state autonomy in the United States in the Progressive
and New Deal eras is massively contradicted by the immediate, direct, and
continuous role of large plantation owners in effecting federal policy
through the Democratic party and Congress. This may seem like an unusual
starting point given the usual emphasis of class dominance theorists on the
power of bankers and industrialists, but banker/industrialist power is often
mediated through foundations, think tanks, and policy discussion groups,
making the argument more indirect and harder to see at first glance. The
usefulness of southern plantation power for my purposes is that it was so
blunt, obvious, and brutal: the African-American work force was dealt with
by force and excluded from the voting booths, and the planters were often in
Congress, representing themselves. Whether as members of Congress or by

other means, they undeniably dominated key congressional committees when Democrats were in the majority. If this segment of the American capitalist class penetrated the state, as it indeed did, then it is all over for state autonomy theory from the outset.

Second, I will repeatedly show that the influence of the corporate rich over the experts celebrated by state autonomists is far more direct and limiting than they allow. This influence on experts is of both the carrot and stick varieties. For carrots the corporate rich offer foundation grants and positions at corporate-controlled think tanks, both of which are considered more lucrative, prestigious, and challenging than mere teaching at a university, except for an occasional graduate seminar. For sticks they have (1) replacement of dissident experts with more reasonable ones, (2) exclusion of dissidents from the policy discussion circles they finance, (3) demotions, and (4) firings. These carrots and sticks will be demonstrated throughout this book on specific cases.

Third, there are strong limits on the legislative responsiveness of political parties to voters. These limits are set by the need for financial donations and other types of support provided by wealthy property owners as well as by the incentives for tacit collusion between party leaders in a two-party system (e.g., Wittman 1973; Domhoff 1983:117–25). Perhaps most important of all for the years before the passage of the Voting Rights Act of 1965, a great many citizens in the South were excluded from participation in elections, making the party system a very imperfect instrument of popular expression (e.g., Key 1949).

In addition to pointing out the empirical and theoretical inaccuracies of the state autonomy theorists, I want to challenge the way they have been able to legitimate a style of work requiring virtually no original empirical research, instead relying almost exclusively on secondary sources in making new and controversial claims. I think this approach is the kiss of death for the development of sociology and political science, a strategy that will turn these disciplines into debating societies better labeled social studies or textual criticism. Originally, when she was studying the revolutions in France, Russia, and China, Skocpol explained her lack of research in primary sources by claiming that "the comparativist has neither the time nor (all of) the appropriate skills to do the primary research that necessarily constitutes, in large amounts, the foundations upon which comparative studies are built" (1979:xiv). More recently, now that she and other state autonomy theorists are studying countries where they have the requisite language skills, she has rationalized their use of secondary sources by claiming their work "is not different from survey analysts reworking the results of previous surveys" (1984:382). But to compare the use of secondary sources to reanalyzing original survey data is a grossly false analogy, as sharply pointed out by British sociologist John Goldthorpe: those who do secondary analysis are returning to the original data, whereas state autonomy theorists are doing what Goldthorpe calls "interpretations of interpretations of, perhaps, inter-pretations" (1991:224–25).

Even if we leave aside the problematic nature of reinterpreting interpreta-tions, secondary sources usually discuss the issues in contention between rival power theorists only tangentially because they are written for other purposes. Not even good descriptive histories aiming to be theoretically neutral can include everything. If they are political, diplomatic, or govern-mental histories, one thing they often do not include is information on the role of business leaders. This absence is then taken by state autonomy theorists as a confirmation of their theory. Not eager to find the owners and managers of plantations and corporations having an impact, they do not search for contradictory data, settling for what the secondary sources pro-vide them. I will be able to provide several good examples in later chapters of what this flawed investigative procedure overlooks.

By this point some readers may be asking, Isn't there at least a little something to what the state-centered theorists say about the United States? Yes there is, but no one ever denied the obvious fact that "state structures" and politics make at least some difference in this country. Except for the Marxists, everyone agrees to the "potential autonomy" of the state. That is why empiri-cal research was carried out in the first place, even though it is much harder work than armchair theorizing. But the federalized structure of American government, the separation of powers at the national level, the role of regulatory agencies, and the rules generating the strong tendency to a two-party system—all this and more were taken for granted as starting points by those who were studying the location and concentration of power in the United States before the rise of the state autonomy school. Nor is it news to say that each government institution comes with an operating manual, i.e., its own routines, customs, and procedures, such as the congressional committee structure, seniority system, and other accepted ways of doing legislative business developed over time (e.g., Potter 1972). The goal was to understand if and how class dominance operated in this governmental context.

To the degree that state autonomy theorists seem to have made a contri-bution, it is because they were able to switch the debate from a general interest in social power (which encompasses state power) to one of state power alone. In so doing, they have in fact repackaged many standard concepts from traditional studies of public administration and political par-ties within political science. But if the real issue is social power, as it is, then all they have done is to remind us of the obvious.

## CONCLUSION

My most general purpose in this book is to defend all society-centric theorists against the state autonomy theorists, but I also want to make the best case I can for the strongest version of that genre, the class dominance perspective. Although class dominance theory is often identified as an aspect of Marxian theory, this is not necessarily the case. A class dominance theory can be developed that is independent of claims about historical materialism, the labor theory of value, the historical pervasiveness of class conflict, the class conflict origins of the state, and the inevitability of socialism. It has been my goal to develop such a theory throughout the course of my work, and this book represents another step in that direction. In the next chapter I will provide a rigorous set of definitions, concepts, and power indicators that make class dominance theory refutable by empirical evidence.

# Defining and Testing the Class Dominance View

2

## INTRODUCTION

Now that I have introduced the two theoretical viewpoints that will be compared in this book, I want to provide a more detailed theoretical context for my class dominance view and then explain the several steps necessary for empirical studies of it. My most general assumption is that social power is rooted in organizations. I define organizations simply as sets of rules, roles, and routines developed to accomplish some particular purpose. I borrow this starting point from the two founding figures of systematic power studies in American sociology, Floyd Hunter (1953) and C. Wright Mills (1956), and even more from the new framework for thinking about power developed by Michael Mann (1986, 1993), whose many virtues I have extolled elsewhere (Domhoff 1990:chap. 1).

Since human beings have a vast array of "purposes," they have formed an appropriately large number of organizations. But only a few of these purposes and organizations weigh heavily in terms of generating social power. According to Mann's analysis, Western civilization and the current power configurations within it are best understood by determining the intertwinings and relative importance at any given time of organizations based in four "overlapping and intersecting sociospatial networks of power" (1986:1). These networks are labeled ideological, economic, military, and political, and placed in that particular order only because it makes for a handy memory device—IEMP. This lack of concern with order of presentation is possible because no one of these organizational networks is more fundamental than the others. Each one presupposes the existence of the others, which vindicates philosopher Bertrand Russell's (1938:10–11) earlier demonstration that power cannot be reduced to one basic form; in that sense, says Russell, power is like the idea of energy in the natural sciences.

This starting point immediately puts Mann at odds with schools of thought operating in terms of the ultimate primacy of historical materialism or the state, but it allows him to have agreements with the Marxists for some eras and the state autonomists for others. Mann's view thus puts an enormous emphasis on history, and hence on empirical studies.

Before I explain each of the four major organizational networks, I want to stress that the theory is not derived from any psychological assumptions about the importance of different human purposes. Instead, the point is strictly sociological: these four networks happen to be the most useful organizational bases for generating social power. In Mann's words, "Their primacy comes not from the strength of human desires for ideological, economic, military, or political satisfaction but from the particular organizational means each possesses to attain human goals, whatever they may be" (1986:2).

In the American vernacular, we can say each organizational network is in the business of selling some service or product needed by many members of a society. The ideology network sells meaning, answers to universal concerns about the origins of humanity, death, the purpose of life, and other existential questions. Churches are the primary salespeople in this area, and some of them have developed into formidable power generators, such as the Catholic church in Europe for many centuries. In the United States, secular organizations like self-help groups and psychotherapy cults have enjoyed some success in marketing meaning to the college-educated middle class, but churches remain the most important organizations in fulfilling this human need for Americans. Protestant churches in particular always have had an enormous role in producing American morality and culture. However, their constant splintering into new denominations, and then further schisms within the dominations, has limited them as a source of social power. The historical role of churches also has been limited through the separation of church and state by the Founding Fathers, reflecting both the weak nature of the church network at the time and the Founders' own secular tendencies. True, the Catholic church was a power base in some urban areas in the late nineteenth and early twentieth centuries through the Democratic party, often making alliances with the political machines, but more recently its power has been limited to realms like abortion and school prayer. Religious values end up for the most part as one of the many hooks used in the symbolic politics played by economic rivals in trying to further their own interests.

The economic network is in the business of selling material goods and personal services. It creates classes defined in terms of their power over the different parts of the economic process from extraction of raw materials to manufacturing to distribution. Since these economic classes are also social relationships between groups of people who often have different interests, the economic network also can generate class conflict, by which I mean disagreements over such matters as ownership, profit margins, wage rates, working conditions, and unionization that manifest themselves in ways that range from workplace protests and strikes to industrywide boycotts and bargaining to nationwide political actions. However, class conflict is not always present because both owners and workers, the most likely rival classes in recent times, have to have the means to organize themselves over an extended area of social space for conflict to occur. For much of Western history, there have been "ruling classes," defined by Mann as any "economic class that has successfully monopolized other power sources to dominate a state-centered society at large" (1986:25). However, because nonowning classes usually find it difficult to organize, class conflict has been important only in certain periods of history, such as ancient Greece, early Rome, and the present capitalist era. In other words, Mann does not see class conflict as the "motor" of history, putting his theory in disagreement with Marxism once again.

In the United States, the economic network leads to the corporations, banks, plantations, agribusinesses, and trade unions of primary concern of this book. The nationwide nature of the transportation and communication systems, and the commonality of language, education, and culture, mean that the bases for class solidarity and class conflict are present in the United States. Moreover, I believe that such class conflict has frequently manifested itself since the late nineteenth century and has been the single most important factor (but not the only factor) driving American politics in the twentieth century. This standpoint may seem to put me at odds with the great majority of social scientists and historians, who see the basic conflict as one between conservatives and liberals, but I will try to show that this conservative/liberal conflict is more fully analyzed as a class conflict. Conservatism is the ideology of the corporate rich and their allies, liberalism the ideology of the working class and its allies. More specifically, I will try to show that a corporate-conservative coalition contends with a liberal-labor coalition for the allegiance of voters from the many occupational, ethnic, and religious groups comprising the American working class. As historians emphasize, the content of conservatism and liberalism does evolve over time: one side is the party of order, the other the party of hope, as the saying goes, but I think the different interests of capitalists and their employees are at the heart of the conflict. These two rival coalitions and their disagreements will be discussed more fully a little later in the chapter. We need to have a look at the other two basic organizational networks before plunging into the thicket of American politics.

The third network of social power, the military, is in the business of organized violence, sometimes for the benefit of its own members, as in what Mann calls empires of domination, but more often in recent centuries as a service to ideological, economic, or political networks. Organizations of violence are most often attached to a state, but they are sometimes separate from it, which is one reason why the state autonomy theorists' emphasis on the monopolization of legitimate coercion in defining the state is not general enough as a starting point (Skocpol 1993:43). In the United States in the late nineteenth century, for example, corporations often created their own organizations of violence to break strikes or resist unions, or else hired private specialists in such work. The largest of the private armies in that era, the Pinkerton Detective Agency, "had more men than the U.S. Army" (Mann 1993:646). The state did not interfere with organized corporate violence until the 1930s because most of the unionization efforts by workers were defined by judges as violations of property rights and/or the right to freedom of contract; employers thus had a legitimate right to "defend" their property and hire replacement workers and private armies (pp. 645–48).

As for the American government's own army, it had a large role historically in taking territory from Native Americans, Spain, and Mexico, but it was never big enough for long enough until the Second World War to be considered a serious contender for social power. True, several famous generals became presidents starting with George Washington (who was also a large landholder of his day), but there has been no sustained organizational base for turning military power into social power. The generals who became presidents had "name recognition" and prestige as war heroes, but it was not the military who carried them to political victory.

The fourth and final network, the state, which Mann calls the political network, is in the business of selling territorial regulation, which means order, dispute resolution, and regularity within a fixed area of land. This task of regulation within a bounded area most fundamentally defines the state and makes it potentially autonomous. The economic network, and people in general, desperately need this service, but no other network is capable of providing it for sustained periods of time.

The lack of emphasis on coercion and domination in explaining the origins of the state once again places Mann's theory in historical disagreement with Marxism, which sees the origins of the state in class conflict between owners and workers, making it an organization of class domination from the outset. Archaeological and historical evidence does not presently support the Marxist view (e.g., Claessen and Skalnik 1978; Cohen and Service 1978; Mann 1986:49–63, 84–87). Lest I seem to be giving hostages here to state autonomy theorists, let me quickly add that Mann sees the American state of the late nineteenth and early twentieth centuries (which is where his account ends for now) as a capitalist-liberal formation embodying basic capitalist principles, using its courts and armies to crush labor organizing, and responding to political parties wherein capitalists have at the least a large amount of influence (1993:635–59, 705).

Historically, states were not highly important in the Western world in the one thousand years following the fall of the Roman Empire. They gradually grew in power in the fifteenth and sixteenth centuries in the context of the growth of capitalism on the one hand and the development of an arms race on another. A highly competitive system of nation-states arose in Europe in which only the militarily powerful states survived, usually in alliance with economic elites willing to pay for the necessary armies in exchange for protection of property rights and the regulation of markets. Within this context, states usually came to have the monopoly on legitimate violence that state autonomy theorists emphasize (i.e., armies capable of policing the state territory and defending it against outsiders). States also gained dominance over ideology networks: nationalism and idolization of the head of state gradually mingled with Christianity in providing meaning for the lives of ordinary citizens. The question of social power narrowed to the relative power of economic and state elites, which is a good part of the story of Western history in the past few hundred years. Thus, the American case I am focusing on here is but one in a much larger set, and the outcomes vary greatly from country to country (Mann 1993).

In the United States, the political network has been decentralized and fragmented to a degree unique among industrialized societies for a variety of reasons taught in junior high school. It also is highly unusual in the degree to which it is staffed by a certain kind of specialist, the lawyer. Lawyers already were important in colonial America, and thirty-three of the fifty-five delegates to the Constitutional Convention in 1789 were lawyers, although they were well-born property owners as well (Mann 1993:157). They remained equally important ever after as the Constitution and the Supreme Court became central features of the American state, and involvement in a political party became the main avenue to a judicial appointment. Twenty-six of the forty-two American presidents have been lawyers, as have a majority of national-level legislators (Eulau and Sprague 1964). In 1972, for example, 70 percent of the senators and 51 percent of the representatives were lawyers (Zweigenhaft 1975).

But are these lawyer/politicians acting primarily in terms of the independent interests of the state, as the state autonomy theorists would say, or instead making sure that the needs of the top economic class are being met even while doing the necessary minimum of regulating and adjudicating? Are lawyer/politicians specialists in smoothing over class conflict? With those questions we can take leave of this general discussion of the four networks of social power and turn to the issue of how we study the class dominance theory of power in the United States.

## MEMBERSHIP NETWORK ANALYSIS

The empirical study of social power begins with a network analysis—a tracing of various kinds of social connections between specific people and organizations in the city or nation under study. More exactly, we begin with what is called a *membership network analysis,* a phrase used to emphasize

*Table 2.1.* A Hypothetical Membership Matrix

| | | Organizations | | | | |
|---|---|---|---|---|---|---|
| | | V | W | X | Y | Z |
| | 1 | | x | x | | |
| | 2 | | | x | x | |
| People | 3 | | | x | | x |
| | 4 | x | | | x | |
| | 5 | | | | | |

that the connections are not merely among people, as in the old sociometric studies of friendship or kinship circles. A membership network is most readily constructed as a simple matrix, as in Table 2.1, with the people arrayed from top to bottom and the organizations arrayed from left to right. The "cells" or boxes created by the intersection of a person and an organization can then be filled with "membership" or "relational" information—member, director, and owner are examples, but later we will expand *relational* to include "attitude toward an organization."

The membership information in the cells can be used to create two different kinds, or levels, of networks: organizational and interpersonal. The organizational network shown in Figure 2.1 is based on connections created by people who belong to two or more organizations. When we look at the configuration we immediately see that organization X is the most central one in the network. As an empirical fact, we do find certain organizations are very central in American power networks. Now we can turn Figure 2.1 inside out and make it into an interpersonal network where the connection is the fact that two or more people are part of the same organization. Figure 2.2 shows that person 2 is more central—connected to more people—than the others. It also shows one person as an *isolate.* Most Americans are isolates in terms of the social, corporate, and other networks that connect to government in the United States.

A membership network may seem very simple, and in some sense it is, but in fact it packs a theoretical wallop because it contains the two types of human relationships of concern in sociological theorizing: personal relationships and memberships in organizations. It also allows us to abstract to the level of organizations (Figure 2.1) or the level of interpersonal relations (Figure 2.2). Some critics in the past believed that network studies focused only on individuals, but in fact both individuals and organizations are present in any empirical study of power, no matter what theoretical orientation is used (e.g., Gross 1966; Breiger 1974; Domhoff 1983:211–12).

Matrices of people and organizations allow us to study the characteristics

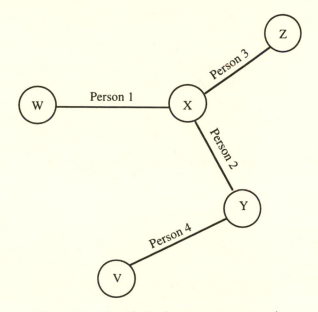

*Figure 2.1* Hypothetical organization network.

of a network with a fair amount of precision. For example, a network can be characterized by a great many connections or only a few; this is its *density* or *connectivity*. Density gives us some indication of the degree of "social cohesion" in the network. Similarly, the configuration of connections tells us about the shape of the network: it can have one or few or no central organizations, it can be *holistic* or *segmented*.

Membership network analysis also can make use of computer programs based on graph theory, matrix algebra, and Boolean algebra to analyze large databases. In theory, we could enter tens of thousands of Americans and their connections (e.g., neighborhoods, schools, clubs, jobs, and political affiliations) into the computer and discover the number, size, shape, and density of their social networks in an instant. In reality, such studies have been done with thousands of corporate directors, as I will report on shortly.

Once basic networks have been established through membership studies, a second step can be taken: a tracing of the size and direction of money flows in the network. In theory, money flows can be thought of as just another kind of relationship or connection between people or institutions, but in practice it is a good idea to consider them separately because they have a quality and role all their own. They are socially distinct in our minds

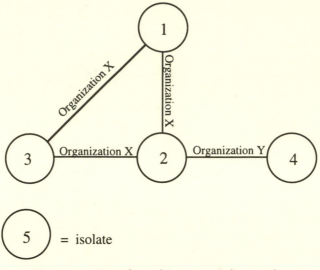

*Figure 2.2*    Hypothetical interpersonal network.

from interpersonal relations or organization membership. As the people/organization matrix implies, there are four kinds of money flows:

1.   people to people (e.g., campaign donations, gifts, loans);
2.   people to institutions (e.g., taxes to government, individual or family gifts to foundations);
3.   institutions to people (e.g., corporate dividends to stockholders, foundation grants to professors, PAC donations to candidates);
4.   institutions to institutions (e.g., foundation grants to policy groups, corporate donations to foundations).

For my purposes in this book, the two money flows that are of the greatest interest are (1) foundation grants to policy groups, and (2) individual donations to political parties and political candidates.

The third step in a network analysis is to analyze the verbal and written "output" of the network, that is, the speeches, policy statements, and legislative acts that allow us to study the goals, values, and ideology of the people and institutions in the network. Technically speaking, this is called content analysis in the social sciences. It may sound a little mundane to those who talk about discourse, but content analysis is in fact what all theorists do, no matter what their orientation, when they make an effort to extract meaning from a text. They can be working from a highly developed theory or intuitive hunches, they can be rigorously quantitative or come away with only general impressions, but any way you cut it, they are doing content analysis. Content analysis has been used on a wide range of topics from plays to newspapers, and has led to many systematic and surprising findings on dream content (Domhoff 1996), but the most interesting findings for power analysts have been the slight difference in ideologies among corporate executives in firms in different industries (e.g., Sutton, Harris, Kaysen, and Tobin 1956; Seider 1977).

But how do we know if any given network of people and organizations is powerful? Readers may have noticed that I have not provided any formal definition of that elusive term up to this point, relying on our shared understandings. Everyone knows what power means, and they prove it with synonyms like clout and juice, or use of a designation for powerful people— rainmakers, big cheeses, head honchos. This sidesteps the issue, of course, and in fact it is very difficult to provide a formal, agreed-upon definition of power. One favorite in sociology, "the ability of A to make B do something he or she does not want to do," smuggles in coercion, for example, without presenting evidence that it is basic or always necessary. When Russell analyzed the matter, building on the knowledge he developed in reformulating the foundations of mathematics, he came away with a simple conclusion: power is "the production of intended effects" (1938:35). Forty years later, sociologist Dennis Wrong covered the same ground with the benefit of the large social science literature created since Russell wrote, then ended up right where Russell did, with a slight specification: "power is the capacity of some persons to produce intended and foreseen effects on others" (1979:21).

But a definition is not what we really need. What we need are indicators of power, outcomes we can point to or measure that are generally agreed to be manifestations of the power of a social organization, group, or class. On this issue we are on firmer ground. Analyzing studies of power by researchers of all theoretical perspectives, I find there are four basic power indicators, although not all theorists accept all of them. To begin with we can call them (1) Who benefits? (2) Who sits? (3) Who wins? and (4) Who shines?

Who benefits? is shorthand for the use of distributions of wealth, income, and well-being in a society as power indicators. The underlying assumption of such an indicator is that people in power would appropriate for themselves disproportionate amounts of what is considered good or important. Even longevity can be a power indicator using this rationale if it can be shown that people in the society value a long life. So too for health, education, vacations, and safe neighborhoods, but the distributions of values most frequently used as power indicators are wealth and income.

Who sits? is a quick way of saying that overrepresentation in important decision-making groups and institutions is an indicator of power. *Overrepresentation* means a percentage of the positions higher than what would be expected by chance in relation to the group's percentage of the total population. For example, if a group makes up 10 percent of a city, but produces 90 percent of the top appointed officials, nine times as many as we would expect by chance if every group won an equal share, then we infer it must have power. Formally speaking, this is the positional method of inferring power.

Who wins? is shorthand for whose ideas are accepted and whose are not in arguments in governmental decision-making processes. If we looked at the outcomes on a range of issues, and then added up wins and losses, we would infer that the most frequent winner is the most powerful. This is the decisional method.

Who shines? is the best short phrase I could think of for what is called the reputational indicator of power. In this approach power is assumed to lie with those nominated as powerful by a cross section of people ("judges") who have been around long enough to be accurate informants. The originator of the method, Floyd Hunter, liked to call it the "take me to your leader" method, a phrase drawn from the image of the anthropologist landing for the first time in a new territory. But the critics called it the reputational method, in an effort to impugn its validity, and the term stuck. Actually, it is as good as any.

Critics from the pluralist persuasion in the social sciences have worried that one or more of these indicators are superficial or misleading, and their views seem to have been accepted by most state autonomy theorists. Nelson Polsby (1963 [1980]), for example, says Who benefits? is not a useful indicator because sometimes benefits are gained by accident, or are purposely given to others by the powerful. Dahl used the fact that "American wheat farmers can benefit from a decision of Soviet leaders to buy American grain" to allege a weakness in this indicator, rightly claiming these farmers "can hardly be said to control the Soviet leaders in their decision to buy American grain" (1982:17), but overlooking the fact that the indicator is for use within societies. Raymond Wolfinger (1960) tried to sink the reputational method by arguing that a reputation is not necessarily reality: media publicity might be leading informants to report fluff instead of real stuff, or a reputation based on power on one issue may not mean power on other issues. Other critics dismissed overrepresentation because a group can win in the decisional arena without sitting in the official seats of power (e.g., Matthews 1954:32), ignoring the fact that we are talking about separate indicators, not processes of governance. In other words, for these critics it all comes down to who wins and who loses on a range of issues, and that remains the prevailing view for most social scientists, including the state autonomy theorists. Dahl stated this point in a critique of Hunter and Mills that became gospel. Note the use of the term *astounding* to denigrate their efforts:

> I do not see how anyone can suppose that he has established the dominance of a specific group in a community or nation without basing his analysis on the careful examination of a series of concrete decisions. It is a remarkable and indeed astounding fact that neither Professor Mills [who used Who benefits? and Who sits?] nor Professor Hunter [reputational method] has seriously attempted to examine an array of specific cases to test his major hypothesis. (Dahl 1958:466)

Dahl then provided a formal statement of what is necessary in a power study that has set the standard ever since:

> To sum up: The hypothesis of the existence of a ruling elite can be strictly tested only if:
>
> 1.  The hypothetical ruling elite is a well-defined group.
> 2.  There is a fair sample of cases involving key political decisions in which the preferences of the hypothetical ruling elite run counter to those of any other likely group that might be suggested.
> 3.  In such cases, the preferences of the elite regularly prevail. (ibid.)

For all the seeming finality of Dahl's statements, the research literature suggests that a more ecumenical approach is used in actual practice. For example, a political scientist very much of the pluralist school of thought twice replicated Hunter's original reputational findings in Atlanta with reputational studies of his own (Jennings 1964), and a decisional study there led to very similar results (Stone 1989). A study of Dallas showed that reputational, positional, and decisional indicators overlapped (Thometz, 1963). A study at the national level showed that the findings of a reputational study overlapped with what would have been found by keying on important positions in large organizations (Moore 1979; Higley and Moore 1981). Ironically, Dahl (1961) himself had to use the Who sits? indicator when he studied the social backgrounds of the mayors of New Haven, Connecticut, from the late eighteenth century to 1953 as one part to his famous study of that city, concluding that power had migrated from the "aristocrats" to the "industrialists" to the "ex-plebes." This set the stage for his "decisional" analysis of events in the 1950s purporting to show the dispersed nature of power there.

A more reasonable assessment of the four power indicators than Dahl provides, based on the many subsequent years of experience with them, is that they all are useful, and all have strengths and weaknesses (Domhoff 1978:136–40). It is therefore best to use as many of them as possible in any given study to compensate for any errors that might happen to creep into any one of the measures for any number of possible reasons. Even the decisional method can have its weaknesses. People's memories are short or they may exaggerate their own role. Interview studies without background documents can be very superficial. When I went back to New Haven fifteen years after Dahl did his study, I had access to documents from the Chamber of Commerce and deceased individuals that showed Dahl to be factually wrong on a number of key issues in his case study of how urban renewal came to the city. More generally, my combination of documents and interviews led me to argue that he underplayed the role of the downtown business community and completely missed the role of the top administrators and trustees of Yale University (Domhoff 1978:chap. 3; 1983:184–96).

However, when in Rome you must do as the Romans do, and the state autonomy theorists are the Romans here, so in this book I will rely primarily on the decisional indicator of power. In fact, I am following every dictum in Dahl's decree on the necessary steps of an acceptable power study.

With the power indicators now established, the earlier discussion of membership network analysis can be used to provide a generic definition of what Dahl called a "ruling elite" and Hunter called a "power structure." The following definition has to be adapted slightly for use with any given theoretical orientation, but it provides a good starting point: a power structure is a network of people and institutions that scores at the top on the power indicators it has been possible to utilize in the study.

I believe that the general methodological framework I have outlined in this section can be used by theorists of any persuasion. It will reveal any concentration and shape of power. It is not biased toward any given theory. It can show that some groups have power in one arena, some groups in others, by discrepancies between indicators. It can show changes in the power distribution through changes on the power indicators.

However, it is not my intent to do a general empirical study of the American power structure. I want to demonstrate the value of a specific theoretical framework: class dominance. Specifically I want to show there is (1) a small social upper class (2) rooted in the ownership and control of a corporate community that (3) is integrated with a policy-planning network and (4) has great political power in both political parties and dominates the federal government in Washington. That may appear to be a tall order because terms like "social upper class" and "corporate community" may seem hard to specify, and evidence for "great influence" in political parties and "domination" of the federal government difficult to come by. But it can be done with a fair amount of rigor in terms of the matrices and power indicators I have presented in this section. Incorporating this general orientation into a class dominance framework is the task of the next section.

## SPECIFYING THE CLASS DOMINANCE FRAMEWORK

### Introduction

In this section I am going to define all the concepts used in my theory, and show how they are studied. I am also going to explain how my theory involves a synthesis of a class theory with what is often thought to be its antithesis in American sociology, an organizational theory, thereby creating what I call a class/organizational synthesis. As I will argue, this synthesis takes place through boards of directors, the legal holders of power in virtually every profit and nonprofit organization in this country. To make this material directly relevant to the rest of the book, I will draw many of my empirical examples from the 1920s and 1930s. This will provide a good background for the case studies in the later chapters.

### Social Class/Upper Class

Formally speaking, a social class is a network of interacting and inter-marrying families who see each other as equals and accord each other social respect. This definition is agreed to across the board by sociologists (e.g., Davis, Gardner, and Gardner 1941:59n; Kahl 1959:12), Marxists (Sweezy 1953:123–24), and pluralist political scientists (Dahl 1961:229). However, that agreement often quickly breaks down because different scholars use different terminology or derive social classes from different roots. Some call social classes status groups, following the lead of Max Weber, while others speak of social elites when talking of the top status group or upper class. Both Weberians and Marxists root social classes in economic classes, but Weberians tend to emphasize the relationship of classes to the market while Marxists insist that economic classes are rooted in relations of production, which usually means ownership or nonownership of income-producing land, machines, or bank capital. Marxists also emphasize that for them the term *class* always includes the relationship between classes as well as the specific categories of class groups.

From my point of view, these disputes involve historic antagonisms that should be resolved empirically, along with emotionally charged suspicions about the alleged political implications of different terminology. Although I do not mind the concept of social elites, I will be consistent in the use of the phrase "social class" in this book. For my purposes, though, social classes as networks of interacting and intermarrying families are only a starting point. If and when such social classes are found, it is then possible to take the next step and see if they are based in one or more economic classes, and to determine the underlying economic and political relationships between so-cial classes. Within this context it also is possible to talk of segments within the underlying economic classes, meaning groupings within an economic class that have somewhat different interests due to their particular position within the overall social structure. In the case of the ownership class in the United States, these segments have different bases of wealth and partially conflicting interests on some issues while sharing strong common concerns in the face of initiatives by nonowners or agencies within the state.

As far as an upper social class, everyone agrees that one exists in the United States, but they disagree on what, if anything, it has to do with economic classes or power. Is it a mere status group with little or no power, or is it also a capitalist (ownership) class whose members dominate the state, as determined by one or more agreed-upon indicators of power? In order to answer these questions, we first of all need an empirical or operational definition of the upper class, that is, a set of indicators of upper-class stand-ing. They have been supplied in the work of sociologist E. Digby Baltzell (1958), himself a member of the upper class, but influenced to join a profes-sion atypical to his class by his experiences during World War II (Schneider-man 1992). Through a careful study of high-status families in Philadelphia from the seventeenth century to 1940, Baltzell established that they lived in the same neighborhoods, went to their own private schools, belonged to their own exclusionary social clubs, frequented their own resort areas, and intermarried. Although he used his findings to show connections outside Philadelphia, and to argue that a nationwide upper class developed in the last quarter of the nineteenth century, his primary focus was on that one city.

It was my fate as a person with strong empirical tendencies to expend many hundreds of my own hours and large amounts of student energy building on, extending nationwide, and updating Baltzell's 1940 findings in a variety of ways (Domhoff 1967, 1970). In terms of my purposes here, one of the most important things we did was to discover a national network of schools and clubs using three very different methods (Domhoff 1970:chap. 1). First, we used a quantitative method called contingency analysis to determine what schools and clubs were related to each other in three thou-sand entries in Who's Who in America. Then we did a reputational study through questionnaires to 317 society page editors across the country, 128 of whom were very cooperative. Finally, we located the school and club affiliations of 3,164 businessmen in fifteen large cities where we had little information from other studies. The schools and clubs on which we found high agreement among the three methods were added to Baltzell's list.

One of the most quaint but useful findings in Baltzell's work is that many members of the upper class subscribe to in-group telephone books called the Social Register. Published originally as separate little books for a dozen major cities, along with an overall index called the "Social Register Loca-ter," they were merged into one large book in 1976 (Baltzell 1966; Domhoff 1983:20–21). We included the *Social Register* in our contingency analysis along with the *Who's Who in America* biographical sketches, showing that it correlated with exclusive private schools and clubs. The society page editors also reported it was an accurate guide to upper-class standing.

The *Social Register* is not merely a useful guide to upper-class standing, but contains valuable information for studies of social cohesion as well, such as the person's schools and clubs. The maiden names of married women are provided in a section called "Married Maidens," and vacation addresses are listed as "Dilatory Domiciles" in a small summer supplement, which we used to show that upper-class families from all over the country go to the same few resort areas each summer (Domhoff 1970:79–82).

The usual dual categories of a membership network analysis emerge from this research. We can talk of the upper class as an institutional network of schools, clubs, and resort areas (Domhoff 1983:17–18). This institutional network has persisted in roughly its present form for a little over one hundred years now, although there have been some additions, subtractions, and alterations. New clubs spring up when the young men do not want to be in the "stuffy" clubs of the older men; a Junior League is developed as women of the upper class gain more independence; a prep school becomes too liberal and loses support; a resort area starts to be frequented by members of the middle class. These are ebbs and lows: the institutional network remains intact.

We know far less about the continuity of the families who create and utilize this institutional network. We found in a sample of 5,900 families in the 1980 *Social Register* that 9 percent listed themselves as members of one of four ancestral societies dating back at least to the American Revolution (Domhoff 1983:22). Baltzell's (1958) work shows continuity back to the seventeenth century in several elite Philadelphia families. Two studies of families in Detroit demonstrated continuity over three generations (Schuby 1975; Davis 1982), as did a study of families involved in the steel industry in the late nineteenth and early twentieth centuries (Ingham 1978:230–31). We know that some members of the upper class marry outside their class, usually someone from the upper-middle class they met at college, but the best general picture for now is a stable family group within the upper class that incorporates new members, including newly wealthy capitalists what-ever their social origins (Domhoff 1983:34–36).

The existence of the network of upper-class institutions makes it possible to determine if and to what extent members of this class are involved in corporations, political parties, government, and other institutions of the society. Through this tracing outward we can determine overrepresentation and discover other institutional networks. For any systematic research seeking to link social class with the power centers of the society, the upper-class institutions are truly the bedrock starting point.

But here I have to enter one caveat before I present the results from such studies: the institutions of the upper class are not perfect as indicators of class standing because they sometimes include people who are not really members of the upper class: the teacher's son who graduates from the private boarding school; the minority student from a low-income community taken into a private school on a scholarship (e.g., Zweigenhaft and Domhoff 1991); the politician or celebrity asked to join the otherwise exclusive club. In sociological terms, these people are known as *false positives*. In theory they could be a problem because they might inflate overrepresentation figures, but in practice they are more than canceled out by *false negatives*, people who are upper class but we do not know it because they choose not to list in the *Social Register* or do not include their schools and clubs in *Who's Who in America*. For example, 37 percent of the alumni of one elite private school, Hotchkiss, did not list their school in the 1976–1977 edition; 29 percent of the members of the exclusive Bohemian Club in San Francisco did not include this affiliation in the same year. So, we can be wrong about upper-class standing for any one person in a large-scale study relying on library sources, but probably accurate overall. Lest readers be shocked by this confession of imperfection, let me add that all indicators in the social sciences have these problems, even if some investigators do not acknowledge them.

Caveats aside, our many studies of the membership networks generated from the *Social Register*, private club membership lists, and private school alumni lists demonstrate beyond a doubt that the upper-class network is nationwide in its scope and surprisingly dense (Domhoff 1970:chap. 4). So does the outstanding study of women of the upper class by Susan Ostrander (1984). It is likely that most members of the upper class have connections in most major cities through common schooling, clubs, or resorts, and can reach a wide array of people through friends of friends. If we think of meetings at clubs, resorts, and alumni gatherings as a series of constantly changing small groups, then research findings in social psychology on social cohesion in small groups become relevant to issues of power because socially cohesive groups are better able to solve problems than less cohesive groups due to a greater desire to reach common understanding. My inference from this research is that social cohesion facilitates policy cohesion within the upper class (Domhoff 1974:chap. 3).

All of these findings on the upper class hold for the 1930s. We know that the gentlemen of that day were usually in six or seven major clubs, not just the three or four of later years. They were graduates of sixteen leading boarding schools, and usually of Harvard, Yale, or Princeton, which did not have many undergraduate scholarships until after World War II (e.g., Farnum 1989:89–90). The *Social Register* was an excellent indicator of upper-class standing. In 1929, for example, the last year before the Great Depression and New Deal created consternation and discord in the upper class, there were thirty-three Roosevelts listed, including the future president, fifty DuPonts, who were to be his major nemeses, and nineteen Rockefellers, one of whom will figure importantly in two later chapters. But just about every other famous high-status family from the past was there as well: Astors, Auchinclosses, Biddles, Mellons, Morgans, Saltonstalls, Tafts, and Vanderbilts, for example.

The findings on the institutional network, along with the number of listings in the *Social Register*, can be used to estimate the size of the upper class. It is probably less than 0.5 percent of the total population, but we will call it 1 percent to be conservative. That also makes calculations easier when we determine if and how much the upper-class network is overrepresented in business, government, and other institutional arenas.

In 1933, the top 1 percent of adults in the United States owned 28 percent of all privately held wealth. This figure includes cars, furniture, and houses as well as income-producing property like stocks and bonds. The figure was at 26 percent in 1956, and probably did not change much until it started upward in the late 1970s (Lampman 1962:24; Smith and Franklin 1974; Turner and Starnes 1976; Wolff, 1995). But is that wealthiest 1 percent the same upper-class 1 percent I have been talking about? Is the high-status network composed of wealthy people? I know it sounds like an obvious question, but the two categories have to be connected empirically for research purposes. Baltzell (1958:20) and Mills (1956:117) compared the best available lists of wealthy families to the *Social Register*, and of course they found a large overlap. So we have evidence that the upper class is a wealth-holding class.

These wealth figures give us our first indication that the upper-class network is powerful because wealth is one of the power indicators in the Who benefits? category. The upper class had twenty-eight times as much wealth as would be expected by chance in 1933; its members also had sixty-five times as much corporate stock as we would expect if it were randomly distributed (Lampman 1962:209). Unfortunately, the state autonomy theorists do not accept this indicator, echoing the kind of arguments made by pluralists Dahl and Polsby. State elites supposedly do not care about wealth. They mostly want to be able to order people around, expand their territory, and make wars when necessary.

**The Power Elite**

Members of the upper class, if they rule America, certainly do not do so alone. There are not that many of them to begin with, especially when half of them have been excluded by sexism from pursuing traditional pathways to power. Moreover, many members of the upper class are not interested in ruling. They prefer to live the good life based on their inherited wealth, even leaving the management of their stock portfolios to hired experts. They spend their time breeding dogs or horses, traveling, or mingling with celebrities at glitzy social events. Now, there are fewer such people than meet the eye, but the first issue we face in claiming that the upper class is a ruling—or governing—class is that many of its members do not seem to be involved in ruling.

Moreover, America seems to be an organizational society, not a class one. What is most obvious about it are the large "institutional hierarchies," as Mills (1956) called them, that developed throughout the twentieth century—large corporations, the Pentagon, the executive branch of the federal government, but also large public university systems like the University of California (nine campuses), hospital complexes like the Mayo Clinic, charitable foundations like the Ford Foundation and Rockefeller Foundation, and more. How could members of a small upper class dominate such a vast array of diverse and apparently independent institutions, each with its own history, traditions, purposes, and internal methods of operation?

At this point the boards of directors of these institutions come into the picture as the official repository of final authority in them. I believe the class and organizational dimensions of American society meet on these boards. Board members from the upper class bring a class perspective to the management of the organization, while the managers of the organization who have risen within it to serve on the board of directors bring an organizational perspective. The board is thus one nexus for a synthesis of the class and organizational viewpoints. Its members strive to keep the organization viable in terms of organizational principles while incorporating the class perspectives of the upper-class directors.

This viewpoint provides an empirical starting point for linking studies of class-based social power to organizations: if there is evidence that a board of directors is controlled by members of the upper class, then we can say the institution itself is controlled by members of the upper class. We can determine this control by studying the history of the board, the funding of the organization, or the composition of the board. In practice we usually end up studying the composition of the board when it comes to the large number of corporations. However, more attention has been paid to history and funding with other organizations, partly because there are fewer of them, partly because the relevant information is more accessible.

Despite the legal importance of boards, they are one of the least-studied aspects of American society, for two main reasons: First, it is hard to gain access to them for interviews or observations, and their records usually are secret until many years later. Just as important, they are dismissed by many social scientists as mere window dressing or rubber stamps. These social scientists are so impressed with the power within organizations that they do not think mere boards could control them. At bottom, this is another manifestation of the kind of theory the state autonomy theorists hold to: experts and specialists run America. What little we have available in the way of observational and interview studies suggests quite otherwise. For example, Ostrander's (1987) observational and interview study of the boards of two nonprofit social service organizations in Boston showed there were several ways in which the upper-class members on the board—often women in this case—used their access to independent financial resources outside the organization and their political contacts to have their way.

Generally speaking, board members wield their power through hiring and firing the leadership level of organizations. They pick and choose among the organizational executives striving to reach the top, whom they know from serving on board-based committees with them, or they bring in a new top executive made known to them by their network of upper-class friends serving on other boards of directors. Boards are especially important in times of crisis or potential mergers (e.g., Mace 1971; Bowen 1994). Board committees often do far more than meets the eye (Lorsch and MacIver 1989).

If boards of directors are given their due, then we have one key to the means by which the upper class exerts its influence: a leadership group I call the *power elite*. I define the power elite as active, working members of the upper class and high-level employees in institutions controlled by members of the upper class. High-level employees are defined as those selected or approved directly by the board of directors, which usually means the chairperson and president, along with a few other high-level employees who may be asked to serve on the board. It follows that all those executives serving on a board of directors in an institution controlled by members of the upper class are members of the power elite. In terms of the membership network matrix, we could say the board of directors is the organizational level, the power elite the interpersonal level, but if we think of the network as one consisting of both people and institutions, as I think we should, then the idea of a power elite encompasses class, organizational, and interpersonal levels. It is not mere individuals, nor is it unrelated to institutions. A few senior members of long standing may have no present institutional affiliations, but for the most part members of the power elite are directors or high-level employees of one or more organizations in the institutional network.

But what institutions in American society are controlled by members of the upper class according to this definition? Every type of institution from major businesses to private universities to cultural and fine arts organizations to private welfare agencies, which is possible because some people sit on many different boards. For my purposes, though, I want to focus on those organizations I think are most involved in the exercise of power.

## The Corporate Community

The corporate community is defined in network terms as all those corporations connected into one network by people who serve on two or more boards of directors. Below this visible level there are also common stock ownership, shared lawyers and investment bankers, and other linkages that help make the idea of a corporate community a sociological reality. The people who create the connections we use for our formal definition of the corporate community constitute 15–20 percent of all directors in the network. They comprise what is called the inner circle of the corporate community (Zeitlin, Ewen, and Ratcliff 1974), and there is evidence showing they are very likely to serve on the boards of nonprofit organizations (Useem 1978, 1979, 1980, 1982, 1984; Eitzen, Jung, and Purdy 1982). The corporate community created by the multiple directorships of those in the inner circle is very large: about 90 percent of the top 797 corporations for 1969 were found to be in the same network, for example (Mariolis 1975; Sonquist and Koenig 1975), and studies of smaller samples from earlier decades reveal the same picture (e.g., Roy 1983, Mizruchi 1982, 1983). Banks and large industrial corporations are at the center; we can say with confidence that the boards of large banks are the main meeting place for those in the inner circle (Mintz and Schwartz 1983, 1985).

The corporate community can be traced back in American history as far as there are adequate records, to 1816, where David Bunting's (1983) important archival work shows that the ten largest banks and ten largest insurance companies in New York City were completely connected; eighteen directors with three or more positions linked 95 percent of the companies in the sample. There were, of course, other interlocks as well. Bunting's sample of the twenty largest banks, ten largest insurance companies, and ten largest railroads for 1836 generated a corporate community that included 95 percent of the sample firms; this time 30 men held 103 directorships linking 73 percent of the corporations (Bunting 1983:133–38). His samples for later in the century show similar results, which are supplemented by Roy's (1983) detailed study of a sample of firms in eleven industries between 1886 and 1904, showing that the corporate community grew out from a core of railroads, banks, coal, and telegraph companies in 1886 to encompass all the industries in his sample by 1904. Work by Mizruchi (1982, 1983) picks up the story at that point and shows the stability of these findings until 1974. Railroads gradually became more peripheral to the network as the importance of railroads in the American economy declined, and industrial corporations became more central, but throughout the seventy-year period the network remained intact, with banks at the center. The four most central banks in 1974 were also the central banks in the 1904 network, created by either the Morgan financial interests or the Rockefeller family (e.g., Mizruchi 1983:176–77).

The corporate community for the era of greatest concern in this book, the 1930s, has been analyzed in great detail by Michael Allen (1978, 1982). Using two different quantitative approaches on a database of the two hundred largest corporations, fifty largest banks, and twenty largest investment banks of the time, Allen found there were several cliques in the network. Several of them were regionally based, not a surprising finding, but the largest one contained corporations from several different cities and coincided with what was thought at the time to be the Morgan Empire (e.g., Carosso 1970; Chernow 1990).

According to our indicators of upper-class membership, the upper class was overrepresented by a factor of fifty-three in a sample of the largest corporations in three sectors for 1963; the figure for the top fifteen banks was sixty-two; for the top fifteen insurance companies, forty-four; and for the twenty largest industrials, fifty-four (Domhoff 1967:52–55). Dye (1976:151–52), using a sample of 201 corporations for 1970, estimates that 30 percent of the directors had upper-class origins. The figure is even higher for the inner circle, where two to three times as many directors are members of the upper class in different samples (Soref 1980; Domhoff 1983:71–72).

The findings on the overlap between the upper class and the corporate community reinforce my earlier conclusion based on the great wealth possessed by members of the upper class: this social group is also a capitalist class. This fact makes the conceptual and terminological arguments between Marxists and other social scientists over class vs. status groups into moot ones for at least the top level of American society in the twentieth century because the highest status group is rooted in the ownership and control of large banks and corporations. In the phrase coined by Mills (1956:147), we are dealing with a "corporate rich." This may not seem like news in the 1990s, but from the 1940s through the 1970s the widespread belief in the alleged separation of ownership and control, with managerial specialists from the middle class supposedly controlling the corporations, was one of the main reasons mainstream social scientists rejected the idea of a power elite or ruling class [see Zeitlin (1974) for a searing critique of what he labels a "pseudofact"].

In addition to the upper-class overrepresentation on the boards of directors, there are many board members who are not members of the upper class. Most of these other directors are executives who have risen through the corporate ranks, but there also are college presidents, academic experts, former politicians, former military men, celebrities, and in recent years, various kinds of "tokens" [see Domhoff (1967:51–52) and Zweigenhaft and Domhoff (1982:25–46) for discussions of the pathways to board status]. The

important point about the upwardly mobile executives is that they are chosen on the basis of their ability to realize goals determined for the corporation by members of the upper class, meaning first and foremost producing a
profit, but also corporate expansion and good public relations as well.
Through their educations at top business schools, their experience in the
corporate world, and their gradual accrual of stock through generous option
plans, they are assimilated into the social life and worldview of the corporate rich (Domhoff 1983:73–76). The upper-class social clubs mentioned in
the previous section also come into play here, according to an interview
study with executives:

> The clubs are a repository of the values held by the upper-level prestige groups
> in the community and are a means by which these values are transferred to the
> business environment.The clubs are places in which the beliefs, problems,
> and values of the industrial organization are discussed and related to the other
> elements in the larger community. Clubs, therefore, are not only effective
> vehicles of informal communication, but also valuable centers where views
> are presented, ideas are modified, and new ideas emerge. Those in the inter-
> view sample were appreciative of this asset: in addition, they considered the
> club as a valuable place to combine social and business contacts. (Powell
> 1969:50)

In terms of the questions I am trying to answer in this book, I will be
placing greater emphasis on the corporate community and its top executives, whether the executives are from the upper class originally or not, than
on the upper class, because the corporate community is the economic class
that underlies the upper class as a social class/status group. I will talk of its
leaders interchangeably as business leaders, corporate executives, businessmen, and corporate leaders, and sometimes I will call the corporate community the business community, adapting to the terms being used by the
theorist I am critiquing. Whatever I call them, they are members of the
power elite, the leadership group of the capitalist class in the United States.

However, I would be remiss if I did not say that there are members of the
upper class who are power actors in the corporate community even without
being on boards of directors. People can exercise their great influence as
owners without being directors or executives. One such person in this study
is John D. Rockefeller, Jr., who quit the several boards his father placed him
on and ran all of his affairs, business, political, and cultural, through a
family office, as many other wealthy families did then and still do now
[Schwartz and Domhoff (1974) on the Rockefeller Family Office; Dunn
(1980) on the Weyerhauser family's office; and White (1978) on family
offices in general]. Rockefeller also hired people who were not part of the
family office to serve as corporate directors for him.

Skocpol and other state autonomists constantly try to narrow the argument to the power of business executives compared to state officials and experts, but my theory is much more general, as the foregoing discussion demonstrates. I am talking about a social upper class and an economic class (i.e., a corporate community in its current form) that are two sides of the same coin, not simply about executives. Further evidence for the greater breadth of my perspective will be presented in the next section on the policy-planning network that is based in the upper class and corporate community. Power in twentieth-century America cannot be discussed in any faintly realistic way without an understanding of the role played by this important network.

## The Policy-Planning Network

Tracing out the nonbusiness directorships of wealthy men and corporate directors led me to the discovery of what I came to call the policy-planning network (Domhoff 1967, 1970:chaps. 5 and 6). It consists of (1) foundations, (2) think tanks, (3) specialized research institutes at major universities, and (4) general policy discussion groups, where members of the upper class and corporate community meet with experts from the think tanks and research institutes, journalists, and government officials to discuss policy, ideology, and plans (PIP) concerning the major issues facing the country (Domhoff 1979:chap. 3; Alpert and Markusen 1980; Useem 1984). If and how the PIP developed in this network ends up in government will be a major theme of the next three chapters. The general way in which I think people, money, and ideas flow through the network is shown in Figure 2.3.

The organizations in the policy-planning network are nonprofit and tax-free, and are therefore portrayed by their leaders as separate from the corporate community. They are also said to be nonpartisan or bipartisan, above the political fray, not tied to either major party. Contrary to these claims, the policy-planning network is, in fact, the programmatic political party for the upper class and the corporate community, a major element in the power elite. There are differences of opinion between different parts of the network, for reasons that I have admitted are not well understood (Domhoff 1983:91), and even between individuals in the same organization, but the general stance of the network ranges from moderate conservative to ultra-conservative. The existence of this network leads me to believe the upper class and corporate community are organized above and beyond the interest group level stressed by most theorists. To the degree that case studies on its operation are convincing (e.g., Weinstein 1968; Shoup and Minter 1977; Domhoff 1979:chap. 3; 1990; Peschek 1987), then my view is supported, but more case studies are clearly needed.[1]

The specification of a policy-planning network also provides us with a way to deal with claims by the state autonomy theorists about the impor-

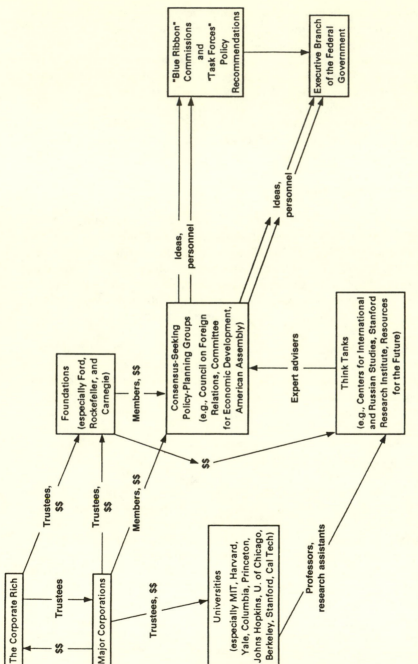

*Figure 2.3* The flow of policy from corporations and their owners to government. *(From G. William Domhoff, "How the Power Elite Set National Goals," in Robert Perrucci and Marc Pilisuk [eds.], The Triple Revolution Emerging, Boston, Little, Brown, 1971, p. 213.)*

tance of independent experts. For them, of course, all experts are independent because they are not capitalists or corporate executives. Thanks to the
policy-planning network, we can say a person is a *corporate expert* if he or
she is an employee of a foundation, think tank, or discussion group in the
network, and even a member of the power elite if on the board of directors
of one of these organizations.[2] Later in the chapter I will add two attitudinal
criteria that also distinguish corporate experts.

The main financial engine for the policy-planning network is a set of
charitable foundations that began to appear on the landscape in the early
twentieth century. They have been conducting studies, funding think tanks
and universities, and providing grants for individual scholars ever since. In
the 1950s, when the huge Ford Foundation joined the network, this foundational complex seemed to be complete, but in the 1970s very conservative
members of the corporate community created a new set of foundations that
fueled the rise of the New Right (Colwell 1980, 1993; Jenkins and Shumate
1985; Allen 1992).

The foundation world during the 1920s and 1930s was not as fully developed as it is today, but it was no less important. A mere twenty foundations
held 88 percent of all the assets in foundations at the time (Lundberg
1937:324). Only a few were concerned with public policy; most foundations gave to local charities, educational institutions, libraries, and museums. The list of the twenty largest foundation donors in 1934 in Table 2.2
shows that four Carnegie and three Rockefeller foundations accounted for
well over half of these donations. In terms of the policy-planning network,
the important organizations in the table are Russell Sage (no. 13), a main
force in creating the profession of social work (Devine 1939:21–23, 30–
31); Rosenwald (no. 10), which worked closely with the Rockefeller Foundation, where its founder, Julius Rosenwald, served on the board of trustees;
the Carnegie Corporation (no. 2); and the Rockefeller philanthropies, with
the Rockefeller Foundation (no. 1) by itself dwarfing the contributions of all
other policy-oriented foundations put together. Moreover, the leaders of the
Rockefeller philanthropies served as an executive committee that met regu-
larly with John D. Rockefeller, Jr., to coordinate his foundational and personal donations, which means that the power of the Rockefeller foundations
was even more concentrated than it appears in the table.

The think tanks in the network are highly specialized research groups
that produce the PIP that are argued about in the policy discussion groups.
They compete with each other for grants from the foundations and government agencies. There is a very limited market for their output—essentially
corporations and government. If think tanks are looked at as if they were
business firms competing in a market, it can be readily understood why they
could not stray very far from the corporate community and the foundations
even if they did not have people from the business and foundational net-

*Table 2.2.*   Grants by the 20 Largest Foundations in 1934

| | Foundation | Grants |
|---|---|---|
| 1. | Rockefeller Foundation | $11,840,719 |
| 2. | General Education Board (Rockefeller) | 5,465,225 |
| 3. | Carnegie Corporation | 4,738,022 |
| 4. | Carnegie Foundation | 1,919,962 |
| 5. | Commonwealth Fund (Standard Oil family) | 1,720,515 |
| 6. | Cranbrook Foundation (Michigan) | 668,296 |
| 7. | Spelman Fund (Rockefeller) | 537,250 |
| 8. | Horace and Mary Rackham Fund (Michigan) | 527,110 |
| 9. | Children's Fund of Michigan | 507,249 |
| 10. | Julius Rosenwald Fund[a] | 505,691 |
| 11. | John and Mary R. Markle Foundation | 420,656 |
| 12. | New York Foundation | 413,913 |
| 13. | Russell Sage Foundation | 267,255 |
| 14. | W. K. Kellogg Foundation | 252,465 |
| 15. | Carnegie Hero Fund Commission | 216,285 |
| 16. | Carnegie Endowment | 205,032 |
| 17. | New York Community Trust (Rockefeller management) | 199,493 |
| 18. | Committee of the Permanent Charity Fund | 197,333 |
| 19. | Cleveland Foundation | 190,179 |
| 20. | Buhl foundation | 176,128 |

*Source:*   Lundberg (1937, 326–327).
[a] Julius Rosenwald served on the board of the Rockefeller Foundation and worked closely with the Spelman Fund on projects.

works on their boards of directors [Alpert and Markusen (1980) provide this insight].

In the 1920s and 1930s only four organizations were recognized as think tanks, although we will meet a less visible one in Chapters 3 and 5. The four visible think tanks were the National Industrial Conference Board (now called simply the Conference Board), the National Bureau of Economic Research (NBER), the Brookings Institution, and the Twentieth Century Fund. (The research institutes at major universities, which train the experts for the think tanks and parallel their activities, will not be discussed because they are mostly a post–World War II addition to the network and do not have any role in this book.)

The Conference Board was created in 1916 with the backing of several trade associations primarily as an organization to gather information on prices, family budgets, hours of work, and other relevant economic statistics, but it also served to some extent as a discussion and conference group as well. Just below the surface, its founders were reacting to what they saw as an overly solicitous attitude toward organized labor on the part of the Wilson administration. However, in 1917 Wilson accepted all their nominees as the employer representatives on the War Labor Board (Eakins 1966:111, 126; cf. Gitelman 1984). After the war, the organization began to be perceived as a partisan and right-wing group, but its president, Magnus Alexander, an executive at General Electric, and its chief economist, Virgil Jordan, were nonetheless active figures as individuals in the policy-planning network in the 1920s. Alexander died in 1932, but Jordan lived to become a staunch opponent of the New Deal.

The NBER, less directly tied to any business groups, and funded by foundation grants and government contracts, developed a solid reputation in the academic community for its careful studies of business cycles and other economic phenomena. Two of its organizers, Edwin Gay, former dean of the Harvard Business School, and Wesley Mitchell, an economist at Columbia, first worked together during World War I in the government's Central Bureau of Planning and Statistics; the NBER was in many ways a continuation of work they started there. The third organizer, M. C. Rorty, an engineer and statistician for AT&T, was the main force in recruiting a distinguished board of trustees and obtaining a twenty-thousand-dollar start-up grant from the Commonwealth Fund (Eakins 1966:128ff.; Alchon 1985: chap. 4). The NBER was managed by Mitchell from his office at Columbia University with only a small staff, often contracting out work to economists at major universities across the country.

The Brookings Institution was created in 1927 through a merger of three independent institutes: the Institute of Government Research, which made its mark in 1921 with the culmination of its five-year effort to create a federal Bureau of the Budget; the Institute of Economics, created in 1922 with a five-year grant of two hundred thousand dollars from the Carnegie Corporation; and the short-lived Robert Brookings Graduate School, which produced many experts who later served in government despite its brief existence. The money for the founding of the Institute of Government Research came from a variety of sources, with the Rockefellers playing a significant role, but in the 1920s St. Louis merchant Robert Brookings was the main fund-raiser for all three organizations and the eventual Brookings Institution (Saunders, 1966; Eakins, 1966; Critchlow, 1985). Once founded, the Brookings Institution staff was never larger than thirty economists and political scientists during its first twenty-five years of existence.

The fourth think tank of the era, the Twentieth Century Fund, was also the most liberal, and it gave out grants as well as doing projects. It was founded in 1919 by Boston businessman Edward A. Filene, a department store owner of great wealth, who was joined shortly thereafter as a donor by another Boston businessman, Henry S. Dennison. The fund put a strong emphasis on issues concerning consumer spending, credit, and product distribution. Its largest single grants until 1935 went to the Credit Union National Extension Bureau, established by Filene and Dennison in 1921 to promote credit unions throughout the country (Eakins 1966:230). In the 1920s it did projects supportive of New Deal initiatives; Filene and Dennison were among the small number of business owners friendly to the New Deal (Eakins 1966:225–56).

The policy discussion groups, consisting of several hundred or even a few thousand members, only some of whom are active at any given time, are the integrating centers within the policy-planning network. They are not places of power, nor even of ideas, but meeting grounds for those with power and those with PIP. Although they sponsor speakers, large conferences, and written policy statements, their most important method of operation is through smaller discussion groups that meet on a weekly or monthly basis. I see these organizations as having several major functions not appreciated by either interest group or state autonomy theorists. If rival theorists took these functions more seriously, they would see why businessmen bring a general power elite perspective when they serve in government and why many experts are known personally by members of the upper class and corporate community.

First, the discussion organizations provide an informal training ground for new leadership within the power elite. The various small discussion groups within each of them are in effect seminars for corporate leaders conducted by experts from the think tanks and university research institutes. Second, it is within these organizations that members of the power elite sort out in an informal fashion which of their peers are best suited for government positions. This is valuable information when they are asked by friends who serve as financial angels to politicians to suggest people for government appointments. Third, corporate experts learn the perspectives of business leaders on the issues of the day, which helps in fitting the PIP to corporate needs. Fourth, the upper-class and corporate members of these organizations have the opportunity to become acquainted with the corporate experts, sizing them up for possible service in government. In a little study I did of members of the Council of Economic Advisers, I found that eleven of its first thirteen chairs came from the policy-planning network; six had been advisers for one policy discussion organization alone, the Committee for Economic Development (Domhoff 1987:195–96).

In addition, these organizations have two major functions in relation to the rest of society: First, they legitimate their members as persons capable of government service and selfless pursuit of the national interest. Members are portrayed as giving up their free time for no reimbursement to take part in highly selective organizations that are nonprofit and nonpartisan in nature. Second, through such avenues as books, journals, policy statements, press releases, and speakers, these groups influence the climate of opinion both in

Washington and the country at large. That is, they have ideological as well as policy functions.

The corporate executives of the 1920s and 1930s had only two general-purpose discussion organizations: the Chamber of Commerce and the National Association of Manufacturers (NAM). Both organizations combined policy discussions with lobbying, giving them a political flavor and a combative image. Both had headquarters in Washington and wide-ranging memberships. They operated through issue-oriented standing committees, magazines and newsletters, and annual membership conferences.

The national Chamber of Commerce was founded in 1912 at the initiative of Filene and other progressive businessmen in the Boston area (Wiebe 1962:35–36; Nelson 1969:42). Due to this Boston influence during the 1920s and early 1930s, the Chamber sometimes took a relatively enlightened stand on new policy proposals, at least compared to the NAM, and its leadership played an important role in supporting proposals enacted early in the New Deal. However, it was taken over by businessmen vehemently opposed to the New Deal in May 1935 and rarely played a proactive role thereafter, except on the creation of the Council of Economic Advisers in 1946 (Collins 1981:chap. 4).

The NAM was founded in 1896 to promote the expansion of overseas sales for American products, but was transformed into an antiunion organization in 1903 and has opposed unions and most social legislation ever since. Its leadership tends to come from the smaller of big businesses in most decades, but the DuPont clan—based in its ownership of General Motors, DuPont Corporation, and U.S. Rubber—took control of it in 1934 and used it to launch attacks on the New Deal (Burch 1973; Burk 1990).

Smaller policy discussion groups based primarily in the largest of big businesses had either lost their way by the 1920s or were very new to the scene in the 1930s. The group that lost its way was the National Civic Federation, formed in 1900 by several of the top corporate leaders of that era. It was a significant force for moderate conservatism in its early years, leading the way on industrial accident insurance, welfare benefits in corporations, and the creation of the Federal Trade Commission (Jensen 1956; Green 1956; Weinstein 1968). Leaders of the National Civic Federation invited officers of the American Federation of Labor (AFL) into their organization, although the role they envisioned even for craft unions was a very limited one. Still, their approach had some differences from that of the NAM. They also sought the advice of academic experts on occasion, and worked with them on some issues.

However, the National Civic Federation drifted to the right during and after World War I, with most of its original agenda fulfilled and business leaders no longer interested in discussing general policy issues with labor leaders. The organization became the creature of its longtime executive director, who joined with his friend Samuel Gompers, president of the AFL, in denouncing liberals as communists and opposing most new legislation. It still served as a meeting group between AFL leaders and some businessmen in the 1920s, but not much else, and was totally irrelevant in the 1930s (Domhoff 1970:168–70).

Meanwhile, the Council on Foreign Relations, today a central organization in the policy-planning network, was only developed in 1921, and did not have any real impact until its War-Peace Studies during World War II, which shaped American foreign policy in the postwar era (Shoup and Minter 1977; Domhoff 1990:chaps. 5 and 6; Wala 1994).

Even more undeveloped, the Business Advisory Council was created in 1933 to aid the Department of Commerce and advise Roosevelt. Its original forty-one members together held over one hundred directorships in the largest banks and corporations, and it had the CEOs of General Electric and Standard Oil of New Jersey as its top leaders. Although the organization did not have a strong general influence until World War II and after (McQuaid 1982), it will figure in the story of the Social Security Act told in Chapter 5.

One of the most central discussion groups of the postwar era, the Committee for Economic Development, was not created until 1942, as an extension of the Business Advisory Council (Schriftgiesser 1960, 1967; Eakins 1966, Collins, 1981). Some of its members had a hand in the industrial mobilization for World War II, but they were members of the Business Advisory Council as well, so it is difficult to assign any measure of influence to the organization until its role in passing a mild form of the Employment Act of 1946 (Bailey 1950; Domhoff 1990:chap. 7).

Two quantitative studies show in great detail how the policy-planning network of recent years is integrated into the upper class and corporate community. Bonacich and Domhoff (1981) analyzed a 36 × 36 matrix of overlapping social club and policy group members, using a hierarchical algebra that revealed two regional clusters of clubs and policy groups, and a nationwide cluster that integrated the two. The integrating cluster included three major policy discussion groups (Conference Board, Committee for Economic Development, Business Council) and social clubs in New York, Pittsburgh, and Chicago. The network was linked to the corporate community through the finding that the most central people in the network were directors of large corporations.

Using a database for 1970 supplied by Thomas Dye (1976) that included 201 corporations, twenty New York law firms, the eleven largest foundations, the twelve richest private universities, seven civic/cultural institutions, six think tanks and policy discussion groups, Harold Salzman and Domhoff (1983) used a centrality measure to analyze the integration of the corporate community with the policy-planning network. As Table 2.3 shows, two foundations and four policy discussion groups joined corporate giants like IBM, General Foods, and General Motors in the top twenty-five. The rankings for the other foundations and policy groups in the study are

*Table 2.3.*  The 25 Most Central Organizations in the American Corporate Community

| | Organization | Size[a] | Organizational interlocks | Centrality |
|---|---|---|---|---|
| 1. | IBM | 18 | 34 | 1.00 |
| 2. | Conference Board[b] | 31 | 53 | 0.87 |
| 3. | General Foods | 16 | 24 | 0.81 |
| 4. | Chemical Bank | 24 | 36 | 0.79 |
| 5. | Committee for Economic Development[b] | 200 | 119 | 0.78 |
| 6. | New York Life | 25 | 36 | 0.77 |
| 7. | Yale University[b] | 18 | 23 | 0.66 |
| 8. | Morgan Guaranty Trust | 24 | 40 | 0.65 |
| 9. | Consolidated Edison | 14 | 22 | 0.63 |
| 10. | Rockefeller Foundation[b] | 19 | 25 | 0.62 |
| 11. | Chase Manhattan | 24 | 33 | 0.62 |
| 12. | AT&T | 18 | 35 | 0.60 |
| 13. | U.S. Steel | 17 | 30 | 0.59 |
| 14. | Sloan Foundation[b] | 16 | 25 | 0.59 |
| 15. | Caterpillar Tractor | 11 | 19 | 0.59 |
| 16. | General Motors | 23 | 31 | 0.54 |
| 17. | Citibank | 27 | 37 | 0.53 |
| 18. | Pan American | 23 | 25 | 0.52 |
| 19. | Council on Foreign Relations[b] | 1,400 | 154 | 0.52 |
| 20. | Metropolitan Life | 29 | 30 | 0.51 |
| 21. | Metropolitan Museum[b] | 44 | 37 | 0.47 |
| 22. | Equitable Life | 37 | 42 | 0.47 |
| 23. | Mobil Oil | 13 | 14 | 0.46 |
| 24. | MIT[b] | 74 | 54 | 0.45 |
| 25. | American Assembly[b] | 19 | 26 | 0.44 |

*Source:*  Salzman and Domhoff (1983: 210).

[a] The size of an organization is the number of directors or trustees on the controlling board of the organization, except in the cases of the Committee for Economic Development and the Council on Foreign Relations, where all members are included. Organizational interlocks are the number of connections an organization has to other organizations in the corporate community through sharing one or more directors with other organizations. The centrality of an organization is a mathematical expression of both the number of organizational interlocks and the degree to which those interlocks are with other organizations that are highly central to the overall network.

[b] Nonprofit organization.

presented in Table 2.4. One of the most interesting findings is the peripheral nature of the National Association of Manufacturers, whose directors by then came from corporations in the top one thousand, but not the top two hundred (vice-presidents from the biggest corporations were active on NAM committees, however).

*Table 2.4.* The Centrality Rankings of Prestigious
Universities, Foundations, Cultural Groups, and
Policy Groups in the Corporate Network[a]

|  | Ranking |
|---|---|
| **University** | |
| Yale | 7 |
| MIT | 24 |
| Princeton | 29 |
| Chicago | 41 |
| Columbia | 48 |
| Harvard | 50 |
| Dartmouth | 56 |
| Johns Hopkins | 60 |
| Northwestern | 63 |
| Stanford | 95 |
| Pennsylvania | 106 |
| Cornell | 145 |
| **Cultural and civic group** | |
| Metropolitan Museum | 21 |
| Smithsonian Institution | 30 |
| American Red Cross | 33 |
| Museum of Modern Art | 59 |
| National Gallery of Art | 90 |
| Metropolitan Opera Association | 200 |
| JFK Center for Performing Arts | 210 |
| **Foundation** | |
| Rockefeller Foundation | 10 |
| Sloan Foundation | 14 |
| Carnegie Corporation | 61 |
| Ford Foundation | 69 |
| Hartford Foundation | 102 |
| Mellon Foundation | 121 |
| Mott Foundation | 151 |
| Duke Endowment | 172 |
| Lilly Endowment | 185 |
| Kellogg Foundation | 187 |
| Kresge Foundation[c] | |
| **Policy group** | |
| Conference Board | 2 |
| Committee for Economic Development | 5 |
| Council on Foreign Relations | 19 |
| American Assembly | 25 |
| Brookings Institution | 42 |
| National Association of Manufacturers | 196 |

*Source:* Salzman and Domhoff (1983: 211).
[a] Out of a total of 256 organizations that were studied.
[c] Isolate (no connections to any other organization studied).

Now that the relationship of the policy-planning network to the upper class and corporate community is clearly established, I want to close this section with a visual representation of how the three networks are interconnected. As Figure 2.4 shows, some people are members of only one of the three, others of two, and a few of all three. Those who are members of all three are certainly at the heart of the power elite, but we also see that people who are neither upper class nor corporate leaders can be members of it by virtue of their high-level positions in the policy-planning network. This diagram reinforces what I explained in my earlier discussion about the relationship of the upper class and the power elite. On the one hand, a person can

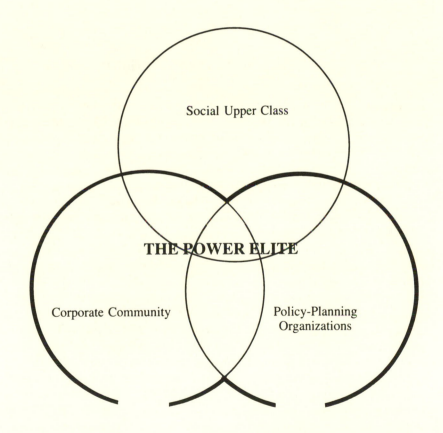

*Figure 2.4* A multinetwork view of the relationship between the upper class and the power elite, showing the overlaps of the social upper class, corporate community and policy-planning network. The power elite is defined by the thick lines.

be a member of the upper class, but not involved in governing. Conversely, a person can be a member of the power elite, but not in the upper class. Thus, this diagram provides a detailed view of the networks that make up the power elite, showing the people involved in the class/organizational synthesis. It warns again that to reduce my view to one of dominance by business executives, as the state autonomy theorists do, is inaccurate.

Now that my multinetwork conception of the American power structure is in place, the sixty-four-dollar question is how it connects to political parties and the state. I want to reserve my general answer until I introduce its main rival in these two arenas: the liberal-labor coalition. Then we can see how the two rivals fare on government appointments, voting in Congress, and, of course, government decisions on key issues, the central topic of this book.

## CONSERVATIVES, LIBERALS, AND CLASS CONFLICT

If we were able to do a membership network analysis that included every person in the United States, we would find very few people in any institutional network. This conclusion follows from studies showing that only one-third participate in any policy-oriented organization even at the local level, and only 10 percent give any money to a political party (e.g., Hamilton 1972:chap. 2; Flacks 1988:chap. 2). However, if we look more narrowly at the networks created by the shared memberships, financing, and policy positions of lobbying and advocacy groups, we find two coalitions competing for the attention, allegiance, and votes of the Great Unorganized (e.g., McCune 1956; Deakin 1966; Ross 1967; Hall 1969; Melone 1977). These two coalitions also are clearly revealed in a comprehensive quantitative analysis of PAC donations to congressional candidates in 1984: business PACs were the heart of one large clique of donors, labor and public-interest groups of the other (Neustadtl, Scott, and Clawson 1991).

The first coalition is based in the upper class and power elite, which reach out to and fund a very large number of conservative groups concerned with tax reduction, patriotism, religion, and morality. It has the support of the real estate and development interests ("growth elites") that dominate local and county governments (Molotch 1976, 1979; Logan and Molotch 1987). As I stated in the first chapter, I call this the corporate-conservative coalition.

The second of these coalitions is based in liberal organizations and trade unions. This liberal-labor coalition is less well financed and is of more recent vintage, roughly the second term of Roosevelt's presidency. It came into being because of the Great Depression as one part of the larger Roose-velt coalition, which already included southern plantation elites, who were the mortal enemies of the liberal-labor coalition. True, there were liberals (often called reformers) before the New Deal, and they sometimes worked with unions, but many of the reformers were still Progressive Republicans, and the unions did not like social policies that brought the federal govern-ment into the picture until well into the depression.

When we compare the corporate-conservative and liberal-labor coali-tions, we can safely say the former is more organized than the latter. How-ever, this kind of a claim is still too strong for historians like Gabriel Kolko and his students, who claim business is highly fragmented (e.g., Kolko 1963; Vittoz 1987; Gordon 1994), or for those participants in the power elite who see nothing but chaos and personal rivalry all around them. To accommodate their concerns, we can approach the point about organiza-tion in terms of how the world looks from the individual viewpoint: the corporate-conservative coalition is slightly less disorganized, confused, and shortsighted than its opponents. Both sides, that is, are made up of strug-gling, muddled, egotistical individuals. However, when it comes to the exercise of power, either perspective adds up to the same conclusion. The corporate-conservative coalition generally is more cohesive than the liberal-labor one. From a sociological point of view, the Kolko school of business history and the participant-observers in the power elite are letting the day-to-day noise of rhetoric and personal ambition obscure the stability of the class and institutional structure of American society.

Like the corporate-conservative coalition, the liberal-labor coalition is made up of only a small percentage of the population. Those liberals who are not from the working class or the union movement are in a minority in the professional social stratum from which they usually come, and union members are a minority in the working class. Moreover, the union move-ment was even smaller at the outset of the New Deal than it is now due to the large number of defeats it suffered in the years after World War I (Bern-stein 1960). Still, it was able nonetheless to influence political parties and the government to some extent, and to grow in the 1930s.

Nor did the liberal-labor coalition develop easily during the New Deal. There were arguments among the liberals about whether to break up large corporations or control them through government planning, for example, and the liberals were not impressed with the AFL leadership. Rexford Tug-well, one of Roosevelt's most liberal policy advisers, writing in 1933, was critical of the unions for their submissiveness to business, their backward leadership, and their unwillingness to listen to experts (1933:5–6, 133). Bernstein (1950:1–4) provides other examples of the negative opinions held by liberals of the time toward trade union leadership. Thomas Emerson, a very liberal New Deal lawyer, later recalled that he was "astonished by the incompetence, narrowness, and stupidity of the AFL traditionalists," then added that the young CIO group was "incomparably more alert, intelligent, and aggressive" (1991:28–29).

When we look at the issues dividing the two coalitions, they add up to what is meant by class conflict, because they involve fundamentally opposed views on how the revenues taken in by corporations, plantations, and other profit-making entities that employ wage labor should be divided up. The liberal-labor coalition wants the corporate rich to pay higher wages to workers and higher taxes to government. The corporate-conservative coalition rejects these two objectives completely, claiming they endanger the freedom of individuals and the workings of the free market. The desire for higher wages and bigger government social programs leads the liberal-labor coalition to take two organizational steps. The first is unionization of the work force, which is opposed vehemently by the corporate-conservative coalition in every way possible. The second is politics, which takes place in the liberal wing of the Democratic party because of the great difficulties in sustaining a third party in a presidential system that also elects legislators from districts (i.e., a series of "winner-take-all" elections makes a vote for a liberal third party a vote for the coalition's least favorite (Republican) choice between the two major parties due to the fact that it is one less vote for the Democratic candidate).

One of the political demands made of the state by the liberal-labor coalition—help in unionizing—is in my view the single most important factor in determining the antigovernment stance of the corporate-conservative coalition. Despite all that the state does for the corporate-conservative coalition in promoting and subsidizing businesses, and in providing protection for private property, it is nonetheless viewed with suspicion and watched with care by the power elite because it is a real threat to corporate control of labor markets, either by employing unemployed workers or supporting unionization.[3] Fear of losing control of labor markets, I believe, is the power issue that links class conflict to the antigovernment orientation of the power elite. Much of this book will be an attempt to demonstrate this hypothesis during both the New Deal and the Progressive Era.

The emphasis on attitudes toward unionization and big government as the defining issues in class conflict in the United States gives us an empirical way to define liberals for the purposes of this book regardless of their social class of origin. This definition deals with a question critics often raise about a class dominance analysis: What about rich liberals? Well, rich liberals are those rare "traitors to their class." They have dropped out of the institutional frameworks through which they normally would participate in politics and governance.

The fundamental differences of opinion on unions and government aid to

*Table 2.5.*  The Similarities and Differences Among Elites, Experts, Liberals, and Trade Unionists

|  | Upper class? | Corporate community? | Policy network? | Rep/Dem? | Pro union? |
|---|---|---|---|---|---|
| Northern upper class | Yes | Yes | Yes | Rep | No |
| Southern upper class | Yes | Yes | Yes | Dem | No |
| Rich liberals | Yes | No | No | Dem | Yes |
| Corporate experts | Maybe | Maybe | Yes | either | No |
| Liberal experts | Maybe | No | No | Dem | Yes |
| Trade unionists | No | No | No | Dem | Yes |

unionization also allow us to distinguish between corporate experts in the policy-planning network and liberal experts. Table 2.5 shows how members of the power elite, wealthy liberals, the two kinds of experts, and trade unionists compare. The table includes an issue I have not discussed yet: southern employers were Democrats for the one hundred years between 1870 and 1970.

The basis for trade unions is obviously in those people who (1) work for a wage or salary, whether wearing a blue, pink, or white collar, and (2) believe in collective action. But what are the backgrounds of those liberals who are not part of the trade union movement? There are four basic sources, in increasing order of importance in terms of their numbers: First, as already suggested, some come from wealthy families. Although they are few in number, they provide the liberal-labor coalition with some of its strongest and most forceful leaders.

Second, employees who work for the mass media, especially journalists, are a source of liberals. They not only contribute financially to liberal causes, but their access to the reading public, through carefully timed exposés and leaks, can make it seem like the liberal-labor coalition has more support than may be the case. This exaggeration of liberal-labor strength, through the magic we attribute to the printed word, often puts pressure on both elected and appointed officials.

However, this does not mean that all journalists are liberals, or even a majority of them. Major national media owners are part of the corporate community (e.g., Dreier 1981), and locally owned newspapers are an integral part of the progrowth elites (Molotch 1976). Moreover, journalists are socialized into the norms and routines of the organizations they work for, like everyone else, and editors exercise control over what goes into the newspapers (e.g., Breed 1955; Gans 1979; Gitlin 1980; Paletz and Entman 1981). All that said, the media remains one of the few places in which liberals are found.

Literary and artistic communities are a third source of liberals (e.g., Lipset 1960:chap. 10; Kadushin 1974). Like journalists, people from these communities can make their voices heard and bring attention to liberal-labor causes.

Fourth, university communities are the most important base for the liberals within the liberal-labor coalition, and this has been true since at least the turn of the century (e.g., Lipset 1960:chap. 10, 1982). These communities include librarians and other staff members as well as professors and students. At the same time, there are dramatic differences from discipline to discipline in the professors' inclination toward liberal causes, with engineers and law professors traditionally at the conservative end of the continuum, natural and social scientists at the other. Through books, lectures, and access to the media, university personnel join writers, artists, and journalists in having the ability to bring their cause to the wider public.

## The Left

My stress in this book is on the liberal-labor coalition as the main opponent of the power elite, but some readers may be surprised that I have not called it the labor-liberal-left coalition because a heterogenous group of socialists and communists often works within or for this coalition. I recognize that this diverse group called the Left exists, but I do not think it deserves equal billing with labor and liberals for several reasons.

First, leftists often work against the liberal-labor coalition. The history of the largest leftist group in the 1930s, the Communist party, is illustrative. Until Moscow changed its stance toward liberals and socialists in 1935, the American party tried to form rival unions to the AFL and denounced every aspect of Roosevelt's program as incipient fascism or fakery. Then, after four years of supporting labor and liberal causes, the Communists again worked against this coalition on some issues in 1939 and 1940 when Stalin signed his peace pact with Hitler. When Hitler attacked the Soviet Union, the Communists once again became fully supportive of the liberal-labor coalition, but were so concerned about the Soviet Union that they would not support a march on Washington by African-Americans for fear it would interfere with military production (e.g., Weinstein 1975; Klehr 1984).

Second, I do not give the Left equal weight because it was so small. Judging by the conservatives' emphasis on it, or the number of books on it, the Left looms gigantic on the American landscape, but in fact the conservatives exaggerate the size, importance, and power of the Left as a way of attacking the liberal-labor coalition, which is a genuine threat to them.[4] As for the books on leftists, we are fascinated with the lives of dissenters, whether we are ordinary readers or academic authors. They attract attention for their human interest, and as possible sources of useful information for people looking for ways to change society.

Third, I exclude the Left from the liberal-labor coalition because very few labor leaders or liberals considered it to be part of their coalition. True, the leaders of the CIO hired Communist organizers to help them build the new industrial unions, but they still saw the Communists as hired hands, not as allies, and they did not trust them.

Nevertheless, the Left sometimes played an important role within the liberal-labor coalition, and that contribution should not be overlooked (Stepan-Norris and Zeitlin 1989, 1991). Steeled by a strong ideology promising a better future for everyone, leftists very often are the activists or exemplars who take bold actions when most people are cowed into inaction by authority figures or fearful of the peer pressure that comes with being part of a group (Flacks 1988:chap. 1). They also do some of the day-to-day organizational work that keeps a movement going. It was leftists, mostly of the Communist party, but some socialists as well, who started the Unemployment Leagues and Unemployment Councils, which helped to overcome the despair and inaction still prevailing two and three years into the Great Depression (e.g., Piven and Cloward 1977). Trotskyists in Minneapolis, followers of A. J. Muste in Toledo, and Communists and fellow travelers in San Francisco led the massive and dramatic strikes in the spring and summer of 1934 that did so much to overcome the lethargic and hesitant positions taken by most of the established AFL leadership (e.g., Bernstein 1970). Leftists also played a big part in the organization of the CIO in the years between 1937 and 1940.

Whether or not readers think it is justified to exclude the Left from the liberal-labor coalition, one final point makes the issue moot for purposes of this book: the Left had little or no impact on the substance of any of the issues I analyze in subsequent chapters.

## POLITICS AND GOVERNMENT

I claim that the power elite impacts government through four separate processes. For individuals, corporations, or specific industries seeking tax breaks, subsidies, friendly regulatory rulings, and other favors beneficial to their short-run interests, there is the special-interest process (Domhoff 1979:chap. 2). It is staffed by lobbyists, former government lawyers, former politicians, and vice-presidents at trade associations. Interviews by Laumann, Tam, Heinz, Nelson, and Salisbury (1992) with vice-presidents and legislative directors at this level hardly tell us anything about the so-called eastern establishment, as they assert, but they do provide evidence for a class conflict theory by finding labor issues the most polarized policy domain in their study.

The second process connecting the power elite to government concerns general policy planning; it is rooted in the policy-planning network outlined earlier in the chapter. The third linkage to government concerns the election of public officials: I call it the *candidate selection process* to emphasize how little political parties in the United States have to do with anything but filling offices (Domhoff 1979:chap. 4). Finally, there is the ideology process, a diffuse network of small organizations radiating out from the policy-planning network and the corporate-conservative coalition. These organizations try to shape public opinion (but do not always succeed) through contacts with middle-class civic organizations, outreach by the public affairs offices of large corporations, direct mailings, and advertising in the mass media (Domhoff 1979:chap. 5). For purposes of this book, I will be concentrating on the policy-planning and candidate selection processes.

I turn now to a consideration of the political parties, which are indeed important in the United States, as state autonomy theorists constantly emphasize. In fact, I think they have in effect become an outreach branch of the state now that they rely almost exclusively on primaries set by legislatures to select their candidates and accept government financing of their candidates in presidential elections. Because American parties have no organizational discipline to speak of, they are highly individualistic. The need to appeal to middle-of-the-road voters in a winner-take-all system reinforces the tendency to blur issues and focus on the personal qualities of individual candidates. The focus on name recognition, personality, and symbolic issues creates the need for financial support, and, of course, no one is in a better position to supply it than members of the power elite. The person with the largest war chest does not always win, but it takes a large minimum to play the game, especially in party primaries (Heard 1962:34; Alexander 1976:44).

Campaign donations, whether from individuals or PACs, fit perfectly into a membership network. Donations are a form of membership in the party or campaign, and they allow us to trace the pattern of corporate allegiances with quantifiable precision (e.g., Clawson, Neustadtl, and Bearden 1986; Burris 1987; Neustadtl and Clawson 1988; Burris and Salt 1990; Su, Neustadtl, and Clawson 1992). These quantitative studies are supplemented by revealing interviews with key participants in the money-raising process (e.g., Alexander 1958; Clawson, Neustadtl, and Scott 1992). Most corporate money goes to Republicans and conservative (usually southern) Democrats, but sometimes liberal incumbents are funded by corporate PACS to maintain access and possible consideration on specific issues. Money from the liberal-labor coalition goes to liberal and moderate Democrats, of course, but the liberals usually are outspent by a wide margin.

Thanks to the work of Louise Overacker (1932, 1933, 1937, 1941, 1945), we have a good picture of campaign finance at the presidential level between 1928 and 1944, and especially for 1936, when she created a name file for every donor of one hundred dollars or more from government records scheduled to be destroyed (they were not, as it turns out). Her studies show most corporate leaders supported the Republicans; the major exceptions were tobacco executives in the South, oil executives from Texas and Oklahoma, and brewers who were grateful for the end of prohibition (Overacker 1937:486–87). Donors of one thousand dollars or more provided 51 percent of the roughly $7.6 million raised by the Republicans, and about 23 percent of the approximately $5.2 million collected or borrowed by the Democrats (Overacker 1937:479, 483, for the figures from which these calculations were made).[5] Southerners provided 37 percent of the Democrats' cash contributions, supplemented by officeholders (several of whom were wealthy ambassadorial appointees), organized labor ($770,000 if its expenditures outside the party are counted), advertising revenues from a convention book, and donations from a few wealthy northern mavericks. In a study of the ninety-three largest Democratic donors for 1932 and 1936, 74 percent of the seventy-eight we could find information on were members of the upper class (Domhoff 1967, 91).

Michael Webber (1990, 1991a, 1991b; Webber and Domhoff 1996) utilized Overacker's data to analyze the patterns of donations by corporate directors in a wide range of industries. His first finding was that surprisingly few gave anything at all at the presidential level, as low as 15–20 percent in some sectors of the economy, which is consistent with findings for corporate officers and directors for 1968 by Alexander (1971) and Domhoff (1972:15). Webber found that many of the rare exceptions to Republican support were due to regional and religious factors. In the tobacco industry, for example, ten of the eleven donors from northern companies gave to the Republicans, but twelve of the fifteen donors from southern companies gave to the Democrats. In large northern department stores, religion proved to be the important factor: nine of the eleven Christian donors gave to the Republicans, eleven of the seventeen Jewish donors gave to the Democrats (Webber 1991b).

Very similar findings are reported for 1936 on 300 members of wealthy families, 250 corporate directors, and 72 members of the corporate inner circle (Allen 1991). Of the one-third of wealthy family members who contributed to either party, only one-twelfth gave to the Democrats, with southern and Jewish families more likely to give to the Democrats. The corporate directors, whether in the inner circle or not, were even less likely to give to the Democrats.

However, there are limits to what we can learn from systematic studies of campaign finance before the 1950s, especially below the presidential level, because of underreporting of donations. We often have to rely on journalistic and biographical sources instead. Take the case of Senator Jimmy Byrnes of South Carolina, who will appear at key points in this study. After losing out in his first try for the Senate, he relied on funding from one of the richest men in the country, Bernard Baruch, to bankroll his successful radio blitz in 1930. The two then became very close friends as Baruch backed Byrnes's bid for a major Senate role by giving personal loans and campaign support to legislators favored by Byrnes (Robertson 1994:101–3, 127–28). This story is prototypical: show me a conservative politician who is not wealthy to begin with and I will show you a financial backer who became essential to his or her career at an early stage.

When we turn to the state itself, there are three kinds of information of interest to us: (1) the previous social, economic, policy-planning, liberal, or union connections of elected and appointed officeholders (for use in positional studies of power); (2) the voting patterns of legislators in the House and Senate (for decisional studies); (3) the substance of presidential orders, regulatory rulings, and congressional legislation (for decisional studies).

There is a very large number of studies on the previous memberships of elected and appointed officials, especially cabinet members. The legislators are lawyers who come from the top 10–15 percent of the social ladder (e.g., Matthews 1954; Zweigenhaft 1975), while the cabinet members come from the power elite (Mills 1956; Mintz 1975; Burch 1981a, 1981b; Sklar and Lawrence 1981; Domhoff 1983:136–43, for a summary). But there is not much use in discussing these findings here because state autonomy theorists do not think such information matters. They believe people act in terms of state needs when they are in state offices. That is, state autonomy theorists are very strong believers in role theory: social background is discounted, not to mention the financially lucrative positions state officials might want to have in the corporate community or policy-planning network in the future (Salzman and Domhoff 1980). The possible pull of past or future roles for the temporary state managers—and most of them are temporary—is not important to state autonomy theorists.

Studies of voting patterns in Congress are quite acceptable to state autonomy theorists, and of great interest to me. Aage Clausen (1973), Barbara Sinclair (1982, 1985), and Mack Shelley's (1983) analyses of congressional voting from the 1920s through the 1970s reveal clusters that in my mind reflect the great influence of employers on the northern Republicans and southern Democrats. Since the late 1930s a majority of northern Republicans and southern Democrats have voted together in opposition to a majority of northern Democrats on the following issues: (1) labor legislation (i.e., legislation that would help unions or benefit workers generally); (2) civil rights legislation (i.e., labor legislation for African-Americans in the South); (3) corporate regulation.

This voting alliance is called the conservative coalition; its history has been traced in detail (Patterson 1967) and its existence as a conscious strategy has been documented (Manley 1973). In the 1960s and 1970s commentators of the moment always claimed it was about to disappear, but studies into the late 1970s showed otherwise (e.g., Shelley 1983:24–25, 34–35), and it was the reason the Reagan tax cuts passed in the early 1980s (Domhoff 1990:280–81). By the late 1980s, however, the Republicans gained so heavily in the South that less than a majority of southern Democrats was needed to block liberal programs. Whatever its party label, the majority in both houses of Congress has been conservative on issues of concern to the corporate-conservative coalition except in the mid-1930s and mid-1960s, when social upheaval and liberal insurgency upset the pattern.

However, the voting pattern studies also show that the majority of southern Democrats sometimes vote with the majority of northern Democrats on certain issues opposed by most Republicans: (1) agricultural subsidies (which go differentially to the South); (2) government management (a catch-all rubric that includes government spending programs like housing). Since both of these issues involve government money for constituents, we can say the Democratic party has been a prospending alliance since the Great Depression. The southern Democrats like the agricultural subsidies and many other federal subsidy programs coming into their region, which even today provide over half of the budget in some southern states. In return for this largesse, southern Democrats support spending programs advocated by Democrats from urban areas in the North (Domhoff 1990:240–43).

I think the overall findings on voting patterns are strong support for my class conflict perspective: the northern Republicans and southern Democrats are united in opposing any legislation that would help employees, and the liberal Democrats support it. However, we will encounter two instances where one part of the conservative coalition abandons the other, thirty years apart, in 1935 and 1964, leading to the two most important victories for the liberal-labor coalition in the twentieth century. But more of that at the appropriate places in our story.

When we come to the third type of useful information on the state, the substantive outcomes of executive and legislative decisions, we have entered a favorite realm of the state autonomy theorists: Who wins and who loses? I have already pledged to play their game by focusing primarily on this power indicator in the rest of the book.[6] What follows, then, are five case studies of state issues claimed by one or more state autonomy theorists as evidence for their claims.

Since the chapters are case studies and critiques, they do not tell the whole historical story for any issue or time period. They are not descriptive histories, but accounts of theoretically relevant events. There always were more things going on than I discuss. For example, there were other titles to the Social Security Act besides the two I analyze in Chapter 5, but the others were not controversial at the time and therefore are not central to my analysis. However, I recognize that the provision for Aid to Families with Dependent Children is of great relevance in understanding why welfare became so stigmatized (e.g., Gordon 1994; Mink 1995), so I am not denying the importance of issues I do not analyze.

New Deal Agricultural Policy

## INTRODUCTION

If there is one research finding by the political scientists and historians of the fifties, sixties, and seventies that seems to have stood the test of time, it is their demonstration that farm and business groups outside the state were able to exert enormous influence over New Deal agricultural policy (McConnell 1953, 1966; Campbell 1962; Conrad 1965; Kirkendall 1966; Baldwin 1968; Perkins 1969; Grubb 1971; Mertz 1978). According to these detailed empirical accounts, farmers and their allies achieved their aims through three very direct means: (1) They enjoyed very close relations with key agencies of the Department of Agriculture, especially the Extension Service. (2) They had the ability to lobby the influential (usually southern) members of congressional agricultural committees. (3) They had access to the White House due to the fact that many of them were part of the Roosevelt coalition.

It would thus seem unlikely that anyone would challenge the established theory on New Deal farm policy, but such a challenge nonetheless has emerged from within the camp of state autonomy theory (Finegold 1981; Skocpol and Finegold 1982; Hooks 1990; Finegold and Skocpol 1995). According to these analysts, it is precisely in the area of New Deal agricultural policy that their general theory of state autonomy can be demonstrated most clearly. As they see it, the major New Deal subsidy program for helping commercial farmers emerged from within the state. This domestic allotment program, and the Agricultural Adjustment Administration that administered it, supposedly were made possible by the state's long-standing employment of agricultural economists, who gave the state the administrative capacity to succeed with the program.

Hooks (1990) goes even further, making three very unique claims that even Finegold and Skocpol (1995) are unwilling to contemplate. First, he asserts that "from 1932 to 1940, the USDA grew stronger and more insulated"; it was therefore able to play "an active role in agricultural legislation" (Hooks 1990:29). His second unique claim concerns the emphasis he puts on a little research agency within the Department of Agriculture, the Bureau of Agricultural Economics (BAE). He sees it as an exemplar of the autonomy of the USDA in the late 1930s. In particular he believes the grass roots land

use planning committees sponsored by the BAE are evidence for his autonomy claims; he asserts that these land use committees "flourished" (pp. 33–
34). Third, Hooks disagrees with most other commentators on New Deal
agricultural policy when he claims that the demise in the early 1940s of the
two most liberal agricultural agencies, the BAE and the Farm Security Administration, was not due to the strength of external forces, but to two
intertwined factors within the state itself: conflict between the new secretary
of agriculture appointed in September 1940 and his inherited staff, and
Roosevelt's unwillingness to protect the liberal agencies from their congressional enemies any longer because his primary focus was on mobilizing the
state for war (p. 36).

These claims by the state autonomy theorists are surprising because they
are based on secondary sources that either disagree with them on state
autonomy or are tangential to the issue. Given the fact that doubt is being
raised about an empirically grounded theory, it might be thought that the
insurgents would do so on the basis of new discoveries in archival sources,
or at least a systematic combing of archival sources for information related
to their hypothesis. Instead, the new claims are based on a very selective
reading and reinterpretation of some of the historical sources cited in the first
paragraph above.

What Finegold, Skocpol, and Hooks see as an example of state autonomy
is actually something very different, an opportunity to show the weaknesses
of state autonomy theory when it is applied to the United States. To accomplish this task, I will begin with a discussion of the book that serves as the
perfect counterpoint to any attempt to claim state autonomy on agricultural
policy, Grant McConnell's now-classic *The Decline of Agrarian Democracy*
(1953). My own analysis will build on, defend, and slightly amend McConnell's path-breaking work. Along with Floyd Hunter's (1953) community
power study of Atlanta, it introduced the notion of a power structure into the
post–World War II social science literature, and its grounding of the farm
power structure in organizational theory is a seminal insight.

Following the discussion of McConnell's work, the chapter will turn to
the origins of the domestic allotment plan, and then to the class conflict in
southern agriculture that the plan helped to generate. From there I will move
to the attempts by USDA officials to gain autonomy from farm interests and
then to a discussion of the outside pressures on the Farm Security Administration. The reasons for the brief rise and rapid decline of the Bureau of
Agricultural Economics are the next focus of attention, followed by a summary of the evidence and arguments that favor a class dominance theory
over state autonomy theory on New Deal agricultural policy. The general
theme of the chapter is that the ability of southern plantation owners and
other commercial farmers to subdue agricultural workers, not the existence

of state capacity, is the primary reason for the success of New Deal agricultural policy.

## MCCONNELL ON THE FARM POWER STRUCTURE

Based in part on his brief experience as an employee of the Farm Security Administration late in the New Deal, and even more on his subsequent dissertation research, Grant McConnell's *The Decline of Agrarian Democracy* (1953) was a theoretical challenge to the conventional wisdom of its day, and it remains the standard against which any new theory of agricultural policymaking must be measured. The conventional wisdom McConnell challenged was expressed in another book published in 1953, Murray Benedict's *Farm Policies in the United States, 1790–1950*. According to Benedict, the farm organizations of the early twentieth century "were, for the most part, followers of administration leadership, rather than creators of new policies and programs" (p. 339) when it came to the origins of New Deal agricultural policies. More pointedly, "the ideas for the new programs came more largely out of the imaginative minds of the group of young policy makers in Washington than from the farm organizations" (p. 346). In effect, it is this public administration theory, as originally applied to the Department of Agriculture by John Gaus and Leon Wolcotte (1940), that the state autonomy theorists are trying to resurrect; Finegold and Skocpol (1995:59–60, 63–64, 265, footnote 153) rely heavily on Gaus and Wolcotte, calling their arguments "highly insightful" and "sophisticated."

McConnell's analysis stressed the ways in which the most prosperous commercial farmers were able to take advantage of the decentralized Extension Service, based in both land grant colleges and the Department of Agriculture, to create their own lobbying organization, the American Farm Bureau Federation. This organization became powerful because it had a strong local base and at the same time could lobby successfully at the national level. In particular this "federation of federations" was able to build an alliance between the cotton and tobacco farmers of the South and the corn and hog farmers of the Midwest. These two regional groupings were the dominant farming interests in the nation in the years before World War II.

The American Farm Bureau Federation (hereafter either Farm Bureau or AFBF) and the county agents employed by the Extension Service were the basis for a "structure of power" or "power structure" (McConnell 1953:7, 72, chap. 16) that bridged the private-public distinction, or what is now called the division between civil society and the state (cf. Selznick 1947).

Although McConnell's primary emphasis is on the fact that there is a symbiosis among interest groups, bureaucrats, some politicians, and expert advisers, he says that in the final analysis the alliance between commercial farmers and county agents meant that "a segment of the public bureaucracy has been captured and made to serve as the bureaucracy of a private association" (1953:176).

McConnell sees political parties as the only serious rivals to this power structure. Indeed, he believes an interest group and a political party are natural opponents because the interest group is based in a "minimum inclusiveness" while the political party is "based on a loose and shifting alliance of diverse elements" (1953:174). Sometimes the two can work in harmony, but if the power structure challenges the party, "the two engage in a struggle for which the formal government is the ground of battle" (ibid.).

Although McConnell (p. 161) notes that a class theory and organizational theory are not "necessarily" incompatible, he puts his greatest emphasis on organizational theory in explaining the operation of the power structure in agriculture. In part he rejects a full-fledged class analysis because most farmers outside the South and California were of relatively modest means and often did not employ workers. Then too, all farmers sometimes were at odds with certain business groups, such as processors and distributors of farm products, over specific issues (pp. 160, 171, 177). Most importantly, the vociferous reaction of the Farm Bureau to the slightest challenge to its power did not seem to be warranted in any economic sense by the small threat that liberal initiatives posed to the "cheap labor market" desired by the growers in the South and California (p. 125). Indeed, his puzzlement concerning this apparent overreaction by the Farm Bureau was a key reason for undertaking the study, and any proposed alternative to McConnell's analysis must deal with this issue to be taken seriously.

For McConnell, the reason for the Farm Bureau's strong counterattack to a weak liberal initiative can be found in the need for organizational survival (pp. 125, 177), or, as he puts it at the end of a chapter entitled "The Rationale of Organization": "Thus, the Farm Bureau, like most organizations, is jealous. It seeks to destroy the basis of its rivals' power and to maintain its own" (p. 165).

However, McConnell does not hesitate to acknowledge the help local business elites, and especially bankers, gave to conservative farm groups early in the twentieth century as an antidote to the populism that had arisen in the 1880s and 1890s (pp. 20, 29–32, 47, 164). This included support for the county agents who played a big role in organizing local Farm Bureaus shortly before and during World War I. Further, McConnell (pp. 170–72, 181) argues that the actions of the Farm Bureau helped to reinforce and increase class differences between large and small farmers within the farm sector. All these points are extremely important in reinforcing a trend toward an alliance of rich farmers and businessmen that was in opposition to small farmers, farm workers, and liberals [see McCune (1956) for information on the support business groups gave the Farm Bureau from its outset].

Although I agree with McConnell that class and organizational analyses can (and should) be intertwined, contrary to him I will be giving the class dimension more emphasis by arguing that southern plantation owners, California agribusinessmen, prosperous midwestern farmers, and general business leaders worked out a modus vivendi that adds up to a classwide political position. This classwide unity made it possible for farm and business forces to use the government to their own advantage in the early New Deal through the domestic allotment program, and then to join in a successful class struggle against a liberal-labor coalition that was trying to organize the depression-generated turmoil among tenant farmers, farm laborers, and unemployed rural people. Further, I believe that evidence to be presented in a later section will show that liberal attempts to create a farmer-labor coalition were in good part energized by the problems early New Deal agricultural policies created for southern tenant farmers and farm workers. I will argue that the possibility of a liberal-labor coalition with poor farmers and farm workers then forced the coalition of prosperous farmers and businessmen to seek greater cohesion. In other words, the stirrings of class conflict led to greater class cohesion and class consciousness among large property owners in farming and business. My analysis thus concludes that New Deal agricultural policy involved both class conflict and a struggle for departmental autonomy on the part of some leaders within the Department of Agriculture. The Farm Bureau was central to both conflicts, but its role can be overemphasized. It was aided by several other farm organizations and the Chamber of Commerce of the United States (cf. McCune 1943:7–12).

In addition, I depart somewhat from McConnell's view in arguing that most previous theoretical accounts of New Deal farm policy have not given enough weight to the role of southern plantation owners in determining the outcome of conflicts over departmental autonomy. These southern plantation owners are an ideal example of a *class segment* that has somewhat different interests from the overall ownership class. The desire of southern plantation owners and their allies to maintain complete control over African-Americans in the South made them extraordinarily sensitive to the slightest challenge to the class/race structure there. This sensitivity manifested itself through the veto power that southern white owners had over agricultural policy thanks to their large role in the Democratic party and Congress. In other words, it was the *potential* for class and race struggle in the South that ensured the defeat of those seeking autonomy for the Department of Agriculture. Moreover, the exceptionally close relationship between the Farm Bureau and local representatives of the Department of Agriculture in the South (cf. McConnell 1953:78; Kirkendall 1966:92–93) served to make southern dominance of the Democrats in Congress an even more potent weapon. It also reduced the possibility of rivalry between the Farm Bureau and southern Democrats. That is, the potential for conflict between an interest group and a political party that McConnell rightly raises did not develop because of the one-party system that southern plantation owners had constructed to protect their unique class structure. Thus, my emphasis on the South provides an empirical answer to McConnell's theoretical point about the possibility of conflict between interest groups and parties.

With or without my emendations, McConnell's analysis of how agricultural policy is created and carried out remains the single best starting point from which to challenge any claims about state autonomy in agriculture in the United States. His deployment of organizational theory to show how the Farm Bureau used the Extension Service to create a public-private power structure that blurs the line between government and private enterprise could not present a more stark contrast with state autonomy theory, and my agreement with him on this issue could not be more complete.

## FARM SUBSIDIES AND THE AAA

The domestic allotment program that is the main concern of this section was a key provision in the Agricultural Adjustment Act, passed early in 1933 in the midst of a major farm crisis and serious rural unrest. The domestic allotment program provided government payments to farmers of major crops like cotton, corn, wheat, and tobacco in exchange for voluntary reductions in the number of acres they planted. In conjunction with the commodity loan and home mortgage programs that were created about the same time, the domestic allotment program played a crucial role in restabilizing rural America.

According to Skocpol and Kenneth Finegold (1982:260, 274–75), the domestic allotment program was primarily the product of agricultural economists within the Department of Agriculture who were working from a "public interest" perspective (cf. Finegold and Skocpol 1995:61). These economists, in turn, were part of the "all-important" BAE, which had been created within the department in 1922 by consolidating several agencies and beefing up their research capability (Skocpol and Finegold 1982:272). More generally, these authors put great emphasis on the state "capacity" available in the area of agricultural expertise, meaning that there were experienced experts within agencies of the department who could formulate the needed policies and then serve as administrators and staff in the Agricultural Adjustment Administration (AAA). This in turn supposedly provided the

AAA with autonomy at its outset, although it eventually came to be controlled by the Farm Bureau (Finegold and Skocpol 1995:188, 194).

Finegold and Skocpol (1995:4, 17, 20, 82) also claim that organized farmers originally opposed the domestic allotment program. This claim is important to them because it allegedly shows that (1) the concepts for the program were not developed by private interests and (2) the state forced these groups to accept a program that was not of their own making. As another part of this argument against the importance of farm groups, they note that the Farm Bureau was a weak force in the South until 1932 (e.g., p. 110).

I think the standard sources and new archival findings that will be cited in this section contradict all of these claims in relation to the domestic allotment plan and the AAA. The domestic allotment program had its origins in private foundations and think tanks funded by wealthy business families, and the program was widely supported by leading businessmen well before Roosevelt was elected. Nor was the idea of production control as contrary to the demands of commercial farmers as Finegold and Skocpol contend. This is especially true for the farmers who mattered the most as far as this legislation was concerned, the cotton and tobacco plantation owners of the South, who were in fact very supportive. Moreover, they had stayed out of the Farm Bureau in the 1920s simply because they preferred their own—southern—organizations as long as their operations were profitable. As far as the AAA, it was administered at the top in large part by businessmen and experts from outside the state. Finally, the state's ability to administer the plan at the local level was intimately linked with large commercial farmers through the Farm Bureau.

The origin of the Extension Service, which played a central role in administering the AAA program at the local level, is the first empirical problem for Skocpol and Finegold. The record shows it was as much the product of private initiative and funding as it was of government efforts. It also was completely intertwined, as I said earlier, with the Farm Bureau. As McConnell explains (1953:24–30), the story of the symbiosis begins shortly after the turn of the century when the leaders of a large Rockefeller family foundation, the General Education Board, began to create the county agent system that provided the basis for organizing the Farm Bureau. Through their involvement in a variety of projects in the South, but especially education, officials of the General Education Board became interested in a farm demonstration project in Texas supported by the Department of Agriculture. In 1906 the General Education Board and the USDA signed an agreement whereby the federal government would fund certain practical aspects of the project, such as boll weevil extermination, and the Rockefeller foundation would fund the educational programs that became the county agent system (General Education Board 1930:25). All of this early work was in southern and border states. Between 1906 and 1914, the Rockefeller foundation donated 23 percent of the funds for the educational programs. State legislatures, chambers of commerce, and community organizations gave another 28 percent, and the federal government provided the remaining half (pp. 48–50). In 1914 the program was formalized through federal legislation, but with both public and private sources supplying funds for the salaries of the county agents. Other funds for the early stages of the program came from the Rosenwalds of Sears, Roebuck through an offer to pay "$1,000 to each of the first one hundred counties to employ a county agent" (McConnell 1953:30).

The involvement of the Rockefellers, Rosenwalds, chambers of commerce, and other private interests in the creation of the county agent system is highly relevant to Finegold and Skocpol's (1995) claims about the capacity and autonomy of the Department of Agriculture, for it was the Extension Service—the employer of county agents—that provided the American state with much of its capacity when it comes to agriculture during the New Deal. If McConnell's earlier-noted argument that the county agents are closely tied to the Farm Bureau is right, then state capacity in the area of agriculture does not lead to state autonomy. Contrary to a state-centric view, the result of this partnership with the state is a public-private power structure that blurs the line between government and private enterprise.

Putting aside the general issue of the autonomy of the Department of Agriculture for the moment, what about the origins of the domestic allotment program? As already noted, Skocpol and Finegold insist that independent agricultural experts—based in the Department of Agriculture and the land grant colleges—developed the ideas and formulated the legislation. They illustrate their point with the work of two agricultural economists, M. L. Wilson and Howard Tolley, who made proposals for production controls and land use planning that went "beyond those directly advocated by farm pressure groups" (Skocpol and Finegold 1982:275). The implication of this remark is that farm organizations are the only way members of the power elite could influence government on farm issues. They thereby overlook several other possibilities: that many big landowners, especially southerners, were in Congress representing themselves, that successful farmers met directly with their legislative representatives, and, most likely of all, as we shall soon see, that the agricultural economists were involved in a "business-foundation-academic complex," not merely in academia and government, as Skocpol and Finegold (1982:274, 277) claim.

In making their claims about the Department of Agriculture's policy-planning capacity, Skocpol and Finegold draw on Richard Kirkendall's (1966) detailed account of how social scientists inside and outside the state were involved in the formulation of New Deal agricultural policy. According to Skocpol and Finegold, Kirkendall "argues that the agricultural experts were more than merely 'servants of power,' that is, paid experts working for farmers' organizations (or, for that matter, for business executives)" (1982:274, note 63). But, for the most part, Kirkendall tells a very different story than the one implied by Skocpol and Finegold. It is a story of "service" intellectuals inside and outside government, not about state autonomy (1966:1). Although Kirkendall sees multiple influences on farm policy, and advocates neither a class-based nor a state autonomy theory, he clearly shows the great influence of business leaders and foundations as well as farm organizations and government officials.

Kirkendall's discussion also reveals the ambiguities of Skocpol and Finegold's claim that the farm intellectuals "were more than merely 'servants of power'" (1982:274, footnote 63). On the one hand he demonstrates that they thought of themselves as independent professionals, had some reformist goals that went beyond the businessmen's or farmers' goals, and refined and disseminated key policies adopted by business leaders. But he also writes, "The intellectuals experienced frustrations, however, in their efforts to be more than mere servants of power" (p. 7). That is, when they tried to go beyond recovery for the better-off farmers to reform for the poor farmers and farm hands, they encountered obstacles. This is the important point for a sociological analysis, and especially a power analysis. Further, Kirkendall concludes that the Farm Bureau was the chief source of this frustration, although he adds that "politicians and bureaucrats were also significant" (p. 7). Similarly, Kirkendall's (pp. 255–61) brief concluding chapter makes clear that he thinks the Farm Bureau and legislators put a stop to reform efforts that were initiated by some of the social scientists. Subjectively, then, the experts were not mere servants of power, but they did find their power was limited when they tried to be more than that. Skocpol and Finegold (1982:275, note 64) also cite William D. Rowley's *M. L. Wilson and the Campaign for the Domestic Allotment* (1970), but that book does not support any claim for successful independent initiatives by the agricultural economists either. If anything, it shows quite the opposite, for the program initiators were working outside the government with the help of foundations and businessmen until 1933.

The actual role of these experts, and the emergence of the domestic allotment program outside the state, is best understood in terms of the financial support the Rockefellers and their associates gave to all aspects of social policy in the 1920s through a number of foundations and programs. For example, several historical studies show that Rockefeller support was vital for developing a network of organizations and institutes in the field of labor relations, including Elton Mayo's famous Hawthorne studies (e.g., Bernstein 1960:159–69; Mulherin 1979:chap. 3). This is an important point that I will build upon in Chapter 5. More generally, several scholars have shown that Rockefeller funds helped shape the agenda for the social sci-

ences in that era, especially through the Laura Spelman Rockefeller Memorial (e.g., Bulmer 1980, 1982; Bulmer and Bulmer 1981; Harvey 1982; Sam-
elson 1985; Fisher 1993).

The Laura Spelman Rockefeller Memorial, which I will call the Memorial
for short, provided the ideas, money, and diffusion network for the domestic
allotment program. With a $74 million capital fund, it contributed about
$41 million to various social policy and social science projects between
1923 and 1928 (Fosdick 1952:199). In the six-year span between 1924 and
1931, it gave the equivalent of $243 million in today's money to a wide
range of organizations, with over half of that money going to Harvard,
Columbia, University of Chicago, Brookings Institution, and London School
of Economics (Bulmer and Bulmer 1981:386–87).

This is a huge investment in social policy and research, and its impact
was appropriately large (Fisher 1993). One of the primary beneficiaries of
this largesse, and one that will figure prominently in this chapter as well as
in Chapter 5, was the Social Science Research Council (SSRC), an inter-
disciplinary organization for social science research formed in 1923 in close
collaboration with the Memorial. The SSRC received 20 percent of the
Memorial's donations from 1923 to 1929. As Table 3.1 shows, most of the
SSRC's funding in its first ten years (93 percent) came from the Memorial and
other Rockefeller foundations. So it is not too surprising that Fisher
(1993:chap. 2) demonstrates in a detailed historical study that the director of
the Memorial and other Rockefeller employees had a major shaping role on
the SSRC's policy initiatives between 1925 and 1935 through its Policy
Planning Committee, a conclusion I will demonstrate in detail in Chapter 5
for SSRC's social policy studies.[1]

The director of the Laura Spelman Rockefeller Memorial, Beardsley

*Table 3.1.*   Funding for the Social Science
Research Council in Its First Ten Years,
1923–1933

| | |
|---|---:|
| Rockefeller philanthropies | $3,932,105 |
| Rosenwald philanthropies | 116,000 |
| Carnegie philanthropies | 85,000 |
| Russell Sage Foundation | 42,000 |
| Service Fees | 13,000 |
| Commonwealth Fund | 5,000 |
| Falk Foundation | 3,000 |
| Revell McCallum (an individual) | 1,500 |
| Total | $4,197,605 |

*Source:*   SSRC Decennial Report 1934, 105.

Ruml, was the pivotal figure in the early formulation of the domestic allot-ment subsidy plan. He brought the idea to the attention of an agricultural economist, financed research on it, and urged it on businessmen and politi-cal advisers. He became interested in the possibility of inducing voluntary restrictions of agricultural production in exchange for higher prices after learning that such a program seemed to be working in Germany. A Ph.D. in psychology and an assistant to the president of a Carnegie foundation before joining the Rockefeller philanthropies in 1922, Ruml first involved himself in agricultural policy in 1923. At that time he had his office make contact with agricultural economist Henry Taylor, the head of none other than the Bureau of Agricultural Economics, to see if there was anything his founda-tion could do in the area of economics. Taylor replied that he had some ideas for dealing with the problems of tenant farming in the dry climate of places like Montana through the use of new scientific methods, so Ruml hired him as a consultant to develop the project (e.g., Rowley 1970:31; Reagan 1982:243). Taylor contacted another agricultural economist, M. L. Wilson, touted by Skocpol and Finegold as one of their independent ex-perts. Wilson became director of the project, called Fairway Farms. He was joined in his efforts by Chester Davis, an agricultural economist who will figure prominently in this chapter, and by several businessmen. Ruml served as the treasurer of Fairway Farms, and John D. Rockefeller, Sr., personally provided a line of credit for one million dollars, a very large sum in those days.

As Rowley (1970:31) explains, the idea was for Fairway Farms to buy up abandoned farms and lease them to tenants, who would work the land with modern machinery and have the opportunity to buy their own land from the project if they were successful. The hope was that such a project would be a demonstration of how tenants could be helped to "climb the 'agricultural ladder' to land ownership" (ibid.). The project was not much of a success, but it did give visibility and legitimacy to Wilson, who was thereafter seen "as a leading authority on the experimental method of research in agri-cultural economics" (Kirkendall 1966:13). Already we see how the careers of experts can become tied to wealthy business groups like the Rockefellers.

Ruml drew closer to the small world of the agricultural economists when the SSRC founded its Committee on Social and Economic Research in Agri-culture in 1925. Taylor became the chair, a position he held until 1929. When Taylor unexpectedly lost his position at the BAE later in 1925 due to a newspaper report that he had allegedly lobbied for an agricultural bill advo-cated by farm organizations, he was hired by friends at the Institute for Research in Land Economics at Northwestern University with special funds provided by Rockefeller philanthropies. Taylor later wrote in his memoirs, which remain unpublished, that the Rockefeller group had "saved my ca-reer" (Reagan 1982:265, footnote 46). I tell this story because it is a microcosm of the relationships that develop between leading experts and the business—foundation—policy group—think tank network.

In 1928 Ruml asked Taylor to do a study of the feasibility of the domestic allotment plan. Taylor declined because he did not have the time, but suggested that Ruml contact John D. Black, an agricultural economist at Harvard University. Black accepted the assignment, and his chapter on the plan in *Agricultural Reform in the United States* (1929) became the basis for a major campaign for the program. Black was no stranger to Ruml because Black, like Taylor, was a member of the SSRC's Committee on Social and Economic Research in Agriculture from its inception, and later served as its chair from 1929 to 1933.

As Black's papers at the Wisconsin State Historical Society Archives make clear, he was in close touch with Ruml while he worked on the project. There are several letters back and forth between them. As Black's eagerness to publish the plan and testify for it before Congress grew in early 1929, Ruml sent him a cautionary letter:

> I think it is very important that we continue to maintain a strictly "academic" attitude with respect to the whole situation. It would be very unfortunate for the opinion to be current that we have a "plan" for which we are agitating. It seems to me that we have fulfilled any public responsibility which we may have had in bringing this plan together with such data as we have been able to assemble, for the people who are responsible for the working out of a national program, and of course the contribution which you will have made in your book is likely in the long run to be far more important than the development of any particular plan which we can envisage at the present time. (Ruml 1929)

The relationship between Black and Ruml also can be tracked from Ruml's side through the papers of the Memorial. They tell the same story with the same letters, except they show Ruml keeping other Rockefeller employees informed, as in this memo to Arthur Woods, president of the Memorial at the time and very close to John D. Rockefeller, Jr., who was in charge of the family's business and philanthropic decisions:

> You will be interested, I think, in the progress which is being made in the agricultural economics matter, which the Executive Committee [the inner circle that met with JDR, Jr.] gave me some assistance on. I think you will agree that I am getting on rather well. (Ruml 1928)

Black also received help from several of his colleagues in agricultural economics, including Taylor, but most especially Chester Davis, who at this point was working for the Illinois Agricultural Association, the Farm Bureau affiliate in that state. Davis sent him eight letters with detailed suggestions, not only on the substance of the issue, but the politics as well. Davis liked the plan very much, but at one point worried that Black had "hung the fodder pretty high for the members of Congress, farm groups, press, etc., to reach"; he therefore counseled simplifying the language (Davis 1929). These letters show, contrary to Finegold and Skocpol (1995:188), that Davis was sympathetic to production control well before 1932.

There was one other source of support for Black: the economists at the BAE. As the tone of the following letter to the head of the BAE suggests, it was as if these experts were at the direct service of Black:

> We shall put in the mails today the remaining chapters of the manuscript. The printers are already at work on the first seven chapters. I want you to farm out the reading of these chapters so as to get them back to me within a day or two. I realize that I am imposing a burden upon your staff, but you will agree that speed is desirable. (Black 1929)

Sure enough, the comments were back to Black within two days. How could Black dare to make such a bold request? Anyone who has spent time in the academic world knows the answer. Black is the professor at Harvard, the BAE staff are the lesser lights who only work for the government. How can the state's capacity become autonomous when the experts providing that capacity are in general highly deferential to Ivy League professors? These mere "status" differences are a very real clue as to the low standing of the state in the United States.

Although Black's hopes for immediate action on the proposal in 1929 were cast aside by the rush of events in Washington, causing him to lose personal interest in pushing it, the SSRC program in agricultural economics continued to provide a larger context for the new ideas that Black and his colleagues were developing. While Black was working on the domestic allotment plan, the Memorial gave the SSRC $158,000 to be used for fellowships between 1928 and 1933. Under this program, 109 agricultural economists received fellowships to study at the university of their choosing. The emphasis was on training people who would make an immediate applied research contribution in policy arenas. Many of those who received fellowships were professors and department chairs at agricultural colleges. Significantly, 50 of the 109 chose to study with Black at Harvard (Klass 1969:158). In effect, Ruml was underwriting the dissemination of the domestic allotment program into the network of agricultural economists seen as independent by Skocpol and Finegold.

Later, when the special fellowship program wound down, the SSRC turned its attention to another project relating to expertise in agricultural economics. From 1931 to 1937 its Subcommittee on Special Graduate Training in Agricultural Economics and Rural Sociology sponsored advanced courses for government workers taught at the Brookings Institution. The chair of the subcommittee was a fellow of the Brookings Institution, and Black was a member. More generally, the membership of the subcommittee demonstrates an intermingling of government and private experts through the SSRC:

- Edwin G. Nourse, Brookings Institution, chair
- John D. Black, Harvard University
- H. C. M. Case, University of Illinois
- Lewis C. Gray, staff member, BAE, U.S. Department of Agriculture
- Nils A. Olsen, head, BAE, U.S. Department of Agriculture

The SSRC ten-year report partially counters Finegold and Skocpol's claims about state autonomy when it assesses its five-year fellowship program as follows: "A very great need of the government, of agricultural experiment stations and colleges, has been met through this grant" (SSRC 1934:15). Similarly, it seems that the graduate courses at Brookings should be given credit for some of the new capacity that the state acquired during the New Deal in the area of agricultural economics. As the annual report for 1936–1937 summarizes:

> During this period a total of forty-six semester courses were offered—thirty-two different courses of which fourteen were repeated. There was an average of forty registrations per semester, a total of five hundred and seventeen. These courses have afforded valuable training to advanced students during six and a half years, and substantially similar courses will in future be offered by the American University. (SSRC 1937:16)

Skocpol and Finegold (1982) do not mention Ruml and the SSRC when they extol the expertise of agricultural economists trained by the state before the New Deal. However, Finegold and Skocpol (1995:169) do acknowledge the role of Ruml and the SSRC, but then try to minimize their importance. They rightly note that there had been an earlier domestic allotment proposal from a state-employed agricultural economist, but they also admit that "the AAA was more directly descended from Black's plan" (ibid.). They also claim that the Memorial "operated with more independence from its benefactors than other Rockefeller family foundations," but we have already seen that Ruml kept the executive committee that coordinated Rockefeller philanthropy well informed on this issue. Nor is it likely that the Memorial had any unusual independence on policy issues (Fisher 1993). In general, Finegold and Skocpol (1995:170) seem very defensive when they conclude that Black and other experts working on this issue "may have been less independent than contemporary university professors, but that does not mean they were completely dominated by the Rockefellers or the Farm Bureau." Why do they stress "completely dominated" when no one has made such a claim?

Putting aside the importance of the Memorial and the SSRC in developing the main ideas in the domestic allotment program, we can see that the policy-planning network also provides part of the context for understanding events beginning in 1930, when the domestic allotment program proposed by Ruml and Black was taken up by M. L. Wilson, by then a member of the SSRC agricultural committee. Wilson modified the plan so that local committees of farmers would administer the program and allow farmers to vote on whether or not they wanted it. He then spent a good part of the next three years championing the program with farm groups, other agricultural economists, and business leaders.

At this point, Skocpol and Finegold go astray once again, for they put their emphasis on Wilson and other agricultural economists as the lobbyists for the plan. However, Ruml continued to play a catalytic role after the plan was completed. Wilson says he first learned of it through Ruml (Klass 1969:90, note 2), and it was Ruml who first explained the plan in the spring of 1932 to one of future president Roosevelt's most important economic advisers, the liberal economist Rexford Tugwell of Columbia University (Kirkendall 1966:44). Tugwell had primary responsibility for formulating Roosevelt's agricultural policy. A conversation with Ruml carried him to Chicago for a crucial meeting with Wilson and other agricultural experts:

> Tugwell, regarding his own thinking on the subject as stale, rather desperately decided to attend a meeting of farm economists held in Chicago shortly before the convention. From Beardsley Ruml in Washington he had heard hints of new developments in the domestic allotment plan; at Chicago he could talk with M. L. Wilson of Montana, who had become the plan's apostle. When he arrived in Chicago, he found not only Wilson, but Henry Wallace of Iowa. For several days they talked late into the night in the dormitory rooms at the University of Chicago where they were billeted. Tugwell was finally persuaded that he had found what he was seeking—a workable means of restricting agricultural production on which the farm leaders might agree. (Schlesinger 1957:403)

Wilson and Tugwell then introduced the plan to Roosevelt, who was impressed by it. He mentioned its basic principles in an important campaign address, and Wilson drew closer to his campaign, describing himself as a "Roosevelt Republican" (Rowley 1970:chap. 8; Hamilton 1991:210–12).

It also needs to be stressed that Wilson did not work simply as a lone-wolf social scientist in promoting the plan. Instead, Wilson's efforts were aided mightily by several businessmen who liked the plan and spread the word about it (Kirkendall 1966:33; Rowley 1970:chap. 7). The first of these was a grain dealer in Duluth, who purchased five thousand copies of Black's book chapter on the plan to distribute around the country. Gerard Swope, president of General Electric, whose one-thousand-acre wheat ranch had been managed for fifteen years by the president of the Montana State Farm Bureau, spread the idea among industrialists because it fit with some of his ideas for solving industrial problems that will be discussed in the next chapter. Then the ubiquitous Ruml spoke of the plan to Henry I. Harriman, a Boston businessman who owned a large ranch in Montana (D. Hamilton 1991:186). Harriman took a great interest in the plan, recommending it to his friends and corresponding with Wilson on how to sell it. Thanks to Harriman's involvement in the Chamber of Commerce of the United States, of which he became president in 1932, Wilson was appointed to the Chamber's committee on agricultural policy in 1930 (Kirkendall 1966:34). By means of this committee Wilson was able to have his views discussed and endorsed by a cross section of the business community. Moreover, Harriman played an active role in shaping the plan because he saw it "as an ideal adjunct to his own plan for stabilizing business" (D. Hamilton 1991:186), which I will discuss in the next chapter. It was he who proposed paying farmers to reduce production. He also suggested imposing "an excise tax on agricultural processors for each bushel of wheat milled, pound of cotton ginned, or unit of tobacco or livestock processed" (ibid.). Both of these proposals became part of the final plan.[2]

One of the people Wilson became acquainted with through the Chamber committee was R. R. Rogers, head of the Farm Mortgage Department at Prudential Life (Kirkendall 1966:35). Rogers was the "leading spokesman on farm matters" for insurance companies, which at the time were "the dominant source of farm mortgage money" (ibid.). They were also coming to own a large amount of farm land as farmers destroyed by the depression defaulted on their mortgages. It was Rogers who "provided most of the money behind Wilson's efforts to influence politicians and pressure groups, and brought him into contact with other insurance men or bankers, and battled against other businessmen who opposed the plan" (ibid.). By 1936 the insurance companies who backed the plan were among the major benefactors from farm subsidies because of the defaulted mortgages (Daniel 1985:170–73).

While all this lobbying for the domestic allotment plan was going on rather quietly behind the scenes, other businessmen and successful farmers were involved in the open promotion of a rival plan, one that had been around since the early 1920s and gained a good deal of visibility. It is in talking about this plan that Kirkendall writes a sentence that state autonomy theorists can seize upon as alleged evidence for the independent power of experts. He says that "the social scientists in farm politics had won a great victory" over a rival plan when the domestic allotment plan was included in Roosevelt's legislation (Kirkendall 1966:57). So we need to stop and take a four-paragraph look at this other plan and meet its creators, two of whom will figure in more than one chapter in this book.

The rival plan, called in the 1920s McNary-Haugen after its two Republican sponsors in the Senate, was the product of a very interesting troika of business executives. Bernard Baruch, a Wall Street speculator born and raised in South Carolina, and one of the richest men in the country, was the financial and policy leader of the trio. During World War I, he was head of the War Industries Board, which coordinated the industrial mobilization. From that commanding position he had come to know most of the businessmen who would figure in the next twenty-five years of American politics, and his success in handling the job gave him great stature with politicians.

One of the people Baruch came to admire at the War Industries Board was George Peek, who had worked his way up to vice-president for sales of Deere and Company, a farm machinery manufacturer, before joining Baruch in Washington as "commissioner of finished products" (Ohl 1985:42). Peek, in turn, saw great promise in Hugh Johnson, a graduate of West Point in 1903 and the law school at the University of California, Berkeley, in 1916. At age thirty-five, he just had become the youngest U.S. army general since the Civil War. When Peek recommended him as the army's representative on the War Industries Board, Johnson came into contact with Baruch and other top business figures running the war effort. Following the war Peek decided to take his chances as president of a failing farm implement company, Moline Plow, and Johnson joined him as assistant general manager and general counsel. Johnson also kept in touch with Baruch, investigating business opportunities for him and helping him lobby the army for his war preparedness plans (Ohl 1985:75).

In August 1920, Peek and Johnson wrote an anonymous memorandum on how to raise sagging farm prices that was edited by officials of the Farm Bureau and then circulated to a small group of politicians. A year later they expanded their ideas into a pamphlet entitled *Equality for Agriculture*. Assuming that farmers could not cut their output nor withhold surpluses from the market, they blamed agriculture's problems on the workings of the tariff. The tariff supposedly forced farmers to pay higher prices for industrial goods, but did not protect the price of farm products, thereby creating an inequality for agriculture. Their solution was to figure a ratio based on average crop prices and average general prices for the ten years before World War I, and then to adjust the tariff based on changes in that ratio. They claimed that farmers would then receive a fair-exchange price, which came to be called the parity price. Perhaps even more importantly, any price-depressing surpluses would be bought by the government at the parity price, and then sold for a loss on the world market. The losses on the world market would be paid for by a tax on the crops farmers sold, called an equalization fee. It sounds complicated to us, but it made sense to farmers back then.

By 1924 the plan was supported by most farm groups and, not surprisingly, businessmen like Peek and Johnson who manufactured farm equipment, and would therefore benefit from increased production. Baruch worked hard for it behind the scenes with Democrats (Fite 1954:55–56, 67–68, 96). Although the bill passed Congress twice, it was vetoed both times by Republican President Calvin Coolidge because industrialists and bankers did not like it. They said it had two fatal defects: it would increase the problem of overproduction rather than curbing it, and it would invite retaliation from angry nations whose farmers would suffer from the dumping of American surpluses overseas. By contrast, the great appeal of the new domestic allotment program as far as most business leaders were concerned was that it reduced surpluses and did not tamper with the tariff or disturb foreign trade. The plan as amended also was genuinely new in that it offered a way to induce individual farmers to take sensible collective action:

> Because the Black-Ruml version of the domestic allotment plan was intended as an alternative price-raising measure to the McNary-Haugen bills, and because Wilson and Ezekiel used the idea of tariff benefits to justify their own measure, the revised plan has often been seen as little more than an extension of the McNary-Haugen fight. But as reformulated by Wilson and Ezekiel, with the help of Henry Harriman, the plan was something very different: it marked a new answer in the long search for a means of achieving cooperative action in agriculture, reconciling individual and collective action on the part of farmers, and sustaining self-government. (D. Hamilton 1991:192–93)

Long-time supporters of the McNary-Haugen plan were often outspoken in their criticism of the domestic allotment scheme. They did not like the idea of curtailing production. This was particularly the case with its main champion, Peek, who fought for his program by claiming that the domestic allotment program was the product of a group of wild-eyed academics. Rather than attacking the businessmen supporting the program, he chose to criticize the allegedly unworldly experts and professors. This kind of talk may be one of the reasons why state autonomy theorists believe that experts are separate from business leaders, but I believe something else is actually going on here. Such an approach is a common displacement tactic in policy disputes where one powerful person does not want to directly attack another powerful person. It is in effect a form of scapegoating that preserves some degree of harmony between the real combatants. In other words, and despite Peek's claims to the contrary, the domestic allotment and McNary-Haugen plans were actually two different business-sponsored plans for dealing with agricultural surpluses. The one developed by the agricultural economists in and around Ruml and the SSRC was favored by the major business leaders of the day because it was more compatible with their general interests. Although Kirkendall seems right to say that "the social scientists in farm policy had won a great victory" (1966:57) because they were central in refining the plan and disseminating it in business and government circles, these experts were hardly independent of big business or part of an autonomous state, as Skocpol and Finegold constantly imply.

I believe the success of these experts should be understood in the context of an argument between rival business and farm leaders, and within parameters that Kirkendall says "harmonized at many points with basic assumptions of powerful farm and business groups" (p. 59). Whatever the intentions and self-images of the experts, I repeat that from a power perspective the agricultural experts ended up serving the interests of big business and large farm owners. They were not merely servants of power, which is the kind of caricature of rival views that state autonomy theorists often employ, but there were severe limits on what they could accomplish, as demonstrated by their subsequent failures in their reform efforts.

The model for understanding policy formulation that I outlined in the second chapter allows for both advice from experts and conflict between rival business plans, and I therefore submit that it is the appropriate one for comprehending the development of agricultural policy as well as the foreign and economic policies I have analyzed elsewhere (Domhoff 1970:chaps. 4, 5, 6; 1979:chap. 3; 1990). It explains how money flows from corporations to foundations, and from foundations to think tanks and policy discussion groups. It shows how experts are supported and brought into contact with business leaders. In the case of the domestic allotment program, this general model can be specified by noting that (1) Rockefeller foundations provided most of the financial support for plan development; (2) an SSRC committee of agricultural economists served as the main think tank; and (3) the Committee on Agriculture at the Chamber of Commerce served as the meeting ground for experts with ideas and business leaders with money and political access.

As I noted earlier, Finegold and Skocpol (1995:4, 17, 20, 82) make much of the fact that the Farm Bureau and other farm groups did not support the domestic allotment scheme until late 1932. However, this only shows that the Farm Bureau did not create the program, as those who have read the records of the Farm Bureau agree (e.g., McConnell 1953; Campbell 1962). From a power perspective, the important point is that Roosevelt was not prepared to enact any program opposed by the major farm groups, and it was the Farm Bureau that played a central role in uniting these groups behind the program (Campbell 1962:51–53). It also should count for something that one of the two drafters of the final legislation was a lawyer hired by the Farm Bureau, Frederick Lee (Saloutos 1982:45). Lee's role does not imply that he or the Farm Bureau was responsible for the substance of the legislation, but it does suggest that there would be very little or nothing in the bill that was objectionable to them. In addition to drafting the legislation, Lee helped in implementing it as the personal lawyer to its first administrator, George Peek (Conrad 1965:39). Peek decided to hire Lee for the post with his own money because he did not trust the liberal "city" lawyers who were appointed to the legal staff of the AAA at the urging of Tugwell (Kirkendall 1966:66).

However, the Farm Bureau and other farm leaders did not simply acquiesce in the bill and hire a lawyer to help refine its language. Instead, they insisted that "the benefit payments should be determined by the fair exchange ratio that originally had been part of the first McNary-Haugen bills" (D. Hamilton 1991:221). Wilson and Ezekiel resisted this change because they feared the "parity formula would undermine the emphasis on production controls and agricultural planning" (ibid.), but to no avail. As subsequent events showed, the act was shaped in practice to reflect the interest group approach of the farm leaders, not the planning approach of the agricultural economists. When the agricultural economists tried to reintroduce planning ideas through other means in the late 1930s, they were defeated by the AAA and the Farm Bureau, as will be shown in a later section. For now, though, the point is that the Farm Bureau and its allies not only had veto power over this legislation, but shaping power as well.

Nor are Finegold and Skocpol (1995:4, 17) correct in implying that all farmers opposed production controls before 1932. In fact, the commercial farmers who mattered the most in terms of the Democratic party, southern plantation owners who grew cotton or tobacco, had understood the usefulness of acreage restrictions since early in the century (Saloutos 1960:160, 277–78). However, they did not push the idea because they did not suffer as much from overproduction and low prices in the 1920s as did farmers in other parts of the country. Even when cotton prices collapsed at the outset of the depression, cotton growers held back from production control schemes in part because they differentially benefited from loans made by the federal government's Federal Farm Board (p. 274).

According to Theodore Saloutos (p. 254), the prosperity of cotton and tobacco growers in the 1920s also explains their relative lack of interest in joining the Farm Bureau: they simply did not need it. As long as their profits were good, Saloutos (p. 259) concludes, planters preferred southern organizations for cotton and tobacco, which usually included bankers and merchants concerned with these crops as well as the growers themselves.

Between 1930 and 1932, southerners pioneered in the use of legislation in limiting production. Texas, Louisiana, South Carolina, and Mississippi passed laws that would allow for acreage controls if other farm states passed similar laws. In late 1932, many plantation owners and their allies made it clear to Roosevelt that some form of production controls was necessary at the federal level. Saloutos concludes his recounting of this story as follows:

> That the South embraced the New Deal farm program as enthusiastically as it did was no mere accident. For years the cotton and tobacco producers were

nurtured on a philosophy of farm relief which the new administration finally adopted and elaborated upon. (1960:281)

Thus, it seems abundantly clear that farmer opposition to production controls is exaggerated by Finegold and Skocpol. When the idea of payments—i.e., subsidies—was then added to induce cooperation more readily, it seems very unlikely that very many farmers would be opposed to the program. It does not take much state capacity to run a program when money is being given to the producers of a few major crops to restrict their production.

As the final part of their argument that the AAA was created and controlled by experts within the government, Skocpol and Finegold (1982:271) imply that independent experts occupied most of the key positions in the AAA (see also Finegold and Skocpol 1984:176; Finegold and Skocpol 1995:188, 194). This claim is made even more directly in an earlier paper on agricultural policy by Finegold (1981:2) to which Skocpol and Finegold (1982) often refer. However, the reality would seem to be more mixed unless Finegold (1981:21) means those staff positions deep in the bureaucracy that provide information on parity targets, processing and benefit rates, and acreage bases. Contrary to Skocpol and Finegold, Saloutos (1982:chap. 5) notes the many business leaders and farmer-connected people who administered the AAA. At the top were Peek, mentioned earlier as a former executive for a plow manufacturing company, and Charles J. Brand, executive secretary-treasurer of the National Fertilizer Association. Peek was shortly replaced by his friend Chester C. Davis, the participant in Fairway Farms and economist for the Farm Bureau in Illinois who had made suggestions to Black on the domestic allotment plan (p. 57). At about the same time Peek left, Brand moved over to become executive director of the fertilizer section of AAA.

The chief of finance was the former manager of a cotton plantation in Mississippi. The chief of processing and marketing was an executive from Sears Roebuck. The chief of the cotton section was a southern journalist close to plantation owners, and M. L. Wilson was chief of the wheat section. An executive from Cudahy Packing Company was in charge of the processing businesses under the jurisdiction of the corn-hog section. A professor of agricultural economics at Iowa State College was chief of the corn-hog section, and a government employee headed the tobacco section (ibid., 57-58). In all, that is six of nine top leaders from business circles, and three academic experts, and only one of the three academic experts had been with the government for any length of time. Rather than supporting Skocpol and Finegold's (1982) claims about autonomy, these appointments are typical of the kinds of appointments that have been made to key government positions throughout American history (e.g., Mintz 1975; Burch 1981a, 1981b; Salzman and Domhoff 1980).

So whether the issue is the origins of the domestic allotment program, the leadership of the AAA, or the autonomy of the Extension Service, it looks to me like this first test case points to businessman/farmer domination of the state, not state autonomy. But there is still the actual operation of the Department of Agriculture during the main years of the New Deal to consider. Maybe Hooks is right that the department was able to gain more autonomy as time went on.

## THE ALLEGED GROWING AUTONOMY OF THE USDA, 1933–1938

Hooks does not go into detail about why he believes the Department of Agriculture became more autonomous during the New Deal. That is because his primary focus is on the BAE and land use planning. Rather than turn immediately to the failings of his characterization of the BAE and its land use planning committees, however, I will first show how the efforts of liberal, second-level department officials to gain autonomy from the Farm Bureau and its allies in 1935 became enmeshed in a class conflict that department policies helped to trigger in the first place. I will argue that by 1938 farm groups had gained such great access to the department that several of its top leaders began a conscious countereffort to regain some independence. The struggle over autonomy between the Farm Bureau and the department became more serious in 1939, and then erupted into open warfare in 1940. But at no time, as will be shown, did any of the department's efforts to increase its autonomy have any success. What Hooks has done is to mistake battles that had within them the potential for departmental autonomy as evidence for actual autonomy.

The USDA became an arena of class conflict because its domestic allotment payments to plantation owners and farmers in exchange for reducing crop acreage had the brutal side effect of bringing greater poverty and disruption into the lives of southern tenant farmers and sharecroppers, who were overwhelmingly similar to wage laborers for purposes of a class conflict analysis. As Michael Schwartz concludes in his study of the southern agricultural system that developed after the Civil War, "the root of all tenant-landlord conflict was in a dispute over who would reap the benefits of the tenant's labor" (1976:21). The program created conflict by forcing farm labor off the land or reducing their income. It had this side effect because the AAA's payments to plantation owners for not growing cotton were an incentive to fire or underpay farm hands. Rather than share payments with tenants and sharecroppers, plantation owners in many cases terminated their leases. This does not mean that every tenant farmer was cut loose, but enough were, especially among African-American tenants and sharecroppers, that Pete Daniel (1985) likens New Deal agricultural policy in the South to a modern-day "enclosure movement."

Although landlords evicted as many as 15 to 20 percent of their tenants and sharecroppers between 1933 and 1935 (Grubb 1971:25–26), they still wanted these people available as low-wage labor when needed (cf. Whatley 1983). They therefore resisted any programs to give unemployed farm workers better welfare payments or to settle them on their own land. Despite what most outside observers and government officials saw as a surplus of labor, the landowners were afraid that they were going to run short of inexpensive employees at peak seasons (Mertz 1978:45–50).

But it was not only evictions that were causing problems for the tenants and sharecroppers. Even those who were allowed to stay on the land were receiving a smaller income from subsidy payments than they had received for growing crops. Through a variety of contractual devices and southern customs, the landlords found ways to keep a very large share of the subsidy payments for themselves. Contracts alone created the following situation:

> Thus the New Deal ordained that the landlord should receive 50 percent more money for not producing than for producing, while the tenant who once kept $15 per acre from the sale of ten-cent cotton should now get only $1.50, his three-fourths of the party payment, a mere tenth of his former income. The way this distribution of government money affected planter and sharecropper income in actual cases was easy to discover. On one plantation called "a very representative cotton farm" by researchers, the landlord's gross income increased under the AAA from $51,554 in 1932 to $102,202 in 1934, while the average gross income of his tenants fell from $379 to $355. (Grubb 1971:20)

However, the power of southern landowners was not so great that they could keep the rural poor in total destitution. There were two countervailing influences: the disruptive potential of the poor people, which was aided and augmented by leftist organizers, and the leverage that liberals gained within the federal government because they were part of the Roosevelt coalition.

Exploited tenants and evicted farm hands were a source of tension and disruption in many ways. They wrote letters of protest about their situation to officials in Washington, generating conflict within the White House, Congress, and USDA. Their poverty was highly visible to journalists and writers, who publicized their plight and thereby caused embarrassment for officials in Washington. Most of all, their turmoil and despair held out the potential for radical action of the kind that leftists were trying to organize (e.g., Conrad 1965; Grubb 1971:27–28).

Liberals within the Roosevelt coalition, both southerners and northerners, responded to this enclosure movement by demanding relief and reform for all southerners, black or white, who had lost their livelihood. In effect, they assumed the leadership of the farm workers' battle with plantation owners. Their role within the Democratic party, along with their ability to stir up public opinion through their access to the media, gave them a toehold in some federal agencies, including the USDA, and a few pipelines to the White House itself. In reaction, there was an attempt by the White House to create agencies and programs aimed at relieving some of the devastating poverty in the South without alienating the wealthy whites who controlled the Democratic party in southern states. Put another way, the Democratic party and plantation owners faced the basic dilemma about relief payments that is analyzed so well by Piven and Cloward (1971): such spending is necessary to forestall disruption, but it must be accompanied by rituals of degradation and eliminated as soon as possible so that work norms and the willingness to work for low wages are not undermined. The harsh way in which this dilemma was handled in the South during the New Deal is demonstrated in detail by Conrad (1965), Grubb (1971), and Mertz (1978), none of whom is cited by Hooks.

The protest movements did not go very far because they were met by racial epithets, violence, and jailings (e.g., Grubb 1971:70–71). Nor did the meager emergency relief payments disrupt the labor market. Despite protests by liberals, local relief administrators cut off payments when more workers were needed for planting or harvesting (Mertz 1978:49; Schulman 1991:31–32). Nonetheless, the southern landlords were extremely disturbed by the farmworkers' protests, and by the involvement of outside agitators (i.e., liberals and leftists). Thus, any understanding of the USDA after 1934 must begin with the fact that the department had to deal with strong pressures from the landlords and liberals outside the state who were the most visible combatants in a class struggle that pitted the better-off farmers and plantation owners against the massive number of displaced farm hands and their liberal allies.

The terrain of what began as a southern class struggle was widened by clashes in California, where there was a long history of large farms and migratory wage labor (McWilliams 1939; Weiner 1978; Daniel 1981; Majka and Majka 1982). Strikes and organizing efforts were frequent in the early New Deal, often led by Communists, and sometimes taking place in labor camps set up by the federal government (e.g., Grubb 1971:162–63). These conflicts were won by a business-farmer coalition called the Associated Farmers (Chambers 1952; Pichardo 1990). The initial funds for creating the organization came from a large public utility company, a packing company, and the Bank of America (McWilliams 1939:232–33).

But farm laborers and class conflict were not limited to the South and California, and here I am taking empirical issue with McConnell on one of his reasons for resisting a full-blown class theory. As farms expanded in size throughout the 1920s and 1930s, there was a growing use of wage workers in the Southwest, Midwest, and even to some extent in the Northeast. These migrant workers were increasingly Mexican and African-American in their origins with the closing off of European immigration in 1924, which heightened the distinction between farm owners and farm hands. In 1935, when 3 percent of the farms were hiring 40 percent of the roughly 2.5 to 3 million farm laborers, the largest 184,000 farms employed 1.1 million workers for some part of the year (McWilliams 1942:353; Majka and Majka 1982:104). For example, the 70,000 growers of sugar beets in Colorado and the Midwest used 158,000 workers, 110,000 of whom were migrant contract workers.

Strikes by these workers, usually to protest wage cuts, but sometimes to demand union recognition, were usually not as large, frequent, or dramatic as in California, but there were many work stoppages in several different states between 1933 and 1936 after virtually no strikes in the preceding three years. These strikes occurred in such varied crops and places as beet fields in Michigan, hop fields in Oregon, onion fields in Ohio, cranberry bogs in New Jersey, citrus groves in Florida, and tobacco fields in Connecticut and Massachusetts (e.g., Jamieson 1945; Reisler 1976; Taylor 1983; Valdes 1991.[3]

In the end, extremely few of these strikes were successful, although some of them won a restoration of wage cuts or even wage increases. As for unions, they "lasted for more than one season in only a few crop areas" (Jamieson 1945:39). However, this labor turbulence between 1933 and 1936 did generate greater class consciousness in farmers in other parts of the country besides the South and California. Because their harvests were at risk if there were strikes or work stoppages, especially with highly perishable crops, the farmers often reacted even more harshly than industrialists to challenges from their workers. The fact that some of the strikes in the Midwest and Northeast were led by organizers from the Communist party, although not as frequently as in California, made it all the easier for the farm owners to become highly agitated about them, and to be successful in enlisting local and state governments against the strikers (pp. 39–42). It is of the greatest theoretical relevance that no labor legislation during the New Deal provided any protection for migrant farm workers.

It is within this general context of highly visible and often violent strikes, along with the prominent Communist involvement, that the spokespersons for two contending social classes battled over policy issues within the allegedly autonomous USDA. Growers from the South and California took command on the employer's side, but they had plenty of sympathy from wealthy farmers outside those regions. Liberal Democrats and leftist organizers aided the farm workers, in effect supplying much of their leadership, and most certainly their connections to the mass media and government. Meanwhile, the Farm Bureau was the means by which the labor-employing farmers from all over the country coordinated their efforts to influence government at all levels, but especially, of course, the Department of Agriculture, congressional committees concerned with agriculture, and the White House. Ready or not, the Department of Agriculture therefore became an arena of class conflict on a variety of issues, even though it is also true that the conflict was fought out in part at the level of pressure groups arguing over the organization and administration of the department.

Class conflict in the South spilled over into the USDA as an argument over how to deal with the low subsidy payments to tenants and the removal of tenants from plantations. In February 1935, these issues triggered a decade-long battle when liberal lawyers within the USDA tried to stem the tide of displaced tenant farmers by ruling that plantation owners receiving subsidy payments could not remove their tenants (e.g., Schlesinger 1959:78–79; Kirkendall 1966:99–103). The ruling caused an immediate firestorm of protest in the South and within AAA. The director of the AAA, Davis, who was far closer to the southerners and the Farm Bureau than he was to the liberals, told Secretary of Agriculture Henry A. Wallace that the liberal lawyers had to go or else he would resign. The liberals thought Wallace would back them (Davis 1986:478), but they were wrong because Wallace feared a confrontation with southern Democrats. The ruling was rescinded and the liberal lawyers were fired. The southern rich won because "almost every major committee in the House and Senate was chaired by a southerner who represented the planter interest" (ibid., 478). Schlesinger puts it even more bluntly:

> The landlords dominated not only the local administration of the AAA, but the sheriffs at the county court house and the Congressmen in Washington. It was this situation that drove the legal staff to the reinterpretation of the contract which led to the agricultural purge of 1935. (1959:376)

The outcome of this conflict was a clear indication, concludes Grubb (1971:59), that liberals would be kept in check in the USDA. Hooks does not realize it, but this incident signals what happened in every major battle within the USDA from that time forward. Every liberal initiative is pared down to the point where it is acceptable to the southern segment of the American ruling class, or else it is rejected. Thus, the seeming autonomy Hooks thinks the department had achieved was illusory, and whatever room it had to maneuver actually existed at the sufferance of the Farm Bureau and the southern landlords inside and outside Congress.

This dominance by owners outside the government is first of all demonstrated by the history of AAA after 1933. It was run at the top in good part, as we already have seen, by outsiders affiliated with businesses (Saloutos 1982:chap. 5). At the local level it was administered by county agents and farmer committees that were intimately associated with the Farm Bureau (e.g., McConnell 1953:75–76; Kirkendall 1966:154). The degree of Farm Bureau involvement in the AAA in 1936, for example, can be seen in the large number of its members on state-level committees. In states where there was a Farm Bureau, which means most major farm states, 117 of the 169 state committee members were members of the Farm Bureau. Further, in some states "90 percent or more of the county and township committeemen are Farm Bureau members" (Annual Report, Farm Bureau 1936, as quoted by McConnell 1953:78).

Legislative changes in the AAA program in 1935 and 1938, the first one necessitated by a Supreme Court ruling the processing tax unconstitutional, tell a similar tale of outside influence. In both instances the Farm Bureau played a large role in shaping the legislation (McConnell 1953:77–78; Campbell 1962:106–14). In addition to giving the program a new justification, soil conservation, the 1935 legislation led to administrative changes that greatly aided the Farm Bureau. There was "a clear organizational gain for the Farm Bureau on three scores," writes McConnell:

> First, administrative organization was now general and not broken along commodity lines. Second, it paralleled the local Farm Bureau structure. Third, it was more amenable to direction through the county agents. In the South the county agent automatically became the secretary of the local association. [which is why the symbiosis between the Extension Service and Farm Bureau is so important to my theory—GWD]. (1953:78)

As for the 1938 act, the Farm Bureau leadership testified before Congress that the farm organizations were asked by the USDA to draft the bill (McConnell 1953:78). To help it with the task, the Farm Bureau once again employed Frederick Lee, the lawyer who assisted in the drafting of the original act (Saloutos 1982:45). Farm Bureau leaders then lobbied very hard for the bill in Congress (pp. 78–79; Albertson 1961:113). McConnell concludes on the basis of the legislative hearings and Farm Bureau reports, "With the passage of the 1938 act, the Farm Bureau had accomplished its basic legislative program" (1953:79).[4]

This account of the general situation of the USDA between 1933 and 1938 hardly accords with Hooks's claim that the department "grew stronger and more insulated" (1990:29) )from 1932 to 1940. However, I have not yet dealt with specific agencies within the department, nor considered the years 1938 to 1940. These possible shortcomings will be rectified in the following sections.

## THE FARM SECURITY ADMINISTRATION

The Farm Security Administration, created in September 1937, is rightly thought of as the liberal agency within the Department of Agriculture (e.g.,

Gilbert and Howe 1991:214–18). It was the heir to the programs of relief, loans, and resettlement that were provided for poor and unemployed farmers and farm workers by the Federal Emergency Relief Administration (1933-1935) and the Resettlement Administration (1935-1937). However, I believe the legislative history of the act underlying this new agency shows that the Farm Bureau and southern legislators set strict limits on what it could do. More generally, a consideration of the FSA in this and later sections of the chapter allows me to contradict Hooks's claim of greater departmental insulation through a detailed look at a specific case where I rely in fair measure on sources not even cited by him (Baldwin 1968; Grubb 1971; Mertz 1978). Whereas the liberals within the Department of Agriculture wanted (1) cooperative farms, (2) resettlement of poor farmers from bad soil to good, (3) the upgrading of tenants to farm ownership, and (4) the unionization of farm workers, the primary emphasis of the FSA was whittled down to such traditional programs as rehabilitation loans to small family farmers, along with an underfunded program to help tenant farmers become owners. Even within this narrow framework the liberals and farm labor suffered further setbacks.

One of the issues liberals inside and outside the state wanted to address through the FSA was the inadequacy of tenancy laws, making it very difficult for tenants to save money and buy their own land. But the President's Committee on Farm Tenancy, appointed in 1936 to suggest programs to be incorporated into the FSA, "side-stepped the problem of obsolete and inadequate tenancy laws" (Benedict 1953:360). The agricultural economists serving as technical advisers to this presidential committee wrote a draft report containing suggestions on a variety of issues that annoyed several members of the committee, and especially the president of the Farm Bureau. These members "regarded the draft as too critical of tenancy, landlords, the South, and race relations and, in spite of objections from some of the social scientists, forced the technicians to alter the draft" (Kirkendall 1966:127). It is another case of experts being cast aside, unlike what state autonomy theorists have led their readers to expect.

Liberals wanted to make it so new farm owners could not sell their farms for several years. They felt such a restriction was needed so plantation owners and speculators could not take the land from the new owners at bargain prices (ibid.). However, the president of the Farm Bureau objected because he thought this provision was a challenge to the basic right to own property "in fee simple" (Campbell 1962:166). The provision never made it to law.

Even the mild legislation proposed by the President's Committee on Farm Tenancy was too much for many southern legislators (Baldwin 1968:chap. 6). They restricted the future agency even further by inserting a provision mandating that any home ownership loans must be approved by what

Grubb calls "local committees of prosperous farmers" (1971:154–55). They also eliminated a provision that would have allowed the government to buy land it could then divide into smaller farms and sell to tenants (Mertz 1978:150). When all was said and done, and very significantly in a theoretical sense, the basic provisions of the law creating the FSA in 1937 ended up as "almost exactly the tenancy 'cure' that southern planters and established, upper-middle-class dominated farm organizations had been advocating" (Grubb 1971:155). This capitulation to southern planters does not suggest state autonomy. Moreover, the FSA actually functioned in part to help landlords shed their traditional responsibility to provide cash, seed, and equipment advances for their tenants. Now the FSA was fulfilling that obligation for the plantation owners with emergency rehabilitation loans and other forms of relief payments (Mertz 1978:198). Perhaps this is why the Farm Bureau and its allies did not block the FSA legislation completely, as the first director of the FSA later said it could have done had it so desired (p. 111, especially footnote 42).

To top it all off, the FSA programs were meager in size compared to AAA programs or what was needed. To give some idea of the magnitudes involved, Kirkendall (1966:129, 131) reports the FSA was authorized to expend $85 million in grants and loans between 1937 and 1940, but that the AAA made $133 million in benefit payments to Texas alone in 1936. Out of 146,000 loan applications received in 1938 and 1939 from tenants desiring to purchase farms, only 6,180 were granted. Tenants were increasing at the rate of 40,000 per year, but the FSA could make "fewer than 10,000 loans per year" (pp. 130–31). This is not exactly progress.

Looked at another way, $500 million of the $644 million in annual appropriations for agriculture in 1938 went for subsidy programs: that is, 78 percent. By contrast, $26 million went to the bureau that supports and inspects the livestock industry, $24 million to the Soil Conservation Service, $18 million to the Forest Service, $13 million to the Extension Service, and only $10 million to the FSA for solving farm tenancy (U.S. Government 1938:145).

In other words, contrary to the impression that can be gained from the FSA's liberal image and the attacks on it by conservatives, the agency was a pale reflection of what its advocates had envisioned, due to the pressures of the Farm Bureau, southern congressional leaders, and commercial farmers (cf. Kirkendall 1966:128–31; Baldwin 1968; Mertz 1978; Alston and Ferrie 1985). Still, the very existence of the FSA can be considered a victory of sorts for liberals and moderates, and its staff often implemented more progressive policies than called for in the legislation for rural poverty programs (Gilbert and Howe 1991:215). Because they understood the power of the southerners in Congress, the liberals' goal at the outset was only to have the programs authorized, and then to increase funding later (Mertz 1978:183).

Thus, the main battles had been postponed, which makes Hooks's claims about why the FSA and BAE declined in the early forties all the more important.

## THE AUTONOMY BATTLE INTENSIFIES, 1938–1941

Because of the great success of the Farm Bureau and other commercial farmers in shaping the major programs of the USDA between 1933 and 1938, tension and then conflict began to develop between some department leaders and the farm organizations. Much of this tension was over seemingly minor issues or out of the public eye at first, but it was there nonetheless. Most generally, the tension involved the desire of the Farm Bureau to be consulted before major decisions were made. In a way, the Farm Bureau was only asking that the department continue to give it the access that Roosevelt and Secretary of Agriculture Henry A. Wallace had granted it earlier, but top officials of the department felt the relationship had become too one-sided (Campbell 1962:158ff.).

Tensions also developed between farm organizations and the AAA because Howard Tolley, the agricultural economist Wallace appointed as its director in 1936, was a liberal who wanted to increase the participation of poor farmers in the management of the program at the local level. He also was concerned that tenant farmers and sharecroppers in the South were not receiving their fair share of benefits. Furthermore, he advocated "a limit on the size of the payment that a farmer could receive from AAA" (Kirkendall 1966:152). These ideas did not sit well with commercial farmers, the Extension Service, or most other leaders in AAA. Kirkendall (pp. 152–54) writes that the opposition to Tolley and his views was especially strong in the South; Saloutos believes that the Farm Bureau and "those who had southern roots were opposed to Tolley's vision for the agency" (1982:241). Cully Cobb, the southern journalist who headed the division for cotton allotments within the AAA, resigned in the summer of 1937, because of conflicts with Tolley. In 1938, Tolley increased the level of tension when he took the state-level administration of AAA away from the Extension Service because he felt he was not receiving the cooperation he needed on new programs. As will be shown shortly, these problems had a direct relation to the elevation of the BAE to a central planning agency and the appointment of Tolley to head it.

Farm organizations and the USDA also clashed in the late 1930s over another agency, the Farm Credit Administration, which made loans to middle-class farmers. It had been created in 1933 to buy farm mortgages from distressed lenders, thereby shoring up banks and insurance companies, and to provide better terms to the angry farmers, thereby diminishing the disruption in the Midwest and Great Plains. The agency originally was independent of the USDA, an arrangement satisfactory to the Farm Bureau and its allies. However, in June 1939, Wallace was successful in having the Farm Credit Administration put into the USDA, and in December 1939 he appointed a new director, agricultural economist Albert Black of Iowa State College. Black already had antagonized the Farm Bureau in the Midwest as head of the corn-hog division of AAA by trying to reduce Farm Bureau influence on his committees (Kirkendall 1966:93; Campbell 1962:172). As soon as he settled into his position at the Farm Credit Administration, Black made legislative proposals opposed by the farm groups. The Farm Bureau, National Grange, and National Coop Council passed resolutions rejecting his proposals. Significantly, the bill put forward by Black and the Farm Credit Administration in 1941 was not reported out of committee in either house of Congress (Benedict 1953:393). Another defeat for the experts.

There were also skirmishes with the FSA. In spite of its limited charter and small budget, the FSA was nonetheless threatening to local power structures in agriculture. As the most detailed analysis of the FSA puts it, the agency was a challenge to the "economic status quo" at the local level even though it was "economically irrelevant" at the national level (Baldwin 1968:263). This challenge to the status quo occurred in every part of the country. In 1938, for example, the FSA upset many businessmen in the Northeast when it decided to continue funding to a few small hosiery factories in resettlement projects in the South started by the Resettlement Administration. Although it was only a matter of $3.05 million to four settlement projects, the outpouring of protest over "unfair competition" to northern industry was very large. Roosevelt and Wallace tried to write off the protests as a minor matter, but Baldwin (1968:264) points out that Congress proceeded to restrict the appropriations to such projects. In the Great Plains the FSA incurred the wrath of the Farm Bureau by giving loans to 9,696 farmers to purchase stock in ninety-nine grain elevators operated by the National Farmers Union, the liberal archrival to the Farm Bureau (Campbell, 1962:170). The Farm Bureau was convinced the loans were an attempt to undercut it. As Campbell wryly comments: "In allying itself with the National Farmers Union, the FSA entered the wars of agricultural politics, and invited political annihilation. The Farm Bureau accepted the invitation" (ibid.).

This attempt to support the National Farmers Union's grain elevators also annoyed the large grain dealers in Minneapolis, who saw the loans as an attempt to undercut them (McConnell 1953:95).

Above and beyond rivalries among farm groups, I believe the FSA was viewed as a threat by most better-off farmers because it might provide organizing assistance to workers. Its camps for workers could be used as organizing sites, for example. FSA was seen by farm owners as prounion, and rightly so.

The most important struggle between farm owners and the FSA over poor farmers and farm workers occurred in the South, but it did not involve the issue of unions. The struggle was primarily in the ideological realm, which is not a minor matter because principle is a basic part of any class conflict. Just the right note is struck by Baldwin when he writes: "Perhaps the most potentially dangerous FSA threat to the southern way of life was the demonstration and dramatization of the relationship between chronic rural poverty, ignorance, social isolation, racial discrimination, and political impotence" (1968:280). In other words, the FSA was out to undermine the southern power structure by helping poor farmers, tenants, and agricultural laborers, six million of whom were African-Americans, and the southern plantation owners fully understood this fact.

The seriousness of the conflict can be found in an exchange between the FSA and Senator Jimmy Byrnes of South Carolina over the appointment of African-Americans to FSA committees in southern states in 1937. The issue and his vehement reaction to it take on great theoretical importance because Byrnes was one of Roosevelt's most important southern allies. He was instrumental in keeping southern delegates behind Roosevelt at the Democratic convention in 1932, and he played an even bigger role in gathering southern support for Roosevelt's program during his first term. By 1937, however, he was in the process of quietly leading the southern revolt against Roosevelt that stopped most New Deal legislation in its tracks and provided the basis for the conservative coalition. Despite this opposition to Roosevelt during his second term, or perhaps because it showed the power of the bloc he spoke for, Byrnes came to figure prominently as Roosevelt's "assistant president" in the industrial mobilization for World War II, a story that will be told in Chapter 6.

Byrnes's clash with the FSA in 1937 came at a time when he was very upset by the CIO sit-down strikes leading to new industrial unions in the North. He also was annoyed by CIO organizing attempts in the South, especially because they were interracial in nature. As one of the many southerners who thought their way of life was under attack, he reacted strongly when he learned about the appointment of African-Americans to state-level FSA committees in the South. He immediately wrote a sarcastic letter to the head of the FSA warning that "the negro will be the one to suffer" if the practice continued (Baldwin 1968:307). He further warned that the FSA should "not disturb the friendly relations now existing between the races." When the FSA refused to back down, Byrnes went to Secretary of Agriculture Wallace, who immediately removed the African-Americans from the committees even though he had originally supported the plan (ibid.).

An incidence of this kind around attempts to help African-American farmers and laborers is essential to understanding the class struggle within the

USDA because the southern segment of the ruling class controlled the legislative branch of government through its position in the Democratic party and, after 1937, its coalition with conservative Republicans of the North and Midwest. The nature of this control had several levels. First, planters and successful commercial farmers served in Congress, making it possible for them to look out for their interests in a very direct fashion. Second, the planters were very close to southern elected officials, as the classic work of V. O. Key (1949) makes abundantly clear. Third, southern control of the Democratic party in Congress involved a complex set of historically developed rules, precedents, and procedures fully explained by David Potter (1972). They included standing legislative committees with powerful chairmen, a seniority system for selecting chairmen, a rules committee that decided what legislation should be considered by the full House, a party caucus for selecting congressional leadership, the assignment of new members to House committees by Democratic members of the Ways and Means Committee, and—in the Senate—the all-important filibuster, which the southerners showed no hesitation in using whenever their subjugation of African-Americans in the South was challenged in any way, shape, or form.

Southern control of Congress was made possible through the long-standing alliance the plantation owners had developed with ethnic and small-business groups in northern cities. The alliance creating this Democratic coalition had nineteenth-century economic and political roots, which I have summarized elsewhere (Domhoff 1990:chap. 9). During the New Deal, as I noted in Chapter 2, this alliance became a prospending coalition in which the northern Democrats voted for agricultural subsidies desired by the South and the southerners in return voted for urban spending programs. Campbell (1962:115ff.) provides congressional testimony on the conscious understanding of this relationship during the New Deal, even though she goes astray in equating the northern Democrats with "urban labor." For example, she reports that the files of the Farm Bureau and newspaper accounts at the time show how northern machine Democrats and farm leaders worked together in 1939 to pass agricultural subsidy legislation in exchange for southern support of urban programs. Similarly, Representative John O'Connor of New York spoke on the House floor in 1938 about how he and other New York Democrats had found the votes to reverse an agricultural subsidy vote that had gone against the farm interests. More pointedly, he explained the "reciprocity" involved in passing a subsidy bill for cotton:

> We got enough changes from New York and the surrounding territory to pass the bill. The McNary-Haugen bill was passed by votes from New York, just a handful. The Bankhead cotton bill was passed by just a few votes from New York. Of course, at those times we had certain assurances of reciprocity. For instance, at the time of the closing days of the first session of this Congress when some of us stood at the door to the Speaker's lobby and got the votes

necessary to pass the cotton bill, we had pretty definite assurances that we
would get considerable help from a certain section of this country on the
wage-and-hour bill. (Campbell 1962:116)

At the same time, the southern Democrats entered into a coalition with
Republicans after 1937 on issues concerning social welfare, labor relations, civil rights, and business regulation. This conservative coalition, as
I stated in the second chapter, came together on the issues that define the
class struggle in the United States at the legislative level. The battle between farm laborers and commercial farmers is most certainly one of
those issues. Furthermore, this rural class conflict was mirrored in conflict
within the department between the AAA and FSA. The overall picture
presents a small irony: while northern Democrats were helping southerners by voting in favor of agricultural subsidies that were opposed by
most Republicans, the southern Democrats were working with the Republicans to dismantle the BAE and FSA. It is at this upper-class level of the
social structure that we can talk about coalitional politics and pluralism
in the United States, but it is coalitions of class segments and pluralism
for the few (e.g., Hamilton 1972:5).

It is of theoretical note that there was no conflict between the Farm
Bureau and two of the most famous and enduring liberal agencies of the
New Deal in agriculture, the Rural Electrification Administration and the
Tennessee Valley Authority. When the Rural Electrification Administration
moved into the Department of Agriculture in 1939 from an independent
status, it quickly reached an accommodation with the Farm Bureau (McConnell 1953:123). Similarly, TVA did not come into conflict with the Farm
Bureau because its leadership chose "to trade control of its large agricultural
program in return for political support for the electric power program"
(p. 116). By giving the Extension Service a large hand in its agricultural
program, the TVA in effect made an alliance with the Farm Bureau and the
most prosperous farmers (cf. Selznick 1947; Baldwin 1968:343). In other
words, whatever autonomy can be claimed for these agencies had a clear
price and limit.

Despite these instances of collaboration, there was an open break between the Farm Bureau and the department in late 1940 and 1941. Different
accounts emphasize different specific events or actions in trying to explain
what led to it. For example, Albertson (1961:136–37) suggests that Wallace's friendly support of the FSA in campaign speeches in 1940 was the
final straw. Benedict (1953:364) mentions the appointment of a more liberal
and confrontational FSA administrator as the tipping point, and we already
have seen that the Farm Bureau was annoyed over changes in the status and
leadership of the Farm Credit Administration. Looking at these and other
actions as part of a general pattern, McConnell concluded that by 1939 the

USDA was making a strong bid for greater autonomy, thereby anticipating Hooks's concerns by thirty-seven years:

> The Department of Agriculture was on its way to emancipation. It is not to be wondered that the Farm Bureau repudiated Henry Wallace and moved toward an open break with the reorganized department. (1953:118)

Thus, Campbell is probably right that no one event or appointment in this "titanic struggle" should be emphasized (1962:156). The important point is that the farm organizations and the department were on a collision course over (1) the degree to which the department should be autonomous and (2) the degree to which the department should aid tenants, farm laborers, and the rural poor. That is, class and organizational issues were closely intertwined. The Farm Bureau and allied farm organizations, along with business groups, southern Democrats, northern Republicans, and most AAA officials, were on one side of the divide, and urban liberals, farm labor, the National Farmers Union, the FSA, and the BAE were on the other. It is in this context that we can look at Hooks's claims about the rise and demise of the BAE as an alleged case study in nascent state autonomy.


## THE BAE AND LAND USE PLANNING

Hooks uses the transformation of the BAE in late 1938 into a central planning agency for the USDA as evidence that the department was enjoying growing autonomy despite criticism by the Farm Bureau and its allies. He quotes Benedict as noting that the BAE went through "an abrupt and fundamental" transformation that gave it "the leadership in shaping policy recommendations, that is, functioning as a general staff for the Department of Agriculture" (1953:395). He further asserts that "each agency was required to submit to the BAE a summary of proposed activities during the next budget cycle" (Hooks 1990:33). However, Hooks does not mention that Benedict follows his statement about the "abrupt and fundamental" shift in the role of the BAE with the judgment that the BAE largely failed in its new mission. Benedict writes that the BAE "made an earnest effort to provide the type of coordination and policy leadership desired, but was unable to make significant headway against the resistance of the various strongly entrenched agencies in the Department" (1953:395).

The questionable accuracy of Hooks's characterization of Benedict's views aside, the issue of land use planning and the role of the BAE must be understood in the class conflict context developed in the previous sections. Land use planning was not simply a BAE plan being pushed by an autonomous department. Instead, land use planning was an amorphous catch-all phrase that included both conservative (proowner) and liberal (proworker) aspects, and the conservative aspects usually were in the ascendancy. From the conservative point of view, land use planning was a way to make commercial farming more profitable by pushing marginal farmers out of the industry. In the late 1920s and early 1930s, many agricultural economists were writing that the only long-term solution to unprofitable farming was to increase the size of farms and reduce the number of farmers (e.g., Rowley 1970:39, chap. 6; Saloutos 1982:31–32; D. Hamilton 1991:184). They suggested the following land use schemes to realize this goal:

1.  eliminate the granting of new homesteads on government lands;
2.  purchase marginal farm lands and turn them into pastures and parks;
3.  encourage industries to move to rural areas in order to employ displaced farmers and agricultural workers.

Liberals, however, had other policies in mind when they talked of land use. They thought a proper land use policy should help turn tenants into owners and that some land could be used more productively if it were farmed cooperatively. Far more than conservatives, they wanted to resettle poor and tenant farmers on good land rather than force them out of farming. They also wanted land use planning to bring low-income farmers into the political process.

When we look at land use planning in a class conflict framework, we find most of the land use policies of the first Roosevelt Administration were of the conservative, pro-owner variety. They were tied to reducing production, not helping poor people (Saloutos 1982:32–33). As for the liberal land use concepts, they largely failed. The idea of resettlement was resisted by all farmers, and it was difficult for the government to buy good land for possible resettlement in any case. Plans for cooperative farming were put on the shelf because of resistance from both poor and prosperous farmers. The FSA did embody the principle of turning tenants into owners, but as already noted, the budget for this program was very small. All that was left of the liberal notion of land use planning was the democratic participation of all farmers in the planning process through membership on BAE committees. It is this remaining liberal policy proposal that Hooks elevates to allegedly important evidence for state autonomy.

Wallace made a number of attempts to bring coordination to the various land use programs administered by the department. He appointed a Land Policy Committee in March 1935 and a Committee on Departmental Coordination in December 1936. In 1937 he created an Office of Land Use Coordination (Kirkendall 1966:151). An agreement worked out between the department and the land grant colleges in July 1938 concerning the structuring of committees created further pressure for a coordinating agency within the department. Thus, there seemed to be a definite organizational need for a planning capability, but it was not foreordained that the BAE would be designated to fulfill the role. Indeed, the agency had been in the doldrums for much of the New Deal. Its holdover chair from the 1920s, Nils Olsen, looked askance at many New Deal agricultural policies, and the AAA therefore developed its own research unit in 1933 so it would not have to rely on the BAE. The situation improved a little for the BAE in 1935 with the appointment of a new director, but not much (Kirkendall 1966:77–78).

Thus, there is reason to be cautious when Hooks talks about the elevation of the BAE strictly in terms of departmental rationales. According to the historians who have looked at the issue closely, political factors may have played a large role. Kirkendall (1966:150) says the motives for upgrading the BAE were mixed, and they included the fact that Wallace had presidential ambitions [see Kirkendall (1990:204–6) for further information on Wallace's presidential hopes]. From a political point of view, the aforementioned conflicts within the AAA over Tolley and his liberal views on subsidies and committee participation were a big liability. To shore up his support with farmers and farm groups, and especially the southern Democrats in those two categories, Wallace decided that Tolley had to go as director of AAA (Kirkendall 1966:160–61).

Saloutos (1982:chap. 17), in a major book more directly focused on the overall functioning of the department than Kirkendall's, but not cited by Hooks, comes to a similar conclusion using a wide range of evidence. It is his strong belief that politics, not land use planning, was the reason the reorganization kicked Tolley over to the BAE. The real problem was to satisfy the growers, planters, and farmers who dominated the AAA so they would support Wallace for president. As Saloutos summarizes, invoking interview materials with several former members of the department:

> The obvious lack of interest of the AAA in the research and planning efforts of the BAE under Tolley after the reorganization of the USDA would tend to confirm that the reorganization was designed not so much for the purpose of achieving better coordination between the land-use planning of the USDA and the states and counties, as it was to aid the political ambitions of Wallace. The observations of John B. Huston, Samuel B. Bledsoe, Rudolph M. Evans, and Tolley in general would support this view. (1982:253)

But Tolley had done nothing to be summarily dismissed, and he was respected by the other agricultural economists in the department. He had been working with agricultural economists inside and outside the department since the mid-1920s, and he and Wallace were close allies who had served together on the Social Science Research Council's special committee on fellowships in agriculture from 1931 to 1933. In other words, Tolley was part of the experts' old-boy network, and it was therefore decided that he would be put in charge of an upgraded BAE. This new BAE would make studies for all agencies and it would report directly to Wallace. Tolley was deeply hurt when he learned of his new assignment, for it was a clear demotion, and he accepted it only reluctantly. In short, the elevation of the BAE was at least to some extent a graceful way to remove Tolley from AAA.

If there is even a little bit of truth to Kirkendall and Saloutos's claim that the elevation of the BAE involved a political dimension, then they have raised a point difficult for a state autonomy theory to handle: the issue is no longer primarily inside the state, but between the leaders of private farm organizations and a politician-administrator (Wallace) who is putting his political ambitions above the development of his department as an arm of the allegedly autonomous state. It is thus that pressure group or interest group leaders and the political ambitions of alleged state managers come together to make the American state so permeable, and hence not very autonomous (Feigenbaum 1985:172; Domhoff 1990:26–27). But Hooks does not even mention the political dimensions involved in the changes in the BAE, let alone try to explain why they do not contradict his theory.

Hooks makes the new BAE sound more like a powerhouse than it was. For example, he claims that the "central offices of the USDA created direct ties to farmers, bypassing the Extension Service, the Agricultural Adjustment Administration, and the Farm Bureau" (1990:34). One of these direct ties was "a BAE training program for USDA staff members and farmers" (ibid.). Hooks here cites Kirkendall in a footnote, but what Kirkendall says is that the BAE "continued and expanded" a program of discussion groups developed in 1935 in consultation with the Farm Bureau (1966:187). When the Farm Bureau expressed concern about any program that might encourage new farm organizations, "department officials took steps to assure the Farm Bureau of their desire to cooperate with existing farm organizations" (p. 141). Thus assured, the president of the Farm Bureau

> sent a letter to all state Farm Bureaus urging them to cooperate. He pointed out that the state units could have confidence in the program, for it had been developed by M. L. Wilson and his staff and they had no intention of setting up new organizations of farmers but planned to work through existing ones. (ibid.)

Kirkendall then quotes a line in the Farm Bureau president's letter: "If properly utilized, this program . . . should result in increasing the effectiveness of our Farm Bureau units in molding public opinion, as well as stimulating interest and participation in local Farm Bureau meetings" (pp. 141–42). In short, what Hooks claims to be a program bypassing the Farm Bureau is actually one the Farm Bureau initially endorsed because it decided it could use the program to its own advantage.

Hooks's belief that the BAE became an important planning agency within the department is contradicted by the massive evidence that it had no power whatsoever to cause other agencies to do anything they did not want to do. Kirkendall stresses that "Wallace had not legally obliged the action agencies to cooperate with the BAE" (1966:168). In other words, its power was purely advisory and hortatory. Since most agencies within the department were angry with the BAE within a year and refused to cooperate with it, even its advisory and hortatory powers were nil. The main exception was the FSA, which looked to the BAE for support. It is within this context that Hooks's (1990:36) claim that action agencies were "required to submit" their proposed activities to the BAE should be understood. In other words, the requirement meant nothing.

The planning committees vaunted by Hooks were resented by the AAA and the Soil Conservation Service. In some states the land grant colleges refused to sign the BAE's memorandum of understanding concerning the functioning of the committees (Kirkendall 1966:174–75). Many officials of the Extension Service remained unconvinced that the department was serious about the planning committees. Thus, it is hard for me to believe Hooks and I are reading the same book when he cites page 174 of Kirkendall's book as the basis for his assertion that "the BAE also gained influence over the Extension Service and land grant colleges in developing state and regional programs" (1990:36). In the first paragraph Kirkendall repeatedly says "were to" do this and that, which does not mean these things were done, as I understand the subjunctive form. In the second paragraph on the page Kirkendall reports that "the degree of cooperation between the bureau and the colleges and the extent to which the schools applied themselves to the project varied greatly from state to state" (1966:174). If there was great variation from state to state, then it is too strong for Hooks to claim the BAE gained general influence.

However, Hooks is right in saying the Farm Bureau did not like the direction in which the BAE was pushing the land use committees in 1939 and 1940. But this does not prove that the committees "flourished" or caused the Farm Bureau any real problems. In fact, the Farm Bureau had a strong presence on the committees as long as they existed. Gross (1943:653–54) flatly states that county land use committees usually were dominated by members of the Farm Bureau. Kirkendall concurs when he writes: "In many counties, the Farm Bureau dominated the committees" (1966:180). Once again, the actual functioning of a USDA agency shows the power of the Farm Bureau more than any alleged state autonomy.

Although Farm Bureau members and other prosperous farmers tended to dominate the county committees in most states, the Farm Bureau saw them as a threat that had to be eliminated. As McConnell explains, this is because the committees "had become potential centers of power" (1953:117). That is, they could become the basis for the development of a rival farm organization if they could attract a wider range of members and become effective. Such a rival organization would make it possible for the department to gain greater independence, and the Farm Bureau understood that point very well. Moreover, that rival organization could advocate very liberal policies that the labor-employing commercial farmers might not like. Once again, class and organizational factors are intertwined.

But the emphasis has to be on the words *potential* and *if*. In 1939 and 1940 the committees only had the *potential* to cause problems for the Farm Bureau *if* they could survive and escape Farm Bureau control. That is certainly a sufficient reason to attack the committees, as a class-and-organization theory of power would predict, but contrary to Hooks, it is not evidence that the committees were effective or autonomous.

When the various problems facing the BAE and its land use committees are added up, it seems highly unlikely that the BAE was autonomous in the two brief years after it was elevated to a higher position in the USDA. Instead, we have to conclude that the BAE was in a formative stage at best, and hanging on by a thread.

## THE DECLINE OF THE BAE AND FSA

The BAE and FSA suffered serious setbacks in the early 1940s. For example, the BAE had its budget cut in battles before the House Appropriations Committee in 1941 and 1942 (Hardin 1946). Then too, employees of the FSA were refused long-sought civil service status in 1941 due to Farm Bureau pressure on Congress. This action kept the pay of FSA employees 10 to 15 percent below that of other government workers, greatly demoralizing the agency and hastening the departure of many of its best employees (McConnell 1953:101–2; Baldwin 1968:315–16). The first head of the FSA, a southern liberal, quit in 1940 in part because he did not look forward to the hostility he encountered at congressional hearings (Kirkendall 1966:132), and his successor resigned in 1943 after members of Congress called for his ouster and trimmed the budget for rural rehabilitation by over half (Baldwin 1968:332, 391–94). The FSA was disbanded in 1946 in favor of the more bland Farmers Home Administration, which became essentially a loan agency for veterans who wanted to purchase farms.

As for the BAE, it suffered a very similar fate. It was officially demoted in 1945 after it was attacked in Congress for allowing its experts to write reports upsetting to the powers that be in Mississippi and California. The report on life in a Mississippi county dared to hint that race relations there might be less than idyllic (Kirkendall 1966:235). The report on two towns in central California claimed that the quality of life in the town surrounded by small farms was better than in the one surrounded by large agribusinesses, and a direct causal link was drawn. The big growers were convinced that the unofficial circulation of a draft of the report was one factor in keeping them from receiving federal water for more than the usual 160 acres. They protested long and loudly, and the BAE decided to withhold the report from publication. But the report cost the BAE a considerable amount of support, and once again experts—sociologists and anthropologists in this case—learned the limits of their tethers while in government service (Kirkendall 1964; 1966:223–24).

Hooks believes the actions of Claude Wickard, who replaced Wallace as secretary of agriculture in 1940, are one key to understanding what happened to the BAE even though scholars who have written on the fate of the BAE and FSA have concluded that the Farm Bureau and southern legislators played the central role in destroying these mildly liberal agencies (e.g., Kirkendall 1966:chap. 11). Benedict (1953:395, note 53), drawing on a report published in 1950 by agricultural economist John D. Black, lists five reasons why the BAE's committees failed. The efforts of the Farm Bureau, along with the innovativeness of the program and the opposition of other departmental agencies, are among the reasons, but Wickard's actions as Secretary of Agriculture are not. For Hooks, however, the problems began in a clash over control between Wickard and one of his inherited staff members, Paul Appleby:

> Just as the waxing of the BAE's power in the earlier period hinged on the active support of Appleby and Secretary of Agriculture Wallace, its decline in the '40s was closely tied to change at the center of the USDA. As Wickard reduced Appleby's influence over "the mechanisms of departmental administrative control" (Albertson 1961:170), the BAE lost its privileged access to the Secretary of Agriculture. (Hooks 1990:36)

In addition to the Wickard-Appleby contest for control, Roosevelt's focus on foreign and military policy meant that he no longer was protecting New Deal agencies from the conservatives in Congress. Taken together, these two problems inside the state weakened the USDA and made it vulnerable to attack by the Farm Bureau. Thus, the state is given primacy over outside pressure groups.

Hooks contrasts his analysis with "the view that Wickard was a puppet of the AFBF" (1990:36), a view no one seems to hold. He tries to establish Wickard's independence and state orientation by saying he was not appointed to "placate the Farm Bureau" (ibid.). His first piece of evidence for this argument is that "Roosevelt first asked agricultural economist M. L. Wilson" (ibid.) to succeed Wallace. For Hooks, the fact that Wilson was a strong supporter of land use planning and the BAE apparently is evidence enough that the Farm Bureau would oppose him. His second piece of evidence is that Wickard allegedly was "not an ally of the Farm Bureau, but remained distant from the AFBF during his tenure as Secretary of Agriculture" (ibid.). His source for this claim is a brief paragraph in Philip Burch's (1981a, 1981b) wide-ranging compilation of the social and economic backgrounds of federal officials.

However, the fact that Wilson may have been asked first is hardly evidence that the Farm Bureau was unimportant on this issue. Moreover, the approach to Wilson by Wallace, not Roosevelt, as Hooks wrongly says, was a very general one in December 1939 that did not go beyond the two men because Wilson declined (Albertson 1961:149). Nor would Wilson's longstanding interest in land use planning necessarily make him unacceptable to the Farm Bureau. In fact, Wilson was on very good terms with it (e.g., Kirkendall 1966:124–25). As for Burch's comments on Wickard and the Farm Bureau, they are a very condensed summary of two sources, McConnell (1953) and Dean Albertson's (1961) biography of Wickard, so Burch's judgment hardly can be taken as the final word. All Burch says is the following. It includes half of a sentence from McConnell (1953:122) in quotations marks:

> Although Wickard had served in the department for the preceding seven years, he was not, interestingly, on good terms with the influential, big-farmer-dominated American Farm Bureau Federation (AFBF). In fact, Wickard soon became anathema to the AFBF, and as a penalty for his independence, he ultimately " . . . paid the price by becoming a nearly impotent bystander in his own department when the main functions of the department were later placed under the War Food Administration headed [initially] by Chester C. Davis," an official who was one of the original trustees of the CED [Committee for Economic Development]. (Burch 1981:77–78)

Albertson's highly detailed biography, based on personal diaries, interviews, and governmental records, presents a very different and more complex picture of Wickard's relation to the Farm Bureau, and the appointment of Chester Davis as "food czar" referred to by Burch did not occur until late March, 1943, nineteen months after Wickard's appointment as secretary. The first surprise is that Wickard helped to found the Farm Bureau in his home county in Indiana in 1919 and took over as its president in 1926. This is hardly the makings of a Farm Bureau enemy. Then, as a AAA administrator from 1933 to 1940, he worked with Farm Bureau officials and lawyers in drafting the legislation of 1938 that helped to reshape the functioning of the agency (Albertson 1961:113). Hooks's claim that the Farm Bureau did not like the selection of Wickard as secretary is contradicted by the fact that

Farm Bureau members were prominent among the groups urging his appointment after Wallace accepted the vice-presidential nomination in August, 1940. In a later context Albertson (1961:271) says Farm Bureau leaders "thought they had 'one of their own' as Secretary of Agriculture" when he was appointed (p. 148). Campbell (1962:184) states that the Farm Bureau endorsed Wickard's appointment when it was announced. Then, too, the liberal assistants inherited by Wickard saw him at the time as an "AAA-Farm Bureau Secretary" according to Albertson (1961:161).

Wickard's relationship to the Farm Bureau aside, the real difficulties with Hooks's analysis begin with the fact that the BAE's problems started well before Wickard bypassed Appleby early in 1941, or even before Wickard was appointed in early September, 1940. By early 1940, according to Kirkendall (1966:chap. 10), the BAE was in trouble with the AAA, the Soil Conservation Service, the Extension Service, officials of land grant colleges, the Farm Bureau, and allies of the Farm Bureau. Its attempts to increase grass roots involvement in the planning committees had alienated all these agencies and groups for one reason or another, and the criticisms it made of the AAA in its annual report were the final straw for that agency.

Kirkendall (1966:191–92) adds another pre-Wickard factor contributing to the downfall of the BAE that may come as a shock to those who have only heard Hooks's version of the story: Wallace in early 1940 was the first Secretary of Agriculture to back away from the BAE, not Wickard. This was because he was too busy with his presidential campaign to give much attention to the BAE:

> In 1940, however, Wallace's attention turned increasingly to the national political situation and away from the matters that interested the BAE. Tolley now seldom received the kind of support that he needed in order to get cooperation from agencies like the AAA. (Kirkendall 1966:191–92)

As it turned out, Wallace had to settle for vice-president because Roosevelt wanted a third term. Although Wallace was supposed to solidify midwestern farm support for the Democrats, the Roosevelt-Wallace ticket lost there to the Republicans. When Roosevelt asked Chester Davis what had happened to cause Democratic defeat in the Midwest, Davis told Roosevelt that Wallace had alienated farmers by ignoring the Farm Bureau and paying too much attention to liberals. He reported his conversation with Roosevelt to the president of the Farm Bureau as follows:

> I gave my impression that for nearly two years the men in the Department had ceased to consult the Farm Bureau, the Cooperatives, or the Grange, on important matters, and that they had elevated Thatcher [of the liberal National Farmers Union] to a position of Chief Adviser for organized agriculture. Under the circumstances, it was not surprising to me that some of the farm leaders

had become lukewarm, even hostile. I urged him [FDR] to get back on the
basis where all the farm leaders were consulted and given the consideration
merited by the interests they represented. (Campbell 1962:181)

However, something more was going on: not only did the Farm Bureau
leadership feel slighted, but it worked quietly against the Roosevelt-Wallace
ticket in the Midwest. Then it privately urged Roosevelt during the campaign
to take steps to reassure farmers of his support for agriculture by decentraliz-
ing the administration of the department's action programs to the Extension
Service, where of course they could be watched more closely by the Farm
Bureau (Albertson 1961:175; Baldwin 1968:342). Thus, the Farm Bureau
was working for greater input into the department well before Wickard had
taken steps to change its administration.

Following the election, the Farm Bureau offered Roosevelt another suggestion: appoint a strong and highly visible secretary of agriculture who was
respected in all farm areas. The Farm Bureau even said who this person
should be: its friend Chester Davis (Kirkendall 1966:199). In December,
1940, the Farm Bureau made its opposition public by announcing its plan to
decentralize the department, a plan resisted very strongly by Roosevelt and
the top leadership of the department. As Campbell (1962:178) is quick to
point out when she mentions the plan, this draconian measure was never
adopted by the government, thereby demonstrating that Farm Bureau power
in this instance was limited by representatives of the state.

Although the Farm Bureau failed to replace Wickard or decentralize the
department, it did accomplish its goal of greatly limiting the independence
of the parts of the USDA objectionable to it. The campaign began in 1941
with the modest aim of cutting back funding for the BAE and FSA, and then
parceling FSA out to the Farm Credit Administration and the Extension Service (Baldwin 1968:343). The fact that the Farm Bureau began so modestly
was in part a function of the developing war atmosphere. As McConnell
points out, the Farm Bureau could not go to its most powerful ally, the
House Committee on Agriculture, because "the wartime situation forbade
consideration of any new farm legislation" (1953:101). Thus, the opening
battle had to be fought at the House Committee on Appropriations, which
listened with a sympathetic ear but did not feel it had the authority to
dismantle the FSA. This little point is important to note because it helps to
explain why the Farm Bureau did not succeed at the breakneck speed that
might convince state autonomy theorists like Hooks that it had predominant
power.

Wickard opposed the attempt by the Farm Bureau to dismantle FSA and
decrease BAE and FSA funding. Directors of the Extension Service in many
states joined in the opposition against BAE cuts, thereby demonstrating, says
Kirkendall, "they were not mere puppets of the American Farm Bureau

Federation" (1966:202). But in spite of this support from state managers, Congress sided with the Farm Bureau on the budget issue, cutting funds for both agencies. In terms of the BAE, this meant its planning committees had to be restricted. At this point Wickard "delegated planning authority to the AAA" (Hooks 1990:36) by creating new committees that relied heavily on it. "In part," explains Kirkendall, "Congress had forced Wickard to move in this direction by blocking plans to expand the planning committee system, but the development also reflected the Secretary's ties with AAA" (1966:205–6). In other words, the decline of the BAE is hardly the unilateral initiative by Wickard that Hooks makes it out to be.

During the next eighteen months Wickard and the Farm Bureau clashed over several issues, but none of them was a life-and-death matter. The Farm Bureau was annoyed that the new committees were not rooted in the Extension Service, and it complained about the wage rates set by the FSA for imported Mexican farm labor. However, there also was cooperation between Wickard and the Farm Bureau because they were in agreement that farmers should receive better prices along with guarantees of postwar price floors if they were to go all out in producing for the war effort. In June, 1941, Wickard worked out a quick compromise with the Farm Bureau on price parity that added $2.5 billion to the pot, causing some outside observers to say Wickard was not a very strong administrator (Albertson 1961:222). In January, 1942, after Wickard condemned unfair price controls on farm products, the Farm Bureau president called to praise Wickard's courage (p. 260). In short, the relationship between Wickard and the Farm Bureau had the kind of give and take we might expect between any departmental administrator and a major pressure group.

When Wickard finally did lose control over most of the USDA in March 1943, it was not only or even primarily because of the Farm Bureau, contrary to Burch. Instead, he looked very bad to his superiors when proposals to reorganize the department that he requested from his staff were delayed by conflict and indecision, and then rejected by him as far too liberal. From Wickard's point of view, it was the liberals who did him in (p. 340), and Albertson presents much evidence to this effect (pp. 342ff.). When Wickard fired a liberal appointee to his agency who was a favorite of Roosevelt's, he ended up in a loud argument with Roosevelt because the president wanted him to take the liberal back. Finally, the conservatives running the war effort, such as the former senator from South Carolina, Jimmy Byrnes, became convinced Wickard was not doing a good job, so they put Farm Bureau ally Chester Davis in charge of agricultural production. Davis, incidentally, lasted only ninety-two days before resigning from what he saw as an impossible job, to be replaced by Marvin Jones of Texas, the former chair of the House Committee on Agriculture.

As for Roosevelt's role in the decline of the BAE and the FSA, I believe he was responding to a new power equation in providing less support for these and other liberal agencies in the government. It was not simply that he "devoted his political power and prestige to shaping foreign and military policy," as Hooks (1990:37) writes, but that an increasingly powerful conservative coalition had developed in Congress with the help of Republican gains in Congress in 1938 and 1942. Moreover, the cooperation of large corporations was essential for war production. In short, Roosevelt needed conservatives in the Congress and corporate community to help him prosecute the war, and their price for cooperation was the dismantling of liberal initiatives such as the BAE and FSA. This point is demonstrated by Albertson's conclusion that Roosevelt ended his stalemate with Congress over the 1943 agricultural budget when he "traded the Farm Security Administration to the Farm Bureau in exchange for the power to control inflation" (1961:286).

Hooks's stress on Roosevelt's change of focus is surprising because he gives considerable emphasis to the rise of the conservative coalition in his study of the development of military autonomy during World War II, a topic on which he will be dissected in Chapter 6. There he points out that "the same Congress that was supplying billions of dollars in excess of the military's astronomical needs" also was doing away with New Deal agencies "in the name of fiscal austerity" (1985:314-15). In that context he mentions the dismantling of the Works Progress Administration, the Civilian Conservation Corps, the National Youth Administration, and the National Resources Planning Board, and adds that the FSA survived only in what he calls "crippled form" (p. 313). Hooks also mentions the demise of the four nonfarm agencies in his article on New Deal agricultural policy (Hooks 1990:38), but he does not seem to notice that the breadth and success of the conservative attack on the New Deal undercuts his emphasis on Wickard in explaining the decline of the BAE.

In short, Wickard's attempt "to consolidate his authority" (p. 36) within the USDA is at best a secondary factor in explaining the decline of the BAE, as is Roosevelt's change of focus. It seems more likely we should focus on the usual suspects, that is, prosperous farmers, plantation owners, and their business allies.

## CONCLUSION

There is ample evidence of conflict between conservatives and liberals over agricultural policy throughout most of the New Deal, and that is how the two sides usually are labeled in the historical literature. I agree that the argument can be considered a liberal-conservative one in terms of values and ideology. However, I would go one step further and say this conflict is also a class conflict because businessmen and successful farmers were on one side, by and large, and tenant farmers and farm workers were on the other. True enough, liberals and leftists from the urban upper-middle and upper classes sided with the tenants and farm workers, and provided most of their leadership, but the fundamental conflict is one of class because employers were pitted against farm workers over the core class issues of ownership, profit, wages, and unionization.

At the same time, this conflict manifested itself in and around the state over issues of organizational growth and survival. The Farm Bureau grew to power due to the county agent system, and it maintained a constant vigilance against any attempt by USDA officials to foster the development of any organizational structures that might provide the basis for a rival farm pressure group to develop. This crucial insight in McConnell's analysis is at fundamental odds with the state autonomy theorists when they implicitly assume that increasing state capacity leads to state autonomy.

Within this context, I think there is overwhelming evidence for an ongoing battle over departmental autonomy between leaders of conservative farm organizations and top officials of the USDA. There also were intradepartmental conflicts and attempts by some agencies of the department to shake free of the influence of commercial farmers in order to aid tenant farmers, farm workers, and the rural unemployed. However, it seems equally clear to me that the department lost this battle for autonomy. It could not escape the bounds set for it by a Democratic party and a conservative coalition dominated by southern plantation elites who wanted (1) subsidies and (2) absolutely no changes in the almost complete subjugation of their African-American work force. In keeping with what a class-based theory would expect, the intradepartmental rivalries within the USDA rather completely parallel the larger class conflict between the conservatives and liberals. The AAA and the Extension Service were closely affiliated with the conservatives, and officials within these two agencies disliked the FSA and BAE largely because the latter two were challengers to their major supporters. It is again noteworthy that the two liberal agencies not challenged in the early 1940s, the Rural Electrification Agency and TVA, were the ones that struck a deal with the Farm Bureau (McConnell 1953:123–24).

This does not mean the USDA was completely at the mercy of the Farm Bureau and its allies on each and every issue. Both government officials and wealthy employers of wage labor have independent bases of power, so the power of one over the other is not an all-or-nothing matter. The question is whether the state has enough independent power to be called autonomous, or whether the owners of large income-producing private properties have enough power to be called dominant. In this particular case, we have seen numerous instances of the ways the autonomy of the Department of Agriculture in general and several of its agencies in particular was severely limited by the actions of the southern plantation owners and the Farm Bureau. Whether it is the 1935 purge in the AAA that sent the liberal lawyers packing, or the restrictions placed on the FSA, or the demise of the BAE's short-lived land use planning committees, the weight of the evidence argues against any significant degree of state autonomy.

But were the owners dominant over the state, or merely able to protect their major interests in a give-and-take fashion, which is the interest group or pluralist position most historians and social scientists would take in this dispute between state autonomy and class dominance theorists? Here the standard of proof on class dominance theorists is higher, especially in a disagreement with those who see the state as the major power rival of the ownership class. If the argument were with other society-centered theorists about the power differentials among rival private groups, then the class dominance position clearly would be supported in the case of New Deal agricultural policy in terms of three traditional power indicators: who benefits, who is overrepresented in key leadership positions, and who wins in an array of policy disputes. No one is claiming liberals, labor, consumer groups, poor farmers, or farm workers scored high on any of these power indicators when it comes to the Department of Agriculture and key agricultural issues during the New Deal.

However, if class dominance theorists point to the tremendous subsidy benefits gained from the state by well-off farmers and plantation owners as evidence of their dominant power over the state, state autonomy theorists might reply that private benefits such as wealth and income are minor issues for state officials. After all, subsidies can be seen as the state's way of paying off business and plantation owners for their cooperation with the state. Similarly, if class dominance theorists note that farm leaders and their allies held key positions in the AAA, and that members of the Farm Bureau were disproportionately represented on local land use committees, thereby invoking the second traditional power indicator, state autonomy theorists could reply that such positions are merely ways for state officials to co-opt the capitalist class. They also might argue that at least some of the people a class dominance theorist sees as members of the power elite, such as plantation owners sitting in Congress, or businessmen serving for one or two years as head of a division of the AAA, are in fact state officials who act in terms of the interests of the state when they are in office. In other words, the only admissible evidence becomes who wins on policy issues where there are distinctly different agendas.

Even here, however, there may be difficulties in agreeing on what is convincing evidence. On most issues, state autonomy theorists might argue, the goals of state officials and wealthy owners may be very similar, in which case state officials simply choose to do the things wealthy owners ask them to do. Some state autonomy theorists might claim this was the case during the New Deal in the agricultural arena. They might argue that neither top state officials nor employers cared much about poor farmers and unemployed farm workers, so the defeats of a few liberals within a large department like the USDA is not evidence that owners dominated the state.

Despite these possible objections by state autonomy theorists, which make some sense in principle, it seems clear to me that the weight of the evidence on all three types of power indicators supports a class dominance theory for the Department of Agriculture, one of the most important arms of the American state throughout the twentieth century. Take the distribution of the AAA benefits through subsidies. It is far more skewed toward the biggest and wealthiest farmers than would make sense if this were simply a matter of the state giving out enough money to cool out dissent in the hinterlands. Nor does it make sense that the state would give these farm and plantation owners so much money if the goal were to keep the state autonomous, for the strengthening of the wealthy commercial farmers meant an increase in their ability to dominate the state. If someone wanted to argue that somehow there once was an autonomous Department of Agriculture, then the account in this chapter shows how the state undercut its own autonomy in the New Deal by giving labor-employing farmers the financial and organizational means to overcome it.

Or take the large number of plantation/farm owners and their representatives in positions of state responsibility. When it is realized that the state is made highly "permeable" (a euphemism used to disguise defeat by Skocpol and Ikenberry 1982:31) by the electoral system, then the overrepresentation of commercial farming interests in the state is evidence of their power, not of their co-optation. This point also holds for appointed state officials because they have close relations with elected officials through campaign finance and other mechanisms. It would be a rare elected official from the South or California, for example, who would cross farm leaders with a government appointment they did not like.

Finally, there is the question of wins and losses on specific policy issues, the most important power indicator for my purposes here because it is the only one state autonomy theorists really acknowledge. Well, the agenda of the commercial farmers, the plantation owners, and their business allies did prevail by a wide margin over that of the top officials of the USDA, whether we look at the operation of the subsidy program or the fate of the BAE and the FSA. The state did attempt to adopt some liberal programs, but the Farm Bureau and its friends forced the state to focus its attention on subsidies for farm owners and stopped it from (1) helping farm laborers, (2) giving a boost to tenant farmers, or (3) developing its planning capabilities. If the Farm Bureau could not decentralize the entire USDA, as it wanted to do in the early 1940s, it could bring about the demise (FSA) or demotion (BAE) of two agencies supposedly backed by the expansion-minded state managers. In other words, if the Farm Bureau did not win on every issue or with a snap of its fingers, it did prevail on most issues of concern to it within a time span of five to ten years, and even Hooks agrees that large commercial farm interests have had their way with the department since World War II. Not a bad won/lost record for private owners against an allegedly autonomous state.

By any count, then, this chapter chronicles a victory for a class dominance theory over a state-centered one in an arena chosen by the state autonomy theorists. They did not dig deep enough, and they did not read very carefully in the sources they did use. They did not see the role of wealthy corporate owners in creating capacity and policies for the state through a private network of foundations and think tanks, and they overlooked the absence of sustained class conflict in explaining the success of the Agricultural Adjustment Administration.

# The Origins and Failure of the NRA

## INTRODUCTION

The National Recovery Administration (NRA), established in June 1933, was supposed to do for trade and industry what the Agricultural Adjustment Administration did for farmers, but it only lasted for twenty-three months and was relatively ineffective after its first year. Based on a two-year suspension of the antitrust laws, it brought together business owners in each sector of the economy, usually through their trade associations, to create codes of fair "competition" to set minimum prices, minimum wages, maximum hours, and levels of productive output. In theory these separate and self-policed codes—called *code authorities* at the time—would eliminate cutthroat competition, reemploy workers, and increase purchasing power, thereby restarting the economy. The NRA began with parades and speeches generating high hopes for a new era of cooperation among business, labor, and government, but when it was declared unconstitutional by the Supreme Court on May 27, 1935, many people rejoiced at its demise for a variety of different reasons.

Given its brief and disappointing career, the NRA has been consigned to the dustbin of history, credited primarily with helping business become accustomed to wages and hours provisions, eliminating child labor, and maybe helping to arrest the downward spiral of prices and wages. It would hardly be worth discussing its origin and demise except that Skocpol (1980) and Finegold and Skocpol (1995:10, 24, 37, 54) claim that its demise is evidence for their emphasis on the lack of state capacity as an explanatory factor, especially when its failure is contrasted with the success of the capacity-laden Agricultural Adjustment Administration. Moreover, Finegold and Skocpol (1995:170–71) assert that my theory cannot account for the NRA's lack of success, making a comparison of our rival views on the issue all the more important.

Once again, I think state-centric theorists are emphasizing the wrong issues. Just as the AAA succeeded because class conflict was kept under control, so the NRA failed in fair measure because it unexpectedly encouraged class conflict that could not be easily contained short of the use of force by the state, which Roosevelt and New Deal governors in the North were generally reluctant to employ. Finegold and Skocpol (1995:99, 113, 138) provide an excellent account of how the NRA created an opening for the liberal-labor coalition, helping to create a revitalized union movement that led an angry corporate community to distance itself from Roosevelt, but they nonetheless emphasize the alleged lack of state capacity as the main reason for the failure of the NRA. They hedge slightly by saying that capacity is not the only issue, and note that the NRA and AAA "incorporated" classes in different ways, but their theory does not encompass the process that they accurately describe (pp. 50, 114).

Moreover, Finegold and Skocpol leave the lack of administrative capacity as an unexplained given, whereas in my view any lack of capacity was due to the fact that business leaders did not want the state to realize its potential for autonomy. Indeed, limiting the capacity of the state is the essence of the power elite's antigovernment ideology. Thus, my class conflict perspective explains the general lack of state capacity as well as the specific failure of the NRA.

In minimizing the power of business in relation to the state, Finegold and Skocpol (1995:36, 67) also emphasize that the NRA was a last-minute program in response to the passage of liberal-labor legislation by the Senate, calling for a thirty-hour work week. However, business leaders' lack of emphasis on an overall regulatory plan was due to the fact that they had not felt as desperate for wide-ranging governmental programs as commercial farmers did. They thought that certain specific reforms, such as those enacted in banking, would be enough. Passage of the legislation by the Senate limiting the work week did catch them by surprise, as we will see, but their general plan for utilizing government if the crisis continued had been germinating for some time.

The chapter begins with the legislative origins and staffing of the NRA, then turns to Skocpol's (1980) and Finegold and Skocpol's (1995) claims about it, and concludes with my analysis of why it failed.


## THE ORIGINS OF THE NRA


There are no mysteries or esoterics when it comes to the origins of the NRA. The fingerprints of various corporate leaders and policy experts can be found on every part of it, thanks to the detective work of several different historians (e.g., Schlesinger 1958; Hawley 1966; Bellush 1975; Himmelberg 1976; Vittoz 1987). The basic idea—a cooperative relationship between trade associations and the federal government in the regulation of the economy—was an important strand of business thinking in the 1920s. It developed as a result of the seeming success of such a relationship during the limited industrial mobilization for World War I under the auspices of the

War Industries Board. It was widely discussed by businessmen through their trade associations in the next twelve years. Roosevelt, as president of the American Construction Council from 1922 to 1928, was one of those "encouraging industrial self-government as an alternative to government regulation" (Schlesinger 1957:374–75).

Two versions of this general idea gained a fair amount of visibility by 1932 in the face of the new difficulties for business created by the unexpected depth and persistence of the Great Depression. The one by Gerard Swope, the president of General Electric, called for industrial self-government with a minimum of government oversight, but with provisions for unemployment, health, and old-age insurance for workers. Labor would have a say-so in administering company-level benefit plans (e.g., Bernstein 1970:20). The second plan, offered by Henry I. Harriman, the Boston businessman, differed only in that labor had less participation, and government even less of a role. Both Swope and Harriman, as we saw in the previous chapter, were advocates of the domestic allotment plan as an ideal complement to their plans to regulate competition within industries. According to Vittoz, the two proposals shared the following key points:

> Both the Swope and Harriman proposals urged that trade associations or their equivalents in industry be given every necessary legal sanction so that they might put into effect their own independently determined controls on levels of output, certain variable costs of production (including wages), and, when it was deemed appropriate, the retail price of goods as well. They also accepted some responsibility for the sponsorship of such generally worthy goals as more stable employment and the adoption of compulsory social insurance for workers. (1987:80)

Ideas like these were on the table when one of Roosevelt's closest advisers, Columbia professor Raymond Moley, asked Senator Robert F. Wagner of New York to help formulate a recovery proposal for industry. Moley was reacting to a bill passed by the Senate that would spread work by limiting the work week to thirty hours. Neither the president nor any business group liked that idea, so the search for an alternative began. To show what Wagner's in-group looked like, and to suggest how important policy groups and think tanks were becoming, here is the line-up of discussants at his meetings:

- Harold Moulton, president, the Brookings Institution;
- Meyer Jacobstein, formerly a New York State congressman, then a prominent banker in Rochester;
- Fred I. Kent, executive, Bankers Trust Company, New York City;
- Virgil D. Jordan, president, National Industrial Conference Board;
- James H. Rand, Jr., president, Remington Rand, and also a leader in the National Association of Manufacturers;

- David L. Podell, lawyer, specialist in work for trade associations;
- Malcolm C. Rorty, the electrical engineer and statistician for AT&T who helped found the National Bureau for Economic Research;
- Senator Robert La Follette, Jr., a Progressive Republican from Wisconsin;
- Congressman Clyde Kelly, from Pennsylvania, a friend of the coal industry and coauthor of an unsuccessful coal stabilization bill that included regulatory ideas;
- W. Jeff Lauck, economist, an adviser to both Representative Kelly and John L. Lewis, president of the United Mine Workers, who also served as secretary of the National War Labor Board during World War I.

Although the Wagner group was overwhelmingly in favor of business planning, it did accept a safeguard for labor that was to play a major part in the splintering of the NRA and creating a major rift between the entire corporate community and the Roosevelt administration. This safeguard consisted of section 7(a) of its plan, which basically said that labor would have the right to bargain collectively through representatives of its own choosing.

There are slightly conflicting claims on how and why section 7(a) was part of the plan, but there is no doubt that labor leaders (Bernstein 1950:chaps. 2–3) and liberals (Schlesinger 1959:99) insisted upon it. It embodied principles that organized labor had demanded in exchange for its participation in the National War Labor Board sixteen years earlier, and in part achieved, but could not convince business to accept once the war ended (Conner 1983:chap. 11). The specific language for section 7(a) seems to have been suggested by Lauck, drawing on his experience with the National War Labor Board and the coal industry, and then agreed to by economist Moulton of Brookings when the two were delegated to write a draft (Vittoz 1987:87). There is also evidence that at least some businessmen and economists joined with the liberals and labor in advocating this provision. They believed unions could play a positive role in stabilizing such highly competitive and wage-cutting industries as coal mining and garment making, thereby giving section 7(a) a patina of business rationale (Vittoz 1987:chaps. 2–3). However, as subsequent resistance to labor involvement in the code authorities shows, most businessmen outside the garment industry allegedly willing to accept some degree of union involvement were in fact highly opposed to them.

Once completed, the Wagner draft went to Assistant Secretary of Commerce John Dickinson, a corporate lawyer from Philadelphia for the sugar manufacturer's trade association, and a professor of law at Columbia University. He and a group of industrialists, mostly from the National Association of Manufacturers and the Chamber of Commerce, had been working on a similar plan. The Wagner and Dickinson groups rather quickly reached agreement on a common draft satisfactory to the businessmen involved. In fact, they were wildly enthusiastic (Himmelberg 1976:204–5). However, the enthusiasm of the business leaders was short-lived because they learned that still another group of Roosevelt advisers was working on its own proposal; they feared it might give too much regulatory power to government and strengthen the prounion clauses (Himmelberg 1976:205; Vittoz 1987:91).

This dreaded draft was being crafted by the same Hugh Johnson encountered in the previous chapter, the former military officer who stayed in close touch with Baruch and worked with Peek on the unsuccessful McNary-Hagen agricultural recovery plan. He was in the thick of things in the White House because in 1927 he became a personal employee of Baruch, by then a major figure in the Democratic party. His main job for Baruch was to go around the country scouting out investment opportunities, but he also wrote position papers and speeches for Baruch, and continued to serve as one of his conduits to the military (Ohl 1985:chap. 5). Baruch also placed Johnson in the 1928 Democratic presidential campaign, where he worked with Peek in a vain attempt to wean farmers from their traditional Republicanism. When Roosevelt won the presidential nomination in 1932 despite attempts by Baruch and other would-be kingmakers to thwart him, Baruch made peace with Roosevelt by becoming his largest campaign contributor (five hundred thousand dollars at today's prices) and giving him Johnson as one of his speechwriters. Some historians see Johnson as a "gift" (e.g., Schlesinger 1957:413), but others believe his presence was a quid pro quo for the campaign donation, a Baruch outpost in the Roosevelt camp (e.g., Rosen 1977:311–12; Ohl 1985:83–85). It is also likely that Roosevelt wanted to neutralize Baruch because he believed Baruch had great influence through his personal loans and campaign contributions to many Democratic members of Congress, especially Roosevelt ally Jimmy Byrnes of South Carolina, Senator Pat Harrison of Mississippi, chair of the Finance Committee, and Senator Joe Robinson of Arkansas, the majority leader (e.g., Robertson 1994:101–3, 127–31). Whatever the reasons for Johnson's presence, he won over Roosevelt's wary academic advisers, including liberals like Adolph Berle and Tugwell, with his hard work, good humor, and ability to turn a phrase (Ohl 1985:85).

Roosevelt shortly decreed that members of the various drafting groups should join together to find a compromise. This final work was done by Johnson, Richberg, Wagner, Perkins, Dickinson, and one person new to the process, Lewis Douglas, director of the budget and scion of a family that owned a large copper mining corporation in Arizona. The businessmen who worked with Dickinson then went to Roosevelt and insisted they be able to comment on the draft before it went to Congress. Himmelberg (1976:206–7) reports that the business advisory committee emerging from this request was generally satisfied with the final draft. Since the drafters were drawing their ideas from basically the same policy circles, there was not too much reconciling to be done, but the Johnson version did prevail in three ways that caused major difficulties later:

(1) Detailed congressional guidelines and loan guarantees for industries rehiring workers called for in the Wagner-Dickinson version were replaced by Johnson's broad delegation of powers to the president, a decision that would be one basis for the Supreme Court ruling the act unconstitutional.

(2) Instead of limiting the codes to a handful of major industries like steel, automobiles, oil, and chemicals, Johnson included all industries engaged in interstate commerce, right down to dog food, ice cream cones, and wigs, costing the legislation the support of Moulton of Brookings and other mainstream economists, who thought such an extension was unnecessary, unmanageable, and likely to lead to too much state control over the economy (e.g., Critchlow 1985:120–21).

(3) The president was given the power to license firms for a period of up to one year in industries where there were widespread code violations, meaning in effect that misbehaving firms would not be given a license; the granting of this power, which Roosevelt used to threaten the steel and coal industries into compromises, was seized upon by businessmen to invoke the specter of a dictatorial state.

Once the bill went to Congress, new trouble arose when the AFL insisted before the House Ways and Means Committee that language from the pro-labor Norris-LaGuardia Act of 1932 be added to section 7(a) stating that labor "shall be free from the interference, restraint, or coercion of employers of labor or their agents" (Bernstein 1970:31). When the House passed the legislation as amended, employers protested vigorously in the Senate, where their amendment to soften 7(a) was defeated, 46 to 31. Although Himmelberg (1976:107) concludes that "few" business leaders felt modification of the new language in 7(a) was an "absolute condition" for their support of the whole bill, the general counsel of the National Association of Manufacturers believed business had been betrayed by Wagner, who agreed to the AFL amendment in his own testimony before the House committee. Still, the provision as passed was sufficiently vague that "the nature of the guarantees extended to labor remained enigmatic" (Schlesinger 1958:136); the section had no penalties for violations attached to it in any case. Thus, everything now depended on who administered the NRA and how the enigmatic guidelines were interpreted.

Given the direct and overwhelming business presence in the creation of this legislation, and the fact that the inclusion of 7(a) had some semblance of a business rationale, and no enforcement mechanism, most historians and social scientists are likely to accept Himmelberg's conclusion to his day-by-day study of its origins: it marked "the triumph of business revisionists"

(1976:chap. 10). The only slight dissent comes from political scientist Donald Brand (1988), who believes that progovernment ideas from the Progressive Era also were behind the act. He therefore makes much of the alleged fact that "[i]n the later stages of the legislative drafting, interest groups even found their official representatives excluded from decision making" (p. 86). Since the final drafting group included Johnson, Dickinson, and Douglas, who fit into anybody's definition of the corporate community, Brand obviously has a very narrow definition of the business world if he restricts its leadership to heads of interest groups. Moreover, the fact still remains, as Himmelberg (1976:206–7) shows, that major business leaders from the National Association of Manufacturers and Chamber of Commerce asked for and received access to the final draft. The claims by Brand notwithstanding then, the way the legislation was drafted does not augur well for state autonomy theory.

Nor did it augur well for state autonomy theory, or the success of the NRA, when Johnson was appointed its director. He immediately made an interpretation of the collective bargaining section that discouraged unionization, and in general accepted every demand made of him by his fellow businessmen, including various mechanisms for setting industrywide prices. Although he staffed the Consumer Advisory Board called for in the legislation with economists and sociologists, many of whom were liberals to boot, he generally ignored their advice. Nor did he pay any attention to suggestions from the Research and Planning Division, also staffed with social scientists. Code authorities were dominated by businessmen; less than 10 percent had even one labor representative, and most of those were in various garment trades (Hawley 1966:56–57, 61; McQuaid 1979; Emerson 1991:13). Johnson also turned out to be a disastrous administrator, interpreting every argument as a personal attack, entering into a highly public affair with his young secretary, and disappearing for days at a time on drinking binges. Many people came to think that the eventual failures of NRA could be laid at his doorstep, but nothing really changed after he was eased out in August 1934, because the businessmen would not agree to the reforms called for by union leaders and liberals.

## THE SKOCPOL ARGUMENTS

It would be stunning indeed if Skocpol could turn what I have said so far into evidence for state autonomy theory, and she does not even try. Instead, she writes, "business leaders and spokesmen" were "all-pervasive" in their presence "with respect to the early, comprehensive measures for economic recovery, the National Industrial Recovery Act of 1933-35, and under the

National Recovery Administration, businessmen in each industry drafted and enforced the regulatory codes" (Skocpol 1980:163). Moreover, she concludes that capitalists were not only involved in creating the NRA and drafting and enforcing codes, but received what they wanted besides: "Capitalists, above all those who ran the major corporations in each industry, were by all historical accounts able to get exactly what they wanted out of the NRA, that is, fixed prices and stabilized production" (p. 164).

How then, does Skocpol make the NRA into grist for the state autonomy mill? With a novel argument: class dominance theorists are wrong because the policies initiated by the business leaders were failures. This supposedly proves they were "*insufficiently* class conscious" (ibid., her italics). It therefore follows for Skocpol that class dominance theorists are all wet because "this part of the New Deal does not measure up as a class-conscious strategy for U.S. corporate capitalism" (ibid.).

Needless to say, I hope, these are not acceptable criteria for either class consciousness or power. If businessmen are organized and put forward a distinctive policy view, that is usually considered to be evidence for class consciousness. Similarly, if the preferences of a group "prevail" (Dahl 1958), that is usually considered one kind of evidence for a group's power. But Skocpol is having none of this. Businessmen may think they know their interests, and they may be successful in implementing policies they believe will forward their interests, but this is not good enough. They have to predict and control the future with great success to have consciousness and power. Skocpol has lapsed into a theory attributing far more potential power to business than class dominance theorists ever have claimed. She makes business leaders into total autocrats and the state into their abject servant. Even sociologist Axel van den Berg, who paraphrases or quotes every criticism she makes of the class dominance view, bridles at this point in Skocpol's attack, stating that "I do not think the theory necessarily implies that *all* policies promoted by corporate liberals are so farsighted as to always be successful" (1988:197, footnote 6, his italics).

But why did the NRA fail? Skocpol and Finegold (1982) present another novel argument that will not stand up. They say it failed because there were too many inexperienced businessmen in the agency and not enough seasoned government administrators. Their main piece of evidence for this claim is the contrast with the Agricultural Adjustment Administration, which they believe to have succeeded, as I explained in the previous chapter, because it had a large number of government experts and administrators in positions of importance. That is, the state had administrative capacity in the area of agriculture, but not in the area of industry:

> Governments that have, or can quickly assemble, their own knowledgeable administrative organizations are better able to carry through interventionist

policies than are governments that must rely on extra-governmental experts and organizations. For historical reasons specified below, the U.S. national state in the early 1930s had greater capacity to intervene autonomously in the economic affairs of agriculture than in industry. (Skocpol and Finegold 1982:260–61)

My reading of the literature on the failure of the NRA puts me at odds with the state autonomy position once again. The person who has studied the administrative apparatus of the NRA most closely, Brand (1988:116–24), flatly rejects the idea that the staffing and administration of the NRA led to its failure. For example, he says the enforcement division set up to help industries not yet able to provide their own enforcement was doing a very good job and that the legal division was "adequately funded and well staffed" (p. 123). He reports that professional economists were heavily recruited to the staff (pp. 123–24). In a three-paragraph footnote in his last chapter he explicitly denies Finegold and Skocpol's argument that the NRA was "administratively inefficient" (p. 311). In fact, he argues that the NRA lost the support of business leaders because "they feared the growing power of the Washington bureaucracy." This implies that the NRA might have received even less business cooperation and been even more inefficient if it were more independent administratively. Brand also questions Skocpol and Finegold's secondary argument—that the NRA would have been more successful with a professional civil-service staff—by pointing out that the Department of Agriculture, which has such a staff, is "one of the best examples of a captured government agency because it has so often placed the interests of farmers above broader national interests" (ibid.). Thus, even a theorist who argues that Roosevelt wanted to give the state a stronger role in good Progressive fashion is highly critical of Skocpol and Finegold's empirical comparison of the AAA and NRA.

## THE FAILURE OF THE NRA

So, how to explain the collapse of the NRA? Most broadly, we have to chalk up its demise to the general failure of New Deal economic policies, for none of them led to recovery from the depression (e.g., Hawley 1966:15; Bernstein 1987:185; Nossiter 1990:chap. 1). The NRA could not increase purchasing power, as it was supposed to do, because the revival of purchasing power was dependent upon massive government deficits and/or a large increase in the money supply. Skocpol (1980) may see such lack of understanding as an absence of sensible class consciousness on the part of the business leaders who created and staffed the NRA, but understanding the economy is not exactly an easy task, and the ability to understand—or apply—the needed remedies may be blocked by even greater needs, such as holding on to power and privilege.

The NRA also failed in a more mundane sociological and organizational sense: it was riven with internal strife, disliked by consumer and labor advocates, and mistrusted by most businessmen within a few short months of its initial burst of energy and enthusiasm. Why could it not at least persist for a year or two as a functioning bureaucracy? Beyond the fear of court challenges, the inadequacies of Johnson's leadership, the sheer size of the effort (over 550 code authorities, two million business enterprises), and the difficulties of enforcing price and wage agreements, two major issues generated interminable conflict: price fixing and collective bargaining.

For most businessmen, the main point of the NRA was to allow them to set prices so they would not be caught in a continuing downward price spiral that might drive many of them out of business. Furthermore, in most cases price controls could not be made to work without control of production, so that had to be regulated too. The net result was that many of the several hundred code authorities set prices at a higher level than seemed justified to liberal experts on the Consumer Advisory Board and in the Research and Planning Division. The liberals argued that prices were rising faster than wages, thereby stifling the recovery by reducing purchasing power. To make matters worse, leaders in the AAA were afraid that high industrial prices would defeat attempts to raise agricultural prices, and the Public Works Administration worried about the effects of rising prices on its construction costs (Schlesinger 1958:135).

In the context of the new minimum wage agreements, the liberals' call for lower prices raised the specter of a redistribution of business revenues from profits to wages, and thus a reduction in the wealth of stockholders, not an acceptable chain of events from an ownership point of view. In this atmosphere the liberals in the Research and Planning Division, led by a very outspoken economist whom we will meet more fully in Chapter 4, Leon Henderson, made the public recommendation in June, 1934, that the NRA should stop regulating "everything except minimum standards covering wages, hours, collective bargaining, child labor, and clearly defined unfair trade practices" (Schlesinger 1958:159). In other words, prices would be set once again in the marketplace (yes, really, the liberal stance at that juncture was back to the marketplace). This policy recommendation deeply angered most businessmen. They made it clear that they were not interested in participating in the NRA experiment if they could not set minimum prices, as they warned every time the subject of market pricing was broached (e.g., Schlesinger 1958:160; Hawley 1966:85–87, 99–101, 111). Under these circumstances the NRA leadership rejected the liberals' proposal.

Most of all, though, the NRA failed because too many businessmen resisted any concessions to organized labor, which did in fact benefit from its existence, as Bernstein (1970:chap. 2) and Brand (1988:chaps. 9–10) rightly argue and demonstrate. True enough, as all the evidence I have presented thus far indicates, Johnson was promanagement in his decisions, the codes were made and administered by businessmen, and the recommendations of liberals inside and outside the agency were ignored. Moreover, hundreds of corporations short-circuited the possibility of unions by setting up localized, single-company "employee representation" plans. Known by their critics as company unions, they enrolled more members than traditional trade unions during the period of the NRA's brief existence. In fact, unions had more defeats than victories during the early New Deal despite a high level of militancy (Schlesinger 1958:chap. 23).

However, the short-term victories for the corporate community over labor within the NRA are not the end of the matter, for the inclusion of section 7(a) in the enabling legislation helped to inspire a huge organizing drive in the summer of 1933. The turmoil led employers on the Industrial Advisory Board of the NRA to join with their counterparts on the Labor Advisory Board to create a National Labor Board in order to mediate labor disputes (Bernstein 1970:37; Piven and Cloward 1977:110; McQuaid 1979, 1982; Domhoff 1990:81–91). This board, although mostly ignored or circumvented by Johnson, became the precedent for legislation in 1935 that was anathema for most employers, the National Labor Relations Act (Gross 1974; Irons 1982). It created a National Labor Relations Board to oversee the rights set forth in Section 7(a) and seek remedies in courts of law for employer violations. Changes in the board's composition in 1939 and in the law in 1947 made the act less helpful to organized labor than it was two or three years after its passage (Gross 1981), but the fact remains that, by one of the criteria I use to assess power, the industrial capitalists of the North had suffered a major setback (Domhoff 1990:chap. 4).

On this issue Skocpol and I have one of our strongest and most enduring agreements: corporate leaders resisted the National Labor Relations Act because it gave the state the potential to help unions organize the entire labor force (Skocpol 1980:181; Domhoff 1990:88–89). Here we see very directly why businessmen fear the state despite all it does for them: it threatens their power on the issue of greatest concern to them as power actors, the control of labor markets. As I said in the first chapter, I believe this problem is the nub of the power equation in a democratic capitalist society. It is the main reason why business leaders will not risk for a minute the development of the autonomous state that Skocpol and her associates believe to exist. From my theoretical perspective, and with historical hindsight about what followed from section 7(a), it is not surprising that the NRA would be torn apart in 1933 and 1934 by conflict over government support for unionization and collective bargaining.

The conflicts within the NRA over price/production controls and collective bargaining reveal the irrelevance of Skocpol and Finegold's (1982:260–61) comparison of that agency with the Agricultural Adjustment Administration in terms of administrative capacity. The AAA succeeded because its main constituency, large-scale farmers, often employers of Mexican and African-American migrant labor, were united behind it, whereas its main critics, the liberal-labor coalition, were unable to have very much influence within it after the liberals were purged in 1935 for challenging labor relations in the South. Further, the AFL had little or no interest in helping farm labor. It had in effect made the following deal with farmers concerning farm labor:

> Most of our social legislation, in fact, has been enacted as the result of a political "deal" between organized labor and the farm groups. The basis of this deal has always been: we, the farm representatives, will not object to this legislation, if you, the representatives of organized labor, will agree to exempt agricultural employees. (McWilliams 1942:356)

It was this deal that allowed southern and California Democrats to support the National Labor Relations Act of 1935, despite the opposition of virtually every business executive in the country. The northern industrialists lost, but only because they were deserted on a labor issue by their usual allies, the plantation owners of the South, that is, class solidarity broke down. A rare division in the power elite at a time when liberals and labor were united allowed the liberal-labor coalition to win an important victory. Finegold and Skocpol (1995:171) claim that the National Labor Relations Act is the "hardest case" for my former views, and they are right, but I think I have now presented a far more convincing explanation than they realize because they underestimate the power of the southern segment of the ruling class in the Roosevelt coalition and Congress (Domhoff 1990:chapt. 4). Put another way, the liberal-labor coalition could make a bargain with Roosevelt and his allies in the executive branch because southern plantation owners acquiesced in the legislation once their own work force was excluded from its protection.

In sharp contrast to the relatively smooth functioning of the AAA, the price and production controls of the NRA increased intraclass conflict between large and small businesses, and both the price controls and labor provisions heightened interclass conflict. Given the potential for liberal-labor influence within the NRA, corporate leaders insisted there would have to be even less government interference in NRA code authorities in the future. In contrast, the cotton and tobacco growers were so pleased with the AAA that they asked for government enforcement of its provisions for their crops, leading in 1934 to the Bankhead Cotton Control Act and the Kerr-Smith Tobacco Control Act. When the Supreme Court struck down the act establishing the AAA because of the tax on processors, Congress quickly passed a new law rationalizing payments to farmers for not growing crops as in the interest of soil conservation (Hawley 1966:192–193). By way of contrast, no serious attempt was made to revive the NRA when the court found it unconstitutional.

The AAA ended up an agency that primarily gave money to several million farmers growing a few major commercial crops in exchange for acreage limitations. The large-scale farmers were joined together in essentially one organization, the Farm Bureau. They supported the AAA because it gave them cash for consumer spending and for investment in new equipment while at the same time raising their prices. Although they were forced to cut acreage to share in this bounty, they could intensify production or their remaining land and then obtain even more government money via a commodity-based "loan" from the government's Commodity Credit Corporation. I put *loan* in quotes because a loan turned into a government purchase of surplus production at a set price when the market price was not as high as the government's loan price. All of this adds up to an incredible bonanza for farmers and plantation owners (or the insurance companies that came to own the land when farmers defaulted on mortgages).

This AAA largesse is a far cry from the task facing the NRA, which did not give money to anybody, but instead tried to fix prices, control production, set minimum wages, and enforce work regulations in two million firms in hundreds of different business sectors, in a context where the incentives for individual businesses to cheat on price and wage agreements were enormous. Moreover, consumer groups were angry over the fixing of prices at a high level, labor leaders were upset by the failure to enforce 7(a), and the businessmen who dominated the code authorities became wary of the potential power of the state to shape labor markets. In short, administrative capacity pales in importance as an explanatory factor in the demise of the NRA when we look at the very different ways the constituencies of the AAA and NRA used and viewed the two agencies. The AAA subdued class conflict while giving away money. The NRA generated class conflict. To the degree that the NRA lacked administrative capacity, it was because the power elite opposes the growth of the state on the basis of its antigovernment ideology.

## CONCLUSION

The NRA failed primarily because the policies set by the businessmen who dominated it unexpectedly generated too much conflict with the liberal-labor coalition over price fixing and collective bargaining. Within the context of what seemed to be a gradually improving economy, most business leaders soon decided the NRA was more trouble than it was worth. They showed their power not only in molding the agency to their expectations on the basis of their World War I experiences and subsequent discussions in their trade associations, but in hamstringing the agency once these expectations proved to be flawed. However, the liberal-labor coalition also showed power in relation to the NRA. It was able to keep section 7(a) in the enabling legislation and use the hope and legitimation generated by the NRA to bring about the creation of the National Labor Relations Board, despite the vigorous opposition of the corporate-conservative coalition.

In terms of my argument with state autonomy theory, the NRA failed because the state was not autonomous enough to control class conflict. Johnson and his colleagues could not convince the corporate-conservative and liberal-labor coalitions to enter into compromises over their differences. Nor was Roosevelt prepared to risk the alienation of business or labor by dictating the terms of agreement, as the leader of an autonomous state surely would have done under the dire circumstances created by nearly four years of increasing economic despair.

Why, then, was Roosevelt unwilling to assert the power of the state as head of its executive branch? It might be in part because of his upper-class background, or the opposition of financial backers such as Baruch and political allies such as the southern Democrats, who might defeat him in the next election. Unfortunately, those arguments do not count for much in a debate with state autonomy theorists. However, if we grant the assumption that Roosevelt did envision an American state with at least the power to create a regulated capitalism, then the deeper answer to his hesitancy to use his executive powers seems to lie in a combination of (1) his ideological convictions and (2) the ideology and composition of the Supreme Court in the early 1930s.

First, Roosevelt was limited in his actions as a state manager by the fact that he did not believe in large-scale government spending. That is, he had a business ideology, not a statist one. It can be argued that the big public works program advocated by many liberal Democrats would have made it much easier to gain business support for NRA, but Roosevelt personally limited such spending to a meager $1.5 billion per year and gave authority over it to his cautious secretary of interior, Harold Ickes, who moved very slowly. Furthermore, Roosevelt believed even less in deficit spending by government. As late as 1937, when the economy was barely recovering, he insisted on balancing the budget for 1938, creating a sudden new depression within the Great Depression. He then proceeded to blame it on businessmen who allegedly refused to make investments because they opposed his administration. Only after seven harsh months, with unemployment growing rapidly, did Roosevelt finally decide to follow the policies advocated by his Keynesian advisers (e.g., Nossiter, 1990:16–26; Davis 1993:chap. 6). How, we might ask, is a president to build an independent state if he is a believer in the prevailing capitalist ideology, i.e., if he is antispending and insistent on a balanced budget?

Second, Roosevelt was limited in his actions by his understanding of what the Supreme Court was likely to do if the executive branch tried to regulate the economy. Since Roosevelt and his advisers feared that the court would rule wages and hours legislation unconstitutional, the only way to obtain the minimum wages and maximum hours he and Secretary of Labor Frances Perkins eagerly sought was through agreements freely negotiated by businessmen in each industry. Unfortunately, the only way to induce those agreements was to give business something it wanted even more, the ability to set minimum prices and restrict output without fear of antitrust prosecution (e.g., Schlesinger 1958:101). Once it became likely that the NRA would fail, Roosevelt started to look for a way to deal with the court. In August 1934, he confided in a note to one of his key advisors, Harvard law professor Felix Frankfurter, that he only wished to salvage "(1) minimum wage, (2) maximum hours, (3) collective bargaining and (4) child labor" provisions; Frankfurter then passed this information to Supreme Court Justice Louis Brandeis in a handwritten note (Davis 1986:517).

As I mentioned earlier in the chapter, the legislation also seemed highly vulnerable to constitutional challenge because Congress gave the president such a large and unspecified delegation of its power over the economy; this was another reason why Roosevelt felt constrained by a court whose great majority (liberal and conservative) consisted of former corporation lawyers committed to laissez-faire principles, not exactly a statist ideology. We thus have the irony that one of the three branches of the allegedly autonomous American state, a branch consisting of nine lawyers appointed for life, did not believe the national state should be allowed to interfere in the business of business. Such a doctrine is not conducive to the autonomy of the executive branch when it is trying to cope with a huge depression while at the same time placating a massive corporate establishment. As Harvey Feigenbaum (1985:172ff.) argued in a telling critique of state autonomy theory, there has to be a unitary state—one not divided within itself—before it makes sense even to begin talking about an autonomous state.

So, granting Roosevelt the best of statist intentions, we can say the NRA failed because the American state is divided and permeable. Never mind the fact that the NRA's policies would not have worked in the long run because a radical measure such as deficit spending was necessary to restart the economy, as the balanced-budget depression of 1937–1938 and the quick recovery during World War II were to show: the NRA could not even last long enough to demonstrate its irrelevance. Conflict between the corporate-conservative and liberal-labor coalitions inside and outside the state, not lack of administrative capacity, was the major undoing of the NRA, powerless to act independently within a divided state dominated by industrialists, financiers, planters, and successful commercial farmers who employed wage labor.

# How the Rockefeller Network Shaped Social Security 5

## INTRODUCTION

The origins and contours of modern welfare states have been just about the sole focus of state autonomy theorists, with a special emphasis on the Social Security Act of 1935 when it comes to the United States. As so often, Skocpol and one of her students (1980; Skocpol and Ikenberry 1983) laid the early groundwork for what a state-centered explanation should look like by giving precedence to politicians, middle-class reformers, and earlier legislative successes at the state level, but in recent years the banner has been carried by another of her students, Ann Orloff, who makes most of the same points while comparing the American case to what happened in Canada and Great Britain (Orloff and Skocpol 1984; Orloff and Parker 1990; Orloff 1993).

Perhaps recognizing that her analysis cannot sustain a case for a "state-centric" theory in the United States, Orloff says she is merely emphasizing the "institutional context" for policymaking, which means "the ensemble of political and state organizations in each country" (1993:86). She joins with those she calls the "new institutionalists" in claiming that political institutions have an autonomous role, but at bottom all this means is that "the logics of state-building and the international states system are not reducible to an economic or class logic" (Orloff 1993:85).

Generalities aside, Orloff confidently asserts the weakness of business during the 1930s: "Despite business (and Republican) opposition, the act passed overwhelmingly, showing the weakness of U.S. business as an interest group at this juncture of American history" (p. 297). She further concludes that "the activities of party officials, elected leaders, state bureaucrats, social scientists, charity workers, and social reformers," the heroes and heroines of her story, "were largely separate from those of businessmen" (p. 76). Just for good measure, she adds that the failure to use a comparative approach by those who think businessmen powerful in the shaping of the Social Security Act shows they have an "ethnocentric bias" (p. 62). This amazing accusation will come as stunning news to all those who have tended to focus on historical studies in the ongoing discussions of the relative merits of comparative and historical approaches to social questions.

117

I do not think Orloff could be more wrong in any of her empirical assertions in the previous paragraphs, as this chapter will attempt to demonstrate.
Corporate leaders set the terms of the debate, they were directly involved
with the elected officials and social scientists, and it is not ethnocentric to
believe history can tell us more about business power than comparative
studies on the issue, or that owners and managers of income-producing
property are more powerful in the United States than in Canada or Great
Britain, for that matter. By switching the question from who holds major
social power in America to questions on how and why the attitudes and
roles of business leaders differ on social welfare policies from country to
country, Orloff and other state autonomy theorists can argue for their rein-
terpretations of secondary sources as a methodological advance, but the
important point is that they have changed the question. Having changed the
question, they then assail class dominance theorists for not having the right
answer.

My earlier views on the origins of the Social Security Act are a twice-told
story (1970:207–18; 1990:chap. 3), so I will not repeat those analyses here.
I only need say I claimed in my first effort that corporate moderates had
significant involvement in the process through an organization called the
American Association for Labor Legislation (hereafter AALL) and the Business Advisory Council (hereafter BAC), and that Gerard Swope, a member of
both forenamed organizations, familiar to readers from previous chapters,
was influential in reinforcing Roosevelt's business-oriented views on how
old-age pensions and unemployment compensation should be funded. I
also said that ultraconservative businessmen, epitomized by the National
Association of Manufacturers, and southern plantation owners made the
legislation even more conservative, leading to my conclusion: the act was
shaped by rival segments of the ruling class within the context of the pressures of major social disruption. That is, there was both intraclass and
interclass conflict.

In my effort of 1990, I provided greater detail on the funding of the AALL
by some wealthy corporate owners as well as on the personal wealth of
several of its expert members, thus placing them in the upper-class circles
from which they originated. I added that two of the main experts involved in
writing this cautious, regressively financed legislation were employees of an
industrial relations consulting group created by John D. Rockefeller, Jr. In
addition, I invoked new research by Jill Quadagno (1988) on the importance
of southern plantation owners and smaller northern manufacturers in limiting the scope of this legislation.

Skocpol (1986/1987; Skocpol and Amenta 1985) and Orloff and Parker
(1990) rejected my kind of claims out of hand. Their paragraphs are often
dismissive in tone and laced with disdain, as if the thought of capitalist
power were ridiculous on its face even though the wealth and income

distributions are highly skewed, politicians have to go around begging corporate leaders for campaign finance support, and a large number of cabinet positions in both Democratic and Republican administrations are filled by businessmen and -women. They claim that the AALL was an organization of middle-class reformers, independent of even the moderate business leaders providing the funding. As for the members of the BAC involved in the Social Security Act, they are said to be mostly liberal mavericks, not representative of their kind. Some of them supposedly quit the BAC to protest social security legislation, and those who remained were not influential anyhow. As for the experts from the Rockefeller industrial relations outfit, only one of them is commented upon by Orloff and Parker, who call him a "noted Canadian social scientist," and the organization is said to have become "self-supporting" by the "early 30s" (1990:306). Besides, the Canadian expert's advice was rejected in favor of advice by reformers and experts from Wisconsin, presumably not affiliated with any institutions of the power elite. Moreover, the politicians and reformers in control of this legislation were functioning on the basis of precedents and laws in the public sector, not on the basis of any business initiatives prior to the New Deal.

Rather than rehash the usual sources in response to the claims of the state autonomy theorists, I am going to bring forth new information obtained in several different archives. Furthermore, I am going to use this information to claim that the richest and most powerful corporate empire of the early twentieth century, what I will call the Rockefeller network, played a major role in shaping old-age pensions and unemployment insurance, the two most important titles of the Social Security Act. This is in many ways a risky assertion because it may call to mind exaggerated claims made in the past about Rockefeller power. It is one I would have rejected out of hand myself until I made use of the treasure trove of detailed documents now available on Rockefeller influence in the 1920s and 1930s at the Rockefeller Archive Center.

In order to build my case, I have to take three steps. First, I need to establish that several very large companies were controlled by John D. Rockefeller, Jr., and his many lawyers and advisers even though no hereditary member of the Rockefeller family was any longer an officer or director in any of them. Second, I will show that there existed by the time of the New Deal a network of foundations, think tanks, and industrial relations groups connected to Rockefeller and his companies through funding, trusteeships, and direct involvement in personnel appointments.

Once it is clear that the Rockefeller economic empire sustained a large network of policy-shaping organizations, my third task will be to show how the overall Rockefeller network was involved in shaping the Social Security Act, particularly in the case of old-age pensions, a topic to which Orloff (1993) devotes an entire book without coming close to any of the people or organizations in the Rockefeller network. We will see how Rockefeller employees at Industrial Relations Counselors, Inc., building in part on plans they developed at the Social Science Research Council, created a design for social security before Roosevelt appointed his famous Committee for Economic Security in June 1934, and that most of the businessmen involved in Roosevelt's effort were part of the Rockefeller network as well. These businessmen worked closely with several of the people Orloff sees as independent middle-class reformers and experts. We will see the SSRC as the main contact point between the Rockefeller network and the government on social security, but the Rockefeller Foundation was standing closely behind it, with an occasional assist by the Spelman Fund, all under the watchful eyes of close Rockefeller advisers like Raymond B. Fosdick, Arthur Woods, Clarence J. Hicks, Beardsley Ruml, and Walter Teagle.

Before I begin my story, however, I want to stress that the Rockefeller network behaved in exactly the opposite fashion on the other piece of precedent-setting social legislation of 1935, the National Labor Relations Act. As I said in the previous chapter, that act truly was opposed by almost all businessmen, including every member of the Rockefeller network. For example, a Rockefeller industrial relations employee coordinated the huge battle the corporate community mounted against its passage, a battle making the opposition to the Social Security Act look like the grousing and grumbling it actually was. This contrast in approaches to the Social Security and National Labor Relations legislation once again brings into stark theoretical relief just how important class conflict is in capitalistic America, and to what length corporate leaders will go to control workers. They will fight unions to the last breath, but pensions and other welfare policies are accepted when they do not jeopardize control of labor markets. In fact, they are often thought to be of use in improving labor markets and controlling labor militancy. It is no secret that the rise of welfare capitalism at the turn of the twentieth century came as a response to the seeming threat from the growth of unionism and the Socialist party (e.g., Weinstein 1968; Brandes 1976).

## THE ROCKEFELLER ECONOMIC EMPIRE

Orloff and Skocpol repeatedly say that only maverick, marginal capitalists supported Social Security. It is therefore necessary to establish the economic standing of the Rockefeller economic empire. The argument begins with the fact the Rockefeller family was the richest of its day, even more so if the nieces and nephews of John D. Rockefeller, Sr., are included. In the early 1920s the twenty-one Rockefellers paying taxes at the time were worth an estimated $2.5 billion, 2.5 times as much as the Fords, Mellons, or DuPonts, whose estimated fortunes were $1 billion each (Lundberg 1937: 26–27). The Rockefeller fortune was based primarily in five of the oil companies created in 1911 out of the original Standard Oil, broken up by antitrust action. The Rockefellers held the largest blocks of stock in these companies and had great influence on their management.

In addition to the Rockefellers, several other families were worth hundreds of millions due to their partnerships with the original Rockefeller in these ventures, and they tended to be close to the Rockefellers economically, socially, and politically in the time period we are discussing. They include the Harknesses and Whitneys, both among the richest ten families of the era, along with the Archbolds, Bedfords, Benjamins, Cutlers, Flaglers, Pratts, and Rogers, who taken together were in the top ten as well.

Given the size of these fortunes, it should come as no surprise that the Standard Oil companies controlled by Rockefeller were among the largest in the country. Their rankings by assets in 1933 are as follows (Burch 1981b:14):

| Company | Rank |
| --- | --- |
| Standard Oil of New Jersey | 2 |
| Standard Oil of New York | 4 |
| Standard Oil of Indiana | 6 |
| Standard Oil of California | 11 |
| Ohio Oil Company | Not in top 20 |

Despite the huge amount of wealth the Rockefellers retained in these companies, they had in fact diversified their holdings. Most importantly, they controlled the largest bank in the country, Chase Manhattan, chaired by Rockefeller's brother-in-law, Winthrop Aldrich. They also controlled several smaller companies, the most direct evidence for which for my purposes is that one of Rockefeller's main lawyers, Raymond Fosdick (1956:182–83), reported he sat on the boards of directors of three of them for his boss: Consolidation Coal Company, Davis Coal and Coke, and the Western Maryland Railroad. There was also one small Rockefeller company on whose board Fosdick did not sit: Colorado Fuel and Iron. It will have a large impact for such a small company, as will be seen shortly.

The Rockefellers also had diversified into real estate. Rockefeller Center, the largest development of its kind at the time, opened in New York City in the early 1930s. By the 1970s it was at the center of the stagnant Rockefeller fortune. All involvement in the oil companies (the first three now called Exxon, Mobile, and Chevron) is long in the past. With the retirement of David Rockefeller from Chase Manhattan Bank in the 1980s, after many years as either president or chairman, there is no longer a controlling Rockefeller presence in that entity either. Thus, these huge corporations have become a general basis for the corporate rich, but in the 1920s and 1930s they were the heart of a Rockefeller economic empire controlled very directly by John D. Rockefeller, Jr., his relatives, family friends, and personal lawyers.

The facts I have recited here were once very well-known. They establish the Rockefeller network as far from marginal—it was central. The main address of the Rockefeller empire, 26 Broadway, was the most famous address in the world. Some Rockefeller advisers simply listed "26 Broadway, New York, New York" on their letterhead, with no company name. Everyone who was anyone knew what this address meant.

## THE ROCKEFELLER NETWORK

The Rockefeller network I am going to outline in this section is built around the economic core described in the previous section. The economic core dominates the rest of the network through funding and direct involvement on the board of directors of the other organizations.

The most important and tightly controlled organizations in the Rockefeller network were the three major foundations created by the family: the Rockefeller Foundation, the General Education Board, and the Laura Spelman Rockefeller Memorial.[1] As demonstrated in Chapter 2, the weight of these foundations in the world of philanthropy was very great, and Chapter 3 showed the role of the General Education Board and the Memorial on agricultural policy. Rockefeller did not take a direct role in all of the foundations, although he chaired the Rockefeller Foundation. However, as noted briefly in Chapter 2, he had an executive committee of his main employees from each of them who met with him to determine whether he should give his own money directly to a project or if the project should be assigned to a foundation.

Rockefeller and his foundations supported a wide array of policy-planning organizations within the larger context of financial donations for medical research, education, and museums. The largest and most extensive involvement in policy-planning came at the urban level, where donations to bureaus of municipal research early in the century gradually created an array of organizations encompassing every aspect of city government and public administration (Domhoff 1978:163–67). Most of this work was accomplished by Ruml as director of first the Memorial and then the Spelman Fund. In conjunction with political scientist Charles Merriam of the University of Chicago (itself a Rockefeller creation), Ruml encouraged a coordinating organization for the urban network, the Public Administration Clearing

House (PACH). Founded in 1930, PACH's organizers were Richard S. Childs, president of the National Municipal League; Luther Gulick, head of the Institute of Public Administration in New York, also Rockefeller funded to a large extent, and Louis Brownlow, a former city manager who worked closely with Ruml and Merriam. Brownlow served as its director until 1945 (Brownlow 1958:chap. 22–24; Karl 1974).

With the founding of PACH, virtually every municipal organization in the country moved its headquarters to 1313 East 60th Street in Chicago, where PACH was located, and then developed in importance with the help of Rockefeller philanthropies. Several of these organizations assisted with relief administration in the New Deal. Brownlow, Gulick, and Merriam served as Roosevelt's Committee on Administrative Management; it led to the strengthening of the White House in 1939 that Hooks (1991:47–48) sees as a lesson in state building (Karl 1963; Fisher 1993:142–44).

Two of the major think tanks of the 1920s and 1930s discussed in the first chapter, the Brookings Institution and National Bureau of Economic Research (NBER), were part of the Rockefeller network even though they were in other networks as well. As shown in Chapter 2, Rockefeller employees and monies helped in the founding of the Institute of Government Research, one of the organizations absorbed by the new Brookings Institution in 1927, and Rockefeller philanthropies gave the institute grants for specific projects in the 1920s (Saunders 1966:14–16, 25, 49). The Memorial alone gave Brookings $2,771,000 between 1924 and 1931 (Bulmer and Bulmer 1981:387). Rockefeller employees Jerome Green and Raymond Fosdick sat on its board of directors as well. Despite these large donations, the Rockefeller philanthropies had a complex relationship with Brookings because Moulton became increasingly skeptical of the New Deal after 1934. Even so, sixty-five former staff members or graduate students were serving in government by 1938 (Saunders 1966:60). Moreover, the Rockefeller Foundation remained involved with Brookings on agricultural policy, as shown in Chapter 2, and financed its oversight studies of the NRA and AAA (p. 54). It also funded Brookings's work on foreign policy in the 1940s (p. 71).[2]

As recounted in Chapter 2, the Rockefeller network had little or nothing to do with the founding of the NBER, but from 1923 to 1928 the Memorial gave it 14 to 26 percent of its income, and in 1932 and 1933 Rockefeller philanthropies gave it over 60 percent of its income (Bulmer and Bulmer 1981:393). The Rockefeller Foundation and the Memorial were the NBER's largest single contributors in its first thirty years (Fosdick 1952:213; cf. Alchon 1985:117, 157, 165, 217–32).

For all the prominence and visibility of Brookings and NBER, by far the major think tank for Rockefeller involvement in the Social Security Act turned out to be what seemed at first little more than a funding and coordinating organization for social science research, the Social Science Research Council. Created in 1923 by Ruml and his friend Charles Merriam, well over 90 percent of its funding in its first ten years came from Rockefeller philanthropies, as shown in Table 3.1 in Chapter 3, and that pattern of support continued into the 1940s. Nominally governed by a thirty-two-person board whose members were provided by the professional associations for each social science, the organization was run in practice from 1925 on by a six-member Policy Planning Committee and the president. The Policy Planning Committee determined new programs and negotiated with foundations for money. It was a self-perpetuating body whose members often were selected by Rockefeller advisers from within other organizations founded or funded by the Rockefeller network (Fisher 1993:49–50, 194, 211). Among the original six members of the Policy Planning Committee were Edwin Gay, one of the founders of the NBER, and Moulton, representing the institutes that became the Brookings Institution in 1927.

The first Policy Planning Committee created a series of advisory committees on topics ranging from the encouragement of quantitative methods in the social sciences to the creation of the *Social Sciences Abstracts* to the study of culture and personality; the SSRC provided many millions of dollars for fellowships and research projects in these areas. Fisher (1993:111) calls the years between 1925 and 1930 a "gilded age" for the social sciences because of the enormous amount of funding they received from the Memorial, either directly or through the SSRC. However, the advisory committees relating to social problems are of the greatest interest for my purposes, and they were the only SSRC committees continued into the mid-1930s.

One of these problem-oriented committees was the Advisory Committee on Social and Economic Research in Agriculture, shown in Chapter 2 to be the think tank for the early version of the domestic allotment plan. Another was the Advisory Committee on Industrial Relations, the critical one for this chapter, especially through its various subcommittees. Its first activities in the late 1920s were two surveys, one on the extent of industrial relations research in universities, the other on the problems between employers and employees most in need of investigation, i.e., research on dealing with class conflict.

In the early 1930s the SSRC decreased its number of advisory committees and put more emphasis on the immediate social problems created by the depression. One of the two domestically oriented committees to survive, the Advisory Committee on Industrial Relations changed its name to the Advisory Committee on Industry and Trade. The other was the Committee on Public Administration, where Gulick of the Institute of Public Administration became chair. SSRC's focus became even more narrow in 1935 when it limited itself to work on public administration and social security, eliminating its international relations committee. The Rockefeller Foundation gave the SSRC's Advisory Committee on Public Administration $386,000 between 1935 and 1940, with most of the money going for studies of the new Social Security Board during the first two years (Fisher 1993:139). These studies were done in conjunction with a new Committee on Social Security, coordinated by the Advisory Committee on Industry and Trade, which received a three-year grant for $225,000 from the Rockefeller Foundation in 1935. The goal was to help coordinate the new social security system.

Fisher (1993:150–54) demonstrates that these two SSRC committees were immensely helpful to the new Social Security Board from 1936 on in establishing administrative procedures, providing personnel, and doing research studies. Although the following sections of this chapter will show that the Rockefeller network had a large role in creating the legislation, Fisher's work shows its impact was even greater once the Social Security Board was in existence. When this supportive role for social security is contrasted with the reaction to the enactment of the National Labor Relations Act, where no programs in collective bargaining or union management were offered, it can be seen just how different the two pieces of legislation were in the eyes of moderate conservatives in the power elite.

Two or three more pieces of the Rockefeller network need to be added in order to complete the picture, especially Industrial Relations Counselors, Inc., but that is best done within the context of the case study itself. For now, it is enough to have shown that the Rockefeller network loomed as large in policy-planning circles as the Rockefeller corporations did in the economy.[3]

It is time for a brief look at the origins of the social insurance movement in the Progressive Era as a context for the involvement of the Rockefeller network in the issue in the New Deal.

## BACKGROUND TO SOCIAL INSURANCE

It is generally agreed that the original movement for social insurance in the Progressive Era was spearheaded by the AALL, the little organization mentioned in my introductory comments to this chapter (e.g., Lubove 1968:29; Domhoff 1970:170–78; Skocpol 1992:176ff.; Orloff 1993:38). Created as a small research and legislative drafting group in 1905, and expanded to do advocacy work in 1910, its record of successes and failures will be analyzed in Chapter 7. In terms of the Social Security Act, its first contribution was the public education it provided through its two decades of legislative campaigning, and its training of many of the experts and business leaders involved as individuals in the drafting of the act.

The AALL is also important because it was the main embodiment of the *Wisconsin approach,* the focal point of a major controversy among the experts and reformers who drafted the provisions for unemployment compensation in the Social Security Act. The AALL/Wisconsin approach was in fair measure the product of one of the most famous economists of the early twentieth century, John R. Commons, a practical reformer who taught at the University of Wisconsin from 1904 to the 1930s after several years of work with reformist business leaders and corporate lawyers at the turn of the century (see Domhoff 1990:48–50, for details).

Based on his experience working with businessmen, and convinced that the secret to reform was appealing to the profit motive, Commons liked to build his reform measures on business principles. In terms of unemployment insurance, this meant any new plan should provide incentives (lower premiums) to those businesses who organized their production so they did not have to lay off their workers from time to time. Insurance funds therefore should be kept in individual accounts rather than pooled by the state or federal government. In addition, since employers are responsible for unemployment, it followed that workers should not have to contribute to the unemployment insurance fund. The Commons approach was a very individualistic, nonsystemic one, suggesting that unemployment was not a function of general economic forces like a decline in aggregate demand.

The AALL/Wisconsin group tended to be oriented toward state-level reforms rather than national ones. Part of this orientation grew out of the successes of Progressives early in the century at the state level in Wisconsin and a few other states, but it was reinforced by the AALL's many failures at the federal level over the years. Then too, the AALL/Wisconsin group was fearful of constitutional challenges to federal legislation due to bitter experience with past labor legislation, including state minimum wage laws for women, struck down by the Supreme Court in 1923.

As for political clout, the AALL/Wisconsin group had the backing of such Progressive Republicans as Phillip LaFollette, governor of Wisconsin, and Robert LaFollette, Jr., a senator from Wisconsin in the early 1930s. Furthermore, as we will see, several of the experts involved in drafting the Social Security Act were AALL members who studied with Commons at Wisconsin and then gained experience in government working for the state of Wisconsin. Most importantly, the AALL/Wisconsin group was directly connected to a very powerful behind-the-scenes player in Washington in the 1920s and 1930s: Supreme Court Justice Louis Brandeis.

Born into wealth in 1856 and a graduate of Harvard Law School, Brandeis worked as a conventional upper-class corporate lawyer from 1879 until the late 1890s, when he became a critic of the "curse of bigness" and legal counsel for the liberal National Consumers' League, where his sisters-in-law, Josephine and Pauline Goldmark, were top leaders (e.g., Baltzell 1964:188–92; Gordon 1994:83–84). He also joined the AALL's Advisory Council, and in 1911 wrote draft legislation for unemployment insurance containing the incentive feature meant to induce employers to minimize unemployment. By then known as a Progressive Democrat, he was appointed to the Supreme Court in 1916 despite opposition by many bankers and industrialists, who combined negative comments about his policy orientation with an anti-Semitic whispering campaign (Baltzell 1964:192–96).

Brandeis conveyed his policy ideas in the 1930s through a number of different people, the most important of which for social insurance was his daughter, Elizabeth Brandeis, who became a professor of economics at Wisconsin in the late 1920s after studying with Commons. He also talked with her husband, Paul Raushenbush, also an economist at Wisconsin, then in charge of administering the state's new unemployment insurance law, complete with the incentive system, passed in 1932. Both Elizabeth Brandeis and Paul Raushenbush were members of the AALL. Brandeis also had an extensive network of legal and political contacts by then, especially among lawyers who had clerked for him or Justice Oliver Wendell Holmes (e.g., Carter 1934:315–16). His most important contact was Felix Frankfurter, a professor at Harvard Law School and a confidant of Roosevelt's since working with him during World War I, famous for sending his students to both corporate law firms and the New Deal (e.g., Irons 1982). One of those students, Thomas Corcoran, who clerked with Holmes, worked very closely with Roosevelt, and served as a direct communication link between Brandeis and Roosevelt. In short, the AALL was not merely a group of academic experts off somewhere in the hinterlands of Wisconsin by the time of the New Deal, but an appendage to the Brandeis/Frankfurter network rooted in the stature and resources of the Supreme Court and Harvard Law School.

Over and beyond the AALL efforts so closely linked to Wisconsin and Brandeis, there existed precedents for pensions in the federal civil service, the teaching profession, and some large corporations. As William Graebner argues in his history of retirement, these precedents are important because they gave Americans of the 1930s over fifty years of experience "in which retirement of older persons had been consciously employed to encourage mobility, efficiency, and social control" (1980, 1982). Moreover, these precedents were based on business models. For example, the pension program for federal civil service employees enacted in 1920 was influenced by the Institute of Government Relations, one of the forerunners of the Brookings Institution (Saunders 1966:25; Graebner 1980:77, 87).

Graebner's emphasis on retirement as a labor strategy is of great relevance to the issues addressed in this chapter because it leads to the possibility that the Social Security Act was not the work of antimonopoly decentralizers in the AALL/Wisconsin/Brandeis tradition, but of corporate-oriented industrial relations specialists concerned with the twin goals of shaping labor markets and reducing labor militancy. This alternative hypothesis is most clearly and briefly stated by Wilbur Cohen, who became the right-hand man to the executive director of the government's social security study shortly after his graduation from the University of Wisconsin and then worked for the Social Security Board for many years before culminating his government career as secretary of Health, Education, and Welfare under President Lyndon Johnson. Here is Cohen's analysis:

> The roots of the social insurance movement came out of the work and consideration of the people in the field of labor legislation. Social insurance was to them a form of remedial legislation to deal with the problems of labor unrest in industrial society which grew out of labor-management problems. (Graebner 1982:25)

Cohen's blunt claim, so sharply at odds with all the uplifting talk in the state autonomy literature about "social provisioning" for "citizens," is an ideal transition to my discussion of the Rockefeller network's involvement in the Social Security Act.

## THE ROCKEFELLER NETWORK AND LABOR

The Rockefeller network first became involved in labor relations and social insurance in 1914 as a result of a disastrous strike at Colorado Fuel and Iron leading to major troubles and embarrassing publicity for Rockefeller, who quietly backed his managers in their desire to break the strike and resist unionization, all the while insisting he had taken a hands-off attitude. He ended up facing ultimate responsibility for over fifteen murders by both sides as well as for what came to be known as the Ludlow Massacre, a gun battle between strikers in a tent city and state militia that caused a fire and the deaths of two women and eleven children. Rockefeller then endured grueling appearances before a presidential commission on industrial relations that released many damaging and incriminating documents about his involvement in the events leading up to the violent confrontation (e.g., Weinstein 1968:191–98). Shortly thereafter he was pilloried for using the recently established Rockefeller Foundation, already under fire as a device to escape the new income tax laws, to pay for allegedly neutral research on industrial relations related to the strike and massacre (Fisher 1993:46).

This sequence of events had a dramatic impact on Rockefeller personally and on the subsequent shape of the Rockefeller network, including its desire to work quietly behind the scenes. These points are best demonstrated by Gitelman (1988), who provides the most detailed account of Ludlow and its aftermath based on documents at the Rockefeller Archive Center. Rockefeller's first step in the midst of this crisis was to hire public relations expert Ivy Lee, who worked for the Rockefellers from then until his death many years later. His second was to hire a Canadian labor relations expert, McKenzie King, who then served as one of Rockefeller's closest advisers until he became prime minister of Canada under the Liberal party in 1921. It was King who acquainted Rockefeller with the basic tenets of welfare capitalism and urged him to foster "company representation plans," whereby workers within a plant could elect their own representatives to meet with management to discuss issues of concern. These representation plans, called company unions by their critics, were designed as a way to resist national labor unions.

When the installation of this plan at Colorado Fuel and Iron seemed to work, and brought Rockefeller considerable praise in the media as a statesman and reformer, he urged its adoption at the other companies where he had major stock interests. In fact, the trail of adoptions for the plan is another piece of evidence for Rockefeller's control of the companies listed earlier as part of the Rockefeller economic empire. The plan also was adopted at International Harvester in Chicago, owned by his brother-in-law's family, the McCormicks. The industrial relations executives trained within the Rockefeller companies and International Harvester supplied Rockefeller with the personal labor relations advisers he acquired in the 1920s and 1930s.

Shortly before King turned his full attention to his political career, he and Fosdick advised Rockefeller to form an industrial consulting group to generalize the results of the experiences within the Rockefeller-influenced companies and develop a program of research on industrial relations. Rockefeller accepted this idea during two days of discussion in the summer of 1921, and Industrial Relations Counselors, Inc., was born, first as a subgroup of Fosdick's personal law firm, and in 1926 as an independent entity with a little over twenty employees, financed almost entirely by Rockefeller's personal fortune at the rate of what would be nine hundred thousand dollars a year in today's money (Gitelman 1988:331ff.). For all its formal independence from Rockefeller companies, though, it was in fact an adjunct to those companies. The board of directors for IRC at its formal founding is analyzed in Table 5.1. Board members Arthur Woods and Raymond Fosdick will make appearances later in this chapter.

Shortly after IRC first was established, the Rockefeller network contacted two prestigious universities to create research programs on industrial relations. One was the University of Pennsylvania, where a Department of Industrial Relations was founded within the Wharton School of Business. Its chair was Joseph Willits, who became involved in SSRC work from that time forward and director of the Rockefeller Foundation's Division of Social Sciences in 1939 (Fisher 1993:54–55, 121, 183). In 1927, for example, Willits headed the SSRC survey mentioned earlier on the extent of industrial research in universities. Joining him in this effort were Boston businessman

Table 5.1.   Trustees, Industrial Relations Counselors, Inc., 1926[a]

Owen D. Young, chairman, General Electric
  Main directorships: General Motors, RCA, NBC
  Main trusteeships: Council on Foreign Relations
  Representative clubs: Century Association (NY)
  Political affiliation: Democrat

Arthur Woods, vice-President, Colorado Fuel and Iron
  Main directorships: Bankers Trust Company, Consolidation Coal, Colorado
    Fuel and Iron
  Main trusteeships: Laura Spelman Rockefeller Memorial, Rockefeller
    Foundation, General Education Board
  Representative clubs: Racquet (New York), Metropolitan (Washington)
  Political affiliation: Republican

Cyrus McCormick, Jr., chairman, International Harvester
  Main directorships: National City Bank (NY)
  Main trusteeships: Princeton University
  Representative clubs: Chicago Club
  Political affiliation: Supporter of Woodrow Wilson, Democrat in 1912

Ernest Hopkins, president, Dartmouth College
  Main directorships: None
  Main trusteeships: Laura Spelman Rockefeller Memorial
  Representative clubs: Century Association (NY)
  Political affiliation: Republican

Raymond B. Fosdick, partner, Curtis, Fosdick and Belknap
  Main directorships: Consolidation Coal, Davis Coal, Western Maryland
    Railroad
  Main trusteeships: Brookings Institution, Institute of Public Administration,
    Rockefeller foundation, General Education Board, Laura Spelman Rockefeller
    memorial, Rockefeller Institute for Medical Research
  Representative club: Century Association (NY)
  Political affiliation: Democrat (friend of future President Rossevelt)

[a] In The Power Elite and the State (Domhoff 1990, 57), I said that the chairman of U.S. Steel was on the IRC board in the 1930s, but it was a vice-president of U.S. Steel who joined the board at that time.

Henry S. Dennison, cofinancer of the Twentieth Century Fund and later a member of the BAC; they first met at the government's Division of Planning and Statistics during World War I (Fisher 1993:54). John R. Commons was on the committee, as were the president of the Taylor Society (a scientific management society), two labor leaders, and several others.

The second new program was at Princeton, where direct overtures from Rockefeller and Fosdick (Fosdick was a graduate of Princeton, John D. Rockefeller 3rd was then a student there) led to the creation of an Industrial Relations Section of the Department of Economics to do research and hold conferences. This subgroup was developed under the guidance of Clarence J. Hicks, the top industrial relations officer at Standard Oil of New Jersey after similar work at Colorado Fuel and Iron. Over the next few years Rockefeller gave several hundred thousand dollars for this effort.

The first director of the Industrial Relations Section, and in fact its only academic employee, resigned after one year to move to another university. He was replaced by J. Douglas Brown, later to be one of the three experts involved in the drafting of the old-age provisions of the Social Security Act. The son of an industrial executive in Somerville, New Jersey, Brown received his B.A. in 1919 and his M.A. in 1921 in economics from Princeton. Then he served as an assistant professor for one year at Princeton and another at Penn before returning to Princeton in 1925 as an assistant professor and director of the Industrial Relations Section. He received his Ph.D. in 1927 and became a full professor in 1934.

Another drafter of the old-age provisions, Barbara Nachtrieb Armstrong, who will be introduced more fully at the appropriate time, recalled in her interview for the Columbia Oral History Project on the Social Security Act that Brown knew the Rockefellers and their friends quite well, and "they seemed in turn very devoted to Doug Brown" (Armstrong 1965:159). By my reading of Brown's papers in the archival library at Princeton, Armstrong is exactly right. He knew the employees at IRC well and often visited their offices in New York. He planned conferences with them. He was in regular contact with Hicks and helped him write his autobiography (Hicks 1941). There are four files of correspondence between Brown and John D. Rockefeller 3rd, who became involved in IRC in the late 1920s, at the Rockefeller Archive Center. The following letter from Hicks to Rockefeller, Jr., gives the flavor of one of Brown's roles in the Rockefeller network, not to mention the range of his contacts by 1930:

Mr. John D. Rockefeller, Jr.

Dear Mr. Rockefeller:

During this past summer Mr. J. Douglas Brown, who has charge of the Industrial Relations Section at Princeton, has been making a trip as far west as California, interviewing representatives of a large number of corporations and getting in personal touch with the industrial relations situation in various sections of the country.

Tomorrow, Friday, he is coming to take luncheon with me to review his trip and to discuss the work of the Industrial Relations Section for the coming year. This appointment has been made at his suggestion and with the approval of

President Hibben [of Princeton]. I am sending you this word because of your interest, with the feeling that perhaps you may wish to see Mr. Brown for a few moments, provided you see an opportunity any time between eleven and two or three o'clock. He does not have any idea that I am making this suggestion, but I am sure that this personal touch with you would be an inspiration and help to him in the important relation that he bears to the work that you have made possible. (Hicks 1930)

Brown did not publicize his Rockefeller connection, at least in the early years. For example, when he spoke to the New Jersey Federation of Labor about the new Industrial Relations Section at Princeton, he asked for their cooperation and said his work was made possible by a "generous endowment," but did not mention its source (Brown 1927). By the same token, there is evidence the Rockefellers did not want Brown characterized as a Rockefeller man. In the following letter, John D. Rockefeller 3rd is mostly explaining to his father why a three-hundred-thousand-dollar endowment should be enough for the work at Princeton, but in the process he notes how important it is to maintain Brown's legitimacy in the eyes of the economics faculty by making sure he is paid by the university, not the Rockefellers. I reprint the bulk of the letter with the thought that such intimate entré into the day-to-day world of a family long mysterious to Americans may be as fascinating to readers as it was to me:

Dear Father:

Mr. Hicks got back to the city yesterday and I saw him this morning. We went over together all the questions in your letter of March 6th. To date the salary of the Director of the Industrial Relations Section has been paid from your grant. Mr. Hicks feels that even if you were to increase your contemplated endowment it would not be wise to have the Director's salary paid from it. Letting the university pay the salary helps to bind the university closer to the Section and also to make the faculty of the Economics Department feel that the Director of the Section is really one of their number and not an outsider paid with outside funds. Mr. Hicks thought that this last was a very important consideration. The success of the Section depends a lot on cooperation between the Economics Department and the Director of the Section. It would be fatal to have the Director thought of as a Rockefeller man. In regard to your giving more than $300,000 Mr. Hicks thought that it would be a fine thing and that the possibility of it should be mentioned when you make the gift now. He feels that it would be wisest not to mention any definite sum beyond the $300,000 now only telling the university authorities that if the work should expand as we hoped it would that we would be glad to consider increasing the endowment as their needs become greater. No definite commitment should be made beyond the $300,000 for if they felt that more money was forthcoming they would feel that they had to find some way to use it. The growth of the Section should be entirely spontaneous Mr. Hicks felt, having the need develop first and then let the money come. (Rockefeller 1930)

With the IRC/Penn/Princeton nexus in full swing by the mid-1920s, IRC hired two new employees, Murray Latimer and Bryce Stewart, who were destined to join Brown as major figures in the drafting of the Social Security Act, Latimer on old-age pensions, Stewart on unemployment insurance. Their employment was a clear indication that IRC was going to involve itself in more than company representation plans. In fact, its pension and employment work came to have far greater significance than the company unions, which largely collapsed after passage of the National Labor Relations Act in 1935, although Standard Oil of New Jersey never was unionized (Gitelman 1988:335).

At the time he was hired in 1926, Latimer was a twenty-five-year-old instructor in finance at the Harvard Business School. Born and educated in Clinton, Mississippi, he received an M.B.A. at Harvard in 1923 before joining the faculty. During his years at IRC he helped to establish pension plans at Standard Oil of New Jersey as well as three other Rockefeller oil companies and an independent steel company, American Rolling Mill. His 1932 book for IRC on *Industrial Pension Systems in the United States and Canada* was well-known and respected at the time, and is still frequently cited in historical accounts (e.g., Orloff 1993:100–2, 278–279). Latimer was an employee of IRC until 1936, although he continued to do studies for the firm and advise its clients until 1941. He worked in Washington as chairman of the Railroad Retirement Board from 1934 to 1946, where he installed the fully integrated social insurance system for old age, disability, survivors, and unemployment that he and his IRC associates wanted, but could never quite attain, for employees in all industries. In 1946 he established his own private consulting service for corporations, unions, and government agencies. It was Latimer who suggested to the Executive Director of the government's social security study in 1934 that J. Douglas Brown should join him on the team drafting the old-age pension plan (Witte 1963:30).

Stewart, forty-four years old when he joined the IRC staff in 1927, was a Canadian with a world of experience in employment and labor issues. A graduate of Queens University in Kingston, Ontario, he was director of the National Employment Service of Canada from 1914 to 1922 after a large role in establishing it. He came to the United States in 1922 to develop and administer the Amalgamated Clothing Workers' unemployment insurance fund, jointly financed by labor and management, but controlled by the union. He completed his Ph.D. in labor economics in 1926, then joined IRC. He became its director of research in 1930 and worked there until his retirement in 1952, except for a return to Canada as deputy minister of labor during World War II. Like Latimer, he was well known in the early 1930s for a book on social insurance (Stewart 1930). He did work for the SSRC and state agencies in Wisconsin and New York before serving the New Deal in various capacities, most famously (and contentiously) as director of unemployment insurance studies for the Social Security Act. Stewart, as we will see, was a strong critic of the AALL/Wisconsin approach.

The predepression thinking of the Rockefeller network on pensions is best exemplified in a pamphlet for the American Management Association in 1928 by Edward S. Cowdrick, a former journalist from Colorado who joined the Rockefellers as a public relations person after he wrote a favorable magazine article in 1915 on company representation plans (Gitelman 1988:185). In the early 1920s Cowdrick became secretary of the then-secret Special Conference Committee, made up of the CEOs and industrial relations vice-presidents for ten of the largest companies in the country, including Standard Oil of New Jersey, AT&T, United States Steel, General Motors, General Electric, and DuPont. The main function of the conference was to exchange information and ideas on labor relations, and to meet once a year for general discussions. Cowdrick and the Special Conference Committee coordinated the all-out battle against the National Labor Relations Act in 1935, as later revealed in documents subpoenaed by a Senate investigating committee (Auerbach 1966; U.S. Senate 1939:16806–809). According to Gitelman (1988:332–33), the industrial relations executives from these large companies were still meeting in the 1980s as the Cowdrick Group at Organization Resources Counselors, Inc., in New York, the current incarnation of IRC.

Because of his role with the Special Conference Committee, Cowdrick was an employee of neither the IRC nor Standard Oil of New Jersey, where he had his office. He was simply "Edward S. Cowdrick, 26 Broadway, New York, New York," but he worked with the other industrial relations experts in the Rockefeller network on many projects, including the planning of the annual conferences at Princeton beginning in 1931.

According to Cowdrick's pamphlet, which contains discussions of all the moral, economic, and technical issues involved in industrial pensions, a pension is part of a good personnel program. Especially in the case of corporations that have been around for many years, a pension is "a means, at once humane and approved by public opinion, of purging its active payroll of men who, by reason of age or disability, have become liabilities rather than assets" (Cowdrick 1928:10). Pensions also provide the "opportunity to promote their younger subordinates" (p. 11). Cowdrick concluded with the prediction that industrial pensions will be "increasingly valuable to employers" (p. 21). Marion Folsom, an executive at Eastman Kodak, later to be involved in shaping the Social Security Act, was advocating pensions for the same reasons at this time (Jacoby 1993).

The Rockefeller network's first government involvement with an employment issue came through the 1921 President's Conference on Unemployment, created by then–secretary of commerce Herbert Hoover in conjunction with experts from the AALL, Taylor Society, and NBER (Alchon 1985:77). The primary Rockefeller representative was Woods, a friend of Hoover's since they met during World War II. Woods worked closely with both Rockefeller and Ruml in the Rockefeller network. The Rockefeller network became even more involved after the conference as research funders because the ensuing report advocated the study of the business cycle and various ways to combat unemployment: employment bureaus, advance planning of public works, and elimination of waste. Although the subsequent research by the NBER on business cycles was financed primarily by the Carnegie Corporation, Ruml supported a small study on the business cycle and immigration after Fosdick and Rockefeller said the NBER should be high on the Memorial's list of priorities (Fisher 1993:37–42).

The financial relationship between the Memorial, the NBER, and Hoover became closer in 1928 when the Memorial and the Carnegie Corporation each contributed seventy-five thousand dollars to an update of the previous study, done under the rubric of the President's Conference on Unemployment once again, with Hoover himself chairing the committee (Alchon 1985:137ff.). The further visibility Hoover gained in policy circles through this effort was seen by some observers at the time as a boost to his chances for the presidency. The report that appeared in May 1929, *Recent Economic Changes in the United States*, was far less critical of the economy than the first one, and attributed the new prosperity to better management and an improved balance between production and consumption (pp. 148–49). With the economy growing and the labor movement moribund, it didn't look like there was much need for social insurance.

The Rockefeller network did its first service for the state of New York on an employment issue in 1928 when the industrial commissioner, Frances Perkins, Roosevelt's future secretary of labor, appointed an Advisory Committee on Employment Problems "to effect some improvement in the State Employment Service" (Perkins 1930). The chair of the advisory committee was Arthur H. Young, the executive director of IRC since 1925 after experience with International Harvester and Colorado Fuel and Iron as an industrial relations executive. His committee recommended that demonstration projects be developed to test the effectiveness of public employment centers. In 1931 the Spelman Fund provided a seventy-five-thousand-dollar grant over a three-year period to help with the project. Stewart of IRC was put in charge of the project as chair of the Committee on Demonstration, through which he came to know Perkins. He worked on the project over a three-year period (Stewart 1933; Moffett 1933). The Rochester project also brought Stewart into contact with Marion Folsom, by then the treasurer of Eastman Kodak, who had taken a leadership role in experimenting with forms of unemployment insurance.

In 1929 Ruml entered into another project with the state government of New York, this time in a study of older workers, where the goal was to find

out at what age male and female workers begin to have difficulties in holding on to their jobs or obtaining new ones, "thrown on the industrial scrap
heap," in the words of the letter requesting the funds (Mastick 1929). This
study was done by Gulick at the Institute of Public Administration for the
New York Commission on Old Age Security. The grant was for $33,500.

Given the recommendations for dealing with unemployment by the first
President's Conference on Unemployment, it might be thought that Hoover
would be ready to act when the stock market crashed on October 1929,
initiating what eventually became the Great Depression. However, the prevailing wisdom among economists and business leaders alike said it was
best to let the business cycle take its course, and Hoover agreed with this
approach. He also was philosophically opposed to very much direct federal
government involvement in the economy, although he did more than is
claimed by liberal historians, as recognized by later accounts (e.g., Nossiter
1990:chap. 1). Leaders of the Rockefeller network also accepted this hands-
off approach, but by the early 1930s there were new initiatives being developed at the Rockefeller Foundation, which became the center of Rockefeller
efforts to help combat the developing depression.

The first step in this new direction was the creation of an Economic
Stabilization Program, a framework used to fund a variety of initiatives over
the next three years. The second step was to tell the SSRC there would be no
further monies for general research. Shortly thereafter, in February, the SSRC
created a committee to consider unemployment. It was chaired by Woods,
whom we met earlier as an IRC director and friend of Hoover; his vice-chair
was Willits (Fisher 1993:122). Stewart of IRC was a member, as was a
Wisconsin-trained economist, William Leiserson, a well-known labor medi-
ator and a professor at Antioch College. The committee also included Morris
Leeds, a Philadelphia businessman and AALL leader. Leeds traveled across
the country speaking for unemployment insurance in the 1920s and
coauthored a book on the topic with fellow businessman and AALL participant, Samuel Lewishon in 1925. (Leiserson, Leeds, and Lewishon figure
later in the story.)

By October 1930, Hoover was becoming less certain that prosperity was
just around the corner, so he appointed a President's Emergency Committee
on Employment, drawing heavily on the Rockefeller network. Fearful that
such a committee might contribute to an atmosphere of pessimism, and call
for greater involvement by the federal government in creating employment,
Hoover stressed the temporary nature of the committee and limited its op-
tions to voluntary efforts at the state and local level.

Hoover chose Woods as the chair, who then dovetailed the work of his
SSRC committee with that of the emergency committee (Fisher 1993:122).
Joining him on the thirty-three-person presidential committee from the
Rockefeller network were Walter M. Stewart, a trustee of the Rockefeller

Foundation and chairman of the investment firm of Case, Pomeroy, and Company; Beardsley Ruml, by then in charge of the new incarnation of the Memorial, the Spelman Fund; Willits; Bryce Stewart; and J. Douglas Brown. To aid the committee in its work, the Rockefeller Foundation gave it fifty thousand dollars in 1930 and seventy-five thousand dollars in 1931 as part of its Economic Stabilization Program. The Spelman Fund provided an additional twenty-five thousand dollars in 1931.

The committee's experts drafted a proposed message to Congress for Hoover, calling for "a public works program, including slum clearance, low-cost housing, and rural electrification" (Schlesinger 1957:170). They recommended speeding up a large program of highway construction. They advocated a national employment service. These suggestions were resisted by Hoover, however. When Woods asked the president to start an emergency program in the near-starvation conditions of Appalachia, he was sent to the Red Cross, which refused to help because the problem was not due to a natural disaster like flood or drought. At that point the Rockefeller network provided money to charitable and community groups for the Appalachian relief effort (Bernstein 1960:310).

Blocked by Hoover's unwillingness to involve the federal government, the Woods committee was reduced to messages of hope and suggestions that had no impact. It encouraged local governments and businesses to undertake needed construction, asked homeowners to make repairs, and urged consumers to stock up while prices were low. Frustrated by his inability to achieve even the limited efforts he was willing to undertake (Woods was no liberal or deficit spender), he resigned at the end of April, 1931, and the committee disappeared in mid-August [see Hayes (1936) for painstaking and retrospectively hilarious details on the exhortations and activities of the committee].

Despite the overt failures of the emergency employment committee, it had longer-term research consequences, not at first apparent, through an Advisory Committee on Unemployment Statistics chaired by Willits, with Bryce Stewart as its technical adviser. The committee sent out questionnaires to businesses and government agencies all over the country; its main finding was the inadequacy of unemployment figures and the impossibility of determining the number of people needing direct relief (Hayes 1936:29). This finding supported later SSRC efforts to develop better data-gathering capabilities under governmental auspices.

The work of the emergency committee also led to research collaboration between the IRC and the Economic Stabilization Research Institute at the University of Minnesota on a pilot program on the usefulness of employment centers. The Rockefeller Foundation's Economic Stabilization Program awarded a two-year grant for $150,000 to the research institute for this work, which was supplemented by smaller grants from the Spelman Fund and Carnegie Corporation. One of the outcomes of this collaboration was a book presenting a plan for unemployment insurance, written by Stewart in conjunction with three University of Minnesota employees. The first was economist Alvin Hansen, soon to be appointed a professor at Harvard, where he became persuaded of the correctness of Keynesian theory in 1937 and went on to be the leading American Keynesian of his generation. The second was Merrill Murray, trained in economics at Wisconsin and previously employed by the Wisconsin Industrial Commission; he was in charge of the actual field study and took part in an unsuccessful campaign to pass an unemployment insurance bill in the state. The third author was Russell Stevenson, the dean of the School of Business Administration, who was mostly along for the ride. Hansen and Merrill will pop up again later in this chapter.

Although the book is only of historical interest now, its preface has one noteworthy comment for my purposes. Hansen, Murray, and Stevenson report that they changed their minds on the usefulness of the Wisconsin idea about creating incentives for businessmen to reduce unemployment. They also tended to favor a national plan. They credit their change of view to Stewart: "Many of the modifications in the original plan are the result of the research and thought brought to bear upon the subject by Bryce M. Stewart of the Industrial Relations Counselors, Inc., and his staff" (Hansen, Murray, Stevenson, and Stewart 1934:v).

At this time the Rockefeller Foundation's Economic Stabilization Program made the first in a series of grants to the IRC, drawing what had been a business-oriented consulting group further into the policy arena. The first grant, for $30,000, on February 21, 1931, was provided at the request of Woods for a study of unemployment insurance plans in Great Britain. A $16,000 grant on September 10, 1931, went for a study of the administration of employment offices, supplemented in May 1932, with $7,500 to support the IRC's role in the demonstration projects on employment offices in Rochester and Minneapolis. Another $16,000 was provided in March 1933, for a study of employment offices in Europe. In June 1935, $10,000 was granted so IRC could help in setting up the New York State Employment Service. As these grants show, the IRC was on its way to developing unique expertise on the administration of employment offices and on unemployment insurance.

The wide reach and visibility of the IRC at this time even extended into Wisconsin. When the legislature there passed the unemployment insurance law in 1932, the State Industrial Commission hired the IRC to draft a plan for administering the law. Stewart played a central role in this effort, traveling to Madison to confer with the commission, headed by Wisconsin-trained economist Arthur Altmeyer, soon to depart for Washington to serve in the New Deal (Stewart 1933). In all, three reports were written by IRC for the Industrial Commission.

During this time the IRC continued to receive the great bulk of its funding directly from Rockefeller, who was well aware of its activities through Hicks, Fosdick, and his son John D. 3rd. The following letter from Fosdick to Rockefeller early in 1933 shows how positively the work of the IRC was regarded by a major figure in the Rockefeller network:

Dear Mr. Rockefeller:

In re Industrial Relations Counselors, Inc.

I hesitate to bother you while you are at Hot Springs about the budget of the Industrial Relations Counselors and I do it only after talking the matter over with John.

You will, perhaps, recall that the fiscal year of this organization begins on May first. For five years up to May 1, 1932, you contributed $150,000 a year. This last year you cut your contribution to $100,000. In addition to your $100,000 gift, the receipts for the year 1932-1933 were as follows:

| | |
|---|---:|
| Rockefeller Foundation (for research) | $12,000.00 |
| Service Revenue | 4,247.26 |
| Retainers from Firms | 10,050.00 |
| Sale of Books | 1,513.40 |
| Bank Interest | 235.51 |
| Rental Revenue | 200.00 |
| | $28,246.17 |

For this coming year the Rockefeller Foundation will continue its support for research, and we estimate that the retainers from firms will remain at approximately the same figure.

As to the value of the work of this organization I cannot speak too highly. In reviewing the current year's work, I would mention the completion of our series of reports on Unemployment Insurance, which are everywhere acclaimed as authoritative and timely, and the publication of the report on Industrial Pension Systems. A measure of the importance of this book is had by stating that the New York Times has devoted nearly a column of important space in five different issues to complimentary discussion of it, and the New York Herald-Tribune gave it a half-column favorable editorial comment. Industrialists, actuaries, insurance companies, sociologists and financiers, without exception, have referred to it as a profoundly valuable and serviceable treatise. Furthermore, our work in these fields has led to engagement of our staff by the Wisconsin Industrial Commission and the Minnesota Employment Stabilization Research Institute to assist in shaping and administering legislation. Negotiations to the same purpose are under way with the government of the Dominion of Canada and also two other U.S. state commissions. These are valid evidence of the character and importance of the work of the staff.

There is much concern over the problem of funding of pensions plans just now, and in the last two years we have directly aided the New York Transit Co., National Transit Co., Buckeye, Northern, Indiana, Cumberland, Eureka, Southern and South West Pennsylvania Pipe Line Companies, Standard Oil

Company of Ohio, Solar Refining Co., Ohio Oil Co. and other clients in
revising and refunding their plans on a sound basis, in nearly all cases securing
adoption of a plan providing for assumption of part cost by the employees, and
other desirable and conservative provisions that have aggregated several millions of dollars in savings to those companies as well as affording greater
security to the employees. This work has required intimate consideration of
the financial status of the companies and on several occasions has permitted
us to make suggestions of general management and economic value which I
believe Mr. Debevoise or Mr. Cutler [other Rockefeller lawyers] could attest.

I realize, of course, that all organizations must face the reality of the present
moment. On the other hand, both John and I feel that Industrial Relations
Counselors is serving a unique purpose in the existing emergency and that it is
one of few organizations whose work ought to be stimulated rather than
curtailed at a time like this. You have already made a cut of 33 1/3% in your
contribution, and I am speaking for John as well as for myself in expressing the
hope that you will renew, for the year beginning May 1, 1933, the gift you
made last year.

Arrangements have practically been concluded for Industrial Relations
Counselors to move to Rockefeller City, but of course we cannot take definite
action until we know what your contribution is going to be. (Fosdick 1933)

Working from memory many years later, Fosdick wrote "By 1933 Mr.
Rockefeller was confident that it [the IRC] was now capable of supporting
itself on a nonprofit basis and that further financial backing from him was no
longer necessary" (1956:186). Orloff and Parker use this single statement as
their main basis for dismissing the possibility of any Rockefeller influence on
the Social Security Act, claiming "by the early 1930s, IRC was a self-
supporting industrial relations consulting firm" (1990:306). This is one of
those instances where state autonomy theorists didn't find evidence that
might contradict their view because they did not look for it. Whatever
Fosdick may have remembered, the reality is that Mr. Rockefeller's support
for the IRC tapered off gradually in the 1930s, as shown in Table 5.2. There
also is more to the decrease in support than meets the eye; Fosdick became
concerned that the IRC might become embroiled in the rising conflict with
trade unions, and he so warned Rockefeller (Fosdick 1934). Although the
IRC escaped public criticism on this issue, one of its former directors did
become embroiled in controversy.

In 1933 the Rockefeller Foundation created a Special Trustee Committee
to administer emergency funds of up to one million dollars in an expeditious
manner. The committee consisted of Rockefeller, Fosdick, and Walter Stewart, mentioned a few paragraphs ago as a member of the President's Emergency Committee for Employment. However, Ruml, Woods, or other
advisers were sometimes present for its deliberations. The largest of ten
projects for that year was one hundred thousand dollars for work by the
SSRC's Committee on Governmental Statistics and Information Services,

*Table 5.2.*  Mr. Rockefeller and Industrial Relations Counselors, Inc., Budget, 1926–1936

| Year | IRC Expenditures | Rockefeller Contributions | Percentage from Rockefeller |
|------|------------------|---------------------------|-----------------------------|
| 1926–1927 | $139,600 | $125,000 | 89 |
| 1927–1928 | 166,400 | 150,000 | 90 |
| 1928–1929 | 170,700 | 150,000 | 88 |
| 1929–1930 | 177,900 | 150,000 | 84 |
| 1930–1931 | 189,500 | 150,000 | 79 |
| 1931–1932 | 176,600 | 150,000 | 85 |
| 1932–1933 | 163,200 | 100,000 | 61 |
| 1933–1934 | 145,100 | 80,300 | 55 |
| 1934–1935 | 134,800 | 67,300 | 50 |
| 1935–1936 | 149,900 | 35,000 | 23 |

*Source:*  IRC (1936).

following up on the concerns Willits, Bryce Stewart, and others expressed about the dismal state of government statistics. This project, the largest undertaken by the SSRC to that date, led to the creation of a new Central Statistics Board for the federal government (Fisher 1993:128–29), an exercise in state building by the private sector that should not go unnoticed. Grants were also given to the Brookings Institution for a study monitoring the administration of the AAA and NRA. Then, too, the Committee on Unemployment of the SSRC was given five thousand dollars for a study of unemployment reserves by Bryce Stewart.

Perhaps the most intriguing and subtle of the grants by the Special Trustees Committee was earmarked to bring two of Great Britain's leading expert on social insurance, Sir William Beveridge and Sir Henry Steel-Maitland, to the United States for a series of conversations and dinners. Moulton of the Brookings Institution was asked to host a dinner and a luncheon at which Beveridge and Steel-Maitland met with various New Deal officials and experts. Swope, in his capacity as chair of the BAC, hosted a dinner "for important industrialists and Department of Commerce Officials" (May 1933). If ever a program seemed designed to create the proper atmosphere for contemplating a government social insurance program, this was it. Perkins later recalled that Beveridge and Steel-Maitland's speeches "before Chambers of Commerce, Rotary Clubs, Church organizations, and their discussions of the practicability of unemployment and old-age insurance did a great deal to allay the fears and doubts of the business and conservative part of the community" (1946:299).

Members of the IRC gave their first direct official service to the New Deal in 1933. Stewart headed a committee to advise Perkins on membership on her Advisory Committee to the Department of Labor. He also was a member of the Advisory Council of the United States Employment Service, within which he chaired the Committee on Research (Stewart 1933). Latimer provided the Department of Commerce with estimates on the amount of pension income paid out in the country and then became a member of the Advisory Committee of the Department of Labor, where he spent part of his summer months assisting "in the revision of the employment and payroll indexes and in making studies which would lead ultimately to the revision of the price indexes" (Latimer 1933).

Most interesting of all, however, late in that year Stewart, Latimer, and Brown worked together to create a social insurance system for railroad workers as members of an Employment Advisory Council appointed by the federal coordinator of transportation. As Brown tells the story:

> The group of us that went down [to Washington] on that centered very much on Industrial Relations Counselors, in New York. . . . So Latimer and I began working on the old-age protection of railroad workers. We put Hawkins [a student of Brown's] to work on the dismissal compensation. Bryce Stewart worked on the unemployment insurance. (Brown 1965:6)

Latimer and Brown lacked the information needed for the actuarial studies on which to base a sound program, and they did not have the army of clerks at their disposal necessary to develop the information. The way they solved the problem shows the triviality of the emphasis on state capacity by state autonomy theorists. Where there's a will, there's a way, as the old saying goes, and it may contain more theoretical insight than state autonomy theory when it comes to power in America. Latimer and Brown applied for a three-hundred-thousand-dollar grant from the recently established Civilian Works Administration, then contacted the railroads for the names of laid-off clerks who had dealt with the relevant employment records for their respective companies. They put 1,500 people to work collecting records on 400,000 employees and 110,000 pensioners, hired a staff of 500 in New York to analyze the data, and in a flash the state had a new set of records (Latimer and Hawkins 1938:111; Brown 1965:8–9). Because of this work Latimer was appointed chairman of the three-person Railroad Retirement Board in the summer of 1934 upon passage of the Wagner-Hatfield railroad retirement bill.

The Wagner-Hatfield bill was written by the leadership of the railroad labor unions and a strong grass-roots movement of aging and retired railroad workers (Graebner 1980:171–76). However, the benefit levels established by the legislation were lower than those originally proposed because the Brown-Latimer study showed that the original actuarial assumptions were unsound (Latimer and Hawkins 1938:123–27). Although the federal coordinator of transportation advised Roosevelt to sign the legislation because "it is in line with sound social policy" (Latham 1959:160), he would have preferred delay to improve it. When the act was declared unconstitutional in early May 1935, it provided the opportunity to bring about agreement between the warring owners and unions on new pension legislation. However, the agreement was not reached until 1936 after another round of legislative and court battles between the two sides. The final agreement was pleasing to the workers because it established a uniform national system, but it was even more satisfactory to the railroad owners because

> the tax rate was temporarily lowered from 3.5 percent to 2.75 percent, because the taxes were not payable until January 1, 1937, instead of March 1, 1936, because they were relieved of the cost of private pensions, and because the provisions of the plan could be financed without any continually increasing tax rate, in fact, at a tax rate not much higher than the one required in title VIII of the Social Security Act. (Latimer and Hawkins 1938:274)

In the end the Railroad Retirement Act was a victory for all concerned, but especially Latimer, who took the central role in the negotiations (p. 234).

The fate of the original railroad retirement bill of 1934 is extremely important to my claims about the importance of industrial relations experts: it was struck down precisely because it was based on labor market rationales, which meant such rationales would have to be replaced in new legislation. First, "two of the stated aims of the legislation—retirement of aged employees and relief from unemployment—were not in themselves proper objects" according to the court (Graebner 1980:160). Second, the alleged positive effects of pensions on the efficiency and morale of the work force were too tenuous to be an adequate basis for pensions. According to a very convincing argument by Graebner, the Supreme Court's opinion on the railroad legislation made it necessary for the drafters of the Social Security Act to drop arguments about unemployment relief and efficiency, and instead emphasize the contribution that old-age pensions would make to the general welfare of the country, which the government had the constitutional right to support through its taxing power. A new ideology of social security had to be created:

> Now, to achieve the original purpose, the administration turned to the taxing power and the general welfare clause of the Constitution. In the process, the ideology of social security was given formal sanction. After May 1935, proponents of retirement legislation talked less about efficiency, economy and unemployment relief than about social security and the needs of older workers, which were now a central policy goal rather than ancillary to some larger purpose. (Graebner 1980:162–63)

This court-induced change in rationale obscured the labor-market basis of the Social Security Act under smarmy talk about "social provisioning" and "social security." Always ready to take rhetoric at face value when it is found in government documents, the state autonomy theorists are uncritical of the emphasis on general welfare, which is why Orloff (1993:76) can believe that social reformers and charity workers were an important part of the story, far more so than businessmen.

The large amount of time being spent in government service by IRC employees led to the next series of IRC grants from the Rockefeller Foundation, beginning in January, 1934. The first grant request, entitled "Grant from Rockefeller Foundation to Cover Expense of Cooperation with Government Agencies," captures much of the argument I have been making for the growing importance of the IRC in the policy-making process. But it also relates to a process close to the hearts of state autonomy theorists, state-building, so I want to quote from it at some length:

December 22, 1933

Dear Mr. Fosdick:

The timeliness and character of the research work of Industrial Relations Counselors, Inc., has resulted in inescapable demands on the staff for service to various government agencies and officials arising out of the emergency problems confronting them. For several years we have been gradually drawn into this important work, and increasing inroads have been made on our time by such agencies as the New York State Advisory Council on Employment Problems, the Labor Statistics Committee of the American Statistical Association and the Social Science Research Council.

Since June, 1933, there has come what amounts to an overwhelming demand for personal participation by staff members and the conduct of special research studies from cabinet officers, federal departments and bureaus and special committees having to do with federal and state legislation and administration, and from our State Industrial Commission, etc. A partial list of the various projects is as follows. (Young 1933:1)

The proposal then outlines the many governmental and SSRC tasks undertaken by Stewart and Latimer, and in addition reports that another employee was "detailed as assistant director of the United States Employment Service as of July and has been serving in that capacity full time since" (p. 2). The director of IRC, Arthur H. Young, who became the vice-president for industrial relations at U.S. Steel shortly thereafter, where he brought notoriety to IRC by saying he would rather go to jail than comply with the National Labor Relations Act, then lists his own government involvements:

I have personally accepted appointment as a member of the Federal Advisory Council of the United States Employment Service, as a member of the Executive Committee, and chairman of the Committee on Veterans' Placement Service and, since June, have been serving as a special representative of the United States Department of Labor, actively assisting the Director of the

> United States Employment Service in the organization and administration of the National Reemployment Service.
>
> In addition, I have responded to requests from the National Labor Board and other agencies in connection with the preparation of labor provisions in industrial codes, the nomination of mediators and investigators, etc. (Young 1933:2)

All of this service, the proposal continues, has been voluntary, and it had been costing IRC money in both salary expenses and lost opportunities to do paid consulting work for businesses. It concludes with a request for "an emergency appropriation of twenty-five thousand dollars," granted by the foundation a few weeks later (p. 3). Similar grants were approved for ten thousand dollars in June 1935 and six thousand dollars in February 1936. Even when Latimer began to be paid by the government, he stayed on the IRC payroll and turned over his fees to the organization, one reason why the Rockefeller Foundation grants for 1935 and 1936 could be smaller (Latimer 1934).

I think the theoretical implications of this series of grants are very great, although Orloff and Parker (1990:306) make light of mere payroll matters, as we will see. In effect, the Rockefeller network became part of the state by paying the salaries of men who were de facto state employees. The Rockefeller network provided the capacity to build new processes and agencies into the state through the expertise of its private consulting firm, Industrial Relations Counselors, Inc. It then continued this process with the new Social Security Board through the Rockefeller Foundation grants to the SSRC committees on administration and social security that I mentioned earlier in the chapter, citing Fisher (1993:150–54). I believe this series of events can be classified as state-building by the class that dominates the state.

By November 1933, the experts in the Rockefeller network who had been working on social insurance for nearly four years felt confident enough with what they had accomplished to bring it to the attention of experts just outside their circles. They did so through a small conference at the Cosmos Club in Washington under the auspices of the SSRC. The arrangements were made by Meredith Givens, the executive secretary to the SSRC's Advisory Committee on Industry and Trade since 1929, and the main force behind the successful state-building effort by the Committee on Government Statistics and Information Services with the Central Statistics Board. He also staffed the Committee on Unemployment Insurance, often working with Stewart. Trained in economics at the University of Wisconsin, Givens joined the research staff of the NBER in 1928 and then added his SSRC role to his other duties. He too ends up working for the government on the Social Security Act.

Eighteen people attended this conference, representing a wide range of social service organizations. Five were social workers, including Edith Abbott, one of the most famous women reformers of the Progressive Era, and dean of the School of Social Service Administration at the University of Chicago since 1921. The only business executive present was Leeds, from the SSRC's Committee on Unemployment. The most important government official was Harry Hopkins, a former social worker who headed the Federal Emergency Relief Administration. The names and occupational backgrounds of the attendees are presented in Table 5.3, along with any connections they had with the Rockefeller network. Many of the names will be familiar from what I have said up until this point. Fourteen of the twenty-two served on an SSRC committee or were connected to the Rockefeller network in some way.

The starting point for the discussions at the SSRC conference was a document prepared by Stewart listing the kinds of studies needed to decide some of the issues that had to be resolved in designing a social insurance program. There was a stress on issues dividing the proponents of various kinds of social welfare, such as existed on unemployment insurance. Although the attendees were unanimous in encouraging the SSRC to move forward in refining its proposal, Abbott did express disagreements based on her preference for "one welfare statute," paid for out of general tax revenues and "available to all without stigmatizing qualifications" [Witte (1963:15–16) for the fact of disagreement; Gordon (1994:261) for Abbott's general views]. Moreover, neither Edith Abbott nor her equally famous sister, Grace Abbott, director of the Children's Bureau of the Department of Labor from 1921 to 1934, liked the idea of employee contributions to unemployment compensation. They spoke for many social workers when they expressed disagreement with the "insurance crowd," which was to be a problem for Stewart later. However, Grace Abbott lobbied very hard for the act in 1935 at crucial moments before Congress (Gordon 1994:261–63).

The same group met for a second SSRC conference in early April, 1934, to consider a second version of Stewart's proposal, this one coauthored with Givens. There was once again general approval, so Stewart and Givens began explorations concerning the possibility of government involvement or sponsorship (Stewart and Givens 1934:1). Learning that Perkins and Roosevelt were thinking about the possibility of general legislation in the area of what was then called economic security, Stewart and Givens decided not to submit their report to the SSRC leadership until they could see how events unfolded. Once the Roosevelt initiative was announced, and they saw what was likely to be its outcome, they revised their proposal to call for a large SSRC study paralleling the government effort. They argued that it was very unlikely any new legislation would be thoroughly satisfactory, so the SSRC studies would be important in making inevitable revisions in the program (Stewart and Givens 1934:11–13). This proposal became the basis for yet

*Table 5.3.* Occupations and Affiliations of Those Who Attended SSRC Conferences in 1933 and 1934

| Name, Affiliation | Rockefeller Network involvements, pre-1933 | Role in New Deal |
|---|---|---|
| Edith Abbott[a] Dean, School of Social Service Administration, University of Chicago | Major grants from Memorial and Rockefeller Foundation to her School of Social Service Administration in 1926 and 1927 | None |
| Arthur Altmeyer Director, Wisconsin Industrial Commission | Hired IRC to do administrative studies for Industrial Commission | Assistant secretary of labor; chair, CES Technical Board |
| Mary Anderson Director, Women's Bureau Department of Labor | None | Director, Women's Bureau |
| Frank Bane[a] American Public Welfare Association | American Public Welfare Association created by PACH and Spelman Fund | Lobbyist[b] Executive director, Social Security Board |
| J. Douglas Brown, Professor of Economics, Princeton | Rockefellers created Industrial Relations Section at Princeton | CES research staff |
| Louis Brownlow, Director, PACH | Spelman Fund created and financed PACH; chair, SSRC Committee on Public Administration | Member, President's Committee on Administrative Management |
| Stanley Davies[a] American Association of Social Workers | None | None |
| John Dickinson Professor of Law, Columbia | Member SSRC Committee on Public Administration | Assistant secretary of commerce |
| John Gaus Professor of Political Science, Wisconsin | Member, SSRC Committee on Public Administration | None |
| Meridith Givens Economist, NBER | Committee on Industry and Trade | CES research staff |
| Luther Gulick Director, Institute of Public Administration | Member, SSRC Committee of Public Administration | Member, President's Committee on Administrative Management |

(continued)

*Table 5.3.* Continued

| Name, Affiliation | Rockefeller Network involvements, pre-1933 | Role in New Deal |
|---|---|---|
| Harry Hopkins[a] Social Worker | None | Federal Emergency Relief Director; Member, CES |
| Parker Lee[a] Director, New York School of Social Work | None | None |
| Morris Leeds President, Leeds and Northrup | Member, SSRC Committee on Industry and Trade | CES Advisory Council |
| Simon Leland Professor, University of Chicago | Memorial funding made him a full-time research professor in 1927 | None |
| Isador Lubin Research staff, Brookings Institution | Brookings Institution | Commissioner of labor statistics; CES Technical Board |
| R. S. Meriam Professor, Amherst College | None | None |
| Edwin Nourse Research staff, Brookings | SSRC Committee on Social and Economic Research in Agriculture; Brookings Institution | None |
| W. Frank Persons Field representative, American Public Welfare Association | American Public Welfare Association | Director, U.S. Employment Service |
| Bryce Stewart Director of Research, Industrial Relations Counselors, Inc. | IRC; SSRC | CES research staff |
| Oscar Weigert Consultant from Germany | None | None |
| M. L. Wilson Professor of Agricultural Economics, Montana State University | SSRC Committee on Social and Economic Research in Agriculture | Director, Wheat Section, Agricultural Adjustment Administration |

[a] Person is self-identified as a social worker.
[b] When the Social Security Act seemed to be delayed in the House in the spring of 1935, Bane's American Public Welfare Association hired John Andrews, director of the AALL, to organize a lobbying campaign by prominent liberals and social insurance experts (Witte 1963, 97).

another conference, this time directly under the auspices of the Rockefeller Foundation, on March 22-23, 1935, in Atlantic City. This conference unanimously recommended funding for the aforementioned studies of the Social Security Board to be carried out by the SSRC's committees on social security and public administration.

So, as this brief history proves, the Rockefeller network was actively involved in developing plans for social insurance right up until the moment the government process began, and then made plans to monitor the outcome. But did any of this really matter? Was this network involved in the drafting processes inside the state? If it was, did it have any impact?

## THE DRAFTING PROCESS

To begin at the beginning of the legislative process on this issue, Roosevelt announced his plan for a comprehensive study of a possible program for economic security on June 8, 1934. The decision-making body for the proposal to be presented to Congress was a cabinet-level committee called the Committee on Economic Security, which I will call CES, following the usual custom in the literature. The CES was chaired by Secretary of Labor, and Perkins it included the secretary of treasury, secretary of agriculture, attorney general, and federal emergency relief administrator.

The CES was assisted by what was called the Technical Board, a group of twenty government-employed experts drawn from several different agencies. It also had the input of an Advisory Council made up of twenty-three private citizens who were supposed to be window dressing, but inserted themselves into the process nonetheless. In addition, there was a research staff made up of experts brought in from outside the government for this special task. It was their job to draft the proposals to be discussed by the appropriate committees of the Technical Board, and by the Advisory Council, before being passed up the hierarchy to the CES (and always Roosevelt behind the scenes) for disposition. Finally, there was an executive director to lead the staff and serve as secretary to the CES; he ended up the coordinator of the whole drafting process, a witness before congressional committees, and even a staff consultart to legislative committees.

The most detailed firsthand account of the process is provided by Edwin E. Witte, the man who filled the difficult role of executive director. Born and raised in Wisconsin, he received his B.A. in history from the state's university in 1909, then studied economics with John R. Commons in graduate school. He did collaborative work with Commons and wrote reports on labor law for him. He became executive secretary of the Wisconsin Industrial Commission in 1917 and chief of the Legislative Reference Library, a service for state legislators who needed help in writing their bills, in 1922, where he worked until he was hired to direct the drafting process. Due to all this investigative and legislative work, he did not finish his dissertation until 1927. Witte was recommended to Perkins to coordinate the social security studies by Altmeyer, another Wisconsin native, equally a product of Commons and the University of Wisconsin (B.A., 1914, M.A., 1921, Ph.D., 1931). He succeeded Witte as executive secretary of the Wisconsin Industrial Commission in 1922 and worked there until he joined the New Deal in 1933. I recite this information on Witte and Altmeyer for a reason, of course: the upcoming disagreement between the Wisconsin approach and what the research staff suggested.

Although Witte's book did not appear until 1963, it is in fact based on a diary he kept during the drafting process for his own benefit in keeping things straight in a complex situation. The diary became the basis for a memorandum he wrote in 1936 at the request of none other than the SSRC's Committee on Public Administration, which used it as part of its study of the new Social Security Board (Witte 1963:xi). When the memorandum appeared as a book, it became the basis for just about everyone's analysis of the origins of the Social Security Act since that time. It remains a valuable book, but it does not tell the whole story.

With this background material in mind, we can open our inquiry into the impact of the Rockefeller network on the Act with the fact that the structure and process for the program were developed by Altmeyer, Givens, and Stewart, according to Witte's biographer (Schlabach 1969:99). This conclusion, based on interviews and a statement in the CES files written by the three men for the president, is consistent with a claim in the introduction to Stewart and Given's SSRC report: "In June, 1934, these draft materials were made informally available in the definite consideration of plans for a government inquiry" (1934:2). We also can note that Witte himself reports he made "some little use" of the research suggestions in this report, "in outlining the fields to be covered by various members of the staff" (1963:15–16). We then can add that Stewart was put in charge of unemployment studies and Givens in charge of the study of employment opportunities (Witte 1963:13–14, 31). It is also worth noting that Latimer and Brown were the first two people to be asked to head the research staff on old-age pensions. All in all, this is impressive preliminary evidence that the Rockefeller network was an integral part of the governmental process.

## OLD-AGE PENSIONS

The Rockefeller network's involvement in the substance of the matter is most impressive on old-age pensions. In describing his search for a staff to study old-age pensions and draft a proposal, Witte writes: "[I]t was agreed by everyone consulted that the best person in the field was Murray Latimer, who was unavailable because he was chairman of the Railroad Retirement Board" (1963:29). Still, Latimer was able to serve as chair of the Technical Board's Committee on Old Age Security, an important policy role in itself, and in any case he worked with the research staff in drafting a proposal: "[T]hroughout [he] was in closest touch with the development of the program for old-age security" is the way Witte (ibid.) puts it. Latimer also was given the opportunity to recommend a leader for the staff, and his suggestion was his collaborator in the railroad study, J. Douglas Brown, whom he had known through IRC and annual conferences at Princeton on social insurance as well (Witte 1963:30). When Brown decided that he could only give part of each week to the work at hand, Professor Barbara Nachtrieb Armstrong of the School of Law at the University of California, Berkeley, was placed in charge of the old-age study, although she originally thought she would be working on unemployment compensation (Armstrong 1965:36). Latimer and Brown worked very closely with her, along with Otto Richter, an actuary on loan from AT&T.[4]

Little has been written about Armstrong and her involvement in the process, but the Oral History Project on the Social Security Act at Columbia University contains materials suggesting that she was the most interesting and talented person in the whole process. Born in 1890, she received her law degree in 1915 at the University of California, Berkeley, and went to work for a state Commission on Social Insurance, producing a report on sickness as a cause of poverty in California that earned her a Ph.D. at Berkeley in 1921. She then taught both law and economics there for the next several years before being appointed what is thought to be the first woman professor of law in the United States. During the 1920s she immersed herself in the study of European social insurance systems and produced one of the best books in the field at the time, *Insuring the Essentials* (1932), with the help of an SSRC grant.

Armstrong (1965:38) reports in her oral history that she knew no one in Washington when she was asked to join the research staff, and never found out who wanted her on it. She says she had received positive letters about her book from Roosevelt intimates Swope and Frankfurter, and speculates that Swope may have been responsible for her selection (p. 30). However, she did know many of the experts in the field from her work on the California commission, and many experts knew of her book. It therefore seems more likely to me that one of the other experts who knew of her work recommended her, possibly someone connected with her SSRC grant, but that detail is lost to history for the time being.

In any case, Armstrong is the kind of independent expert that state autonomy theorists emphasize. She is described by a slightly younger coworker on the project, Eveline Burns, a British woman from the London School of Economics who taught economics at Columbia, as "brilliant, outspoken and effective" (Burns 1966:28). Brown said she had "a brilliant legal mind" (1972:8). Altmeyer (1966:5–6) also calls her "brilliant," but said she was "difficult" for Witte, and in fact she didn't believe either Witte or Altmeyer knew very much about social insurance (Armstrong, 1965:46–47). She had contempt for the Wisconsin ideas on incentives for employers, labeling them "absurd" (p. 42). She fought tenaciously for her ideas on both old-age pensions and unemployment compensation, driving Witte to distraction, contrary to the usual claim that he always was calm and collected (pp. 67–68; Burns 1966:28). She had little use for Perkins, who never bothered to meet with her, which Armstrong attributed to Perkins's preference for the cautious Wisconsin approach (Armstrong 1965:31).

Armstrong also fought with young New Deal lawyers, particularly Perkins's twenty-six-year-old right-hand lawyer, Thomas Eliot, when they asserted that national-level insurance plans were unconstitutional. She firmly disagreed and then pointed out that she knew more about law than they did, gathering written statements from leading constitutional law professors at Berkeley, Harvard, and Duke to buttress her point (Armstrong 1965:75; Brown 1972:10–12). When Eliot claimed his former teacher at Harvard Law School, Thomas Reed Powell, thought national-level old-age pensions were unconstitutional, Armstrong took the night train to Boston, where she obtained a personal letter to Eliot from her friend Powell, saying he believed no such thing. At the next meeting of her group where Eliot was present, she handed him a copy of the letter and asked him if he wanted to read it aloud [Armstrong (1965:90–93); see Powell (1934) for his postvisit letter to Armstrong and a copy of his letter to Eliot]. By way of contrast, Armstrong had the highest regard and affection for Brown and Stewart, whom she describes as kind and gentle people. She felt sorry for Stewart because he was not as tough as she was; she reports "he suffered awfully at their hands," meaning Perkins, Altmeyer, and Witte (Armstrong 1965:36).

After playing a central role in the drafting process, Armstrong returned to California to resume her roles as a professor, mother, and wife (to a San Francisco businessman), writing important legal books on family law, community property law, and labor law. She never returned to Washington, in part because of the pressure of time, in part because she feared she might be too acerbic as a witness before congressional committees (Graebner 1980: 187). However, she stayed in close touch with the twists and turns that congressional sentiment took toward her handiwork at various moments of the legislative process; her impassioned letters to Brown and Latimer in their collected papers at Princeton and George Washington universities, expressing her anger and frustration with those who tampered with the proposal in any way, still make for enjoyable reading.

The plan prepared by Armstrong and her colleagues sailed through the Technical Board's Committee on Old Age Pensions, although two features of the plan made the CES a little nervous: its national scope and the insistence on employee contributions. However, the original plan prevailed on both issues. So far the process would seem to be a clear victory for the Rockefeller network in terms of policy preferences.

However, the plan faced an even bigger challenge. There may have been some inclination on the part of Witte, Perkins, and Roosevelt to exclude it from the final package sent to Congress because there was too much controversy swirling around old-age pensions due to the more radical plans being advocated by the Townsend Movement and other militant groups. Perkins and Witte later denied there was any such move afoot, but Armstrong, Latimer, and Brown were convinced there was, and they spoke off the record to reporters to that effect after an ambiguous line in a speech to a national conference by Roosevelt. The uproar in the newspapers led to the assurance by all concerned that old-age pensions would be included in the legislative proposal (Armstrong 1965:88–89; Brown 1966:13; Latimer interview in Schlabach 1969:iii).

Shortly thereafter, business leaders came into the picture in a supporting role as members of the Advisory Council. According to Armstrong (1965:82–83) and Brown (1972:21), these businessmen were critical in convincing Roosevelt and Perkins to retain the old-age provisions in the legislation. As Brown put it:

> The likelihood of gaining the support of the Cabinet Committee for our proposals was still in doubt. At this critical time, December, 1934, help came from an unexpected source, the industrial executives on the committee's Advisory Council. Fortunately included in the Council were Walter C. Teagle of the Standard Oil Company of New Jersey, Gerard Swope of General Electric, and Marion Folsom of Eastman Kodak, and others well acquainted with industrial pension plans. Their practical understanding of the need for contributory old age annuities on a broad, national basis carried great weight with those in authority. They enthusiastically approved our program. Just as the newspaper writers had carried us through the November crisis, the support of progressive industrial executives in December ensured that a national system of contributory old age insurance would be recommended to the President and Congress. (1972:21)

Swope and Folsom are familiar names by this point, Swope through his many roles, Folsom from his involvement in the Rochester employment centers project. Morris Leeds and Samuel Lewishon, who also should be on Brown's list as business members of the Advisory Council, are also familiar names, Leeds as an SSRC participant, Lewishon as his coauthor on a book on unemployment insurance. But a word needs to be said about Teagle. He was in many ways the critical person in the Rockefeller network in Washing-

ton in the first two years of the New Deal, not only because of his stature as a
business executive, but as a person very close to Rockefeller. The grandson
of one of John D. Rockefeller, Sr.'s, original partners, he had been an
executive for Standard Oil companies for fifteen years when he became
president of Standard Oil of New Jersey in 1917, serving in that position
until he retired in 1937. He was a director of White Motors in Cleveland and
Coca Cola in Atlanta due to personal friendships with their CEOs. He served
on the Petroleum War Service Board in World War I and chaired a Share-
the-Work campaign for Hoover in 1932, making dozens of speeches across
the country (Wall and Gibb 1974:chap. 15).

Immediately following Roosevelt's inauguration, Teagle was named to
the new Business Advisory Council as a member of its nine-member executive committee. He also chaired the BAC's Industrial Relations Committee,
where he installed Cowdrick as secretary and made all members of the
Special Conference Committee members of that BAC committee. As Cowdrick explained in a letter to an AT&T executive:

> Each member is invited as an individual, not as a representative of his compa-
> ny, and the name of the Special Conference Committee will not be used. The
> work of the new committee will supplement and broaden—not supplant—
> that of the Special Conference Committee. Probably special meetings will not
> be needed since the necessary guidelines for the Industrial Relations Commit-
> tee's work can be given at our regular sessions. (U.S. Senate 1939:16800)

The Industrial Relations Committee then wrote a report for the BAC supportive of employee representation plans and critical of unions. By the time
he was appointed to the Advisory Council for social security legislation,
Teagle was chair of the Unemployment Insurance Committee of the BAC as
well. For this committee he called on Stewart and his staff at IRC for advice.

Shortly after joining the BAC, Teagle was asked by Hugh Johnson to chair
the NRA's Industrial Advisory Board. He then brought Clarence Hicks, his
industrial relations vice-president at Standard of New Jersey to join him in
Washington as his personal assistant. Teagle spent the summer of 1933,
along with Swope, Henry Harriman, and other business executives, over-
seeing the development of the NRA. According to McQuaid (1979:688),
Teagle suggested at a joint meeting of the Industrial Advisory Board and the
Labor Advisory Board in August, 1933, that they create a labor mediation
board to settle the strikes for union recognition in response to section 7(a).
He then joined the new National Labor Board and used Hicks as one of its
mediators.

In other words, Teagle was a visible, active corporate leader at the center
of the corporate/labor/government nexus in the crucial early years of the
New Deal. Since both he and Hicks were very close to Rockefeller, it is my
conclusion that these three men served as the collecting point for all the

work by the Rockefeller network on social insurance up until that time, as well as its leaders in relations with the New Deal. Here we can see in microcosm the relationship between members of the power elite and their hired experts. The experts are employed to create plans within general guidelines set out by corporate leaders. They then show the plans to the corporate leaders for modification or approval. Once the plans are satisfactory, the corporate leaders make their approval of the plans clear to politicians and other state officials.

In this particular case, Teagle and Hicks clearly coordinated the work of Stewart, Brown, and Latimer in favor of social security and the work of Cowdrick in opposition to he National Labor Relations Act.[5] Hicks even attended at least one meeting of the drafting group on old-age pensions. I therefore believe Armstrong and Brown were entirely right when they asserted that Teagle, Swope, and Folsom had the clout and stature to make sure the old-age plan was included in the Social Security Act.

The old-age provisions of the proposed Social Security Act were explained and defended before Congress at length and in detail by Witte, Brown, and Latimer. Latimer and others believe that Witte was the most creditable witness for most congressmen (Schlabach 1969:144). However, Brown and Latimer's testimony is of greater theoretical interest here because it supports the claim I cited earlier by Wilbur Cohen: the legislation reflected the labor market concerns of industrial relations experts (Graebner 1980:187–89). Latimer's only concern was that larger benefits might be needed to induce a greater amount of retirement. Armstrong's oral history shows the same kind of emphasis, which is worth adding to the argument because she speaks from an independent, liberal perspective. She told her interviewer that the objective "was not only to protect the older worker, but it was also to get him out of the labor market" (1965:255). When the interviewer asked in effect if this was her perspective alone, she replied that Latimer, Brown, Richter, and "anybody who ever worked on social insurance" understood this objective (p. 260).

The importance of shaping labor markets through this legislation also is attested to by another participant in the process, Jane Hoey, who went on to be the director of public assistance for the Social Security Board from 1936 to 1954. Her testimony is important because she was trained as a social worker. She had known Roosevelt for decades because one of her brothers served in the New York State Assembly with him (Hoey 1966:4–5). She worked in New York in social welfare. Her oral history makes it very clear that the idea of the old-age provisions of the act was to induce older workers to retire so younger men would have work (p. 10).

Brown (1972:chap. 6) later summarized this "American philosophy of social insurance" in a retrospective book. One of his clearest statements of the heart of the matter is the following:

The acceptance by the larger American corporation of the obligation to pay contributions to a social insurance program, although influenced by the traditional concept of employer responsibility, was probably more directly the result of the need for a perpetual corporation to assure a flow of effective and well-motivated personnel for the year-by-year operation of the company. Retirement programs with adequate pensions became necessary; to prevent an excessive aging of staff or the loss of morale which the discard of the old without compensation would involve. Such programs became a charge on current production to be passed on to the consumer. (pp. 90–91)

Orloff is, of course, aware of the important roles assumed by Armstrong, Brown, and Latimer, but for her they are elite experts independent of the corporate community. She seems unaware that Latimer was an employee of IRC, or else does not think it is worthwhile to deal with the fact, perhaps because she believes the IRC was self-supporting by the early 1930s. Given her prior convictions, she also would be unlikely to pursue the possibility that Brown might be closely linked to the Rockefellers. But if we assign Latimer and Brown to their proper places as part of the Rockefeller network, and recall that Richter worked for AT&T, then Orloff is left with Armstrong. Now, Armstrong truly was an independent expert, but on this particular issue her views were quite in accord with people like Latimer, who certainly could have exercised veto power over her selection, given the deference Witte showed to him at the outset. In support of this point, Armstrong (1965:36) claims she was taken off the unemployment study when her views became known to Witte; that is, she was assigned to a task where her views were compatible with what Witte had been convinced of early in the process by Latimer (Schlabach 1969:115).

In short, Orloff does not have any support for her theory when it comes to old-age pensions because the issue was shaped by the Rockefeller network. Labor, liberals, and government officials may have created old-age pensions in Great Britain and Canada, but they didn't have much to do with it in the United States.

## UNEMPLOYMENT COMPENSATION

When we turn to unemployment compensation, the other major title of the Social Security Act of theoretical interest, the story begins as even more of a triumph for the Rockefeller network than old-age pensions were. Not only was Stewart put in charge of the staff study, as I mentioned earlier, but he installed his coauthor from the Minnesota study, Merrill Murray, as his principal assistant, and then insisted on using employees of IRC to make the study. As Witte explains, Stewart would only take the position if he could also stay with IRC in New York and use his own staff as well:

It developed that he did not feel that he could leave his position and would consider only an arrangement under which his work for the committee could largely be done in New York, and under which he could use his own staff to assist him. Such an arrangement was objected to by some members of the technical board, but was finally made. Almost the entire research staff of the Industrial Relations Counselors, Inc., was placed on the payroll of the Committee on Economic Security, so that the arrangement in effect amounted to employing the Industrial Relations Counselors, Inc., to make this study. (Witte 1963:29)

Witte then explains a little further in a footnote:

Dr. Stewart himself was never on the payroll of the Committee on Economic Security, pursuant to his express request. Instead, his staff was put on the payroll, with the understanding that both he and the staff would work simultaneously for the committee and the Industrial Relations Counselors, Inc. (p. 29, footnote 24)

This seems to me to be a rather amazing set of demands for an autonomous state to accept. To retain the services of the expert it wants, it has to hire the staff of a private firm everyone knows is a Rockefeller outfit, and it has to let them work at home besides.

It would thus seem the story would have a similar ending to the one on old-age pensions, but it didn't. Stewart recommended that unemployment compensation should be a national system, not a state-by-state one, to ensure adequate and uniform standards of taxation and benefits, and that employees should contribute to it as well as employers, to make higher benefit levels possible. This made the plan parallel to the old-age plan. But as might be expected by now, these recommendations generated enormous conflict, and the CES opted for a federal-state system and no contributions by employees. Just as Latimer and Brown had won for the Rockefeller network, Stewart lost.

But the preceding paragraph makes the outcome seem too cut-and-dried, and we have to determine why Stewart's plan lost, which has important theoretical implications. That is, there needs to be a lengthy discussion of what today seem like fairly small details. The process leading to the defeat had many twists and turns, and toward the end it seemed like Stewart might win out after all. Here is how the early stages of the battle unfolded:

1. September 26, 1934. Stewart gave his report to the Technical Board's Committee on Employment, headed by another of his colleagues from the Minnesota project, Alvin Hansen. Also serving on this committee were Edward Jensen, the executive secretary of the BAC; William Leiserson, whom we met earlier as a member of the SSRC's Committee on Unemployment, where he served with Stewart; Jacob Viner, an economist at the

University of Chicago and an adviser to the Department of Treasury; and Eliot, the young lawyer who annoyed Armstrong (and a strong believer in the Wisconsin approach).

2.   The committee was unanimous in its support of Stewart: the program should be national, both employers and employees should contribute, and contributions should be put in one pot, not kept separately, as in the AALL/Wisconsin incentive plan of past years (Witte 1963:112–13).

3.   Late September. The committee's recommendations then went to the executive committee of the Technical Board, where Altmeyer presided. The board made a very general statement of endorsement to the CES, but expressed worry about the constitutionality of a national-level system (p. 114). This worry planted the seed of doubt and unraveled Stewart's plan.

4.   October 1. The CES discussed the issue, but said it wanted more definite recommendations before it reached any conclusions.

5.   October 2 to November 9. General discussions brought in staff and Technical Board members from outside the group of people who had considered the issue up until then, including Armstrong and Brown, who weighed in on Stewart's side. There was increasing disagreement and acrimony on all the usual issues (pp. 114–15). However, one new idea did develop as a compromise on the federal versus state question: the federal government would collect the money, but return it to each state "subject to the state's compliance with standards to be prescribed by the federal government" (p. 115). This became known as the "subsidy" plan, even though there were no subsidies involved. It was seen as an acceptable fall-back position by Stewart, Murray, Armstrong, and Brown (p. 116) because it gave some assurance of federal standards.

6.   In early November the unemployment insurance committee of the Technical Board met again and completely reversed itself, now unanimously supporting the cooperative federal-state system favored by many Wisconsin experts, especially Witte. This plan differed from the subsidy approach in that states would collect the money and set their own tax levels and benefit payments. Questions of constitutionality and political viability seem to have influenced the committee (Schlabach 1969:118).

7.   November 9. The CES met with Hansen, Viner, Stewart, Altmeyer, and other experts to hear a debate on the issues. The CES members concluded that a fully national system was out of the question, but the issue of a subsidy plan versus the cooperative federal-state one was left somewhat open.

8.   Perkins immediately told Roosevelt the sentiment was primarily in favor of the federal-state system. Roosevelt liked that recommendation, and supported it in a speech on November 14, the same speech mentioned earlier in which he gave the impression that the old-age plan might not be included in the legislative package (Witte 1963:118–19).

This would seem to be the end of the matter, for the president had spoken, but Stewart and his colleagues would not accept the decision, to the great annoyance of Witte. The next day Stewart discussed the issue with a group of experts that he personally invited to an informal discussion. They voted 14 to 3 in favor of a national plan over a state-federal one (p. 121). Stewart also lobbied the businessmen on the Advisory Council, which was not hard because the IRC had been serving as consultants to the Business Advisory Council, to which three of the five (Teagle, Swope and Leeds) belonged. Stewart also had access to the nonbusinessman chair of the Advisory Council, Frank Graham, the president of the University of North Carolina, through a staff member mentioned earlier, Eveline Burns of Columbia. Burns knew Graham well in London after World War I, and was able to use their friendship to arrange a dinner at Graham's house where she, Stewart, and Armstrong lobbied him for a national plan (Burns 1966:44).

There then followed a battle within the Advisory Council, much to the consternation of Witte, Perkins and Roosevelt. The council heard directly from Stewart, Murray, and Armstrong, and even created a committee on unemployment insurance to draft its own proposal with the help of Stewart and Murray (Witte 1963:56–57), but the attempt went nowhere because the same divisions appeared. Finally, on December 9, the Advisory Council voted 9 to 7 in favor of the nationally oriented subsidy plan over the federal-state plan. Three liberals and the president of the AFL joined with the five business executives in supporting the subsidy plan. Voting in the opposition to a national plan were the representative from the Fraternal Order of Eagles, which had stumped for old-age pensions since the 1920s, the president of the Wisconsin Federation of Labor, and five people from charity and social work backgrounds who were not big supporters of the insurance crowd, including Grace Abbott. The key problem for the insurance crowd, obviously, was its inability to sway the social worker/charities crowd that Stewart and Givens first tried to co-opt at the SSRC conference in November 1933.

However, not too much should be made of the social work/charity opposition, although Perkins came from this network and worked with some of the women on the Advisory Council for several decades, because the CES agreed to reconsider the issue even before it received various reports from the Advisory Council, as well as a new report from the BAC to Roosevelt (written by Stewart) urging the subsidy plan (Schlabach 1969:140). The CES now decided on a federal system, but then changed back again (p. 125). As Perkins later explained:

> After long discussion we agreed to recommend a federal system. We went back and informed colleagues in our own Departments. Within the day, I had telephone calls from members of the Committee saying that perhaps we had

better meet again. There was grave doubt, our latest interviews with members of Congress had shown, that Congress would pass a law for a purely federal system. State jealousies and suspicions were involved. So we met again, and after three or four hours of debate we switched back to a federal-state system. (Perkins 1946:291–92)

In the end, then, Stewart lost on both a federal system and employee contributions.

According to Orloff, this story proves Stewart's ineffectiveness, even though he was a Rockefeller employee, and she and Parker (1990:306) say so with an exclamation point:

Yet what all this concern about who was on what payroll obscures is that Stewart was unable to get the plan he and the welfare capitalists on the Advisory Council favored incorporated in the bill! Note that the subsidy plan in favor of which Stewart and other expert members of the American Association for Social Security testified in 1935 is simply not the unemployment plan incorporated in the Social Security Act. Note also that the federal social security tax paid by employees went for old-age insurance; only employers were taxed for unemployment insurance under the tax-offset solution developed by the CES.

Contrary to Orloff, the Rockefeller network lost out on the specifics of unemployment insurance for reasons not given sufficient attention in earlier accounts. True enough, there was a Wisconsin influence, as I have agreed all along, and it was reinforced by the fear that a national-level law might be unconstitutional. However, I don't think the Wisconsin idea or the fear of a constitutional challenge would have won out if it had not been for another factor. The southern plantation owners bitterly opposed a national plan, even if it allowed for regional wage differences, because such a plan might give the federal government a way to help the African-American work force in the South. As Latimer wrote to a professor at the University of Virginia early in 1935:

Almost without exception, congressmen and Senators from the South indicated extreme skepticism of the wisdom of any legislation of a social character which would concentrate further power in Washington. Behind this feeling was obviously a fear that unsympathetic administrations in Washington would require southern states to pay Negroes a benefit which would be regarded locally as excessive. (Latimer 1935)

Following Latimer, I think southern worries are the "state jealousies and suspicions" Perkins (1946:291–92) was referring to when she explained why the CES rejected a federal plan the second time around. However, I am going to wait until I have discussed other evidence for the alleged powerlessness of business in general on social insurance before I present the argument and evidence for my southern emphasis.

In concluding this section on unemployment compensation, I want to point out that Orloff's emphasis on the defeat of Stewart on unemployment compensation undercuts her argument on old-age pensions. If she wants to claim Stewart of IRC lost on unemployment insurance, then she has to admit that Brown and Latimer won on old-age pensions, for the two situations are parallel. The victory of the Rockefeller network on old-age pensions is overwhelming evidence that the moderate conservatives from the heart of the corporate community, joining with liberals like Barbara Armstrong, had the lead role in creating and shaping the most important title in the Social Security Act.

Moreover, Orloff is wrong about more than just the Rockefeller network. I want to show how poorly she understands the rest of the business community before turning to the role of southern landlords as the major reason for the defeat of national unemployment compensation.

## WAS MOST BUSINESS OPPOSED?

Orloff claims there was huge business opposition to the Social Security Act, and it is true that manufacturer associations testified against it in January and February 1935. However, Harry I. Harriman, as president of the Chamber of Commerce, testified in favor of the bill even though offering some amendments, as did a representative of the National Retail Dry Goods Association (Witte 1963:88–90). As Altmeyer put it, "Employers' groups were divided in their attitude toward the proposed legislation" (1966:33). How, then, does Orloff develop her false impression of the attitudes of business as a whole toward the Social Security Act? In this section I will identify and analyze the variety of sources for her claims, including her questionable use of several sources and her lack of empirical information.

The first problem with Orloff's analysis is that she talks about information from the 1920s as if it were relevant to events following the depression and the election of Roosevelt. For example, she cites Louis Leotta's (1975) article, "Abraham Epstein and the Movement for Old Age Security," as evidence that even corporate moderates opposed pensions, giving the impression that the article reports on business groups (Orloff 1993:282). Except for passing mentions of the "opposition of State Chambers of Commerce" and "the hostility of business groups" (Leotta 1975:360, 365, 374), the entire article presents original research only on nonbusinessman Epstein's efforts in the 1920s to pass old-age legislation at both the state and national levels. The efforts had no success; the burden of the article is that agitation by Epstein and his group helped to create a favorable climate of opinion for later passage of the Social Security Act. It is an irrelevant citation in terms of business.

While putting forth her negative claims based on the 1920s, Orloff does not make any attempt to counter a contrary argument in the most detailed history of unemployment insurance, which says that AALL business leaders Ernest Draper, Morris Leeds, and Sam A. Lewisohn, two of whom ended up on the Advisory Council, traveled widely during the 1920s telling other businessmen about the virtues of unemployment insurance, and were taken seriously (Nelson 1969:43–47). Why, then, did nothing happen? Nelson points out there was no real pressure at the time from high unemployment, so businessmen decided to take a wait-and-see attitude. Drawing the opposite conclusion from Orloff, Nelson says it was not "extraordinary" that so few firms did anything, "but that any did anything at all" (p. 47).

Orloff's (Orloff and Parker 1990:307; Orloff 1993:292) next argument concerns a claim by Berkowitz and McQuaid (1978:132–33) that the drafters of the Social Security Act were following precedents drawn from corporate experience with their own pension systems. She calls this claim misleading and says the experience with pension plans in other countries was far more important. But she does not stop to ask what precedents seemed most important to the drafters themselves. Here Brown's testimony becomes relevant. In his oral history he explains the basic principles of the Act by the fact that Armstrong knew everything about the European experience, which fits with Orloff's point, and then adds "I had experience with company schemes and so had Latimer—that by contributory arrangements, we could provide these people with benefits as a matter of right," which does not fit with Orloff at all (Brown 1965:12). More generally, the whole thrust of this chapter, showing the great importance of the Rockefeller network in general and the IRC in particular, refutes Orloff's attempt to dismiss this kind of evidence for a business role in creating the American version of social security.

Within the context of their critique of Berkowitz and McQuaid, Orloff and Parker (1990:307) insist that business leaders wanted voluntary pension plans. Their citation is to Lubove (1968:132, 140). But Lubove is talking about the 1920s, not the 1930s. His footnote on page 132 is to a study by the National Industrial Conference Board in 1925. The discussion on page 140 concerns the reactionary National Civic Federation in 1923, and the Chairman of General Electric, Owen D. Young, in 1928. As noted in Chapter 2, I wrote long ago that the National Civic Federation was largely dead and irrelevant by 1918 (Domhoff 1970:168–69). As for Young, he did not oppose his younger colleague, Gerard Swope, when he called for compulsory pensions through the government in the 1930s. Conditions changed drastically between 1929 and 1933, and so did the businessmen when it came to pensions, humbled by the failures of their programs, educated by Brown, Latimer, Stewart, and the rest of the IRC staff.

As part of her claim that business leaders remained enamored of voluntary pensions, Orloff (1993:278–79), cites work by Latimer in 1932 as reporting that such plans were insecure. Calling Latimer a "Roosevelt official," she does not seem to realize Latimer's conclusion is a good indication of where the moderates in the corporate community were headed: to the kind of government pension plans Latimer helped to institute. Sure, Latimer probably had to explain the facts of life to some hesitant and hidebound executives, but that was his job. He was their employee, paid to advise them on pensions, and they took his advice. Latimer's book is therefore evidence for my theory, not a state autonomy one.

Orloff (and Parker 1990:306; Orloff 1993:292–93) holds to the mistaken notion that business opposed contributory programs, and lost on this issue to the state officials who wanted contributory plans. Like Roosevelt, business leaders in fact preferred a system based on contributions by business and employers, which they obtained on old-age insurance, as my analysis makes clear. More generally, many businessmen were reconciled to compulsory and contributory social insurance by early 1935. If it was not their favorite legislation, they knew it was cautious, as the press made clear when the plan was first released on January 17 (Schlabach 1969:134–35). However, the attitude of most businessmen toward the New Deal in general changed dramatically between February and May of that year, and the Social Security Act was caught up in the fervor. I think the real issue was the National Labor Relations Act, but Orloff tries to draw evidence for her specific claims from the general uproar.

The actual attitudes of business groups toward the Social Security Act can be seen in what they said before they launched their general political attack on Roosevelt. In December 1934, for example, the NAM convention was positive toward the idea of social insurance legislation (Jenkins and Brents 1989:900). In March 1935, the Chamber of Commerce's committee on the topic endorsed the administration's general proposal, then went one step further by favoring the subsidy plan (Nelson 1969:214).

## THE BUSINESS ADVISORY COUNCIL

Orloff paints the BAC as an organization riven with division due to disagreements on the Social Security Act. She says it "nearly broke up and did lose several of its members in the course of the drafting and congressional consideration of the law" (1993:296). "Key members," she claims, "already had resigned by mid-1934," and she names John Raskop of General Motors and Pierre DuPont of the DuPont Corporation as examples. She asserts that more resignations occurred in the spring and summer of 1935, shortly after Roosevelt allegedly inaccurately cited a BAC memo as evidence for its support for the Social Security Act. Three members supposedly resigned "immediately" and another three within two months (p. 296). But every one of these assertions is wrong to one degree or another.

First, the conflicts Orloff refers to were not primarily within the organization, but with Roosevelt over events in May and June 1935, which I will discuss in a moment. The biggest potential policy disagreement within the organization concerned support for majority rule in determining union representation in collective bargaining, but the BAC members on the National Labor Board who originally supported this provision did not dissent when the BAC harshly criticized Wagner's proposed legislation making majority rule a matter of law. As McQuaid (1982:46–47) recounts, the moderates now sided with the ultraconservatives on this issue or remained silent.

There is one sign of disagreement over social security in the BAC records at the National Archives. In October 1934, the organization printed a pamphlet for members in which several members expressed their opinions on a report on unemployment insurance presented by Teagle. Nine of the opinions were supportive, six were negative (BAC, 1934). However, a majority then voted to set up a committee to consider social legislation (Jenkins and Brents 1989:899).

Second, there is no evidence of resignations in protest from the BAC in mid-1934. Any resignations at that point were part of a normal rotation after one year of membership decided upon when the organization formed in 1933 (Swope 1934). Pierre DuPont's resignation was from the Industrial Advisory Board of the NRA to protest the direction in which labor relations seemed to be moving (Burk 1990:133–35). Indeed, he served on a BAC committee unanimously opposed to the National Labor Relations Act in May 1935, working with industrial relations experts from several companies in the Special Conference Committee (BAC, 1935). He did not leave the BAC until January 1936, although he was inactive in 1935 except for the antiunion committee (Burk 1990:189–90). As for Raskop, he served on a BAC committee on social legislation that made a report on relief policy in December 1934, then took an extended leave of absence in January 1935, when he went on a four-month world cruise in frustration over the New Deal (p. 169).

Third, the BAC did not come into conflict with Roosevelt over Social Security. Although the general body did disagree with its social legislation committee in May 1935 by suggesting delay on old-age pensions, its general report on social insurance was by far its most positive report of the spring. The real conflicts concerned Roosevelt's sudden emphatic support for the National Labor Relations Act, his unexpected call in mid-June for a new tax on the extremely wealthy, and his attack on the holding companies through which Wall Street financial interests controlled many public utilities around the country. These points were reported in the *New York Times* and *Business Week* at the time, but they are also summarized fairly well in Collins's (1981:59) work on the BAC and Burk's (1990:183–91) study of the DuPont interest group between 1925 and 1935.

Fourth, none of the six resignations in the summer of 1935 came "immediately" after Roosevelt announced BAC support for much of the social insurance program in early May 1935, nor did they concern his alleged mischaracterization of BAC views on that issue. The *New York Times's* (1935a, 1935b, 1935c, 1935d) accounts, for example, made clear that the support was "in general" and "in principle"; they also accurately state that the BAC was completely opposed to the National Labor Relations Act and supported a two-year extension of the NRA only if changes were made giving the government even less power over the corporations. In fact, the resignations of late June, early July, and early August were made in the face of the issues already mentioned as the sticking points: the labor act, the wealth tax, and the attack on holding companies (*Business Week* 1935a, 1935b). They came in the context of a call by ultra-conservatives for general resignations from the BAC that was not at all successful (Burk 1990:189).

The BAC and the corporate community are often portrayed as ineffective in 1934 and 1935 because legislation they opposed on stock exchange regulation, public utility regulation, the Federal Reserve System, and wealth taxes were passed, but I think these claims are overdrawn. The modifications made in these pieces of legislation in Congress suggest business was successful in removing the most stringent forms of regulation [e.g., Parrish (1970) on the regulation of stock exchanges and public utilities]. The Federal Reserve bill ended up acceptable to the American Banking Association, and the wealth tax had very little impact once it was eviscerated in Congress (e.g., Schlesinger 1960:300–1, 333–34). The biggest and most bitter defeat suffered by the BAC and other business organizations, as I have said several times, was the National Labor Relations Act. Social insurance legislation was a mild irritant for very conservative businessmen, not the divisive issue Orloff imagines. The BAC was not the driving force for social security, as this chapter shows, but it made a difference through its leaders, especially Swope and Teagle.

## THE ADVISORY COUNCIL

Orloff emphasizes the fact that the Advisory Council did not have a major role in the drafting of the legislation. She does so because she thinks "much" of the class dominance argument rests on the presence of business leaders on it (Orloff 1993:288–89). But she is wrong on several counts even though the Advisory Council did not have a central role in the proceedings.

1.    First, the case for class dominance on the Social Security Act hardly rests on the role of the Advisory Council, as this chapter has shown.

2.    Second, Roosevelt had consulted with one important member of it, Swope, before he formed the Committee on Economic Security. When Roosevelt said from the outset that his plan would be contributory, meaning no government funding, and would maximize federal-state cooperation, he was well within the bounds of what was acceptable to moderate businessmen like Swope.

3.    Third, Witte consulted with two future members of the Advisory Council, Swope and Teagle, before the studies began, so he was well aware of their thinking and of the fact they would be players in the process. However, these points are relatively minor within the context of the involvement of the general Rockefeller network in the process.

4.    The fourth and final point is not so minor. From Armstrong and Brown's standpoint, it will be recalled, the Advisory Council, and particularly the businessmen on it, played a major role in assuring that the old-age pension plan would stay in the legislation. They were convinced that Witte, Perkins, and Roosevelt were wavering on the issue, and they went to the businessmen for support. Evidence for their concerns can be found in Armstrong's (1965:82–83) oral history, but Brown (1972:21–22) said it well in his earlier-quoted comment about Teagle and the other business leaders saving the day for the plan.

Why would this business support for old-age pensions seem minor to Orloff? Because the Witte-Altmeyer-Wisconsin viewpoint has dominated the historiography on the Social Security Act, and she follows it uncritically, as her citations reveal. Witte denied there was lack of enthusiasm for the old-age pension plan, and Perkins denied it, too, meaning the fuss kicked up by members of the Rockefeller network supposedly was unnecessary (e.g. Schlabach 1969:110, 111). If we allow the testimony of Armstrong and Brown to be admitted into the record, then we can see that Orloff has downplayed the role of the Advisory Council too much, with her usual eagerness to give little or no weight to the influence of business leaders.

## THE CLARK AMENDMENT

A Philadelphia insurance man who did a brisk business in installing retirement programs for corporations, Walter Forster, became worried that the new law might hurt his business. He therefore invested considerable time and effort in lobbying for a simple amendment saying that any corporation that developed its own equivalent pension plan could be exempted from the statute ("contracting out," it was called). He convinced Bennett Champ Clark, the conservative Democratic Senator from Missouri, to introduce this amendment, and it became known as the Clark Amendment. The Senate passed it, but Roosevelt sent word it was unacceptable because it would make it impossible to determine how much the government would have to collect from employers and employees in the government program, among several problems. The Clark Amendment caused a two-month delay in the signing of the bill. The deadlock was broken in August when it was agreed that the amendment would be reconsidered the following year after experts had a chance to see if contracting out could be made compatible with the overall system.

I have explained this situation at length because Orloff claims, "Almost all of the welfare capitalists backed the Clark Amendment" (1993:293). Furthermore, she uses this instance as a basis for her more general claim that business leaders were still in favor of a voluntary approach in the 1930s: "[E]ven the business leaders most sympathetic to social reform were not enthusiastic about provisions for compulsory employee and employer financial contributions" (p. 180). The Clark Amendment may be the most important evidence she believes she has for what business was thinking and doing at the time.

Orloff's only sources for her claim are Altmeyer (1966:40–42) and Witte (1962:157–61). But these two sources are not supportive of her conclusion. The two pages in Altmeyer say nothing of any businessmen until a footnote at the end, which merely states that "employers and insurance companies" lost interest in the Clark Amendment and did not push for it the following year. Surely this loss of interest should have stirred Orloff's interest if the businessmen were so adamant for voluntarism. As for the Witte account, it only says that the insurance man Forster and two representatives of Equitable Life were the primary proponents, and that Forster "circularized all employers known to have industrial pension plans and urged them to demand an exemption" (Witte 1962:161). Witte goes on to write that Senators "then heard from home," but that is the extent of his analysis. Furthermore, he doubted whether "more than a half-dozen employers" had been interested in the amendment before the final push by Forster (1962:160). This is very thin evidence for Orloff's claim about "Almost all of the welfare capitalists."

In point of fact, there was very little interest in this amendment by welfare capitalists. It was seized upon by conservative Senators to hamstring the Social Security bill without seeming to oppose it in principle, as they in fact did. My evidence for the lack of business support for the Clark Amendment comes from the correspondence of Brown and Latimer, and a report by the Social Science Research Council.

There are three different statements on the issue in Brown and Latimer's papers. On February 13, 1935, well before the issue became visible, Brown wrote to Witte about his participation in the annual meetings of the American Management Association. After reporting that the executives were favorable to his presentation on the contributory old-age plan, he wrote that they were opposed to contracting out and that Forster "stands practically alone as an insurance broker" (Brown 1935a). He added that only two large insurance companies were in sympathy. Shortly thereafter, on February 23, Brown (1935b) reported to Witte that U.S. Steel, AT&T, DuPont, U.S. Rubber, Union Carbide, and Western Electric had no interest either. The inclusion of DuPont and U.S. Rubber on the list are especially interesting given the DuPont clan's general opposition to the New Deal in the name of voluntarism.

Brown also corresponded with Latimer on corporate interest in contracting out. While traveling in the West, he reported he had talked to "scores" of executives, but found "never even a wishful thought for the Clark Amendment" (Brown 1935c). In the fall he wrote Latimer a letter revealing the thinking at IRC:

> I was at the Counselors yesterday and the general feeling there is that Forster is foolish to keep pressing the Clark Amendment since any Company that studies costs would be entirely disinterested in contracting out. Have you seen the chart which Teuful [an IRC employee] worked out? He had it checked by the Equitable and every interpretation makes the figures more favorable to government protection. (Brown 1935d)

In addition to these letters from Brown, we have the results of a study commissioned by the SSRC's Committee on Social Security to determine the extent of corporate interest in the Clark Amendment. The author, Rainard Robbins (1936), reported that he could find only a few corporate executives who supported the Clark Amendment once they understood it.

Combining these reports with his own observations, Latimer wrote a report for the Social Security Board on March 23, 1936, on the Clark Amendment in which he said, among other things: "With the possible exception of Standard Oil Company of New York, I know of no industrialists favoring the Clark Amendment, if such amendment has all or most of the following features" (Latimer 1936:1). The memo then lists several basic features, such as being at least as favorable as the Social Security Act.

The conclusion was obvious to Brown, Latimer, and IRC: companies should put their old programs on top of the government's plan, making employment at the company all the more attractive. The corporate executives caught on fast, although some used it as an opportunity to shrink their plans (Quadagno 1988:118). Latimer's files show that as a continuing IRC employee he helped companies adjust their plans even while working for the government. Brown also helped out. On July 12, 1935, he wrote to Latimer that he "had an interesting time at the Counselors Wednesday discussing with Horlick [an IRC employee] and the others the possible means of adjusting company plans to the security bills" (Brown 1935e).

The foregoing evidence presents a considerable problem for Orloff's conclusion. Since Brown, Latimer, and the IRC opposed the Clark Amendment, and are representatives of very important welfare capitalists, and can name many such companies opposed to the amendment, it seems to follow that Orloff could not possibly be right when she concludes the amendment was supported by "almost all" such capitalists.

Despite considerable effort by Eliot and his team of experts to make the amendment compatible with the overall act, they were not happy with what they drafted. Not only were there actuarial problems, there would be difficulties in transferring records when privately contracted workers changed jobs, and in guaranteeing pensions if companies failed. Eliot recalled he was not looking forward to the second meeting with Forster and the Senate committee in 1936. Then he received word that the meeting was canceled. Forster had lost interest, or so a senator told Eliot: the new law actually stimulated his business (Eliot 1992:130–31).

I tell the story of the Clark Amendment in detail, of course, because I think it reveals the weaknesses in Orloff's evidence when she is talking about business or business involvement. Instead of doing new research on the issue to support her suppositions, she directs us to sources like Altmeyer and Witte even though they have little or nothing to say about her issue.

## WHO WON, WHO LOST, AND WHY?

Always remembering that the corporate leaders and their associated experts in the Rockefeller network were in support of the basic principles of the Social Security Act, I turn now to the details of who won and lost on various specific issues. According to Orloff and Parker (1990:306–9), business lost on two key issues: (1) employee contributions to unemployment insurance; (2) national-level control of unemployment insurance.

### Employee Contributions

As we have seen, most business leaders wanted employees to contribute to both old-age pensions and unemployment insurance. Lest readers assume this must be the conservative position, it should be stressed that some very independent liberal experts like Armstrong and Paul Douglas, an economist at the University of Chicago, and later the senator from Illinois, thought the smart thing was to have employees contribute to both so benefits could be higher. Although the original Wisconsin position was to oppose employer contributions, many of its adherents changed their minds. Thus, the most adamant opponent to the business plan on employee contributions turned out to be the AFL, which accepted employee contributions to pensions because aging is natural and inevitable, but opposed them for unemployment because it is supposedly the fault of business. So Orloff can chalk this one up as a loss for business at the hands of labor with an assist from social workers and some Wisconsinites, but it should be kept in mind that it was not a very wise victory for labor. Saying he agreed with the Business Advisory Council's position on the matter, Altmeyer regretted the CES decision to side with labor on this one:

> If employee contributions had been included in the 1935 bill, I believe that the adverse effect of employer rating ["incentives"] in keeping benefits low would have been far less. I also believe that the adversary character of existing state laws would have been avoided, as it has been under the old age, survivors', and disability insurance system. (1966:258)

So maybe we should say it was a Pyrrhic victory for labor.

## Federal Control

The disagreement among the drafters that has the most theoretical relevance today concerns the degree to which there would be federal control of old-age pensions and unemployment compensation. As we know, the Rockefeller network wanted the greatest possible federal control and the experts from Wisconsin wanted a federal-state system. Since the CES decided on less federal control on unemployment insurance despite the relentless lobbying by Stewart, Orloff claims business was not powerful on this issue, and that politicians and experts won the day.

Putting aside for the moment that the Wisconsin view is explicitly rooted in business principles and caters to the most conventional business views on states' rights, there are two pieces of evidence for the emphasis on politicians and experts. First, Wisconsin's two most important political leaders, Governor Philip LaFollette and Senator Robert LaFollette, Jr., lobbied Roosevelt for a system that would preserve the Wisconsin unemployment law, and Senator LaFollette might have been able to rally the support of several other Progressive Republicans in the Senate as well. Second, Witte felt very strongly on this issue; his biographer believes he exerted more influence on it than any other (Schlabach 1969:114ff.).

However, there is more to the Wisconsin group than experts and elected political figures. It had the backing of the Brandeis-Frankfurter network discussed earlier in the chapter. Brandeis and Frankfurter were wary of both big corporations and big government, and they sought ways to decentralize as much as possible. In fact, a new idea that made the state-federal plan even more attractive to Perkins and Roosevelt—called the *tax-offset plan*— was developed by Brandeis in 1933 and conveyed to his daughter and son-in-law. It called for the federal government to pass an unemployment tax on employers that could be offset (canceled, deducted) if the employer had to pay a similar tax to the state. In other words, the law was meant as an inducement to states to set up their own unemployment insurance statutes. The precedent for this approach was a 1926 Supreme Court decision up-holding a similar federal tax, this one on inheritance, passed so states with inheritance taxes would not be deprived of revenues by aged millionaires who moved to tax-free states in their declining years.

Those who were writing during the 1930s or in the early postwar years often downplayed Brandeis's policy role because it supposedly would not fit with the image of a Supreme Court justice [e.g., Perkins (1946) does not mention Brandeis at all]. However, later accounts, drawing on the oral histories provided by Elizabeth Brandeis and Paul Raushenbush, make clear that the tax offset idea came from Brandeis (Murphy 1982:165–75; Baker 1984:301–3). Moreover, Eliot says in his memoirs that the idea came from Brandeis, which helped convince him this approach was the best way to avoid a constitutional challenge. According to Eliot, Elizabeth Brandeis sold the idea to Perkins and Senator Robert Wagner for her father at a dinner party given by one of his old friends, Boston department store owner Lincoln Filene, at the home of his daughter:

> On New Year's Day, 1934, Mr. Filene was visiting his daughter, Mrs. Jouett Shouse, in Washington, DC, and "E. B.," as Mrs. Raushenbush was called, was visiting her parents, the Brandeises. Mr. Filene persuaded the Shouses to let him invite several people to dinner, including Secretary Perkins, Senator Wagner, and E. B., who explained how the tax-offset device would solve the problem. The others agreed, and said that a bill should be drafted accordingly. Wagner promised to introduce it in the Senate, and approved of Miss Perkins's suggestion that David J. Lewis of Maryland should introduce it in the House. Next morning the Secretary, full of enthusiasm, told [Charles] Wyzanski [a lawyer in the Department of Labor] what had transpired at the dinner. And this is where I re-enter the picture. (Eliot 1992:77)

Eliot and Raushenbush soon drafted the Wagner-Lewis Act, introduced a few months later, then withdrawn, because Roosevelt decided on the more comprehensive study leading to the Social Security Act. We also know that Brandeis's view on this issue was supported by Frankfurter, who conveyed his opinion to Witte in personal correspondence (Schlabach 1969:122). Witte also was hearing the same pitch from Eliot and Perkins, and Roosevelt was hearing it from Frankfurter and Corcoran.

From the other side of the fence, Armstrong (1965:58) firmly believed Brandeis and Frankfurter were the biggest influences on Eliot, Perkins, and Roosevelt on this issue; she reports that Frankfurter would not talk to her about the national view she espoused. Folsom (1970:18, 21, 29–30) also believed Brandeis had a role.

There is a small irony in this evidence for Brandeis's influence on the state-federal issue: he could not savor his victory because he was disappointed that the incentive system he and Commons favored, giving lower premiums to employers who did not lay off workers, did not have an equally prominent place in the CES plans. He even lobbied Witte directly on the issue (Murphy 1982:175; Baker 1984:303), but by then most participants in the drafting were unwilling to believe incentives mattered very much.

Given the stature of the Brandeis-Frankfurter network, and Roosevelt's respect for it, it is entirely conceivable to me that it could have been the tipping point on the federal-state issue. If so, this is hardly a victory for Wisconsin experts alone. Nor does a defeat by such formidable opposition suggest that the Rockefeller network is powerless.

Having said all this, I still want to contend that something more was going on: the power of the southern segment of the ruling class in Congress through the Democratic party. Southerners played a key part in helping Roosevelt win the nomination in 1932, and their control of most major committees in Congress (nine of fourteen in the Senate, twelve of seventeen in the House) made their support essential if Roosevelt's general legislative package was to pass. Always keeping in mind that the CES reconsidered the issue in December under lobbying pressure from Stewart, the BAC, and the Advisory Council, and that Perkins (1946:291–92) said political concerns about resistance from state-oriented legislators were the deciding factor, here is my evidence for resistance by southern employers as the critical factor in the final decision.

1.   Witte constantly expressed concern about the southern influence in Congress. For example, he claimed that the president of the University of North Carolina was named chair of the Advisory Committee "because it was thought that the South was the section of the country in which the social security program would have the greatest opposition" (Witte 1963:50). In January 1935 in a private letter to a friend, he said, "[O]ur hope for carrying the whole program is a strong stand by the President to coerce the southern Democrats into lying" (Schlabach 1969:146). Even after the program passed the House by a large majority in April, he wrote a letter saying he was fearful of "very strong opposition on the part of influential southern senators against

any action," and in May he wrote privately, in words similar to those I quoted from Latimer (1935) earlier, claiming that southern congressmen "feared that someone in Washington would dictate how much of a pension they should pay to the Negroes" (Schlabach 1969:146, 148).

2. According to Eliot (1992:88), southern Democrats were the major opposition to the plan. He recalls leaving the hearings with the following thoughts:

> I was glad that I'd so vehemently opposed the subsidy plan. I had done so in part because I thought the Court would strike it down; now I came to feel that its safe passage through Congress would have been problematical at best. (p. 111)

3. To the surprise and dismay of staff experts, the CES included virtually no federal standards for state unemployment compensation. Tax and benefit levels were entirely at the discretion of the states (Witte 1963:125). Since Brandeis and the cautious reformers from Wisconsin believed in setting minimum standards (Schlabach 1969:115), it follows that they were not the main concern of the CES in giving states carte blanche.

4. Senator Harry Byrd of Virginia, backed by other southerners, made sure there would be no federal standards even in managing old-age pensions when he removed a stipulation saying states must choose their pension administration by the merit system (Witte 1963:143–44). Since Witte considered this provision extremely important, its removal suggests that southerners were more important than Wisconsinites in giving as much control as possible to states (Schlabach 1969:149).

By contrast, Orloff claims this change by "Congress" shows "the resilience of the patronage system" (1993:274). Her citation on the issue is to Altmeyer (1966:35–36), who says nothing about patronage, but does make clear the southern influence on other changes made at the same time. Orloff's argument may have some reality, but it is best described as superficial. The basic concern was to eliminate any federal or bureaucratic interference with employer subjugation of African-Americans in the South. As Senator Fred Vinson of Kentucky told Altmeyer at the time, "No damned social workers are going to come into my state to tell our people whom they shall hire" (p. 36).

5. By the late 1980s Skocpol realized the Social Security Act would not have passed without the acquiescence of southern Democrats, and that southern Democrats were closely tied to southern plantation owners (1988:303). In a somewhat similar vein, Orloff almost concedes the power of southern employers on the act, but muffles her admission by speaking in terms of "southern lawmakers and other conservatives" (1993:294–95). Her even stronger statement talks about a states'-rights perspective rather than anything so materialistic and economic as a landowner or cotton planter:

In addition, they [Roosevelt and the CES] had to cope with the political exigen-
cies represented by the distribution of power within the Democratic Party,
which favored the representatives of conservative and states'-rights viewpoints
as much as or more than those of urban liberalism. In particular, the extraordinary political leverage of southern representatives in Congress, out of propor-
tion to the population and economic might of their states, was a fact that could
never be neglected as FDR and the CES formulated the bill. (p. 289)

But just who does Orloff think stands behind these representatives if not
plantation owners and other employers forever vigilant against any federal
interference in the superexploitation of African-American labor? Are they
not owners who put together land, labor, and capital to create a commodity
they sell on a market in an attempt to realize a profit? Did not V. O. Key
show long ago how closely southern "representatives" of that era were tied
to southern elites, when only a small percentage of white voters decided
elections? Is there really anyone who would deny that the Democratic party
in the South in the 1930s was the instrument of southern plantation and
business owners?

Once power elite control of the Democrats in the South is admitted,
Orloff's argument concerning the fight over unemployment compensation
collapses because it becomes apparent that the conflict is between northern
corporate moderates in the Rockefeller network and southern plantation
owners (cf. Quadagno 1988). And so, of course, does any claim about state
autonomy fall by the wayside.

## CONCLUSION

When we step back and look at the overall picture, we see old-age and
unemployment insurance provisions founded very explicitly on "business"
principles:

1.  benefits are tied to salary level, thus preserving the values established
    in the labor market;
2.  no government contributions;
3.  employee as well as employer contributions for old-age pensions;
4.  incentives to business to stabilize employment.

On the major issue of disagreement, the degree of federal control on
unemployment compensation, we see a battle between the corporate moderates of the Northeast and the southern landed elites, with the Brandeis-
Frankfurter network on the southerners' side on this one. To the degree that
the Rockefeller network was unsuccessful, it was because of this potent
southern-Brandeis coalition.

Put another way, the limits of the debate were set by rival segments of the ruling class. Middle-class experts, liberals, social workers, trade unions, and pressure groups for the elderly had little or nothing to do with the general shape of the legislation. Due to the disruption and militancy everyday people were beginning to generate, they certainly had something to do with the fact that there was some sort of Social Security Act, but I have not stressed this critical point here because it is accepted by all theorists (e.g., Orloff 1993:284–87). In particular, the efforts by the supporters of the Townsend movement were thought by many observers of the day, including Brown (1972:6–7, 56), to be a key factor in moving the legislation through Congress. But we also have seen that the act was designed as much to deal with labor-management problems as with the income needs of those who were elderly, disabled, or without jobs. In terms of the specifics of the act, the only victory for unions was the fact that employees did not have to contribute to unemployment insurance. It was a shortsighted and self-defeating victory because it limited the size of benefits, but it was a victory.

And where was the state in all this? It certainly had very little expertise of its own on the issues. The staff had to be drawn from the Rockefeller network, along with universities and non-Rockefeller think tanks. As for the Technical Board, most of its members had joined the state only in the past two years as part of Roosevelt's victory; they too came from think tanks and universities.

In other words, the state's purposes had to be carried out almost entirely by elected officials, which meant primarily the president, because most members of Congress had little understanding of the specific issues or the time or staff to draft complex legislation. So, the question is, to whom were these elected officials beholden? Well, yes, to the people for their votes, as most pluralists, state autonomy theorists, and American citizens would say. It was voters who replaced Hoover, who was wary of further federal involvement, with Roosevelt, who was willing to experiment in the face of impending disaster, despite initial impulses to cut government spending and a persistent desire to return to a balanced budget. But it is also the case that the choices offered to the voters had been shrunk to a very narrow range because of the overwhelming influence of northern and southern employers through campaign finance and other resources.

By the above line of reasoning I arrive at a point of agreement with state autonomy theorists concerning the importance of the political parties, but immediately diverge from them because of our differing emphasis on who controls the parties: voters or rival segments of the ruling class. Put differently, we agree that the parties bring together two different coalitions, but I believe both coalitions are controlled by owners who have far more in common with each other on economic and labor issues than they do with the voters in their respective coalitions. I think the emphasis on voters ignores the power structures within each party and the electoral rules creating a two-party system. At a time when there were few primaries and bosses ruled the political machines, the parties were corporate- and plantation-controlled at the top, leaving ordinary people with no place to go because there was no possibility of creating a viable third party that might represent their needs more fully. The critique of a voting emphasis is all the more powerful for the time period under discussion because African-Americans and poor whites in the South, a majority of the population, could not vote. The power of the southern segment of the ruling class through the Democratic party unquestionably skewed the two-party system as a whole.

I do not see how state autonomy theorists can squeeze out from under this argument until the middle 1960s, when African-Americans won the right to vote and party primaries gradually became more important throughout the country in selecting party nominees (i.e., when the potential for turning the Democratic party into a liberal-labor party developed). In other words, even a party-oriented emphasis for the 1930s, the period many state autonomy theorists are trying to explain, is necessarily an argument for class domination of the government. Stated more generally, the limits of the American welfare state, and of liberal-labor politics in general, were set until very recently by the interaction of the political economy of the South with the presidential/single-member-district method of electing public officials.

Industrial Mobilization and                        6
the Military in World War II _____


## INTRODUCTION

This chapter is the story of how a state autonomy theorist tried to claim the growth of the Pentagon during World War II as evidence for the theory even while overlooking all of the major studies relating to his thesis. But first I have to set the scene by describing the work escaping his attention.

The tale begins with the appearance in 1956 of C. Wright Mills's analysis of how the events of World War II reorganized and solidified the dominance of the United States by a *power elite*, which he defined as those who sit atop the major institutional hierarchies of the society. According to Mills, the "warlords of Washington" became part of the American power elite for the first time because the hot war of the early 1940s and the ensuing cold war brought the military as an institution to the same high level as the large corporations and the executive branch of the federal government [see Moskos (1974) and Gillam (1975) for the antecedents Mills drew from for this theory]. Such previously important institutions as the schools, churches, and Congress were now at a secondary level when it comes to power. The decline of small property owners and unions, along with the rise of the mass media, meant that the great majority of people were relatively powerless.

The overall picture was a stark one that called into question both pluralism and class analysis. In contrast to the shifting coalitions of interest groups portrayed by the pluralists, and the ever-evolving class conflict seen by the class dominance theorists, there was an interlocking institutional elite of corporate, rich, political directors, and warlords who shared advantaged social backgrounds and common bureaucratic experiences, and sometimes moved from one institutional realm to another. Below this small power elite there were disorganized masses, with not much in between. Mills's new claims, coming at a time when most Americans were basking in the victories of World War II and a reasonably healthy economy, generated a large amount of commentary in both the popular press and social science journals, mostly critical, but sometimes sympathetic on one or another aspect of his thesis. However, there was one subject all of his critics agreed on, whatever their theoretical orientation: he had overemphasized the independence and power of military leaders [see Domhoff and Ballard (1968) for a compilation of these critiques].

Moreover, the studies in the ten years following the appearance of Mills's provocative book provided no support for his claims of a "military ascendancy." When the sociologist with the overall perspective closest to that of Mills, Floyd Hunter, published his mid-1950s reputational study *Top Leadership, USA* (1959), only five former military leaders, counting President Dwight D. Eisenhower, were nominated as top leaders by his hundreds of informants. Similarly, sociologist Morris Janowitz (1960), in a book-length study of the military and its leaders, could find no evidence for any major postwar role for military leaders, nor for their ascendancy during the war itself. Detailed historical studies of important decisions during World War II by historian Barton Bernstein (1965, 1967), using interviews and archival materials, lent no support to the thesis. Nor did careful case studies of major defense decisions in the years after World War II (Hammond 1961; Huntington 1961).

My own studies supported Mills's critics. I was able to show that two of the five military leaders on Hunter's list of top leaders were from wealthy families or had been corporate employees before the war, and that the civilians appointed to run the Department of Defense were disproportionately from the upper class and corporate community. Reanalyzing one of the key episodes of the industrial mobilization seen by Mills as a turning point in the rise of the military, I concluded that the few military men involved in it had strong prewar connections to the upper class and corporate community (Domhoff 1967:115–26; 1968:257–59; 1970:137–39).

By the 1970s the idea of military leaders as equals to the corporate chieftains and top political appointees in the power elite seemed to be a dead issue. Moreover, studies of the Vietnam War showed that headstrong corporate and political leaders escalated the war, often against the advice of the military, and then decided to cut back on American troops in 1968, once again against the advice of top brass (e.g., Shoup and Minter 1977).

The few studies appearing in the 1970s on the power of the military came to conclusions similar to the earlier ones. Diana Roose (1975) used minutes from meetings of the Industrial Advisory Committee of the Department of Defense for the years 1962 to 1972 to show convincingly how the business leaders had their way on the nuts and bolts of military contracts, procurement policies, and methods for determining profit rates. Historian Paul Koistinen (1973:447) published original research on the role of labor during World War II, concluding that big business was the dominant partner in an "industrial-military" complex. A good summary of the literature supporting the case for corporate dominance during World War II (Feagin and Riddell 1990) did not find much new research on the issue after the mid-1970s.

Given this history, perhaps readers can imagine my surprise when I learned that Hooks (1985) had written a Ph.D. dissertation claiming the military establishment as new evidence for state autonomy theory. Surprise turned to shock when I read the dissertation and learned there was no mention of the arguments presented by Mills, nor of my counterarguments. Nor was there any reference to the essential work by Janowitz, Bernstein, Huntington, and Roose just cited. By the time Hooks's work appeared as a book in 1991, it had undergone a major rewrite and now included references to most of the literature I have cited, especially Mills, who is cast as a great, but flawed precursor of Hooks's thesis. Sadly, the explication of Mills is inaccurate and the contradictory studies made no dent in Hooks's earlier conclusions. He repeatedly portrays Mills as a classical elitist who puts too much emphasis on individuals, and at the outset even says that Mills's ideas need to be "restated in terms of institutions instead of elites" (1991:4).[1]

I hope my brief recounting of the literature finding no support for the independent power of the military will help readers to see why the rest of this chapter is so thorough and detailed in its refutation of Hooks's claims about the military as evidence for state autonomy theory. Before turning to a full challenge to Hooks's claims, however, it is necessary to state his thesis at greater length. Then it will be possible to focus on the validity of his claims by presenting a chronological account of what most authors have said about the events he purports to analyze. In the process I will show how a corporation-military coalition led by investment bankers, lawyers, and corporate executives controlled the industrial mobilization for the war by defeating the initiatives of the liberal-labor coalition that had solidified its place within the Democratic party by that time and taken on the label New Dealers, which is what I will sometimes call them in this chapter. To show the power of the corporate community and its military allies in terms of the three major indicators of power, I will demonstrate that business policies prevailed in the decisional arena, that corporate lawyers, executives, and investors were overrepresented in positions of authority in the alleged military bureaucracies, and that the large corporations benefited greatly from war contracts.

## THE HOOKS THESIS

The main concern of Hooks's theorizing is a dual one focused first on the effects of the war mobilization on the American state, and second on the effects of the increasingly powerful and insulated Pentagon on the postwar economy. He believes the American military gained significant independence and bureaucratic insulation because of the need for a large industrial mobilization for World War II. He claims the Pentagon became increasingly autonomous due to its "control over the sources of investment capital and the letting of procurement contracts" (Hooks 1991:5). In his view the Penta-

gon is a "self-sufficient autarky operating independently of most other federal agencies" (p. 6). The defense program is said to be "first and foremost an
exercise in industrial planning, with decision making lodged in the Pentagon" (p. 7). Speaking of the military officers themselves, he writes that "the
Pentagon's budgetary resources, power, and insulation, coupled with the
distinctive worldview among professional military officers, allowed them to
operate as 'relatively autonomous bureaucrats'" (p. 17).

In the aftermath of the war, the Pentagon allegedly was in a position to
have a large effect on aspects of the civilian economy due to its expertise
and control over resources. Hooks believes the Pentagon's role in the economy is evidence for planning by a state that is much stronger than most state
autonomy theorists realize.[2] True enough, it is not planning for the commercial success of large national corporations, but it is planning nonetheless
even though its purpose is not profit (p. 226). At the same time, Hooks
makes clear he does not believe the Pentagon's growth in power made all
private firms dependent upon it. He argues that large "monopoly-sector"
firms like General Motors, U. S. Steel, and General Electric actually increased their independence from government due to contracts during World
War II. It was small firms in industries like aircraft that became (1) dependent
upon the Pentagon and (2) the core of a postwar military-industrial complex
(pp. 126, 133, 135).

Although Hooks's main focus is on the industrial mobilization and its
aftermath, he also has claims to make about the legacy of the New Deal in
terms of state building in World War II. He argues that the growth of the
executive branch and the enlargement of the president's staff left a legacy of
agencies and policy tools that could be used in building the new national
security state. More exactly, the New Deal brought about "shifts in budget-
ing priorities, decision premises, and staffing tendencies" (p. 43). There was
a strengthening of the federal bureaucracy, greater influence on capital
markets, and a "new era in labor relations" (ibid.). Hooks believes this trend
toward autonomy in the New Deal was so strong that he disagrees with
those many historians who think the New Deal was stalled by 1938 because
of such factors as Roosevelt's attempt to pack the Supreme Court, the alienation of all-important southern Democratic leaders due to biracial organizing
in the South by the CIO, and the election of a significant number of Republicans to Congress. Contrary to this view, Hooks claims the essential point is
that New Deal executive agencies remained in place until Roosevelt turned
his attention to building a national security state (pp. 10–11, 49). Hooks
thinks the best demonstration of his point about the persistence of New Deal
agencies is to be found in the area of agricultural policy (pp. 70–72), which
should give those who have read Chapter 3 of this book an idea of how
seriously to take his analysis of the New Deal.

Most of the claims made by Hooks about the development of the state during the New Deal are peripheral to his main thesis concerning the effects of the industrial mobilization. He could be mostly wrong about the New Deal and still be right about the industrial mobilization and its aftermath. Granting his point that the growth in strength of presidential executive powers was important, I would nonetheless note that members of the Rockefeller network outlined in the previous chapter played the major role in this development, not state managers (Karl 1963; Fisher 1993). Moreover, the important government agencies for the war, the Reconstruction Finance Corporation and the War Production Board, were legacies of World War I. More exactly, the Reconstruction Finance Corporation was created by Hoover on the basis of the War Finance Corporation.

But even granting Hooks some of his precedents and legacies, his argument does not speak to the issue of autonomy. A bigger and more bureaucratic state is one thing, an autonomous state is another. Hooks, like other state autonomy theorists, in effect makes the implicit assumption that state capacity can be equated with autonomy, but that does not follow in an automatic fashion. Demonstrating a state has capacity does not spare state autonomy theorists the task they often avoid, establishing just who—capitalists, workers, experts, state managers, or some combination of these groups—controls given agencies of the state.

In summary, here are Hooks's main claims in the order and manner he presents them. He says he has "four hypotheses:"

**Hypothesis 1:**   Administrative advances and strategic policy tools forged by the New Deal were absorbed by and adapted to the nascent national security state during and after World War II (1991:5).

**Hypothesis 2:**   The federal government was able to guide the mobilization of the economy for World War II by virtue of its control over the sources of investment capital and the letting of procurement contracts (p. 5).

**Hypothesis 3:**   Monopoly-sector firms in civilian industries gained political and economic advantages in the World War II mobilization that increased their autonomy from the federal government in the postwar era (p. 6).

**Hypothesis 4:**   The World War II mobilization provided the material foundations for a vast postwar industrial planning effort centered in the Pentagon and devoted to national security goals. (p. 6)

I now turn to my critique of Hooks's claims. As noted, I will present it in the context of a chronological account of the industrial mobilization and its aftermath, starting with some of the legacies of World War I and the institutions and practices developed during the interwar years.

## THE BACKGROUND TO DEFENSE MOBILIZATION, 1920–1940

With Hooks's assumptions and claims clearly in mind, it is now possible to examine key events and decision-makers relating to defense mobilization during World War II, the period of the alleged military takeover of a significant portion of the economy. The story will be interspersed with a running commentary on the way Hooks interprets it. As one aspect of this commentary, I will argue that Hooks has misused texts in several cases by not characterizing accurately what they say on the pages he cites.

Everyone agrees, including Hooks (1991:76), that big business dominated the industrial mobilization during World War I through the War Industries Board. The success of the mobilization in terms of productivity and efficiency is probably far less than the ebullient businessmen later claimed, and it was far from an all-out mobilization, but the effort did give business, military, and government officials experience and legitimacy helpful to them in World War II. This was particularly the case for financier/speculator Bernard M. Baruch, chair of the War Industries Board and an adviser to the military and industry on industrial mobilization from then on, as well as a major contributor to Democratic politicians, including Roosevelt, as we already have seen in Chapters 3 and 4. However, many other businessmen and lawyers involved in the World War II effort were called upon because of their experience with the War Industries Board.

The first attempt to utilize some of the lessons of World War I was contained in the Defense Act of 1920, which placed the assistant secretary of war in charge of planning for any future mobilization. This position became a link between industry and the military. (When the War Department was reorganized in December 1940, the title of the person carrying out these responsibilities was changed to under secretary of war.) As a second step in preparing for any future war, an Army and Navy Munitions Board was created in 1922, putting the services in closer touch with some parts of the business community. Although it was not an important body until the war began, this board became a key interface between the military procurement bureaucracy and big business for a brief time during the early phases of the war, when a Wall Street investment banker, Ferdinand Eberstadt, became its chair (e.g., Millett 1954:202–6, 290–91). As a third outcome of the World War I experience, the War Department created an Army Industrial College in 1924, which was focused on preparing career military officers to deal with industrial mobilization. Businessmen were among the primary lecturers at this school, including Baruch (Schwarz 1981:335; Ohl 1985).

The army produced its first industrial mobilization plan in 1930. Baruch worked on the plan with Dwight D. Eisenhower, at the time an assistant to the army deputy to the assistant secretary of war. The plan was not comprehensive enough to satisfy Baruch, nor was it of great interest to most business leaders at a time when no major war seemed likely, but the point for now is the basis it provided for the business-military nexus that came into existence later. The mobilization plan was updated in 1933 and 1936, but serious organizational preparation for World War II did not begin until August 1939, when a new assistant secretary of war, corporate lawyer Louis Johnson, another confidant of Baruch's, asked Roosevelt for permission to create a mobilization advisory board.

The resulting War Resources Board (WRB) was a business-dominated group noteworthy primarily for the protest its membership caused in the liberal press. Chairing the War Resources Board was the chairman of U.S. Steel. The other members were a former chair of AT&T; the chair of Sears, Roebuck; a senior partner in Lehman Brothers; a director of General Motors; the now-familiar president of the Brookings Institution; and the president of the Massachusetts Institute of Technology. The board produced a report calling for the adoption of a mobilization structure much like that used in World War I, as suggested in the other Baruch-inspired mobilization plans produced by the War Department. In particular, the War Resources Board called for a czar with considerable independent power to oversee the economy and control production priorities.

Roosevelt buried the plan and dismissed the War Resources Board within six weeks of its creation for two reasons. First, he saw the mobilization plan as a direct challenge to his authority; he called it "a second government" (Schwarz 1981:361). Roosevelt wanted to keep as much direct control of the war effort in his own office as possible (Blum 1972). Only when the war started in late 1941 did he adopt a plan somewhat similar to that offered by the War Resources Board, and only in late 1942 did he delegate power over all war-related agencies to one person, Jimmy Byrnes. Second, the plan and the board were very upsetting to New Dealers. They were concerned that the "economic royalists" so recently criticized by Roosevelt would use the mobilization effort to strengthen their authority and roll back the New Deal.

When Roosevelt took his next overt step toward war mobilization in May 1940, it was through an Advisory Commission to the Council on National Defense. Unlike what we might expect from Hooks's emphasis on New Deal legacies, the president set up this body using a law passed in 1916. Known at the time as the Defense Council, this advisory group had eight members, each of whom gave Roosevelt advice in a specific area of the economy. The commission had no power as a body, and it did not vote on issues. This commission was more reflective of the Roosevelt coalition, but still dominated by corporate executives. Three top business leaders— Edward R. Stettinius of U. S. Steel, William Knudsen of General Motors, and Ralph Budd of the Chicago Burlington & Quincy Railroad—began the process of letting contracts and organizing raw materials and transportation.

Chester Davis, a name familiar due to his role in the AAA, gave advice in the area of agriculture. Labor leader Sidney Hillman of the CIO advised on labor issues. Harriett Elliott, a dean of women at the University of North Carolina, did the same on consumer issues, and Leon Henderson, the outspoken New Deal economist who made his mark in the NRA, was in charge of price stabilization.

The Defense Commission was not very effective due to its lack of leadership. Shortly after its creation, Roosevelt took a more concrete step toward mobilization when he appointed two prominent Republican businessmen to his cabinet. The first was Henry Stimson, a Wall Street corporate lawyer since the turn of the century who had served as secretary of war under Taft and secretary of state under Hoover. He in turn appointed Judge Robert Patterson, another Wall Street lawyer, as assistant secretary of war (within a few months his title was made under secretary of war). The second cabinet appointment was Chicago publisher Frank Knox as Secretary of the Navy; he had been the Republican's vice-presidential candidate in 1936. Knox in turn accepted as his under secretary a Wall Street investment banker from Dillon, Read, James Forrestal, recently working as an assistant to Roosevelt in the White House. These appointments made clear that Roosevelt was prepared to create a bipartisan government and make peace with Wall Street in order to prosecute a war.

The New Dealers and the corporate community continued to spar during the thirteen months between November 1940 and December 1941, when the United States entered the war. During that time the New Dealers were for a more intense mobilization effort; they were known as "all outers." Business was resistant to such an effort. It was enjoying the prosperity created by increased government spending, and it was not convinced war was a certainty. Its leaders expressed fears about creating an excess of industrial capacity. Business was mostly for "business as usual" (Stone 1942). Roosevelt, too, resisted pressures for a stronger mobilization organization because he did not want to be too far ahead of public opinion. However, he did tighten up the mobilization structure a bit in December 1940, when he replaced the amorphous Defense Commission with an Office of Production Management (OPM) that had Knudsen of General Motors as its director general and Hillman of the CIO as its associate director general. When that system did not prove workable, he overlaid the Office of Production Management with a Supply Priorities and Allocation Board (SPAB) to provide the OPM with direction. This board had Donald Nelson, a vice-president in charge of purchasing at Sears, Roebuck (who becomes prominent later in this story) as its executive director. Vice-president Henry Wallace was a member, along with Knudsen, Henderson, and Harry Hopkins, Roosevelt's right-hand man and former head of the Works Progress Administration.

Nelson, known as a protégé of Hopkins, was gradually gaining favor with New Dealers as a reasonable businessman (e.g., Schwarz 1981:375–76).

Hooks accepts much of the picture I have painted up to this point. He agrees that big industry and the military purchasing bureaucracies had a close relationship prior to World War II; that the Army Industrial College created bonds between businessmen and military officers; and that the army preferred to make purchases from big companies (Hooks 1991:75–78). He rightly notes that the conservative coalition in Congress heartily approved of the business/military coalition (pp. 88–92). But despite all this, Hooks believes the military became autonomous and insulated as the industrial mobilization continued. It is thus necessary to look closely at what supposedly changed in the next few years. When did the military become autonomous, and on what issues?

## CONTRACTS AND INVESTMENTS

As pointed out in the section on Hooks's thesis, he bases his claim of Pentagon autonomy in good part on the fact that during World War II the military had the power to give out procurement contracts and provide capital for new plants and equipment. That is, the state had control over "strategic resources" (1991:22–25). Hooks is thereby emphasizing that corporations needed the state, and therefore could be controlled by the state, but he never explores the other side of the coin, that the state had to do business with the corporations to manage the war effort. More broadly, he cannot seem to grasp theoretically that the businessmen wanted the state to survive and the state leaders believed in private enterprise.

Big corporations carried the following advantages into any conflict with the state over military production. First, they had the ability to do large-scale production, which the state did not. This is a fatal weakness for a state facing war. Second, the military wanted to work with big businesses, not with a myriad of small contractors whose reliability was uncertain. Third, a few large steel, aluminum, and auto companies had such a monopoly on machinery, resources, and skills, and such close ties to major banks, that most small businesses could not have been successful in war production even if they had tried. In reacting against the idea that America was controlled at that time by a few rich families like the Morgans, Rockefellers, Mellons, and DuPonts, it should not be forgotten that a relative handful of large companies did control most industries at the time [e.g., Lynch (1946) for a summary of the TNEC hearings of the 1930s on economic concentration]. In short, if Roosevelt expected to have tanks, airplanes, and other big weapons in a reasonable period of time, he was going to have to reach an accommodation with the big corporations, and he knew it (e.g., Catton 1948:29–30, 121; Blum 1976:118–19).

Hooks agrees that at the outset the businessmen were able to obtain legislation and rulings giving them the tax breaks and subsidized private investments they sought; he says that "the federal government's initial efforts at mobilizing for World War II conformed to the wishes of the business community" (1991:131). However, he discounts these victories for the business community because private financing was not heavily utilized as the war drew closer. He says there was a "surprisingly limited role" for private financing during the mobilization and that this "runs counter to the expectations" of a class dominance perspective (p. 131). Since he cites no class dominance theorists asserting anything about war financing, it would be more accurate to say these are his expectations, that is, a straw issue based on a narrow economism argued by no one. I know of no class dominance theorist who would expect that the state would be kept from financing war plant and equipment during a major war.

Nonetheless, Hooks believes business failed to achieve its goal of private financing of the war effort because it was not united enough to force the issue. That is, some of its members were hesitant. Reinforcing this hesitancy, says Hooks, were the efforts of New Dealers in planning agencies to block subsidy requests and contracts that "would enrich the nation's largest corporations but not promote the interests of the state" (p. 132). His favorite example concerns the efforts of lawyer Clifford Durr and his colleagues at the Reconstruction Finance Corporation (RFC) in early 1940 to create a type of contract that would give the federal government ownership of the defense plants it built. Hooks begins by emphasizing that New Deal lawyers had "accumulated seniority and clout in the RFC legal offices" (p. 136). According to Hooks, Durr objected to an arrangement proposed by his conservative boss, Houston magnate Jesse Jones, that would have allowed a war contractor to own the plant the government would build for it. Durr thought this a complete giveaway of government funds. He expressed his concerns to his counterparts at RFC and to members of Congress, and then drafted legislation that would create a Defense Plant Corporation (DPC) within the RFC. The DPC would build plants and lease them to war contractors. The bill "called for the creation of an RFC subsidiary devoted to financing the mobilization and urged federal ownership of production facilities," reports Hooks (p. 137). Strangely enough, however, the military opposed this important advance for the state, but the bill passed anyway. Hooks does not pause to tell us if military opposition to a bill proposed by other state officials is any problem for his theory (p. 137).

Now, Durr was indeed a liberal, although he was a somewhat atypical one in that he came to the RFC in 1933 as an upper-class southerner who attended Oxford as a Rhodes Scholar after graduation from the University of Alabama and then worked as a corporation lawyer in Montgomery, Milwaukee, and Birmingham for eleven years. What Durr had in common with other New Dealers was his training as a lawyer, his government position, and his growing conviction that business was opposing necessary reforms (Salmond 1990). It is also the case that he did collide with Jones over a specific contract, but even Hooks's own sources tell the story differently than he does.

First, the idea for a lease contract was put forth by Durr and accepted by Jones independently of the specific contract over which there was an argument (Salmond 1990:63). As Durr himself wrote, the job of convincing Jones "turned out to be somewhat less difficult than we had contemplated" (1952:294). Jones then testified before Congress in favor of the enabling legislation. At the same time as this general plan was about to pass Congress, Jones and Durr argued over a specific contract for the manufacture of airplane engines proposed by Knudsen of General Motors and the corporate lawyers who assisted him at the Defense Commission. They brought the contract to Jones and asked that it be "adopted as a standard procedure for the financing of all defense plants where government was required" (ibid.; cf. White 1980:20). Jones wanted to accept the contract, but Durr opposed it, and the majority on the RFC board sided with Durr. It is this defeat for Jones, which did annoy him, that is the kernel of truth in Hooks's account (Salmond 1990:65). With the RFC behind Durr on this one, the next stage of the battle pitted the New York corporate lawyers of the Defense Commission against Durr and his staff. Surprisingly, in terms of Hooks's account, it turns out that the aircraft engine contractor in question, and most other businessmen, came to like the lease arrangement for a wide variety of reasons. It was simple, kept banks out of the picture, had certain tax advantages, and insured that the corporations would not be criticized after the war for windfall profits (White 1980:24–33).

Still, Knudsen and his lawyers at the Defense Commission resisted in favor of their kind of contract, which would avoid government ownership and give a role to private banks. So the RFC lawyers and the Defense Commission lawyers had to go to high officials at the War Department to settle the issue. At first, Under Secretary of War Patterson angrily criticized the RFC contract, siding with the Defense Commission, but within a few minutes—a few minutes, mind you—he decided that the RFC contract made sense (Durr 1952:307–8). Soon there was a meeting of representatives of RFC, the War Department, and the Defense Commission. At this point Jones switched sides, at least temporarily: "Much to my delight," Durr reports (p. 308), "Mr. Jones backed me up completely." The upshot was that manufacturers could choose either the RFC lease contract or the Defense Commission contract, and most of them opted for the RFC contract (pp. 308–9).

Nor were most bankers very upset by all this. As Hooks himself reports, private lenders were "fearful of financing the expansion of emerging industries during World War II, especially in the case of those that would be heavily dependent on military sales in peacetime" (p. 132). Moreover, as Durr (p. 293) points out, the capital needs were massive, and therefore beyond what any one or few private banks could do in most instances. When four New York banks worked out an arrangement whereby they would organize consortiums of banks to take care of a given large contract, it turned out that other bankers were not interested in deals where the big New York banks would dominate. As White puts it, "Neither banks nor contractors could work up much enthusiasm for a plan that would place the New York giants in a favored position athwart the stream of defense financing" (1980:33).

It is hard to see how preference for government ownership of defense plants and for government financing by the RFC, the War Department, and manufacturers runs counter to a class dominance perspective, as Hooks claims. The capital needs were huge, the bankers were hesitant, and the manufacturers liked the government contract, even if it was thought up by a liberal corporate lawyer. As far as any alleged fears of government control were concerned, the contracts carefully specified that the companies that leased government plants would have the first option to buy them after the war and that the government could not use them for any postwar production in competition with private enterprise (Durr 1952:302; White 1980:10). There never was a chance in the world of the state's direct involvement in the private economy through industrial mobilization.

Finally, and again undermining his own arguments, Hooks reports that the New Dealers at the RFC who created the new contract were pushed aside, apparently in spite of their much-heralded seniority and clout. Jones still had the upper hand, bargaining with individual contractors and giving them what Durr saw as sweetheart deals within the context of the general DPC arrangement. Hooks rightly says that Durr himself "bitterly resigned from the DPC less than two months before Pearl Harbor" (1991:139). He watched the war as a commissioner at the Federal Communications Commission, where he took the liberal side for seven years before becoming a famous civil rights lawyer in his native Alabama. Meanwhile, most of the new defense plants of greatest value were leased to such giant corporations as DuPont, General Motors, U.S. Steel, Alcoa, Ford Motor, Bethlehem Steel, Chrysler, and General Electric (pp. 133, 135).

Hooks recognizes that this story appears to support a class dominance thesis. He therefore makes the following rhetorical concession before saving the day for his theory:

> On the face of it [the rhetorical concession] the pattern of lending between the DPC and monopoly-sector firms in civilian sectors conforms to the expectations of corporate liberal [class-dominance] theory: business leaders and their allies in the government successfully controlled the state's resources to further their interests. This pattern is striking in the case of Jesse Jones's personalized negotiations with the directors of major corporations. (p. 139)

Then comes the big "however" that smites the class dominance view:

> However, the DPC also contributed to the strength of the Pentagon and the emergence of a sizable state sector. The military procurement agencies—not the DPC and not private firms—had the authority to initiate industrial expansion. (p. 139)

Hooks goes on to explain the advantages of DPC leases to the military, but one wonders why he bothers if the DPC's role was as minor as the above quote suggests and if, as he then claims, the military "dominated" decision-making "regardless of the funding mechanism" (p. 140). One also wonders why military leaders seeking to build an autonomous state would have opposed such a useful leasing arrangement when it was first proposed (p. 137). Contrary to Hooks, I think White, the historian who has written the most about the issue, is right when he says the development of the DPC involved "a deep conflict between liberal New Dealers and conservative leaders in business and government over the scope and shape of DPC operations that abated only with the outbreak of war" (1980:viii). Put another way, what sense does it make to say the New Dealer's leasing plan was in the interest of the state when the major state actor in Hooks's scenario, the military, joined with businessmen at the Defense Commission in opposing the arrangement? Surely it is more reasonable to analyze the conflict as one within the state between New Dealers and the business-military coalition over how to manage the state's business. When Hooks says the New Dealers represent the real interests of the state, he is enshrining his own particular political or theoretical preferences as somehow inherent within the state. This will not be the last time Hooks resorts to such an equation.

After saying control of contracts is what matters, Hooks then discusses defense contracts for several more pages (pp. 143–46), concluding that the Pentagon indeed controlled them. Once again, however, there is a strong business involvement that must be shown to be an illusion:

> On the face of it [yes, again], the history of the administration of the procurement program provides strong support for the corporate liberal view. Dollar-a-year men in the planning agencies typically sided with the military in these

disputes [with the New Dealers]. They endorsed the military's control of procurement and frequently assisted the armed services' sabotage of contract
clearance procedures. (p. 146)

The apparent business-military alliance chronicled in this quote, and the
seeming power of business within that alliance, is beside the point, according to Hooks, because "the offices letting defense contracts were dominated
by military officers, not business executives"; besides, the contract program
"strengthened the Pentagon" (ibid.). So, it suddenly turns out that who runs
an agency is an important issue for Hooks. As for his point that the contracts
strengthened the Pentagon, this once again smuggles in the implicit assumption that strength equals autonomy, and avoids the issue alluded to in his
point about military officers dominating the contract offices: who controlled
the Pentagon?

In short, Hooks's account of contracts and investments during World War
II does not support his theoretical claims. There was a brief struggle within the
state between New Dealers and the business-military coalition. The New
Dealers may have scored a point with the DPC contract, although Durr (1952:
294) stresses they needed Jones to do so. The contract was then taken over by
conservatives and used for their own purposes. Nor did the contract keep the
large corporations from retaining any plants they wanted after the war or from
eliminating any potential competition from government-owned companies.

As for who received the contracts, the answer is big business. Hooks
(p. 149) summarizes the evidence showing that the 1.3 percent of industrials
accounting for 38.4 percent of civilian industrial output produced about 70
percent of all war materiel. A stunning 30 percent of the contracts went to
the top ten corporations and two-thirds of the contracts went to the top one
hundred corporations. Conversely, smaller businesses were underutilized.
Hooks says, "Smaller concerns frequently worked at less than full capacity
during the war because they could neither secure defense contracts nor the
authority to produce civilian goods" (ibid.). The net result of war contracts
was to strengthen big business and to reinforce market concentration. Many
smaller businesses became dependent upon subcontracts from large corporations in order to survive. It is thus safe to say that big business benefited in
an economic sense from the war, but I do not want to limit the benefits to the
corporate community to a narrow economism. The corporate community
also benefited in that the nation in which it is the dominant power group
prevailed over formidable military enemies.

## REORGANIZING THE WAR DEPARTMENT, 1941–1942

A major reorganization of the War Department took place in late 1941
and early 1942. The reorganization made the under secretary of war far

more of a policymaker and took him out of the direct line of running an office, grown to 879 civilians and 257 military officers by November 1941 (Millett 1954:20–21). The reorganization created a division first called Services of Supply (soon changed to Army Service Forces, the name I will use) responsible for the army's involvement in the industrial mobilization. For our purposes, the most important divisions of the Army Service Forces were procurement and ordnance, but it also included divisions for transportation, medical personnel, military prisons, and many other noncombat services.

Hooks explains the reorganization in terms of an alleged conflict between civilians and the military. He also personalizes the reorganization by saying it reflected the desire of the military officer in charge of the Army Service Forces, Brehon Somervell, to aggrandize his power. Hooks uses Millett (1954:29) as his source for claiming that "Somervell resented the authority of the civilian under secretary of war over economic affairs." (1991:96). This is an amazing assertion, for there is not the slightest hint of resentment or civilian-military conflict on the page Hooks cites. There is discussion of the need for reorganization, but not of resentment or any other personal motives.

In fact, the story of the reorganization is much more prosaic and mundane. Contrary to Hooks, who says "this change was initiated by insiders within the officer corps" (p. 96), it began with the fact that everyone connected with the office of the under secretary of defense, including the under secretary himself, knew there were organizational problems due to the rapid growth of the office and the size of the task that lay before the procurement agencies. In the summer of 1941, before Somervell was in charge of supply and procurement, Patterson hired the management consulting firm of Booz, Frey, Allen, and Hamilton to study the problem. Most of the recommendations in its report of December 20, 1941, were adopted (Millett 1954:28). Was this famous New York consulting firm, which did a similar study for the navy (Connery 1951:113), advocating a military takeover at the expense of its many business clients?

One of the problems identified in the report had not been resolved. It concerned "the relationship between the Under Secretary's office and the General Staff Supply Division (G-4)" (Millett 1954:28). Somervell, put in charge of G-4 on November 25, received permission from Stimson and Patterson to ask Wall Street lawyer Goldwaithe Dorr to make a study. Dorr was a close friend of both Stimson and Somervell. He had known Stimson since serving as Stimson's assistant in the attorney general's office in New York in 1906, and he came to know Somervell when they worked together on an economic survey of Turkey in 1934. He also was involved in the push for the NRA in 1933 as a lawyer for the cotton textile manufacturers (Himmelberg 1976:175–78, 187–89). Thanks to his many government connections, Dorr was named chair of a study group with the unwieldy working title of the Informal Group in Connection with Supply Reorganization in the

War Department. The other members of the Informal Group were as non-military as Dorr:

> Mr. Dorr became chairman of an informal group which at first consisted of Mr. Robert R. West, director of the Bureau of Industrial Research at the University of Virginia, and Dr. Luther Gulick, who had served on the President's Committee on Administrative Management in 1936 and was then a consultant to the National Resources Planning Board. Subsequently, the group included Brig. Gen. Arthur H. Carter, previously a senior partner in the accounting firm of Haskens and Sells and then director of the Administrative Branch in the Office of the Under Secretary, and James H. Graham, dean of the Engineering School of the University of Kentucky, who had been associated with General Somervell during World War I. An officer of General Somervell's staff, Lt. Col. Clinton F. Robinson, was the principal assistant to the informal group. (Millett 1954:29–30)

Dorr's group worked "in a 'hush-hush' atmosphere after regular working hours" (p. 30). Its discussions were kept "secret" (ibid.). Meanwhile, a regular army general, Joseph T. McNarney, was working on a reorganization plan at the request of General George Marshall, army chief of staff, but Dorr and Somervell did not think the plan went far enough (p. 32). McNarney then asked Somervell to draw up a plan for the supply side of the relationship (Ohl 1994:61).

Millett devotes five pages to the details of how the final arrangement was worked out. It is a complicated story. It includes the fact that Patterson wondered at one point whether Somervell was suitable to head the Army Service Forces given his grating personal style (1954:36). Although I will discuss Somervell and his career in depth in the next section of this chapter, the details of his particular role in these negotiations are not important for my purposes because the important point is this in terms of Hooks's major thesis: there is no evidence that military men were lined up against civilians in this policy discussion. The Dorr group, along with Somervell, received most of what it wanted, but this was not a military group and there is no sign of deep conflict. The real lesson is that there were genuine organizational problems difficult to solve in a huge and rapidly expanding operation that had to move very quickly. Hooks is far off base to reduce this problem to one of civilians versus the military.

Although the reorganization meant a military man, Somervell, was directly responsible for army procurement, he was hardly in charge of a military bureaucracy in the sense that regular commissioned officers dominated decision-making and carried out the bureaucratic operations. First, Patterson remained in charge in terms of overall decision-making; he and Somervell had adjoining offices to symbolize the closeness of their relationship (Millett 1954:174). Second, Somervell took many of the aforementioned civilians from Patterson's previously large operational staff into his agency (Millett 1954:38, 174; Smith 1959:112).

There seems to be nothing about the reorganization, then, that supports Hooks's theory. It is now time to look more closely at the military bureaucracies created in 1941 and 1942.

## CONTROL OF THE MILITARY BUREAUCRACY

Hooks returns numerous times to the idea of the Pentagon as a military bureaucracy controlled by military men. Indeed, this claim is one of the main underpinnings for his entire theory. He therefore repeatedly says that this bureaucracy is "insulated" and subordinates the civilians who are in it (e.g., 1991:31, 37, 126, 140, 164, 172, 263).

However, at one point Hooks (pp. 147–48) states there were many businessmen in uniform, too, which suggests that some of the military bureaucrats might be civilians for all intents and purposes. Still, he downplays their presence because (1) these businessmen "served under career officers" and (2) some of them were drawn from "less prestigious positions" (p. 148). Both of these arguments are false. The first argument opens him up to having to deal with the fact that the career officers of whom he speaks were serving under civilians like Stimson, Knox, Patterson, Forrestal, and other Ivy League lawyers and investment bankers (e.g., Blum 1976:120; Schwarz 1981:428). That is, if the businessmen in uniform can be dismissed as evidence for the quasi-business nature of these bureaucracies simply because they serve under career officers, why is it then possible to simply dismiss the fact that these career officers serve under Wall Street lawyers and investment bankers?

As to the second point, about the prestige of the positions from which the businessmen in uniform came, it is irrelevant and inaccurate. It is irrelevant because these men were put in uniform precisely because of their positions in specific corporations or their contacts in the business world. It is inaccurate because many of these men were in fact from highly prestigious positions. Knudsen of General Motors, for example, became a lieutenant general and served as a special adviser to Patterson on production problems.

Hooks is also inaccurate on this issue because he once again misuses a source. He says, "Even in the navy, where civilian control was more effective, military bureaucrats harnessed the skills of businessmen without losing control of their agencies" (p. 148). His citation is to Hammond (1961:157–58), but those pages argue just the opposite, which should have been apparent because they are part of a discussion subtitled "The Basis for Civilian Control" (p. 156). Most of page 157 is about centralized control within the context of a decentralized bureau system. The only sentence dealing with civilian versus military control during the war says: "The key to Forrestal's control was the independence of the legal and business technicians assigned to the bureaus" (ibid.). This independence, in turn, was said to be "due largely to temporary conditions." These legal and business technicians were not making a career of the military, so they did not fear a showdown with a bureau chief, and they knew they could go right to Forrestal. As for the eleven lines on page 158 closing out the chapter, they merely say that the wartime organization leading to civilian control might not work "under other conditions or in the long run."

To give further flesh to my general arguments about civilian dominance, let us look more closely at the Army Service Forces (ASF) headed by Somervell. It employed 1,022,074 civilians at its peak on June 30, 1943; this was 75 percent of all civilians employed by the War Department within the continental United States (Smith 1959:112). Thirty-two thousand of these people were employed in the command's headquarters. It still can be argued, of course, that these civilians were under the command of military officers, but when we turn to the part of the Army Service Forces of greatest moment to Hooks's thesis, the procurement division, we see that its military officers were overwhelmingly businessmen in uniform. The authorized army history by Millett (1954:290) claims that 96 percent of all officers in army and air force procurement "had been recruited from civilian life." Millett (p. 370) later lists the major corporate positions held by key members of General Lucius Clay's staff in the army procurement bureaucracy. They seem prestigious enough to me to cast doubt on Hooks's claim that the businessmen in uniform often came from less prestigious positions:

> When Clay went to the Office of War Mobilization and Reconversion in the autumn of 1944, his successor was Mr. Howard Bruce, Baltimore businessman and chairman of the board of the Worthington Pump Company. Mr. Bruce had been a leading figure in the ASF since the beginning, one of a number of businessmen brought in by General Somervell. Other prominent staff officers on procurement matters were Maj. Gen. W. H. Harrison, formerly vice-president of the American Telephone and Telegraph Company; Brig. Gen. Frank R. Denton, a Pittsburgh businessman; Brig. Gen. A. J. Browning, formerly president of the United Wall Paper Factories, Inc.; Col. Fred C. Foy, of a large New York advertising firm; Mr. W. C. Marbury, a prominent Baltimore lawyer; Mr. Joseph M. Dodge, president of a Detroit bank; and Col. Maurice Hirsch, prominent Houston lawyer. (ibid.)

Once the contracts were set by the procurement division, supervision and delivery of the war materiel were turned over to the ASF's ordnance division, honeycombed with businessmen. This agency has been chronicled by its chief, Lt. Gen. Levin H. Campbell, Jr., in a book he titles, significantly enough for my thesis, *The Industry-Ordnance Team* (1946). He begins with the fact that he had a personal advisory staff of four businessmen: Bernard M. Baruch, investor; Lewis H. Brown, president, Johns-Manville Corporation; Benjamin F. Fairless, CEO, U. S. Steel; K. T. Keller, president, Chrysler Corporation (pp. 3–4).

Campbell (p. 9) reports that he met with one or more of these men twenty-three times in 1942, twenty-nine times in 1943, and eighteen times in 1944. He also reports the size of his "military bureaucracy." He had "only 350 Regular Army Ordnance officers"; seventy-five of them had less than three years of experience (p. 5). Since the Regular Army Ordnance officers he started with soon had to concern themselves with training the ordnance personnel to go overseas with combat divisions, they had to be replaced by "trained industrialists and former officers" on the home front (p. 54). By V-J day, only 10 percent of the total ordnance personnel in the United States were Regular Army officers (ibid.). There were also local advisory councils that were predominantly businessmen; the title of Chapter 8 is "Industry Integration Committees." More generally, Campbell gives numerous examples of deep business involvement in his agency.

So far I have been stressing the ways businessmen are integrated into the military, but there is another aspect to this integration: individual military men, especially those in the Corps of Engineers, were often integrated into the upper class and corporate community through family and/or work. This point is best seen with the two military men who figure most prominently in all accounts of the industrial mobilization: Brehon Somervell and Lucius Clay. Both were from the upper levels of society, and both had significant organizational experience with business leaders and politicians because they were officers in the Corps of Engineers.

In fact, the Corp of Engineers is primarily a small contracting bureau that in effect spent most of its time in the 1920s and 1930s administering public works projects for the government. As Hooks rightly says, the Corps "nurtured powerful private-sector allies among contractors and subcontractors" (1991:78), especially in the South. In my terms, the Corps of Engineers was part of the "growth machine" at the state and local levels, helping "place entrepreneurs" prepare the land for manufacturers and retailers (Molotch 1976, 1979; Logan and Molotch 1987). But in the 1930s the Corps was far more than an adjunct to local growth machines; its officers helped run the Civilian Conservation Corps and Works Project Administration for Roosevelt, and in that capacity they were very close to his administration, as we will now see by turning to the life stories of Somervell and Clay.

Somervell was from an upper-class southern family. His paternal grandfather was a wealthy planter-politician, his father a physician. His mother's family is described by his biographer as "equally prominent" (Ohl 1994:9). When Somervell was fourteen, his parents moved from Arkansas to Washington, D.C., where they founded Belcourt Seminary, soon a prominent private school in the area. Once Somervell expressed an interest in a military career, his parents were able to secure him an appointment to West Point through an Arkansas congressman. The above information is what is meant by the term "social capital" (i.e., connections).

By all accounts, Somervell was arrogant, abrasive, and ambitious. Few of his fellow officers liked him, but the civilians he often worked for appreciated the fact that he finished assignments quickly. The first of these civilian sponsors was a New York railroad and cotton textile lawyer, Walker D. Hines, who, like Somervell, was originally from the South. Somervell served as his aide when Hines was assigned in 1920 by President Woodrow Wilson to arbitrate conflicts concerning riverboat shipping in Central Europe (Ohl 1994:14). After two years in the office of the Chief of Engineers in Washington and then further training at a select army school, Somervell's next good break was a second tour of duty in Europe as an aide to Hines. This time he did a special survey of navigational conditions on the Danube and Rhine rivers. From 1926 to 1930, Somervell served as the Corps's district engineer in Washington, where he oversaw a civilian staff, met with government officials, and negotiated with the contractors who did the actual digging and building. Then he worked in Mississippi and Tennessee on flood control. The point I am making, of course, is that Somervell's career does not fit our everyday image of a military officer.

Once again, in 1933, Somervell went to work for Hines, this time on an economic survey of Turkey that took him out of the country for a year. Unfortunately, Hines died just as the project was about to be completed, to be replaced by one of his law partners, the aforementioned Goldthwaite Dorr. Nothing came from the report, but Somervell gained a useful contact in Dorr, as we already have seen.

After losing out on an assignment he wanted in Washington, we next find Somervell in late 1935 and early 1936 building a canal across northern Florida, using relief money meant to fight the depression. When asked what his hurry was, he replied, "We've got to clean up the relief rolls; that's the hurry" (p. 24). Actually, he also was trying to outrun opposition from growers and railroaders, but the canal was stopped. However, Somervell had shown once again that he could manage a project, so he was put in charge of one of the Works Progress Administration's largest and most difficult districts, New York City, employing over two hundred thousand workers.

Somervell was chosen for this job by the director of the WPA, Hopkins, a well-known liberal and former social worker very close to Roosevelt. This selection, Somervell's biographer points out, "was part of a large pattern of bringing army engineers into the New Deal relief program" (p. 26). Hopkins needed experienced administrators who knew engineering and could handle public money, and the army needed good assignments for its overly large office corps. So a deal was struck, an important one in terms of why military officers later had such good access to Roosevelt and his aides. In effect, these officers were part of the work-relief machine put together by the New Dealers to soak up some of the huge unemployment that continued until war spending began.

From the politicians' point of view, Somervell did an excellent job in his four trying years at the New York WPA, taking all the heat for the firing and rehiring of workers caused by the constant changes in their relief policies (pp. 29–30). Somervell learned how to deal with unions as well. Small wonder that after World War II he was tapped by the Mellon family to run their Koppers Company from 1946 to 1954. More immediately, his construction work in New York, and in particular La Guardia Airport, caught the eye of Army Chief of Staff George Marshall, who earlier had worked for the New Deal organizing camps for the Civilian Conservation Corps (Schlesinger 1958:339). When it came time to build the supply services that Somervell eventually would head, he first was brought to Washington to a position where Secretary of War Henry L. Stimson could "get a look at him without Somervell being aware of this" (Ohl 1994:38). Once again we see how corporate lawyers and business executives select the army leadership that best suits them.

With a good word from Hopkins, Somervell was placed in charge of the army's Construction Division, where he replaced a career officer who had disregarded the advice of a New York City engineer serving as a special assistant to Under Secretary of War Patterson (pp. 39–40). His immediate superior in the military gave him "practically a blank check to run the division" because he knew Somervell was supported by Stimson and Marshall, and had "direct access to the White House" through Hopkins (p. 40). Even if Hooks were right about Somervell pushing aside Patterson, which he is not, the story of Somervell's power is hardly one that suggests a military ascendancy. He already was part of the White House network; according to Ohl's (p. 40) later interviews with Somervell's peers, everyone knew it. Nor would it be bad to have a southern gentleman testifying to a southern-dominated Congress on appropriations for supplies.

On the other hand, many regular officers were surprised and annoyed when Somervell was put in charge of the Army Supply Services within a year of his recall to Washington. For Millett he was an unexpected choice because he was "relatively young and unknown in Army circles" (1954:6). Millett does not provide any details on this unusual choice for a key position, but Lucius Clay's biographer, Jean Edward Smith (1990:111–15), says Hopkins recommended Somervell to Army Chief of Staff George Marshall. So much for Somervell's military autonomy.

As for Clay, he too was from the southern segment of the ruling class. His father was a three-term Senator from Georgia when Clay was growing up, giving the younger Clay many connections in Washington when he arrived there in 1932, twenty-two years after his father's death. Like Somervell, Clay graduated from West Point and joined the Corps of Engineers. He married a northern woman from a wealthy business family. Once assigned to Washington, he became a liaison with southern Democrats, especially with a house leader, Sam Rayburn of Texas. Clay also helped Hopkins create the Works Progress Administration, then sided with Hopkins when he feuded with Secretary of Interior Harold Ickes over New Deal relief programs (p. 3). Like Somervell, he became a corporate executive after the war, serving as CEO for Continental Can in the 1950s. He is one of the five former military leaders on Hunter's list of top leaders for the 1950s.

With his strong emphasis on institutions, Hooks makes no use of biographical information on family backgrounds, friendships, and business contacts. But I believe these social networks, when rooted in institutional and career frameworks, do count for something. As Mills liked to say, sociology exists at the intersection of biography and history. In this instance, the biographical information helps account for why the military seemed to win out over the civilians at the War Production Board, which Hooks sees as evidence for military autonomy. At the very least, the following argument by Smith deserves some consideration by those who make what he calls a "simple military-civilian dichotomy":

> From General Marshall down, the Army's high command had worked with the New Deal, trusted it—and in turn were trusted by it. Hopkins recommended Marshall to FDR, just as he recommended Somervell to Marshall, and he had known Clay since the very beginning of the WPA. All three were as much a part of Roosevelt's political team as Morgenthau and Hopkins. In the later squabbles the Army had with Donald Nelson and the War Production Board, the simple military-civilian dichotomy does not fit. For the fact was that Marshall, Somervell, and Clay were usually closer to the White House, and certainly closer to Hopkins and Morgenthau, than Nelson and the WPB. (p. 115)

For all intents and purposes, the biographies of Somervell and Clay obliterate Hooks's superficial argument about the civilian-military distinction, but there is more to come. So now we leave the Pentagon for the War Production Board, where Hooks lodges the civilian side of his false dichotomy. There we will see that the big businessmen in that agency were often fighting the New Dealers within it, and were often in cahoots with the businessmen and military officers over at the Pentagon.

## THE WAR PRODUCTION BOARD

Once the United States entered the war, there were dramatic changes in business and New Dealer attitudes toward industrial mobilization. Now big business wanted a total mobilization with full controls on the economy. It wanted very little business as usual. It wanted to freeze everything as it was at that time for the duration of the war; stabilization was its creed. The New Dealers, on the other hand, wanted war production and as much civilian production as possible. They were for guns *and* butter, and believed both were possible. They now feared cartelization by big business and a rollback of the New Deal. They wanted to battle business and fight the war, while big business worried (rightly it turned out) that the New Dealers would try to expand government involvement in all aspects of the economy (e.g., Schwarz 1981:377, 387, 401–2).

In January 1942, Roosevelt announced the creation of a War Production Board (WPB) to replace the Office of Production Management and the Supply Locations and Priority Board as the structure to organize the wartime economy. It would have the authority the previous agencies lacked. Nelson from Sears, Roebuck was put in charge. He had an advisory board that included Under Secretary of War Patterson and Under Secretary of the Navy Forrestal, but it was only a sounding board. His decisions were final at the WPB. The creation of the WPB and the appointment of Nelson seemed to be the final link in the business-military-conservative coalition power structure that ran the war, but it was not, as we will soon see.

Under the new arrangements, New Dealers were frozen out or pushed to the fringes. However, they were able to do battle from several outposts:

1.   Within the War Production Board, there were liberals on the Planning Committee that advised Nelson and in the Office of Public Information, where liberal journalist Bruce Catton (1948) was in charge and reported to Nelson. New Dealers also had a voice through the chairman of the Small War Plants Commission within the WPB. A CIO official and an AFL official were among the several vice-chairmen under Nelson. None of these positions was one of great influence, but those occupying them did have an official status, and they did have access to liberals in Congress and to the mass media.

2.   The Office of Price Administration (OPA) was in good part a liberal stronghold. It was chaired at first by New Deal economist Henderson, who had been part of the original Defense Commission, but he soon was forced out by conservatives (Catton 1948:189).

3.   Although the conservative coalition was dominant within Congress during the war, there were one or two committees in the House and Senate where the liberal Democrats were sympathetic to the New Dealers at WPB and OPA. These committees often investigated the complaints and claims of the New Dealers. In particular, the liberals on Nelson's staff had a direct pipeline to Senator Harry S. Truman's Special Senate Committee to Investigate the National Defense Program.

For the most part, the business-military-conservative coalition was in complete charge of the industrial mobilization. However, the presence of Nelson as chair of the WPB made things more complex, controversial, and seemingly tenuous, for he developed more sympathies for the New Deal than most corporate leaders. He was thus open to discussing some New Deal initiatives. At the same time, he knew the ins and outs of purchasing as well as anyone in the corporate community, and at the outset was acceptable to fellow businessmen.

Nelson's position between the New Dealers and big business was made even more difficult by his personal and administrative weaknesses. He procrastinated, changed his mind, and appeared weak. He went out on the town, and was known as a drinker and womanizer in some quarters (e.g., Smith 1990:145). New Dealers themselves had their doubts about Nelson's suitability as early as 1941; Schwarz (1981:429) speaks for many sources when he says these doubts "abounded." Still, New Dealers decided it was better to support a known quantity somewhat friendly to them rather than risk an unknown business leader as chair of WPB. Unfortunately for them, Nelson did not do a good job. He "alienated his doubters and disappointed many of his friends" (ibid.). In other words, the battles between the New Dealers and the corporate community were complicated by Nelson's personal failings and his inability to make difficult decisions.

To the consternation of his New Deal friends, one of Nelson's first major decisions was to leave the power of procurement within the purview of the military departments. That is, he sided with the business-military coalition on an issue regarded as crucial by the liberals, arguing it would take too long to build an alternative civilian organization. Nelson also insisted that dollar-a-year executives working for the government while being paid full salary and benefits by their home corporations were essential to the functioning of his operation, again to the great disappointment of the New Dealers (U.S. Bureau of the Budget 1946:107; Catton 1948:115ff.).

Hooks discusses Nelson's decision to delegate procurement authority to the military in the overblown context of a complete battle between civilians and the military. He frames his discussion with the claim that "the WPB failed to tame the insulated and well-financed military bureaucracies" (1991:104), but later he rightly says Nelson delegated this authority because he believed it was the best thing to do (p. 145). Moreover, the decision did not mean regular military officers were in immediate charge of the ordering. That task went to Eberstadt, the Wall Street investment banker, as chairman of the Army and Navy Munitions Board. Starting out as a Wall Street lawyer in the 1920s, Eberstadt became a specialist in corporate mergers for Dillon, Read, where he worked with Forrestal, and later started his own company. At the Army and Navy Munitions Board he "coordinated procurement among the services, securing raw materials for munitions, and advocating military requirements before the WPB" (Schwarz 1981:432). It was

Eberstadt and his staff who did battle with the New Dealers at the War Production Board over the division of materials and manpower, with Eberstadt invariably opposing the "expansionist" desires of the New Dealers. While some New Dealers liked to claim that Somervell dominated Eberstadt, Schwarz concludes from his careful examination of archival records and the papers of several of the participants that the civilians controlled the military, at least on this score:

> Some liberals often assumed that Eberstadt's "Prussianism" ran interference for Somervell. Actually, however, because Eberstadt followed Baruch's mobilization scheme with its defined supremacy for civilian industrial leadership, he prevented the army from running amok. Somervell's quest for an inordinate amount of power encouraged the illusion of a civilian-military conflict, but the bull never got into the china shop. (ibid.)

The liberals and experts within the WPB urged Nelson to reclaim some of his delegated authority from the Pentagon, but he was unwilling and/or unable to do so. From this Hooks (1991:107) concludes that business did not control the mobilization. Further, Hooks claims this shows "business executives are rarely unified and rarely do they possess a shared vision for society" (ibid.). He then cites Skocpol (1980) with approval as the source of this general critique of class dominance theory, but I think I have shown throughout this book that Skocpol and Hooks are wrong on this score.

Whatever the unity of the corporate community during the New Deal, it was very united on the key issues related to the mobilization, and it worked very closely with the military in opposition to the New Dealers. The corporate community knew what it wanted, and it knew it preferred to have more decisions made at the Pentagon if there were going to be problems elsewhere with New Dealers. Hooks fully understands this conflict between big business and the New Dealers, but he does not see its connection to decision making at the Pentagon (1991:143, 165, 169) because he is blind to corporate control there (Stimson, Patterson, Forrestal, Eberstadt, etc.).

New Dealers, quite naturally, were dismayed by the defeats they were suffering. They decided their best strategy was to call these setbacks a military or Pentagon takeover. Two members of Congress introduced a bill to create an Office of War Mobilization to replace the WPB and "restore" civilian control. Hooks then accepts this liberal ploy as a statement of reality when he writes: "To salvage civilian control, liberal congressmen Kilgore and Pepper introduced a bill calling for the creation of an Office of War Mobilization" (p. 107). But the issue was not civilian control. It was corporate and military control versus New Deal control. Hooks has uncritically accepted liberal rhetoric as history, legitimizing claims about military control that are untrue.

Concerned that the passage of the Kilgore-Pepper bill might limit his flexibility, Roosevelt reacted to this liberal initiative by issuing an executive order on May 27, 1943, creating an Office of War Mobilization (OWM). According to Somers, "he gave its director authority over virtually all domestic phases of the wartime government" (1950:1). Sixteen months later, in October 1944, "Congress reaffirmed and extended these powers in an act which rechristened the agency, The Office of War Mobilization and Reconversion (OWMR)" (ibid.). Roosevelt put Byrnes, whom he had appointed to the Supreme Court in 1941, in charge of the agency. This appointment symbolized the further marginalization of New Dealers, not the reassertion of civilian control over the military, because Byrnes was very close to the corporate community through his long friendship with Baruch and many other businessmen, and had been a leader of the southern Democrats in Congress. He was respected and trusted by military leaders.

In actuality, Roosevelt had given Byrnes a central role in the White House only a few days after the war started. Although Byrnes stayed on the Supreme Court until October 1942, Roosevelt made it clear in the middle of December 1941 that all defense legislation coming out of the executive branch had to be cleared with Byrnes (Robertson 1994:311–12). Byrnes immediately asserted that an economic czar was needed, defeating Hopkins's suggestion that a three-person leadership team representing "small business and labor as well as large capitalists" should be created (p. 313). It was then that the War Production Board was announced and Nelson put in charge of it.

However, as we already have seen, Nelson quickly was in trouble at the War Production Board and inflation was developing besides. In October 1942, Roosevelt created an Office of Economic Stabilization in the White House and put Byrnes in charge as the new economic czar. "With this development," reports Somers, "it was clear that Nelson was no longer top man on the home front" (1950:35). When there was a conflict on price controls, wage stabilization, or "other aspects of economic stabilization," it soon "became known that the decision of the Director of Economic Stabilization was controlling" (ibid.). In other words, Nelson lasted only nine months as the civilian head of the mobilization, another reason the military leaders felt free to ignore him and go to the White House (meaning Roosevelt, Byrnes, and Hopkins) for the final word on a range of issues (cf. Janeway 1951:291). This is hardly the stuff of a military takeover of the War Production Board. Catton (1948:203) knew right away that Nelson had been demoted when the Office of Economic Stabilization was created. Byrnes became known as the "assistant president," with complete control on the domestic economy, and Roosevelt turned his full attention to military strategy and diplomacy (e.g., Robertson 1994:chap. 12). And behind Byrnes stood Baruch and the southern Democrats.

Here we can note a rather stunning fact given that Hooks relies exclusively on secondary sources in making his claim about military domination of the industrial mobilization. Only one of his many sources even suggests that there may have been military domination. This source, *The United States at War* (U.S. Bureau of the Budget 1946), is a compilation of chapters written by eight separate liberal authors who worked for the Bureau of the Budget, the publisher of the volume. A second source, *Industrial Mobilization for War* (U.S. Civilian Production Administration 1947), written by members of the Civilian Production Administration, the postwar incarnation of the War Production Board, has a slight tendency to blame the problems of the War Production Board on the military, although it recognizes far more than Hooks that there were civilian leaders at the Pentagon. All other sources expressly deny that there was a military takeover, and several of them take issue with the Bureau of the Budget history.

R. Elberton Smith (1959:11), a member of the Office of the Chief of Military History in the Pentagon, whose book is part of the multivolume government study of the United States in World War II, flatly states there was no military takeover. Another official military historian, John D. Millett (1954:284, 289–93), who wrote a detailed history of the Army Service Forces, specifically denies the claims in the Bureau of the Budget and the Civilian Production Administration histories. The official historian of the role of the navy in the industrial mobilization, Robert H. Connery (1951:154–55), who worked for the navy as a historian during World War II, also explicitly rejects the idea of a military takeover in the context of criticizing the Bureau of the Budget history. Herman Somers (1950:75, 137), who worked for the Office of War Mobilization and Reconversion at the end of the war, similarly rejects the military takeover thesis. Economist Elliot Janeway, an editor at *Time* during the war, says the Bureau of the Budget account is "biased and, at the analytical level, self-contradictory and amateurish" (1951:363).

At this point readers must be wondering if these authors might be biased by their experience of working for various military and civilian agencies during World War II. What do recent historians and social scientists conclude? Perhaps to the surprise of those who assume that the military historians would be most blinded by their affiliations, recent scholars conclude there was no military takeover during World War II (Janowitz 1960; Huntington 1961; Bernstein 1965, 1967; Polenberg 1972:216; Koistinen 1973; Blum 1976:120–22; Schwarz 1981:chaps. 7–9). In effect, then, Hooks adopts the perspective of the liberals in the Bureau of the Budget as against that of military historians and recent scholars without feeling any need to explain why he rejects the great weight of scholarly opinion or to collect any new data to justify his position.

However, it is not enough to say Hooks has drawn a conclusion opposite that of the sources he utilizes. It is also necessary to examine several major issues where there was conflict in order to see who was involved and how those issues were resolved.

## THE CONTROLLED MATERIALS POLICY

One of the most important problems facing the mobilization in 1942 was the development of a priority system for the allocation of scarce raw materials, especially steel, copper, and aluminum. The original system of simply giving a contractor a priority rating broke down because there were far more top priority ratings than there were raw materials. Moreover, the contractors had to find the raw materials themselves, so the priority rating was little more than a hunting license. The granting of priorities during 1941 had been the province of the Army and Navy Munitions Board. When the WPB was created in 1942, Nelson specifically delegated that authority to the Army and Navy Munitions Board once again. Given the problems of the old system, the chair of the munitions board, the aforementioned Eberstadt, developed a new system based on a plan advocated by executives at General Motors. Termed the "controlled materials policy," it directly allocated the needed raw materials to prime contractors, who then handed them out to subcontractors when necessary. Nelson agreed to the new system and then went one step further. He asked Eberstadt to administer the program from a new position within the War Production Board. With Baruch acting as an intermediary (Schwarz 1981:433), Eberstadt agreed to a position reporting directly to Nelson in mid-October 1942. The Army and Navy Munitions Board then declined greatly in importance (e.g., Millett 1954:290–92).

However, the New Dealers were wary about this whole process from start to finish. Schwarz says "This method immediately drew apprehension from liberals, who viewed it as a shift of production authority to the military and claimed that it would permit materials to be controlled by giant corporations acting as prime contractors" (1981:433). Still, the Planning Committee at WPB supported the plan after being reassured by liberal economists that there would be plenty of materials for both military and civilian needs. When Eberstadt then came to WPB, the liberals were upset again because they saw him as the military's man, and they "sought to counterbalance his sudden ascendance to power in the WPB with the appointment of General Electric's Charles E. Wilson as WPB program vice-chairman and head of the Production Executive Committee" (p. 434). The New Dealers were under no illusions about Wilson's identification with the corporate community, but they made a "calculated gamble that the production man would side with advocates of an expanding civilian economy against the financial-military combine of Baruch, Eberstadt, and the Pentagon" (ibid.).

Now, as it turned out, Eberstadt and Wilson did clash, and Nelson later fired Eberstadt in a last-minute maneuver in early February 1943, saving his own job for the time being [cf. Janeway (1951:320–21) for a critique of the liberals' intrigue on this issue]. The details of the argument need not occupy us here because Wilson was a strong friend of his counterparts in the Pentagon on all major issues and opposed New Deal initiatives. The important point for now is that the argument over the controlled materials policy is not one of civilians versus the Pentagon. The battle lines are once again between the business-military coalition and the New Dealers.

Hooks (1991:169–73) misunderstands the decisional process on this issue before concluding that the policy "provided the final blow to New Dealers in the planning bureaucracies" and "reinforced the position of both the military and the monopoly sector" (p. 172). More strikingly, he says that "military officers gained control of this nominally civilian agency [the WPB] and the material control program it implemented" (p. 172). Although he begins by talking about the power of the military on this issue (p. 169), he writes about "Eberstadt's proposal" (p. 170) and "Eberstadt of the ANMB and his allies in the Services" (p. 171) when he turns to specifics. He claims that "representatives of the military established the most important WPB policies" (ibid.) as members of the Production Executive Committee chaired by Wilson of General Electric, thereby overlooking that the committee reflected the business-military coalition. Once again, that is, Hooks uncritically accepts the liberals' tactic of calling anyone they disagree with, like Eberstadt, a flunky for the military.

Worse, Hooks quietly abandons the kind of argument he made when he claimed that businessmen-in-uniform did not prove anything because military officers were in charge of them. Faced with a situation where two businessmen, Eberstadt and Wilson, usually described as strong-willed and forceful, are in charge of key agencies or committees, Hooks suddenly says a leadership position does not matter. Eberstadt is a Pentagon representative because the Army and Navy Munitions Board has military leaders on it (actually, Patterson and Forrestal), and Wilson is an agent of the military because the WPB committee he is chairing has strong military representation.

In my view, his argument is totally wrong. The controlled materials policy is not evidence for a military takeover. It is evidence for a business-military coalition in which corporate leaders are dominant. Only by in effect equating civilian with New Deal and overlooking the role of big businessmen in the mobilization can Hooks even begin to make his claims look plausible.

## THE FEASIBILITY DISPUTE OF 1942

Running parallel to the problem of how to allocate scarce resources, an argument began to simmer in early 1942 about the feasibility of certain of the production goals enunciated by Roosevelt. This argument came to a boil in September and October, about the same time the controlled materials policy was being put into place. Since Roosevelt's production goals were deliberately set high and meant in some measure for public consumption, the dispute over them is partly a tempest in a teapot. Still, there were some very real and important issues involved because unbalanced production goals could mean shortages and delays in delivering the most essential weapons. Moreover, the conflict did harbor within it a much bigger issue about the control of war strategy that was smuggled in by New Deal planners to the great consternation of the military; however, that issue disappeared from view very quickly.

Hooks deals with this dispute in his characteristic fashion. It was civilian (WPB) versus military (the Pentagon), with the Pentagon winning out (1991:114, 118). The reality is as follows:

1.  Drawing on a wide variety of inputs, including figures from his industrial mobilization agencies and the suggestions of the British government, Roosevelt set a target of sixty thousand airplanes and forty-five thousand tanks for 1942, higher than what the WPB recommended (Brigante 1950:23–31).

2.  The military took these figures very seriously and pressed hard to meet the goals, even if that meant limiting the civilian economy. The military was very sensitive on the issue because it had been accused in 1940 and 1941 of setting its goals too low, and had only recently been chided for not adjusting its goals.

3.  Meanwhile, the New Dealers in the Planning Committee at the WPB worried that these goals were unrealistic and would do damage to the war effort by causing shortages and bottlenecks in the overall production of military goods. They also worried that the civilian economy would be squeezed more than it need be. Economic statisticians working for the WPB did a very careful study of the economy's capabilities that proved to be accurate and helpful. Since these studies were conducted by Simon Kuznets of the National Bureau of Economic Research, this is another example of how think tanks are a major source of state capacity.

4.  At this point the New Dealers introduced the issue that upset the military. They used the feasibility issue as the occasion to call for a superboard with both civilian and military members to coordinate production and military strategies (e.g., Smith 1959:155). Since this board would have power over the army, navy, and Maritime Commission as well as other agencies, it was a clear subordination of military control over the war itself.

5.  Nelson liked the feasibility report and apparently the superboard idea. He thought the whole proposal should be forwarded to the Pentagon and the White House. However, he asked the chair of the Planning Committee, economist Robert Nathan, to send the report directly rather than sending it himself. It must be emphasized what this signified to understand the military's reaction. A mere Planning Committee that reported only to

Nelson, and had no operating responsibility, was making suggestions to the military about a new committee to control military strategy. According to Brigante, Nelson and the Planning Committee "appear to have been singularly oblivious" to the "far-ranging organizational implications" (1950:4) of the suggestion for a new board, but I wonder about thát seeming naiveté given the ongoing battle between New Dealers and the business-military coalition. Hooks (1991:116) misses all this completely when he says that the WPB proposed this superboard.

6.  Somervell was very upset when he saw the report. It was the superboard in particular that set him off (e.g., Millett 1954:217). He quickly wrote out an angry reply and sent it to Nathan, suggesting in no uncertain terms that the report be buried. He called the idea for a superboard "an inchoate mass of words" (Brigante 1950:83).

7.  Now it was the liberals' turn to scream. There was a meeting at the WPB on October 6, 1942. Hooks says that Somervell "recruited" Stimson and Patterson to support him at the meeting, thereby giving the impression once again that Somervell is in charge of his hapless civilian bosses (1991:117). There was a major debate at the meeting. The New Dealers were very impressive in arguing about the numbers and about the possible bad effects of distorting the economy by striving for unattainable goals. Henderson went into a tirade against Somervell, who did not say a word in reply. Henderson was gone from his position not long after.

Significantly, the issue of greatest concern to the military, the new superboard, was deeply buried, perhaps due to a letter from Marshall saying he did not think much of having economists and politicians helping to decide on strategic matters (e.g., Millett 1954:217). The meeting ended with no decision on feasibility.

8.  Contrary to Hooks's claims about a military victory on this issue, the production goals were lowered at the next WPB meeting and some timetables were stretched out. Moreover, it was Patterson who decided to accept the WPB estimates. As Brigante says, Patterson set the policy for Somervell the day after the big meeting: "For Somervell, however, the issue was presumably settled by a memorandum that Patterson sent him on October 7th, the very next day after the first WPB discussion" (1950:102). Brigante then quotes from the memorandum, the first two parts of which are worth reproducing here because they clearly state what should happen even though written in a very indirect and impersonal language. In particular, note the flat, passive language Patterson uses in the first sentence of point (2) to tell Somervell that the WPB position had prevailed:

Memorandum to General Somervell:

1.   It seems probable that we will be told by WPB that the military production program now outlined for the year 1943 is considerably beyond the capacity of the nation to fulfill within the time objectives. The position of WPB

will be that the military requirements (Army, Navy and Maritime Commission) for 1943 would involve production of some $95 billions and that the maximum military production actually to be expected will not exceed $80 billions. These figures in dollars will be backed up with figures in raw materials and in manpower.

It is also likely that WPB will recommend or direct that the production objective for 1943 be reduced to a point within striking distance of estimated maximum production for that year. The figure specified as the aggregate limit of the military program is apt to be between $80 billions to $85 billions.

2.   The WPB position, that production objectives ought not to be far in front of estimated maximum production, is believed to be sound as a general rule. Otherwise our scheduling of production cannot represent reality, and it is generally agreed that without realistic scheduling we will continue to suffer from maldistribution of materials, thus cutting down the actual output of finished weapons. (pp. 102–3)

9.   Hooks claims that "the armed services ignored Nelson's repeated calls to address the feasibility of the procurement program" (1991:115), and cites Smith (1959:154) as his source. Smith, however, says no such thing. He instead writes that "some adjustments in programs were made" in reaction to requests by Nelson in the spring and summer of 1942. Two pages later, following Brigante (1950), Smith summarizes the memorandum partially reproduced above by saying Patterson wrote Somervell "conceding the correctness of the WPB position." Smith then details the very large reductions in army plans (Smith 1959:157). In short, Hooks is wrong to say the military "ignored" these requests, and wrong to say the military "won."

Brigante does not talk in terms of defeat for either the WPB or the Pentagon. He notes that the WPB won its point in terms of a reduction in goals, but the Pentagon eliminated the threat of a new superboard. However, Brigante does say the dispute led to later problems for Nelson. His handling of the matter led military people to lose confidence in him, and they were henceforth antagonistic toward him. In that sense, Nelson lost. Moreover, the liberal Planning Committee of the WPB lost in a very big way, for it was phased out shortly thereafter. Brigante (1950:106) argues that "the feasibility dispute may well have likewise constituted the largest single factor in bringing about the demise of the Planning Committee." The committee was relegated to a secondary position when Wilson of General Electric reorganized the WPB early in 1943. Due to the reorganization, Nathan and other members of the Planning Committee resigned. Like Durr at the Reconstruction Finance Corporation—and Henderson at OPA, for that matter—Nathan was pushed to the sidelines for his activism. Once he resigned from WPB, he was drafted.

In calling the feasibility dispute a defeat for the WPB, Hooks's view seems to be closest to the Bureau of the Budget history. He cites that study as claiming the outcome was "a crucial resignation of power by WPB" because it "let the general outlines of the production program be determined by the Services without the development of a firm, comprehensive or balanced program related to military strategy or industrial feasibility" (1991:117). Actually, this is another questionable use of a source by Hooks, for the paragraph goes on to talk about the way the WPB put firm reins on the military because of "the failure of the military to plan or to keep reasonably within the productive capacity of American industry." (U.S. Bureau of the Budget 1946:126). That is, after discussing the various delegations of power Nelson *chose* to make, the section of which this paragraph is a part ends up arguing that he later put a series of limits on military procurement agencies. Even the Bureau of the Budget history does not go as far as Hooks does in claiming military dominance.

This misinterpretation aside, Hooks never discusses why he disagrees with the accounts of the feasibility dispute by Brigante (1950), Millett (1954), and Smith (1959). Indeed, Hooks does not even make use of Brigante, who is clearly the best secondary source on the issue, but in effect relies on accounts of Brigante's work by Millett and Smith. Thus, he is doing what Goldthorpe (1991:223) says theorists of the state autonomy school often do: making (1) his interpretation of (2) interpretations by Millett and Smith of (3) Brigante. The net result is a very inadequate account of the feasibility dispute, hardly a victory for the military when it came to production goals.

## THE RECONVERSION CONTROVERSY

No sooner did the allocation and feasibility issues die down than a controversy slowly developed over whether there should be reconversion to some peacetime production even though the war was still going on. The issue in effect became an official one due to a government report in January 1943, but it did not become a controversy within the WPB and War Department until late 1943 and early 1944, and the real showdowns leading to angry denunciations and resignations did not occur until late August 1944.

Hooks deals with reconversion in a cursory way in three overlapping discussions (1991:118–22, 151–53, 173–78). In the end, he does not attach much importance to it because it does not relate directly to his concern about the close relations between the defense industries and the Pentagon after World War II: "The institutional dynamics of the military-industrial complex are not revealed in an examination of reconversion because the defense industries remained in the Pentagon orbit" (pp. 177–78). However, he makes a number of assertions in the course of his discussions of this issue that I do not believe should go unchallenged. The issue also is of relevance because Mills (1956:213) put some emphasis on it in his argument for a military ascendancy.

Discussions about reconversion began to occur in government agencies and in the press in late 1942 when it became clear that both Germany and Japan would be defeated. There are various speeches or articles that might be considered the opening round, but the most important was a report issued in January 1943 by a small White House planning agency, the National Resources Planning Board, to which Hooks (1991:48, 79) attaches much importance. Created as an independent board early in the New Deal, it was moved to the White House in 1939 on the basis of a recommendation by the president's Committee on Administrative Management. Most of its reports up until that point were limited in their scope, but this one was a blueprint for a welfare liberalism or social democracy, deeply upsetting moderates and conservatives. In fact, the conservative coalition in Congress was so annoyed that it abolished the board a few months later by refusing to renew its funding, yet another defeat for a New Deal group challenging the prevailing power structure.

Hooks interprets this report to mean "New Dealers took the lead in representing the state's interest" (p. 119), but he does not explain why social democracy was the interest of the state. Nor is it clear why it was in the state's interest to alienate the corporate community and conservatives in a time of war when there was no threat from a working class not widely organized or deeply committed to class politics. Finally, Hooks does not discuss why the legislative part of the state would find the board and its report so annoying if the report was in the interest of the state. What his claim boils down to is that what he likes—New Dealism, social democracy—is in the "objective interests" of some abstract entity called "the state"; underneath his bias lies the fact that state autonomy theory cannot deal with conflict within the state because a state has to be united to be autonomous.

While the arguments were going on within government over the National Resource Planning Board's report, liberals in the Program Office, filling some of the duties of the defunct Planning Committee, urged Nelson to begin planning for the postwar world. They in effect wanted to ensure continued high employment by allowing some businesses to resume peacetime production when they were no longer needed for war work. The idea, in short, was to phase in peacetime production during the war, especially through small businesses without war contracts. The New Dealers felt this was necessary because they predicted high unemployment after the war, picking up where the Great Depression left off. Nathan, in a book published early in 1944, predicted there would be eighteen million unemployed "unless civilian production expanded immediately" (Schwarz 1981:463).

Just as congressional conservatives did not like the National Resources Planning Board report, businessmen in the Pentagon and War Production Board did not like the idea of reconversion during wartime. The industrialists had two concerns: the reconversion was going to be carried out by the New Dealers in the Program Office rather than through the Production Executive Committee (PEC) responsible for all other industrial operations; and there was to be no regard for the previous market shares held by specific corporations in the awarding of reconversion contracts. Since big corporations were tied up in war production, it was likely that smaller companies would receive the reconversion contracts. However, it did not seem fair to the corporate leaders at WPB that companies should lose market shares simply because they were fully involved in war production. They spoke of this issue in terms of "equity for industry" (Peltason 1952:237; cf. Sitterson 1946:134). According to Catton, this matter of market shares was absolutely fundamental to the business leaders at the WPB:

> One consideration should guide all reconversion planning, as the dollar-a-year men saw it; the old competitive patterns in industry must be preserved intact. When the last traces of the war economy evaporated, each industrialist must be able to pick up exactly where he had left off. . . . WPB should do its programming in such a way that all new manufacturers would be kept out of any given industry until all of the prewar manufacturers had resumed production, and as production was resumed in any industry all of the early starters should be limited to quotas based on their prewar production. (1948:247)

Anything less than this, the industrialists felt, would be unjust. It would be using the war mobilization to help some businesses and hurt others. Thus, they believed the New Dealers' plans for reconversion were an attempt to help small businesses and decrease the importance of large corporations. It was an attack by "government" on their basic principles concerning competition and markets. The arguments coming from the Small War Plants Commission of WPB, a champion of small business and reconversion planning, certainly gave credence to their concerns. Nor did they accept the New Dealers' claim that any breaks for small business would be too small to matter.

At the same time, leaders at the Pentagon were adamantly opposed to any reconversion during wartime because it might lead to less defense production or a psychological letdown on the part of everyone in their war-focused efforts. Thus, there was the basis for the kind of industrial-military alliance on this issue seen by Catton (1948) and Bernstein (1967) as the reason for the delay in any significant reconversion until the war was over in Europe. As Catton says:

> Being violently opposed to Nelson's proposal, the dollar-a-year men began to realize that they had warm allies over in the War Department, who were also

violently opposed. The reasons for the opposition were different; the Army simply opposed reconversion as such, while the industrialists wanted reconversion but opposed the kind Nelson was insisting on. But the common ground of general antagonism to what Nelson was trying to do was broad enough to form ranks on, and the ranks formed swiftly—thus demonstrating, neither for the first nor the last time in American history, the extreme ease with which industry and the military can make book together when the heat is on. (1948:248)

It is important to emphasize that neither the corporate community nor the military opposed planning for the postwar economy, especially if it were done in such a way that it did not give the impression the war was all but over (e.g., Peltason 1952:226; Millett 1954:227). As Somers says, "virtually no controversy existed over the desirability of early planning for reconversion" (1950:174). Instead, the big questions concerned when and how much:

But how much war energy should be diverted to actual reconversion while the two-front war was still in progress? How soon should actual measures be taken and how extensive should such steps be? Here interests and viewpoints clashed violently. (ibid.)

Hooks begins his first analysis of the reconversion issue by giving the impression that liberal businessmen sided with Nelson on the need for reconversion and then backed down to the demands of the military. He overlooks the great difference between planning and implementation stressed by Somers. He starts with the claim, "The most influential proponents of early reconversion planning were 'liberal' business executives associated with the Business Advisory Council and the Committee for Economic Development [CED], especially Donald Nelson" (p. 119). His source for this claim is A. D. H. Kaplan's Liquidation of War Production (1944), which was not a statement of CED policy, as Hooks implies, but a study sponsored by the CED. There is a huge difference from the CED point of view: trustees vote to accept CED policy statements, but not commissioned studies by experts. Two pages later Hooks makes it sound like the military was the main source of the demand that reconversion be delayed: "While the Committee for Economic Development report on reconversion endorsed Nelson and the WPB's emphasis on coordinating reconversion and on minimizing unemployment, it accepted the Pentagon's demand that reconversion be delayed until after Germany's defeat" (p. 121). From reading this one would never know that virtually all businessmen in the CED and at the WPB strongly insisted that reconversion should be delayed. As Hooks says much later, in his third discussion of the reconversion issue, "Nelson was not supported by the dollar-a-year men in the WPB" (p. 175). In fact, the New

Deal economists, along with Catton and the rest of the public relations staff, were his only supporters.

Despite the opposition to wartime reconversion, Nelson moved to implement it in a small way. Shortly after he announced at a meeting of his advisory board on November 30, 1943, that he intended to allow some reconversion in areas where there was a surplus of materials and manpower, industrial leaders at the WPB and military leaders at the Pentagon entered into various stratagems to block any serious efforts. The details of the battles that went on over the next nine months are not relevant here, but they did lead Roosevelt to send Nelson on a special mission to China in August 1944 to ease him out of his position. When the liberals in the Office of Public Information began to leak stories claiming that Wilson had blocked reconversion to protect big corporations, he resigned at the time Nelson left for China with an angry public denunciation of New Dealers at WPB.

These battles within the WPB over reconversion were overshadowed by the fact that the final decision belonged to Byrnes and his Office of War Mobilization. Due to the pressures building in WPB over reconversion throughout 1943, Byrnes asked Baruch and another Wall Street financier, John Hancock, in October 1943 to prepare a report on the matter. According to Hooks, the Baruch-Hancock Report, appearing in February 1944, rejected all of the New Dealers' initiatives and became the "official blueprint for government reconversion activities" (Hooks 1991:121, citing Somers 1950:178). Hooks agrees that "[t]he adoption of the Baruch-Hancock Report to define the goals and policies for reconversion determined the outcome of this debate" (1991:122). However, he does not see this conclusion as strong evidence for corporate dominance on the issue. It seems to me that the complete acceptance of a report written by two Wall Street investors who did not have paid positions in government is powerful evidence for a class dominance hypothesis, but Hooks does not even confront the possibility. Instead, he says the issue now became "the timing of reconversion" (p. 121). As a matter of fact, timing was a major issue all along from the point of view of both corporate and military leaders.

The liberal-labor coalition of New Dealers fought long and hard on this issue, but it had more success in gaining headlines than in implementing its policies. It was successful in pushing Wilson out of the WPB, but not in bringing about wartime reconversion.

## THE REMOVAL OF CONTROLS ON BUSINESS

Although it is not possible from the existing literature to determine the exact influence of leaders in the corporate community as compared to the military on the reconversion issue, a closely related issue followed shortly thereafter where corporate leaders were clearly the driving force. It concerned the removal of all controls on business between late 1944 and 1946. Hooks gives only brief attention to this issue (p. 176). Bernstein (1965), however, has reconstructed it in great detail. His work shows that the corporate community defeated the New Dealers on this issue without the help of the military, which remained silent.

Throughout the summer of 1944, when the reconversion issue was being fought, corporate leaders opposed "any relaxation of WPB priority and production directives" (Bernstein 1965:244). However, in the fall of 1944, with victory in Europe near and Nelson out of power at WPB, business began to push for the removal of controls. It seemed to be a dramatic reversal in the business position on the issue, and it was not opposed by the military. The difference was that the removal of all controls allowed big corporations to compete for raw materials and markets, whereas the plan for gradual reconversion gave preference to small businesses.

The corporate businessmen's desire for a speedy removal of controls was endorsed by the new chair of the War Production Board, Julius Krug, a thirty-six-year-old government official with previous experience at WPB. When he announced in September 1944 that he planned to remove all controls once there was victory in Europe, the only opposition came from experts and New Dealers. Two professors in positions of authority at WPB protested the decision. So did the chairman of the Office of Price Administration, the chairman of WPB's Smaller War Plants Corporation, and the Senate Small Business Committee. Due to this opposition, the corporate leaders did not win everything they wanted immediately, but they won massive decontrols on V-E day and just about everything else upon the surrender of Japan. At one point in the struggle it seemed as if President Harry S. Truman were going to retain the controls, but his orders to this effect were circumvented by the WPB without any protest by Truman's top adviser on such matters, John Snyder, a conservative banker from St. Louis. Snyder had served as executive vice-president of the Defense Plant Corporation at the RFC and then oversaw the Federal Loan Agency before going to the White House as head of the OWMR, replacing Byrnes, who became secretary of state.

There is another aspect of this case that does not accord with the expectations of state-centered theory. The heads of the WPB and its civilian successor, the Civilian Production Administration (CPA), worked hard to shrink their agencies, not to build them. As Bernstein remarks, "In this behavior Small [Chair of the CPA] and Krug were atypical administrators in a government where agency heads were notorious for seeking more power and fighting all attempts to deplete their staffs and reduce their strength" (1965:258–59). I believe this unusual behavior can be explained best by the great outside influence of the corporate community, which has a deep hostility to all forms of government control. It is this kind of evidence contrary to their views that state autonomy theorists never face.

## DISPOSING OF GOVERNMENT-OWNED DEFENSE PLANTS

Hooks's reasoning in explaining what happened to the government's huge capital investment in defense plants after the war is highly unusual. He turns a clear and decisive victory for the corporate community, in close collaboration with the military, of course, into a triumph for the military over civilians. He does so by equating civilians with New Dealers, who surely did lose on almost every count on this issue. But corporate leaders are civilians too.

Hooks begins by claiming that "The powerlessness of civilians to direct federal industrial investments continued into the reconversion period" (1991:154). In the very next sentence he switches to the term "New Dealers": "New Dealers failed to regain the initiative or to secure control of federal facilities to advance civilian-oriented planning" (ibid.). Then he makes it appear that the Pentagon decided what to retain and what to dispose of: "Those industrial facilities *deemed unnecessary* by the Pentagon were made available for sale to the public sector" (ibid., italics added).

After telling of the failed attempts of a few New Dealers to keep some productive facilities as yardsticks to measure the performance of private business, Hooks then makes what should be the primary point in talking about the disposition of war plants and equipment: everything was done according to the reconversion report by Baruch and Hancock (p. 155). This includes setting up an advisory board on the issue that included military and business members. Then Byrnes appointed a surplus property administrator described by Hooks only as "a longtime associate of Jesse Jones" (ibid.). But Will Clayton was far more than that. He was an owner of Anderson, Clayton, the largest cotton broker in the world; in other words, he was a prominent Texas businessman. Moreover, he had been brought into government by Baruch in 1918 as a member of the War Industries Board and was appointed surplus property administrator in World War II at Baruch's insistence and over the liberals' candidate (Schwarz 1981:457–58, 461). He also was a trustee of the new Committee for Economic Development. I think the appointment of such a person to head the agency disposing of factories and machinery built by the government is evidence for a class dominance perspective.

Hooks rightly says Clayton did nothing in 1944 to further reconversion. This was of course the business plan: no reconversion until after the war was over in Europe. Once the war was over, Clayton moved to the State Department and was replaced as chair of the Surplus Property Board by Stuart Symington. Hooks provides no information on Symington. The fact that he came from a wealthy business family, ran various family businesses in his young adulthood, and then purchased a company in St. Louis, Emerson Electric, that made parts for military aircraft, apparently is not deemed relevant by Hooks. Shortly thereafter Symington became secretary of the air force.

Hooks reports that "monopoly-sector firms fiercely opposed any proposal that the government continue to operate the plants after the war, and they rejected the idea of subsidized sales to smaller firms" (p. 155). He also says major defense contractors reaped a "windfall" in the disposal of surplus plants, despite the DPC contracts created earlier by Durr (p. 156). Both of these points are evidence for class dominance, but Hooks says this is not direct evidence for the power of the corporate community because the army kept shipyards and ordnance facilities (p. 158). Moreover, Hooks says the important point is that the military had gained expertise in federal investment. He cites Morris Janowitz as authority for the following claim:

> After the war, the Pentagon took control of a vast portfolio of industrial facilities. Seen in this light, the role of Generals Gregory and Littlejohn in the surplus property-disposal program attests to the growing influence and expertise of military officers. Not only was it military officers who protected national security interests, but it was they—not career civil servants and business executives—who had acquired expertise in federal investment during the wartime mobilization. (See Janowitz 1960:378; Hooks 1991:158)

There is nothing about any of this on page 378 of Janowitz. The page actually states Janowitz's argument that military officers did not have very much influence in the civilian parts of the government after the war. Janowitz claims the appointment of "military personnel to politically responsible posts, although it continues, has declined sharply since 1950," and then says there were "a few conspicuous cases where civilian leadership sought to make use of prestigeful military officers to deal with difficult political problems." He gives several examples, none relating to either mobilization or reconversion. In some respects, this page directly refutes Hooks, but in any case there is nothing about federal investment.

When Hooks gets down to cases about the "vast portfolio" held by the military after the war, he first notes that the government held on to its ordnance and explosive facilities. This turns out to be a handful of factories by 1955: "As of 1955, the Department of the Army (1956) reported thirty-two industrial facilities in its possession, most of which were devoted to the production of ordnance" (1991:158). Hooks turns next to the shipbuilding industry, where the government retained some of its new facilities, but this is not exactly an earthshaking development when it is realized that the government owned such facilities *before* the war as well. Hooks quotes a government study as follows: "About half of the Federal expenditures were for expansion of Federally owned Navy shipyards and drydock facilities" (ibid.). I do not think state autonomy theory gains any support when half of the vast portfolio is an addition to long-standing navy facilities.

The situation is a little different for aircraft. The military kept plants it had not owned before the war. But this is not exactly a power grab either, because there was no desire for the plants on the part of the private sector. First, "the major auto companies that had manufactured aircraft and aircraft parts during the war had no interest in continuing this line of production after the war" (p. 160). Second, the private aircraft companies could not afford more plants and had no use for them anyhow because there was not a big civilian market for airplanes. Moreover, these plants quickly became irrelevant because manufacturers were reluctant to use them during the Korean War (Rae 1968:198–99).

And yet, Hooks concludes his discussion of the disposal of war plants with the following claim: "The Pentagon's command of industrial financing during World War II helped consolidate its *insulation* at the war's end" (1991:160, my italics). It was therefore able to "gain control of a vast industrial portfolio during the reconversion period" (ibid.). In a certain very real sense, I cannot understand this line of reasoning. It makes me feel like I must be missing something somewhere along the line. When reading pluralists in the past, I could understand their arguments and then go look for new evidence. With Hooks I find myself staring at evidence that seems to support a class dominance perspective, but he says it supports military autonomy. If we leave aside for a minute that corporate executives ran the military bureaucracy, as I showed earlier, and assume the military ran the bureaucracy all by itself and was therefore potentially powerful, then how could it be that everything with a possible private market went back to the corporations? Given business aversion to big government or any kind of government autonomy, how come "The Pentagon's expansion into the aircraft industry did not spark howls of protest from the private sector" (ibid.)? Why were the corporate leaders responsible for creating and implementing the disposal policies—Baruch, Hancock, Clayton, and Symington—so relaxed about this new government power via the Pentagon?

The Hooks explanation is that business and the military decided to live and let live. Big business grew and solidified its independence, but the military carved out some state autonomy by creating a separate military-industrial complex (p. 161). Hooks devotes an entire chapter (pp. 197–224) to the postwar strength of the monopoly-sector firms, showing their fast growth and describing their independence from government. He even agrees that this independence had "ramifications within the state" because "[i]t legitimized the state's reliance upon business leaders—rather than professional civil servants—to fulfill the highest posts in the federal bureaucracy" (p. 222). He devotes another full chapter (pp. 225–66) to the independent military-industrial complex that allegedly blossomed after the war.

But what if the military-industrial complex is not separate from the monopoly sector, as Hooks claims? Then we have a single corporate community, which he concedes to have the ability to place its leaders in high government positions. That would put us back to a close military-business partnership in the postwar era, as Mills (1956) claims, or corporate dominance within that partnership, as I have argued (Domhoff 1967:chap. 5; 1968:257–59; 1970:138–39). Rather obviously, then, the next step is to look at the evidence for the separate military-industrial complex Hooks claims to demonstrate in his seventh chapter.

## A POSTWAR MILITARY-INDUSTRIAL COMPLEX?

Hooks's fourth hypothesis, it will be recalled, is that "the World War II mobilization forged the military-industrial complex, that is, a large and defense-oriented state sector" (1991:225). He stresses this is a "planning effort," a "de facto industrial planning policy that continues to this day" (ibid.). It is not a planning effort that involves the whole state or several agencies, but only an "autarkic" Pentagon, a self-sufficient and insulated agency within the state (p. 226). Hooks sees Pentagon involvement in the aircraft and electronics industries after World War II as the primary examples of his point. He thinks a class dominance perspective is contradicted by the fact that "monopoly-sector firms did not dominate defense production and rarely were dependent on defense contracts—which is still the case today" (p. 228). He then presents what he sees as a summary of the evidence contrary to the class dominance view:

> Instead, the major defense contractors of the postwar period have tended to specialize in defense production. Little evidence exists to suggest that these firms are closely interlocked with monopoly-sector firms (Lieberson 1971). (ibid.)

There are three main problems with Hooks's claims about an independent military-industrial complex based in an autarkic Pentagon. First, there is nothing of relevance to the issue in the article by Lieberson (1971) that he cites as his main support on the lack of interlocks between defense and nondefense companies. Second, there is strong evidence that the monopoly-sector and defense firms are very closely integrated into one corporate community. Third, his analysis of the aircraft industry is in good part wrong.

Hooks cites Lieberson (1971) as his source for claiming monopoly-sector and defense firms are not closely interlocked. In actuality, Lieberson's article does not talk about interlocks aside from a finding that in 1965 the top seven New York banks included officers from fifty-one large corporations. What Lieberson shows in relation to the issues at hand is that the one hundred largest military contractors are among the largest companies in the country, which should come as no surprise to anyone. This suggests to me, contrary to Hooks (1991:228), that monopoly-sector firms do dominate defense production, but note that this tells us nothing about interlocks. When it comes to the ties among big corporations, however, we know from numerous studies cited in Chapter 2 that most of these corporations in the United States are closely related through (1) interlocking directors, (2) common sources of loans and legal expertise, and (3) common owners (e.g., Sonquist and Koenig 1975; Mizruchi 1982; Mintz and Schwartz 1985; and sources cited in Domhoff 1983:chap. 3).

Lieberson next turns to the importance of military contracts for big corporations. He repeats the well-known fact that military spending is a very minor part of the business of the very largest corporations even though many of them are the recipients of very large defense contracts. That is, they are big contractors, but contracts are not a big part of their sales because they have enormous civilian markets as well. Lieberson then argues that only a few companies have a strong direct interest in military spending. Once again, this has nothing to do with interlocks between monopoly-sector and defense firms. Hooks goes wrong by arguing that specialization in defense production tells us something about how close defense companies are to civilian-oriented firms.

Contrary to Hooks, there is evidence that the handful of companies specializing in defense contracts are closely interlocked with other large firms. The most detailed and systematic published study of this nature compared the fifteen largest defense contractors for the years 1966 to 1972 with the fifteen largest nondefense industrial corporations (Johnson 1976). This study showed that the 174 directors of the defense companies had 91 interlocks with major banks, which the author converted into a "director interlock percentage" of 56 percent, while the 252 directors of the large nondefense industrials had 138 interlocks with these banks, a director interlock percent of 55 percent. The directors of defense companies had 97 interlocks with other top corporations for a director interlock percentage of 51 percent, while the directors of the big industrials had 183 (73 percent). There is thus a difference for interlocks with other big industrials, but it is not one Hooks could make much out of given the very large number of defense interlocks with major corporations and the fact that the big industrials are so much larger than the defense firms (pp. 86–87, 89).

Johnson also looked at ownership patterns, educational backgrounds, social club memberships, and involvement in policy-planning groups for both samples. He found the following: large blocks of stock in companies in both samples were held by the same giant banks (pp. 71–76, 78–79); 23 percent of the directors of major industrials attended Harvard, Yale, or Princeton, a figure slightly lower than the 28 percent for defense companies (p. 82); and memberships in exclusive social clubs were about the same for both samples (p. 84). The one difference was found in participation in policy-planning groups. The 252 industrial directors had 128 interlocks with such groups (51 percent); the 174 defense company directors had 32 (18 percent) (p. 85). The cumulative impact of Johnson's findings, I believe, is to show that defense companies are owned and directed by people drawn from the same social, economic, and policy circles involved with the largest corporations. Any differences in the two samples, as Johnson (pp. 84–85) argues, are probably due to the fact that the industrials are far larger than the defense companies. That is, the ideal comparison group would have been nondefense industrials of comparable size to the defense companies.

Detailed information on ownership patterns compiled by Stephen Abrecht and Michael Locker (1981) for Corporate Data Exchange corroborates Johnson's conclusion based on congressional reports that the stock of most large defense companies is held by the same financial institutions and pension funds holding the stock of the top fifteen industrials. Leaving aside Hughes Aircraft, 100 percent owned by the Howard Hughes Medical Foundation, and assuming a family has to have at least 5 percent of the stock to assert control, only General Dynamics, 20 percent owned by the Crown family, McDonnell Douglas, 22 percent owned by the Douglas family, and General Tire & Rubber, 19 percent owned by the O'Neil family, were under family control at the time of the study. In addition, the DuPont family held 4.18 percent of Martin Marietta. No other defense company on Johnson's list had more than 2 or 3 percent of its stock in the hands of families or individuals. Nor did the number of family-controlled companies differ from a control group of fourteen industrials of comparable size to each defense company.

A comprehensive study of the top ten defense contractors for the 1970s, looking at their boards of directors, campaign finance contributions, and lobbying efforts, also supports Johnson's overall conclusion (Adams 1982). The directors of these companies come from a wide range of nondefense companies. Their trade associations give them strong ties in Congress, providing them with civilian supporters and leverage against Pentagon officials.

We can add even more impressive evidence for the integration of defense and nondefense firms from the study including both large profit and non-profit organizations that was discussed in Chapter 2 (Salzman and Domhoff 1983). The 1970 database for this study included all directors of the 100 largest industrials, the 50 largest banks, the 18 largest insurance companies, the 21 largest utilities, the 11 largest transportation companies, the 20 largest law firms, the 11 largest foundations, the 12 most richly endowed universities, and 13 prominent policy-planning and cultural organizations (e.g., the Council on Foreign Relations, Brookings Institution, and New York Metropolitan Museum of Art). All possible interlocks among these 256 organizations were analyzed using an algorithm developed by Mintz and Schwartz (1985) and Mizruchi (1982) to ascertain the centrality of each of the organizations that had at least one interlock with the overall network. There were 31 "isolates" with no interlocks in the database, mostly law firms, smaller regional banks, or utilities.

Seven defense corporations also on Johnson's list were large enough to be included in the database. Their centrality scores ranged from 67 for Boeing to 171 for Tenneco, an impressive showing in an interlock network of 225 major organizations (i.e., excluding the 31 isolates). To provide an idea of how favorably their centrality scores compare with well-known nondefense corporations and other organizations, Table 6.1 lists the seven defense companies, the industrial corporation next lowest in rank to each of the defense companies, and the other organization(s) closest to each defense company. The defense companies are as central to this corporate-foundation-university-policy-group network as some of the most prominent businesses and nonprofit organizations in the country. There simply is not a military-industrial complex separate from the corporate community. The empirical evidence supports those who say that the idea of a separate military-industrial complex is conceptually flawed (Wolf 1972; Slater and Nardin 1973; Levine 1973; Moskos 1974), none of whom is cited by Hooks.

Most of Hooks's chapter on the role of the postwar Pentagon is devoted to showing that the military had tremendous influence over the aircraft industry. It owned a majority of the plant and equipment, and supplied a great amount of financing as well (1991:243). It shaped the products produced by these companies to fit its needs and specifications, and financed research and development (p. 244). There are many problems with Hooks's claims about the aircraft industry. First, the ties of this industry to government are not unique to World War II or the postwar era. For example, Anna Rochester (1936:199) starts her chapter on the aircraft industry in the interwar years by saying it is a war industry and always has been subsidized in one way or another by government, not only in the United States, but in other advanced capitalist countries. In fact, the government actually organized the highly competitive small companies of pre–World War I days into an association so they could produce military aircraft for World War I (Mingos 1930:26–29). Thus, there was ample precedent for the continuing close relation between the industry and government after World War II. It was hardly the breakthrough or change of course that Hooks claims.

Government subsidies for the industry began in the mid-1920s. Five-year

*Table 6.1.* Centrality Rankings for Defense Companies and Other Organizations

| Defense companies | | Next lowest industrial | | Closest other organization(s) | |
|---|---|---|---|---|---|
| 1. | 67 Boeing | 68 | Eastman Kodak | 66 | Mellon National Bank |
| 2. | 84 AVCO | 85 | ARMCO | 83 | Olin Corporation |
| 3. | 98 United Aircraft | 99 | Westinghouse Electric | 97 | Bank of America |
| 4. | 114 Sperry Rand | 115 | Celanese | 113 | Sherman & Sterling (law firm) |
| 5. | 136 McDonnel Douglas | 138 | Standard Oil of Ohio | 135 | Detroit Edison |
| | | | | 137 | Marine Midland Bank |
| 6. | 144 General Dynamics | 150 | Getty Oil | 143 | Davis, Polk (law firm) |
| | | | | 145 | Cornell University |
| 7. | 171 Tenneco | 173 | Phillip Morris | 170 | Duke Power (utility) |
| | | | | 172 | Duke Endowment (foundation) |

procurement programs for the army and navy were adopted to stabilize the industry. Even more significantly, the industry was given contracts to carry the mail: "The importance of this subsidy is shown by the fact that in 1932, for instance, the air mail subsidy amounted to 76 percent of the total revenue of the four leading transport companies" (Rochester 1936:200). Here it only need be added that the same companies owned both the transportation and manufacturing segments of the industry until legislation forced them apart in 1934.

The second problem with Hooks's analysis of the aircraft industry is that these companies were not as politically weak as their small size in the 1930s might indicate. This is because they were part of much larger family, industrial, or financial complexes. I. F. Stone (1942:169), one of the sources drawn on by Hooks, writes that the extremely wealthy DuPont family was a "major factor" in the aircraft industry shortly before World War II. A few pages later he notes that "in 1935 the DuPonts, through General Motors, had a sizable interest" in Pratt and Whitney, Curtiss-Wright, and Douglas Aircraft (p. 173). At a later point he reports that General Motors, then jointly controlled by the DuPont family and Morgan financial interests, controlled both North American Aviation and the Vultee Corporation through a holding company (p. 184). Elsbeth Freudenthal (1940:78–83, 96–99) spells out in detail the control structure mentioned by Stone. She shows that the industry was dominated by the same companies in the late 1930s that received the lion's share of the mail subsidies between 1926 and 1934. The only difference was the separation of transportation and manufacturing divisions into separate companies. General Motors, First National City Bank of New York, the Mellon family, and other major financial powers dominated these companies. In short, it is simply wrong to see the small aircraft companies as isolated little supplicants with no basis for standing up to the Pentagon. Given their ownership patterns and connections to banks and other companies, their corporate-based power was considerable.

Third, Hooks's claims about the Pentagon and the aircraft industry are contradicted by the way the air force was cut back in 1945 once it was clear the war was won. In fact, the cutbacks were so great that the aircraft industry fell from the largest industry in the United States in 1944 to sixteenth in 1946 and forty-fourth in 1947. The industry was on the brink of collapse in 1947 when its trade association, the Aircraft Industries Association of America, began to agitate the Truman administration to come to its rescue (Kofsky 1993). This intervention by industry representatives was decisive. It started with industrial advisory groups to the Air Coordinating Committee, an interagency body within the executive branch. From there it progressed until the air force's commanding officers, along with the under secretary of the army, the secretary of the air force and the secretary of defense, had been enrolled in the rescue effort. By the end of the process, not only had the manufacturers been able to defeat air force opposition to dispersing procurement contracts to a larger number of firms, which the industry demanded as a means of preventing any of the major companies from going under, but the head of their trade association had joined the staff of the secretary of defense as his principal adviser on aircraft procurement. Throughout 1947 and 1948, it was civilian bureaucrats, not the uniformed military, who directed the Truman administration's policies with respect to the aircraft industry. Finally, it was the manufacturers themselves who shaped the construction program that the administration won from Congress in the aftermath of a war scare in March and April of 1948 concerning an allegedly imminent Russian invasion of Western Europe.

The details of this influence process, unearthed in the kind of highly original and creative research in many different historical archives that Hooks ought to have done for such controversial claims as he makes, can be found in historian Frank Kofsky's (1993) wonderfully detailed work. Whether or not Kofsky is correct that the aircraft industry and the Department of Defense played the major role in the war scare of 1948, or whether it was more directly tied to the upcoming vote on the Marshall Plan, one thing is certain: he has shown exactly how, down to the person and minute, the aircraft executives and their lobbyists had at least as much influence on military leaders as military leaders had on them.

In short, Hooks is quite wrong about the relationship between the aircraft industry and the Pentagon. The situation is much more interactive than he allows. Whether we look at the history of the industry before World War II or the years immediately after that war, we find the aircraft industry unique in its deep dependency on government contracts. We also see that the companies were part of a larger corporate community able to exercise its influence on the government in general and the Pentagon specifically.

Within this context we can look at statements in the final two paragraphs of Hooks's chapter on the military-industrial complex as examples of what is wrong with his overall viewpoint. He ends the penultimate paragraph with a conclusion fitting very nicely with my view that the corporate community sets the limits within which the American state must operate:

> The vast defense planning effort was rarely attacked by major corporations precisely because it did not threaten to become a centralized planning effort with direct impacts on civilian sectors. Recognizing the limited scope of the Pentagon's de facto industrial planning is essential to understanding its dynamics and its durability. (1991:264)

Exactly so. It reads like a brief for a class dominance perspective. There is no autonomy of any importance if the state cannot go beyond boundaries set by the corporate community.

The final two sentences of the chapter reveal the narrowly economistic view he has of corporations, as well as the fact that he does not take seriously the literature on how the power elite is involved in setting the state's agenda:

> The Pentagon's interventions in the aeronautics and electronics sectors, however, cannot be reduced to the interests of capitalists. This planning represents a clear case of the state pursuing a distinct—but not necessarily hostile— agenda from that of the dominant class. (ibid.)

These words show that Hooks does not take seriously the evidence suggesting that the agenda of the dominant class includes unsurpassed military power and the ability to expand economically all over the world (e.g., Eakins 1969; Shoup and Minter 1977; Domhoff 1990:chaps. 5 and 6; Leffler 1992). Further, he does not tie this agenda to the fact that members of the dominant class are the top policymakers at the state and defense departments, as he almost concedes in his chapter on the monopoly sector. Given that we know the agenda of the dominant class, and that leaders from the corporations, foundations, and policy groups setting this agenda often serve in key governmental positions, there is a strong case to be made that the state's agenda is *not* distinct from that of the dominant class in the United States. Which brings us to the point where we can conclude this chapter with a brief look at the postwar America made possible by the American victory in World War II.

## CONCLUSION

World War II in general and the industrial mobilization in particular did for the upper-class and corporate community in the United States just what Mills said they did. Thanks to the economic recovery caused by massive military spending, and the rekindling of patriotism any successful war generates, American corporate leaders and their policy advisers were restored to their place in the sun. They delivered war materiel from factories and leadership in Washington, serving the government for a mere dollar a year. In the process, the American corporate community became in part a military-industrial complex, that is, developed a significant defense sector. There was, as Mills also said, a reorganization of the power elite through the incorporation of an expanded military establishment, but I hope I have shown that the military leaders were junior partners in the new arrangement. More broadly, America as a whole became a military-industrial complex (Pilisuk and Hayden 1965): military spending at home and the expansion of corporations overseas became one means by which the economic problems of the 1930s were overcome. Furthermore, this defense spending favored some regions over others, playing a "large role" (Schulman 1991:ix) in triggering southern economic development, as did the space program that complemented defense spending in the arc between Cape Canaveral and Houston after 1960. More dramatically,

> in 1964 defense and space work was calculated to account for more than 10 percent of total income in six states: Alaska and Hawaii (where it came largely from bases and installations); Virginia (where a combination of bases and defense industry was the overwhelming cause; and California, Utah, and Washington (where defense industry was the overwhelming cause). (Huntington 1969:12)

In claiming that military spending was an essential boost to the postwar economy, I am not saying the cold war was created as an excuse to justify military spending. I believe the cold war was very real, rooted in a clash between two expanding rival systems, Soviet communism and American capitalism. It concerned geopolitics, economics, values, and ways of life. Nor am I saying that military spending was increased in reaction to temporary economic downturns; work by Huntington (1961) and Goertzel (1985) has shown that is not the case, although I will introduce an important qualification in a minute. I am most definitely saying, however, that the 8 to 13 percent of GNP provided by military spending between 1951 and 1964 was no small potatoes in pumping up the economy (e.g., Huntington 1969:5–80; cf. Nathanson 1969; Reich 1973).

Bernard Nossiter (1990:chap. 7), in his readable and cogent history of economic policy between 1929 and 1990, argues the case even more strongly after stressing that the cold war was "politically motivated," not an economic boondoggle:

> The fact is that arms spending and its related programs for foreign aid and space have been a great bulwark to the postwar economy. In fat years and lean, high levels of military outlays (ranging from 5% to 3% of the economy since 1950) have put a floor under effective demand, a break on every slide. It is spending that can be turned on rapidly, although it is hard to turn off. The mere announcement of a speedup in defense orders will expand hiring, improve the bank balances of large contractors, stimulate the economies of communities where arms plants are located, and multiply its blessings by increasing incomes for the providers of goods and services to the newly hired. (p. 204)

Specifically, military and space spending "now account for about three-quarters of the goods and services bought by the government" (ibid). Nossiter cites the documents showing that speedups in defense orders were used by the Eisenhower administration to fight slumps in 1954 and 1957; these speedups show that the aggregate numbers used by Goertzel (1985) to dismiss military spending completely are not the whole story (Nossiter 1990:76–78, 210–11).

Military spending aside, the postwar era began with the liberal-labor coalition firmly entrenched in the Democratic party, a very big change from the early 1930s. However, it made very few gains in the immediate postwar era, contrary to the impression generated by talk about the continuation of the New Deal coalition until the Nixon era. For example, the liberal-labor coalition was defeated in its attempt to create a means for significant government involvement in the generation of jobs: the proposed Full Employment Act of 1946 was watered down to a Council of Economic Advisers, a joint congressional committee on the economy, and an annual report on the economy (Domhoff 1990:chap. 7). Nor could the unions convince any Democratic Congress to modify the restrictions on the National Labor Relations Act passed by the Republican Congress in 1947. Even the feeble reforms called for in 1977 in the Labor Law Reform Act were defeated.

As was the case before and during World War II, the most immediate problem facing the liberal-labor coalition in the postwar era was the conservative coalition in Congress, behind which stood the northern corporate community and the evolving southern ownership class, meaning a united ruling class on three key issues outlined in the first chapter:

1.   opposition to prolabor legislation,
2.   opposition to pro–civil rights legislation,
3.   opposition to business regulation.

However, this North/South employer unity in the postwar era was finally broken momentarily by a major societal upheaval, the civil rights movement. This movement was made possible by the mechanization of agriculture in the South and the further economic changes wrought there by defense spending (Piven and Cloward 1977; Wright 1986; Bloom 1987; Schulman 1991), but it would not have happened without disciplined organization, patient struggle, and great sacrifice by African-Americans. Faced eventually by the prospect of severe disruption throughout the country, the northern Republicans deserted their southern Democratic friends on this labor issue in 1964 and 1965. They joined with the liberal-labor coalition within the Democratic party in making possible the Civil Rights Act of 1964 and the Voting Rights Act of 1965, but not before obtaining several concessions that made racial equality slower and tougher to achieve (Potter 1972). The situation in 1964 and 1965 was the mirror image of the years 1934 and 1935, when the southern Democrats abandoned the northern industrialists in the face of union organizing and societal disruptions in the North (Domhoff 1990:chap. 4). These were the only two times the employers from the

North and South have broken ranks with each other before or since. Both breaks were precipitated by massive upheaval within the working class itself, albeit aided by liberals and leftists from the middle and upper classes in both instances. That is, these were years of major class conflict.

Once African-Americans won civil and voting rights in the South, southern capitalists no longer could defeat liberal candidates, black or white, as easily in Democratic primaries, so they began to drift into what was becoming their natural home as the South industrialized, the Republican party, taking many working-class whites with them on the basis of appeals to racism, religion, southern white pride, and the usual opposition to an intrusive federal government. But it was not simply that the white capitalists were pushed out of the party; they had lost interest in it as well because its primary function for them had been to maintain African-Americans as a powerless, low-wage work force. (Federal subsidies were its second function.) In power terms, the success of the civil rights movement meant that the South would become more like the North, and as part of that process the southern segment of the ruling class became Republican.

From my theoretical perspective, there is great continuity in the postwar power elite. Whether the conservative, business-oriented politicians of the South call themselves Democrats or Republicans is a relatively minor matter. As long as liberals and unions can be marginalized politically, as they have been throughout the postwar era, and even more so since the mid-1970s, for reasons I explain elsewhere (Domhoff 1990:chap. 9), then little or nothing will change in terms of the overall power structure. African-Americans now have greater rights and opportunities, no small improvement from the viewpoint of these previously excluded citizens, but at the highest levels of society nothing has changed in terms of wealth, income, or tax structure, except to favor the wealthy even more since the mid-1970s (e.g., Piven and Cloward 1982/1985; Wolff 1995).

However, there is one way that the changes brought about by the civil rights movement may have large consequences in the future: the movement of southern capitalists into the Republican party means the liberal-labor coalition can have its own political party for the first time in American history. Given the great difficulty of forming a viable third party within the American electoral system, and the need for an organizational basis for creating policies and ideologies to challenge the hegemony of the corporate-conservative ideology, this possible takeover of the Democratic party is of great potential importance.

To state this structural possibility, however, merely shows what a formidable task it would be to use the Democratic party to challenge the American power elite. Voters and nonvoters alike in the working class would have to be convinced that the antigovernment ideology they usually embrace is self-defeating in terms of their desire for full employment and better educational opportunities. They would have to be convinced to vote their pocketbooks (class) instead of race, religion, or superpatriotism. Enormous amounts of money would have to be raised in small sums to support candidates. The many differences of opinion on policy matters within the liberal-labor coalition would have to be compromised or transcended. Considering the difficulties of mounting a successful liberal-labor challenge to the current power elite under normal conditions, there may be only two possibilities for change: a crash of the economy due to shortsighted policies by conservatives, or major disruption of the system by those who are being ground into even deeper urban poverty by the movement of industrial jobs to low-wage countries and cutbacks in federal welfare spending [see Galbraith (1992) for a sobering treatment of the possibilities of near-term social change in a "culture of contentment"]. But neither of these scenarios is very likely either.

In other words, short of major societal breakdowns or a political mobilization by the liberal-labor coalition through the Democratic party, or some combination of those possibilities, the power elite of the United States will remain much as it was at the end of World War II. Contrary to Hooks, then that war did not increase the autonomy of the state. It increased the strength and cohesion of the power elite by incorporating an expanded military, and hence increased the ability of the power elite to dominate government. The trend since World War II therefore has been toward less state autonomy, not more. As Mills (1956) argued, the "political directorate" had its greatest independence in the 1930s, when the massive failures of the economy discredited corporate leaders and made it possible for liberal and prolabor politicians to gain some electoral and appointed positions in government. But the mobilization for World War II, bringing together military leaders and businessmen in Washington, began the process of power elite reorganization that led to the gradual reduction of the relatively minor political influence of the liberal-labor coalition at the national level. This liberal-labor influence was all but gone by 1977 at the latest.

Is there a state-centric theorist anywhere other than Hooks who would argue that there was a trend toward state autonomy after World War II? Or any signs of state autonomy in the Reagan-Bush or Clinton eras? Just to ask those questions is to reveal the inability of state autonomy theory to account for the fifty years of American political history following World War II, let alone the war years Hooks tries to invoke by making claims that are contrary to what virtually every historian has written about them.

## INTRODUCTION

After the detailed discussion of the New Deal and World War II in the previous four chapters, it might seem a little unorthodox to turn to the Progressive Era (1890–1916) in this one. However, that is where the trail leads in terms of the development of state autonomy theory, because Skocpol unexpectedly focused on it in her 1992 book on *Protecting Soldiers and Mothers*. As she explains in her preface (pp. vii–x), the book was supposed to be primarily about social welfare during and after the New Deal, but she became so fascinated with Civil War pensions and the role of women in the Progressive Era that she did not make it any further. Moreover, what she learned about the well-known women's reform movement of the era caused her to modify her theory to some extent. She found these women to be so successful in their efforts to influence the state from outside it, even without the right to vote nationally or in most states, that she decided she could no longer talk about the American state as autonomous. Instead, she began calling her version of state-centered theory a "polity-centered approach" (p. x), meaning that social movements, coalitions of pressure groups, and political parties must be given their due.

Skocpol insists that her view is still distinctive, but the new version sounds more like the pluralism of the 1950s and 1960s than anything else. We are told, for example, that the lack of government bureaucracies and an established church in the United States left ample space for "voluntary associations," with plenty of highly educated women and men to join them (p. 529). In addition, "broad, transpartisan coalitions of groups—and ultimately legislators—had to be assembled for each particular issue" (p. 368). Now, Skocpol may put a little more emphasis on political institutions and the structured nature of the polity, but in fact voluntary associations, shifting coalitions, and political parties are the essence of mainstream pluralism. One thing is certain: there is little mention of business leaders, classes, or class conflict, so her perspective is even further removed from a class dominance one than it was before. Indeed, it is astonishing that she could give so little attention to business and class in the age that saw the rise of the giant corporation and a nationwide upper class based upon it. Half of the largest corporations in 1899 were created that year and twenty-three new corporations joined the top hundred in 1901 (e.g., Bunting 1986:37–39), but Skocpol barely acknowledges these dramatic economic changes in her discussion of alleged political transformations.

Perhaps sensing that some readers might be disappointed because she does not fulfill her earlier (1988/1989:642) promise to analyze the welfare state in her next book-length effort, Skocpol constantly reminds the reader of how important her findings supposedly are by the use of vivid adjectives. She claims in the first sentence of the preface that she has discovered "startling new facts" (1992:vii). She chides other scholars for allegedly overlooking or ignoring the stories she tells, but she also admits that much of her material comes from secondary sources (pp. vii, 61, 102), which seems to me to make her chastisements a contradiction in terms. She calls many organizations and people "remarkable." Nineteenth-century political parties earn this designation (p. 75), as does the Bureau of Pensions in the 1870s for its clerical capacity (p. 532). The women who worked for reforms in the Progressive Era were even more "remarkable"; she uses the term ten different times to describe them or their efforts. When such glowing terms as "adept," "amazing," "apt," "astute," "bold," "fascinating," "inspirational," and "ingenious" are added to the list, it is clear that Skocpol has an enthusiast's attitude toward her subject.

In the rest of this chapter, I will provide an empirical and theoretical critique of the "startling new facts" and polity-centered theory Skocpol now champions, showing that the position to which she has retreated is no more accurate than the one she staked out for herself and her students in 1980. First, I will provide a brief overview of her general framework, then turn to a consideration of her three case studies: the expansion of Civil War pensions, the failures of male-oriented insurance and pension legislation, and the successes of the women's movement in obtaining legislation benefiting widowed mothers and working women. Whether any of this has anything to do with the New Deal or any other later developments is one of the main questions I will address.

## THE BIG PICTURE

Skocpol's new theoretical emphasis is summed up in a passage she uses twice from James Bryce, one of those nineteenth-century European observers of the United States who mainstream social scientists love to quote in an undisguised appeal to authority: "In America the great moving forces are the parties. The government counts for less than in Europe, the parties count for more" (1992:64, 72). This is, of course, quite a concession for someone who criticized almost all social scientists for overlooking the power of the state in America, but no apologies are offered. She spends a full chapter reviewing standard sources on parties, machines, patronage, and bosses in the nineteenth century, but with no discussion of the role of wealthy campaign donors, who were far more important in the late nineteenth and early twentieth centuries than she realizes (e.g., Overacker 1932; Lundberg 1937:54–64; Alexander 1992:9–13). The fabled political machines were oiled from the top (e.g., White 1905, as reprinted in Chambers 1964; Myers 1917; Zink 1930; Katz 1968).

Another new emphasis in her polity-centered context is on the importance of fit between a group and the polity in understanding the success and failure of rival policy initiatives. If a group happens to have the organizational and rhetorical capacities that "fit" with the structure of the polity and the going cultural discourse, then it is more likely to enjoy success than a group that does not (e.g., 1992:54–57). This is one of the key ways the shapes and contours of the state matter greatly, for these contours determine which groups will have fit and which will not. The potential for a tautological argument with such a vague concept is very great, of course. Those who win must have had fit, those who failed must have lacked it.

In the context of her discussion of contours and fits, Skocpol emphasizes that the United States is a "non-parliamentary polity" lacking "strong civil service ministries" and "programmatically oriented political parties" (p. 253). The presidential system and single-member districts lead to a two-party system. The courts were very important in the nineteenth century as bastions of protection for private property. None of these homilies is news to anyone. They are the reason why few social scientists were ever state centered in trying to understand social power in the United States. There is one further point that Skocpol thinks has escaped most other people. Policies not only flow from institutions, they reshape these institutions (e.g., p. 531).

She often invokes one of her favorite phrases, that the nineteenth-century American state is one of "courts and parties," but I do not think this is a good way to conceive of the state because it makes the courts sound too independent of the parties. If the issue is power, then the question is who has the resources to win the presidency (or governorship), which has the authority to appoint the most important judges. If corporate leaders have the major role in narrowing the field of possible presidential and gubernatorial candidates through the huge weight of financial donations and other favors, then of course the Supreme Court is going to be made up predominantly of corporation lawyers, which Burch (1981a, 1981b) shows to be the case from 1875 to 1937, when Roosevelt started putting politicians, law professors, and members of the Justice Department on it.

So much by way of general overview. It is now time to see what Skocpol claims in her case studies.

## CIVIL WAR PENSIONS: DO THEY MATTER?

Skocpol is extremely impressed with the extent and generosity of the disability and old-age pensions paid to veterans of the Civil War and their survivors, and with the fact that these pensions became "more liberal" over the decades (1992:110). In 1873, extra monies were added to widow's pensions for each dependent child; in 1890 the government extended the pensions to any veteran who at some time had become disabled for manual work; in 1906 the pensions became available for all veterans by reason of being over age sixty-two (pp. 107, 111, 129). By 1915, the percentage of surviving veterans (about 424,000 people) on pensions had risen to a little over 93 percent. A disproportionate number of these veterans lived in small towns and rural areas in the North and Midwest, and many of them could be described as middle class (pp. 136–38). They were Anglo-American and Irish-American, concentrated in a relative handful of states. She thinks this pension system has consequences for understanding old-age pensions in the United States.

Skocpol makes a reasonable case that the increasing generosity of the Civil War pension system was in some part a function of the close party competition between Republicans and Democrats in the 1870s and 1880s (e.g., pp. 115, 118–24, 130). In fact, the competition tended to be closest in those states with the largest number of pensioners, evidence that the pensions had become a form of patronage (p. 124). By the late 1880s, Republicans were the main proponents of a generous pension system for veterans. For Skocpol, this story is important because she thinks it supports her claim that parties were predominant in the nineteenth century.

However, it turns out there is more to it than parties. The original pension disability act of 1862 was extremely generous to begin with because of the uncertainties and difficulties of raising a volunteer army in a hurry (pp. 106–7). Thus, it would have been very difficult to be stingy with these veterans as they aged, especially when we recall the extreme carnage and bitter memories from that war. Moreover, much of the impetus in the 1870s for the increasing number of pensioners came from "a few prosperous pension lawyers" who made a good living by obtaining pensions for veterans and then collecting a fee from them (p. 116). Skocpol reports this fact, then downplays it by saying the parties quickly took control of the action (p. 117). In the 1880s, organized vets played a role in improving their pension plan, but Skocpol argues that their strong organization was the product of legislative changes brought about by the parties, making the vets' organization an auxiliary of the parties as much as a pressure upon them (p. 111).

Beyond all this, one of the biggest factors in the increasingly generous pension system was the growing budget surplus created by the high tariffs instituted by the northern industrialists and Republicans as part of their victory over the plantation South. Skocpol stresses that pensions were taking an "astounding" 41.5 percent of the federal budget in 1893 (p. 128), but from the point of view of the Republicans and industrialists the pensions were killing two birds with one stone. They were siphoning off the budget surplus, thereby reducing some of the pressure to lower tariffs, and they were providing patronage in key swing states, thereby helping to keep Republicans in office (e.g., pp. 125–26). Since pensions for Civil War veterans were a safe and useful way to spend money the industrialists did not really want the government to have (they just wanted the tariff protection), I do not think there is anything astounding about the percentage of the budget spent in this way. By the time Skocpol is done with this case study, it seems like there are several factors involved in Civil War pensions more important than parties.

Moreover, the extent of these pensions may not be as impressive to everyone as it is to Skocpol. In 1900, for example, when the population of the country was 76.1 million, with 3.1 million age sixty-five or over, there were 741,259 veterans with disability pensions (p. 109, Table 2). Skocpol estimates that 35 percent of northern men over age sixty-five had a Civil War pension in 1910 (p. 135), but the figures she presents for veterans and their widows age sixty-five and over in 1910 in Appendix 1 (pp. 541–42) are not as impressive. Only sixteen states had 20 percent or more of their entire age-sixty-five-and-over population on a Civil War pension; Kansas was the highest with 30.4 percent. Only eleven states had 20,000 or more people on such pensions; the highest were Pennsylvania (67,371), Ohio (66,920), and New York (58,670). There were only five states where the 20,000 or more pensioners made up 20 percent or more of the age-sixty-five-and-over population: Pennsylvania, Ohio, Indiana, Missouri, and Kansas. When we recall that a disproportionate number of these pensioners lived in rural areas and small towns, it is hard to see their presence having a social impact. As I already noted, there were only 424,000 surviving vets by 1915, when 4.5 million of the country's 100 million people were sixty-five or older, and most of them were dead by 1920, when a twenty-year-old from 1865 would be seventy-five and the life span was far shorter than now. The pensions rarely went to African-Americans and, of course, they excluded the large immigrant population arriving after the Civil War.

But is any of this important if the goal is to understand the modern welfare state in the United States? According to Skocpol, charges of corruption in relation to these pensions by Mugwumps and other moralists were a big factor in causing the delay of the welfare state (e.g., pp. 59, 285). Quite frankly, I doubt the importance of this factor in explaining why the welfare state was later in the United States than most of Western Europe. The charge of corruption was more likely a rationalization, not a cause. First, there is little or no evidence of widespread corruption (pp. 143–45), and only members of the higher classes begrudged what was in effect an old-age pension to a few hundred thousand "morally deserving" veterans (pp. 148–51). True enough, it is perception that counts in politics, but if there is no evidence for the perception, then it is all the more likely that it was manufactured for political reasons. Supporting this point, there is much evidence that industrialists and plantation owners vigorously opposed government old-age pensions for their employees during the Progressive Era for economic and political reasons (Quadagno 1988).

In terms of the later American welfare state, Skocpol ends up with one possibly usable point from her wrong turn into the dead end of Civil War pensions. Memories of the charges of corruption in relation to these pensions allegedly "helped to shore up the determination of New Deal policy makers to emphasize *contributory* forms of unemployment and old-age insurance in the Social Security Act of 1935" (1992:533, her italics). "Helped" is a weak claim to begin with, but it is too strong on the basis of the evidence I presented in Chapter 4 that industrial relations experts like J. Douglas Brown and Murray Latimer wanted contributory pensions for quite other reasons. I have to conclude that Skocpol's first case study is irrelevant to issues concerning the nature of the American social welfare system.

## POLITY CHANGES OR CLASS CONFLICT?

Skocpol's next stop is the movements for various welfare benefits for workers during the Progressive Era—industrial accident insurance, health insurance, unemployment insurance, and old-age pensions. To make a long story short, they all lost except industrial accident insurance (workmen's compensation). This part of the book makes a good contribution by showing how the differing state systems of Great Britain and the United States contributed to liberal-labor victories on these issues in Great Britain and splits between reformers and organized labor in the United States. We do agree that the structure of the state matters.

Skocpol begins this section with a lengthy history of the small organization of experts and reformers over which we constantly do battle, the American Association for Labor Legislation (AALL), arguing vigorously that it was not dependent upon its handful of wealthy donors (pp. 183–84). While I have argued just the opposite (Domhoff 1990:46–48), for my purposes here I want to emphasize our agreements about the organization. The American Association for Labor Legislation had elitist views and did not try to reach out to grass roots groups. Much of its program was opposed by industrialists and organized labor alike. It lost its campaigns for health insurance and unemployment insurance, and gave up on old-age pensions before it started. Further, I agree that middle-class experts shrank from an alliance with organized labor because labor wanted noncontributory old-age pensions and laws that would improve its ability to organize and strike (Skocpol 1992:209–10). In short, there was not a good fit between reformers and labor in the Progressive Era for a variety of reasons that Skocpol spells out in a useful discussion of trade unions and social legislation in her fourth chapter. In my terms, the liberal-labor coalition was very limited in scope.

Only in the case of workmen's compensation were the reformers in the AALL on the winning side, but by any account except Skocpol's this victory was won by a united business community ready to change the law because juries were deciding too many lawsuits in favor of injured workers (Weinstein 1968:chap. 2; Domhoff 1970:197–201; Castrovinci 1976). Even the National Association of Manufacturers was overwhelmingly in favor of workmen's compensation. Organized labor finally went along reluctantly. The AALL did the leg work.

What does the overall lineup of victories and defeats on social welfare legislation in the Progressive Era demonstrate? I believe it shows that the corporate community was victorious on all four issues of concern. It opposed the three losing programs, supported the one winning program, and no other group can match its record. Not the middle-class reformers of the AALL, who lost three out of four, and not organized labor, which supported a nonstarter, noncontributory old-age pensions, and had to be pushed into supporting workmen's compensation. If we were disciplining our thought by using accepted power indicators, these four victories for the corporate community in the decisional arena would be considered support for a class dominance theory.

However, Skocpol does not think in these terms. She has a much more general explanation for why both reformers and labor lost. There was not a good fit between the movement for welfare legislation and the polity because the polity was undergoing a major transformation: "In clear contrast to contemporary Britain, the United States at the turn of the twentieth century was undergoing a transformation from party-dominated patronage democracy to interest-group-oriented regulatory politics, a transformation that discouraged the inauguration of a modern paternalist state" (1992:285). Then too, organized labor did not trust the state because of the harsh way it had been treated by the courts, so it would not go for the statist solutions advocated by the reformers.

While there is something to Skocpol's polity-centered analysis of the failed welfare initiatives, I do not think she sees the big picture correctly. Still, she almost hits upon the key factor at the very end of her discussion. After going on for many pages about parties, courts, governmental contexts, and the state's lack of "autonomous administrative organs," (1992:310), she says straight out that proworker social policies were opposed by "middle and upper classes" that were "not about to support new social benefits that might lubricate ties between politicians and the state" (1992:310). This comes very close to addressing the basic problem: class conflict. It also comes close to explaining why capitalists then and now want a small domestic state that they can dominate: they were/are afraid that a large and perhaps more autonomous state might help the working class. States that help workers are states that disrupt capitalist control of labor markets, and such disruption cuts into the profits and power of capitalists. If Skocpol and other state autonomy theorists could bring themselves to see the importance of this basic conflict, then they could better understand why the American state lacked autonomous administrative organs. The capitalists and their allies bitterly opposed the development of such organs throughout the nineteenth century. It was their state, and they were not going to let it escape from them without a fight.

Some state-centric theorists might think my analysis is too simple because capitalists elsewhere opposed most social policies sought by the working class and reformers, but at least some of these policies passed anyhow. Why the difference between the United States and the others? Skocpol, as noted, thinks the answer is to be found in the nature of the polity, along with the transformative processes going on in the polity at the turn of the century, but I believe those factors to be secondary. The major issue is that the working class is weaker and the capitalist class stronger in the United States than elsewhere. There are several intertwined reasons for this, all of which were even more salient in the Progressive Era than later.

The first reason for this greater power differential, as I argued at the end of Chapter 5, lies in a region mostly ignored by state autonomy theorists: the South. The American working class never could be united and strong when most of its southern half was completely subordinated and without the right to vote until 1965, giving southern plantation owners more or less complete control of politics in that region (cf. Goldfield 1987:235–40). Second, the political and cultural differences between the largely nativist craft workers of the American Federation of Labor and the largely immigrant industrial workers created another division in the working class (Mink 1986). Third, the structural factors leading to a two-party system meant that northern workers had no place to go except into a Democratic party controlled by the southern plantation capitalists.

Within the context of racial/ethnic splits and the lack of a labor party, we can mix in the fourth factor: the importance of the individualistic ideology of American workers, an explanatory variable largely dismissed by Skocpol (1992:15–22). It is not that this individualistic culture somehow inevitably persists through tradition in some vague fashion, as it seems to for some of the values theorists Skocpol criticizes, but that the working class could not develop the institutional forms—strong labor unions and a labor party—that would make it possible to create and sustain a more collectivist, class-oriented consciousness, thereby overcoming the individualistic ethos, not to mention ethnocentrism and racism. Individualistic ideology persists in the working class, and matters, because it is embodied in the corporate-sponsored institutions dominating the society and because it has not been possible in this country to develop any counterinstitutions to create more communal, cooperative, and progovernment programs and values. Put another way, and contrary to Skocpol and many others, it was not the fact that there was universal white male suffrage in the nineteenth century that led to the absence of a labor party, but the nature of the southern political economy and the near impossibility of creating a third (labor) party in a state system whose electoral rules tend to generate a two-party system.

Fifth, the working class in America has been weak for a reason mentioned by Skocpol: its inability, at least until the New Deal, to form a solid alliance with well-off liberals. This difficulty has its roots in two of the factors already mentioned: the ideology of the working class and the difficulties of sustaining third parties. The liberals of the twentieth century, usually called reformers in the Progressive Era, wanted to use the federal government to solve social problems, but their program clashed with the antistatist views of labor. Moreover, in the absence of a liberal and/or labor party, there were no meeting grounds where liberals and labor could overcome their differences and develop a common program. Only after 1935 did the Democratic party fulfill part of this need as the leadership of the new CIO and liberals formed the liberal-labor coalition within the context of the larger Roosevelt coalition. But even after 1935 the liberal-labor coalition was to be a shaky one, as the fight over the Progressive party in 1948, the reluctance of many unions to support the Civil Rights movement, and the split over the Vietnam War between antiwar liberals and prowar unions were to show.

As for the capitalist class, it is stronger than in most other countries for a number of reasons. It is a commonplace to observe that it had no feudal lords, established church, military, or state bureaucrats to contend with as it grew to power. Everyone knows its leaders purposely created a national state with limited powers, and that the plantation capitalists of the South feared a powerful national state even more than northern capitalists because they worried, rightly, both before and after the Civil War, that such a state might interfere with their complete subordination of their African-American work force. Let us make no mistake about it: state's rights is the antistate ideology of both the Republicans and southern Democrats. Once their Civil War was over, and despite their other policy differences, this ideology united northern and southern employers completely in opposing any federal program or agency that might aid those who worked with their hands in factories and fields.

Building on these strengths, northern capitalists were able to defeat classwide attempts at working-class organization in the 1880s, shrinking the labor movement to the small, nativist, craft-oriented AFL. As Kim Voss (1993) shows by comparing the conflicts between capitalists and workers in the United States, Britain, and France from 1830 to 1887, the working-class movement in this country was very similar to those in the other two until the mid-1880s. Then it suffered a series of defeats at the hands of highly organized and violence-prone employers who enjoyed the neutrality or support of local and state governments controlled by the political parties they dominated. This situation contrasts with what happened in Britain and France, where the employers were constrained in their resistance and forced to compromise with unions by governments still dominated by landed aristocracies and state elites [Voss (1993:237–38, 245–48); cf. R. Hamilton (1991) for evidence that capitalists did not control nineteenth-century European governments]. Here we see the genuine usefulness of a good comparative study, complete with original data developed by Voss for the American case. Mann (1993:648–51) comes to a conclusion similar to Voss's in comparing the United States to Britain and Germany.

## SISTERHOOD OR CLASS POLITICS?

Skocpol devotes four chapters and an appendix to the legislative and state-building efforts of women of the Progressive Era. She chronicles their success in (1) establishing maximum hours for women in most states; (2) making it possible for counties in most states to pay mother's pensions to needy single mothers (usually widows) if they so desired; (3) creating a fact-finding Children's Bureau in the federal government; (4) passing laws that set up minimum-wage commissions for women in a few states between 1912 and 1923; and (5) convincing the federal government to create federally subsidized clinics that provided prenatal and postnatal health advice to mothers.

Skocpol attributes the success of these efforts to several factors. First, both elite and middle-class women were willing to ignore class barriers and coalesce with working-class women (1992:319, 324). Second, the elite and middle-class women came together in nationwide social clubs and policy organizations that could adopt and disseminate a common program, and then lobby effectively in many states at once. Third, the women made excellent use of magazines, books, forums, and media in influencing public opinion, which in turn influenced politicians. Fourth, the activist women used "moralistic" and "maternalistic" rhetoric in influencing male legislators and judges (1992:368–69). Most generally, there was an ideal organizational and ideological fit between the maternalist women's movement and the government at the time, just the opposite of what obtained for male reformers (1992:319, 531). The women could be active in many states at the same time because of their federal organizational structure, and their maternalist ideology resonated with the values of the many legislators and judges who wanted to preserve the family and have women at home raising their children.

In regard to the organizational dimension of this movement, Skocpol's main focus is on the General Federation of Women's Clubs (hereafter GFWC). Founded in 1890 to bring together local women's clubs, the GFWC had biennial conventions, published a journal, maintained a national office, and held regular meetings of elected national officers (1992:320). Once the GFWC was established, there soon followed state federations linked to it that also were socially and politically active. Importantly for my purposes, Skocpol notes that policy flowed from the top down in the GFWC (1992:331). She raises an interesting possibility when she claims the women reformers and intellectuals—overwhelmingly unmarried, she emphasizes (1992:342)—could work with the noncareerist married women in the nationwide GFWC because they all shared "maternalist values" (1992:354).

Although the GFWC was the most general organizational base of the movement, it was joined on some issues by the Congress of Mothers, created in 1897 by the wife of a Washington, D.C., lawyer and other elite women. For example, Phoebe Hearst of the newspaper clan was among its early leaders and backers. This organization focused on the "ideal of educated motherhood," especially through work with public schools (1992: 333). It later evolved into the PTA and narrowed its focus to schools only. The other national-level organization working with the GFWC on many issues was the liberal National Consumers League, formed in the 1890s. Its leaders, according to Skocpol, were primarily elite women, along with a few male professors who rarely attended meetings (1992:352).

As impressive as these women were in their abilities and organizational skills, their power was not as great as Skocpol implies and their successes were not as great as they first appear, as I will document shortly. Nor does Skocpol consider the possibility that some of these groups represent "the feminine half of the upper class" (Domhoff 1970:44–54), reinforcing the efforts made by their husbands, brothers, and fathers, rather than challenging them. Instead, she says the women in this movement had "unselfish" policy goals (1992:319). They wanted "to protect children and mothers and at the same time address the inequities and inefficiencies of an industrial and urban society" (1992:314).

Skocpol does speak of upper-class women in relation to the settlement house movement, the National Consumers League, and a small proworker organization known as the Women's Trade Union League, but mostly she says these women were "elite women" or "highly educated career women." She discusses their educational backgrounds at length. They were from the Seven Sisters, by and large, well-known as schools for upper-class women in the nineteenth century. She says women in these schools were taught they were "superior" to other young women, suggesting to me class consciousness (p. 343). At another point Skocpol notes that only 2 percent of the women between eighteen and twenty-one years of age in 1880 were in college (p. 341). Given the small number, it is likely that the majority were from the upper class. In my own study of these issues, I found almost all the top leaders of the movement came from upper-class backgrounds (Domhoff 1970:48–49), and other studies concur (e.g., Linn 1935; Williams 1948; Davis 1967; Platt 1969:77, 83–95; Payne 1988:50–52; Gordon 1994:chap. 4).

Once their schooling was completed, the well-educated women of the upper class wanted roles in society commensurate with their class and educational backgrounds. It became difficult to teach them they were superior and members of a ruling class, and then not let them share in ruling. Subsequent sociological studies show that upper-class women did carve out a role for themselves in the power structure, primarily in the areas of concern to the women of the Progressive Era (Ostrander 1984; Daniels 1988; McLeod 1988; Odendahl 1990).

In her eagerness to portray women of the era as part of one big movement, Skocpol downplays or ignores the many differences among them, not just class and education, but race and ethnicity as well. She talks as if women were single-mindedly gender conscious in their politics, overlooking their differences related to class, race, and ethnicity on many issues. As her feminist critics point out, gender is not a single phenomenon unrelated to other social characteristics (e.g., Mink 1993, 1995; Abramovitz 1993; Scott 1993).

One final difficulty with Skocpol's perspective on the women's movement must be introduced before turning to an analysis of her case studies. She does not stress enough that the three groups she emphasizes—the National Congress of Mothers, the GFWC, and the National Consumers League—were "quite different" in politics and membership despite their common maternalist orientation (Gordon 1993:150). They therefore should not be lumped together too readily. The National Congress of Mothers, which Skocpol shows to be the most socially elite of the groups, had an exclusive focus on improving motherhood. Its efforts to change child-rearing practices in the working class were endorsed by male politicians, including President Theodore Roosevelt (1992:337). I believe one of its main goals was to Americanize the new immigrants in the industrial working class, that is, convey to them the standards and ideology of the traditional upper class. Its members were conservative maternalists.

The GFWC, on the other hand, was far more wide-ranging in its interests, and probably had more middle-class women in its leadership. Its views on general issues tended to be mainstream and conventional. The National Consumers' League, however, was a liberal maternalist organization even though many of its women leaders had upper-class backgrounds. I think its leaders were part of the nascent and struggling liberal-labor coalition of the era. They are the female counterparts of the liberal men met in earlier chapters. In fact, a great many of them lived long enough to become important members of the liberal-labor coalition during the New Deal (Chambers 1963:254–57). This group also differed in that it had some male leadership. Perhaps the most telling evidence for placing the National Consumers' League in the liberal-labor coalition is its backing of reform legislation for men as well as women, whereas the other women's groups focused exclusively on women and children. As one expert on women in American history concludes, it had "far more radical goals than did the women's clubs," and "would have supported provision for all workers had they thought it politically feasible" (Scott 1993:778).

In the following analysis, therefore, I am going to use the National Congress of Mothers and the GFWC as indicators for acceptable upper-class views and the National Consumers' League as emblematic of the liberal view on an issue. This distinction makes it possible to determine if the two mainstream women's groups ever line up with employers, leaving the National Consumers' League on its own.

We are now ready to consider the case study materials brought together by Skocpol. The first concerns industrial legislation (primarily maximum hours and minimum wages), the second mothers' pensions, and the third the creation of the Children's Bureau and its later program for advice-giving maternity clinics.

## THE CASE STUDIES

### Maximum Hours and Minimum Wages

The most successful of the reforms sought by the women's movement was a restriction on the number of hours women could work during a day or week. Between 1874 and 1920, forty-one states passed what were called maximum-hours laws, most enacted from 1910 to 1920. By way of contrast, the least successful of the reform efforts was in the area of minimum wages, where only fifteen states passed legislation creating minimum-wage commissions between 1912 and 1923; most of these successes were in low-population western states with little or no industry, and two were soon repealed. Moreover, minimum-wage legislation was declared unconstitutional by the Supreme Court in 1923. The large differences in the success rates of the two types of legislation allow us to see what factors may be having the greatest influence on the passage of these laws.

First, it needs to be stressed that maximum-hours laws had far less potential impact on employers than minimum-wage laws because they were not an expense to the employer: hours laws were regulatory in nature, simply limiting the total daily or weekly hours women could work. Minimum-wage laws, however, were redistributive in nature. Employers in most cases would be required to pay female employees higher wages. Thus, the two types of laws were quite distinct. Hours laws did not necessarily pose a threat to profit making (McCammon 1995).

Second, male workers tended to be favorably disposed to maximum-hours laws for three reasons. First, such laws fit with their patriarchal ideology about the fragility of women. Second, such legislation could help to limit women as competitors with men for good jobs, just as protective laws keeping women out of night work or allegedly dangerous jobs helped to monopolize the best jobs for men. Third, unions saw such legislation as a precedent for gaining a similar law for men, a thin entering wedge.

On the other hand, the AFL was bitterly opposed to minimum wages for anyone because it feared minimum wages would in fact become the maximum. However, state federations of labor sometimes favored such laws, so the situation varied from state to state. For example, the state federations were supportive in Washington, Texas and Massachusetts, where the laws passed (Skocpol 1992:412).

A third general factor to be considered is that there were male state officials who favored maximum hours because they wanted mothers at home supervising their children (p. 377). They decided they could not enforce child labor laws unless women's working hours were cut back. Experts in bureaus of labor statistics and factory inspectors were the leaders in this regard.

Fourth, the women's reform movement was not united in favor of both maximum hours and minimum wages. Both the GFWC and the National Consumers' League were in favor of maximum-hours legislation, but the GFWC never endorsed passage of minimum-wage legislation (p. 414). As for the National Congress of Mothers, it "virtually never mentioned industrial regulations beyond the child labor laws that it strongly supported" (p. 382). Skocpol even presents some evidence that the national leaders of the National Congress of Mothers may have opposed regulations for women workers (p. 382). This means the liberal National Consumers' League was the only major national-level organization of women advocating minimum-wage commissions, aided by the National Women's Trade Union League, which was small, organized in only a few states, and of less influence than the other three groups.

In the case of the GFWC, Skocpol follows her statement that it never endorsed minimum-wage legislation with the assurance that "the nationally assembled clubwomen did hear a discussion of the state-by-state movement for female minimum wages" on two different occasions, in 1912 and 1914 (p. 414). Then, too, some state federations did work in favor of the minimum-wage laws passed between 1913 and 1915, but Skocpol concludes that "the state federations do not seem to have adopted the cause of minimum wages in many key states" (p. 417).

Given the differing patterns of support and resistance concerning the two types of legislation, perhaps it is understandable that far more states passed maximum-hours legislation than created minimum-wage commissions. Holly McCammon's (1995) quantitative study of the many factors possibly accounting for the success and failure of these legislative campaigns provides support for the importance of both the women's groups and the employers. Using a method called *event history analysis*, making it possible to assess the influence of time-varying independent variables, she found that hours laws were likely to pass in states where women's reform groups were organized and gubernatorial elections were competitive, but states with large employers were less likely to have such laws (McCammon 1995:231). When it came to minimum-wage laws, however, the presence of the women's groups showed no independent effects. The combination of the National Consumers' League and the presence of the Progressive party, along with the right to vote for women, were the explanatory factors in the few states where these laws did pass. Employer resistance seemed to be the important factor in explaining why minimum-wage laws did not pass (p. 234). Such factors as the degree of unionization, presence of a state labor bureau, and the nature of recent Supreme Court decisions had no effect on the passage of either type of legislation. As McCammon concludes, "The crucial factor for success for the gendered movement was a minimum of employer resistance, and employer opposition was at a minimum when the workplace reforms demanded by the reform groups did not threaten profit making" (p. 239).

We can understand the power dimension of these laws even better if we consider the substance of what they entailed. Did they enact the eight-hour day and living wage the reformers desired? Did they have significant sanctions for violations of them? Were they enforced? In the case of the maximum-hours legislation, the strength of the laws was not impressive. Domestic and agricultural workers were excluded, as were office workers. Only six states limited work to eight-hour days and forty-eight-hour weeks. Another nine set nine hours a day and fifty-four hours a week as the maximum. Ten-hour days and sixty-hour weeks were the standard in most states

(Kessler-Harris 1982:188). Moreover, these limits were easily evaded by employers when necessary through a variety of tactics, such as not counting the time the women workers spent in cleaning or repairing their machinery. Most women workers felt they had to go along with these subterfuges for fear of losing their jobs. There also were numerous exceptions built into the laws for employers with special needs (Kessler-Harris 1982:188). Although there is evidence that these laws helped many women, there is little or no evidence that they were onerous for employers. Employers simply evaded the laws or added more workers in an era when this was not a burden because there were no social security taxes or health benefits to pay.

As for the minimum-wage commissions, they were not very impressive either. For example, in Massachusetts, the one major industrial state with minimum-wage legislation, there were in fact huge holes in the law. The minimum-wage commission was supposed to determine living wages for women and minors, but it set up panels for each industry that recommended widely different levels, and new hearings were constantly needed to consider increases in the face of inflation. Worse, employers could win an exemption if they could prove they would not be able to make a profit if they paid the minimum wage. Most striking of all for the modern reader, the only penalty for noncompliance was adverse publicity, namely, "publishing the names of employers who did not comply" (Kessler-Harris 1982:196).

Whatever way we slice it, maximum hours and minimum wages are not impressive achievements if their enactment is used as an indicator of power. Employers were rarely restricted by them; their power was not challenged.

## Mothers' Pensions

Mothers' pensions, mostly for widowed mothers of children under the age of sixteen, but occasionally for deserted or divorced women, were the second major success after maximum hours for the reform movement. Laws permitting counties to pay such pensions passed in virtually every state outside the South between 1911 and 1920. The campaign was spearheaded by the National Congress of Mothers. The GFWC wholeheartedly supported the effort, as did the National Consumers' League and other women's organizations.

There was little or no opposition to this policy innovation from employers. Skocpol makes this critical point rather obliquely: "Opposition from business, and from economically conservative forces generally, may have been less of a factor in the case of mothers' pensions than it was for hour and minimum-wage laws" (1992:425). Nor was there opposition from any other male group. In fact, the movement for mothers' pensions originated with male juvenile court judges in Missouri, Illinois, and Colorado, who were concerned about both juvenile delinquency and the institutionalization of teenagers from mother-only families (e.g., Lubove 1968:97ff.). The idea then was adopted by the National Congress of Mothers and carried to fruition. The opposition to mothers' pensions came from the established private charitable groups, who vigorously fought government involvement in welfare in the name of voluntarism. The leadership of this opposition was centered in New York at the Charity Organization Society and the Russell Sage Foundation. This opposition included both men and women.

The reform movement won out over the voluntarist opposition with a fair amount of ease. The new law turned out to be a relatively easy one for most state legislators to accept because it primarily involved giving permission to pay such pensions; only 25 percent of the states agreed to help counties with the funding (Lubove 1968:99). Moreover, relatively few counties across the nation took advantage of the opportunity provided by the law, and payments were invariably meager in those that did (Skocpol 1992:472). For example, only 45,800 mothers were funded in 1921 and 93,600 in 1931 (p. 466).

Nor was acceptance into the program automatic for those who were eligible. The mothers had to prove to inquiring social workers that they were fit mothers who were providing a good home and moral atmosphere for their children (pp. 465–70). Although immigrants made up less than one-third of Chicago's population in 1920, "they accounted for more than two-thirds of mothers' pension beneficiaries," which suggests that these pensions were another way the National Congress of Mothers and its allies tried to Americanize the new industrial working class (Mink 1995:31). Skocpol (1992:479) rejects this kind of analysis, saying we should take these upper-class women at "their word" when they say they were "honoring motherhood," but readers should ponder the analysis and evidence in Mink (1995:chap. 2) before they do so.

## The Children's Bureau and Maternity Clinics

The Children's Bureau came into being in 1912 as the culmination of an eight-year legislative effort. It was supported by all the female reform groups. According to Skocpol, its main opponents were "legislators fearful of child labor reforms" (1992:484); one of the early reformers tells us these legislators represented southern mill owners who claimed child labor laws were the work of Yankee agitators trying to kill new industrial rivals in the South (Costin 1983:102–3). But there seems to have been no organized employer opposition to the idea in the North. The main function of the bureau was to carry out studies relating to infants and children, and to issue reports. Within a few years it also was administering programs. The most important of these programs provided advice through maternity clinics set up in cooperation with the states.

The bill creating the maternity clinics in 1921 was supported by the GFWC, National Congress of Mothers, and National Consumers' League, but also by charity groups, churches, unions, and the women's committees of both major political parties. In addition, many legislators were afraid to oppose the bill because they did not know if recently enfranchised women were going to vote as a bloc or start their own political party (Skocpol 1992:505). The opponents of the program were antisuffragist groups, defenders of states' rights, some medical groups at the local or state level, and "forces trying to protect the bureaucratic prerogatives of the Public Health Service" (p. 500). There is no suggestion of any employer opposition. Under the circumstances, the opponents were no match for the reform movement, and a bill passed calling for $1.9 million a year in funding for five years. The program was carried out by public health nurses and women physicians.

By the time the clinics came up for renewal, the circumstances were different and they had acquired an implacable enemy besides, the American Medical Association, which saw them as competition and as a possible precedent for "socialized medicine." No longer fearful that women would desert the two major parties or punish legislators who voted against women's issues, and facing a women's movement now less militant and united, a minority of ultraconservative senators filibustered against the bill. They forced the reform movement to settle for a two-year renewal in the vain hope that the next Congress would be more responsive. Planning began for states to sponsor the program. Most states continued to fund at least some of it, but there were severe cutbacks when the Great Depression began. The functions of the program were taken over by private physicians and the Public Health Service.

## Summary of the Cases

At the outset of her discussion of the women's movement, Skocpol asks the following question: "Why did such maternalist measures succeed during the Progressive Era, even as the first efforts to launch a paternalist American welfare state came to naught?" (p. 317). She says the answer "lies in the heights of social organization, ideological self consciousness and political mobilization achieved by American middle-class women around the turn of the twentieth century" (p. 318). Based on the pattern of success and failure on the five main issues discussed by Skocpol, I suggest a very different answer: the solidarity and power of the power elite, male and female, were determinative.

Employers were highly resistant as a group to only one of these issues, minimum wages, as Skocpol agrees (pp. 411, 417). This was also an issue that the National Congress of Mothers avoided, and on which the GFWC did not make a national endorsement. Even at the state level, Skocpol agrees that the state federations of women's clubs reported "much more involvement" in hours laws and mothers' pensions "than in the campaign for minimum wages for women" (p. 417). This adds up to class solidarity. The fact that the minimum-wage campaign organized by the liberal National Consumers' League was the least successful of the five efforts is therefore supportive of the class dominance view, especially when it is added that employers put up less or no resistance on the other five issues. When the employers were neutral and the National Congress of Women or GFWC supportive, then the program won. When the employers were adamantly opposed, then the program lost, which we can recall is exactly what happened on the male social insurance issues.

Skocpol seems to come to a very similar conclusion at the end of her overview chapter on the various women's groups. There she says that the reformers succeeded when they "seemed to be asking for forms of help for children and mothers that would not apparently severely disadvantage established political, business or labor interests" (p. 372). This is a very different answer from the one she provides at the start of the same chapter, where the victories are credited solely to the "social organization" and "political mobilization" of "middle-class" women (p. 318). From where I sit, the efforts by mainstream middle-class and upper-class women are part of the equation, but the indifference or disinterest of employers as a class is essential, too.

Even where the employers were not an organized stumbling block, however, we should not exaggerate the strength and accomplishments of these programs. The maximum hours were often evaded, the mothers' pensions were small and rarely offered, and the advice-giving maternity clinics did not last very long. I do not think this overall record is one on which a polity-centered or pluralistic theory can be built.

## WHERE DO SKOCPOL'S CASE STUDIES LEAD?

Given all the enthusiasm Skocpol puts into writing about Civil War pensions and maternalist policies, it is stunning how irrelevant her three cases turn out to be in terms of understanding the main features of the American welfare state. It is as if she chose three meandering paths that dry up in the middle of a desert—a desert known as the 1920s. These paths lead nowhere in terms of later developments, at least nowhere very positive. In 1980 Skocpol said she was going to help us understand the origins of the welfare state, and in the preface she reaffirms that this was her original goal for the book, but none of her three case studies comes close to explaining anything major about later welfare legislation.

As we have already seen, the only case she can make for the role of the Civil War pensions is that they "delayed" the welfare state and "helped" reinforce the insistence on contributory pensions through their allegedly bad example. Even if for the moment we accept the delay factor as a partial explanation, it does not tell us about the paths that *did* lead to the main provisions of the Social Security Act. For that we have to turn to William Graebner (1980), Jill Quadagno (1988), and the fifth chapter of this book, which show that the key programs adopted in 1935 were (1) devised by corporate-oriented experts and (2) acceptable to northern Republican industrialists and southern Democratic plantation owners. In this book Skocpol does not really challenge any part of that explanation.

Turning to the maternalist policies that "managed to survive the Progressive Era," Skocpol herself says they were "reworked in unforeseen ways" (1992:320). Indeed, she says they became "subordinate and marginal parts of nationwide social provision in the United States" (ibid.). Furthermore, the Children's Bureau lost most of its influence after 1927. During the New Deal mother's pensions were taken from it and lodged in the male-oriented Social Security Board, where they suffered the "unfortunate unintended consequence" of becoming "demeaning and ungenerous 'welfare' for the poor alone" (p. 536). Based on Mink's (1995) subtle analysis of how maternalist assumptions are in part responsible for the way mothers' pensions became stigmatized as welfare, I question Skocpol's uncritical stance toward maternalist politics, but if what she says about the marginality of the maternalists to the overall social security program is correct, then why study maternalist policies if the goal is to understand the major features of the American welfare state? I agree that many of the women leaders of the Progressive Era are fully worthy of honor and respect, and I paid mine to them in my 1970 chapter on the feminine half of the upper class. Their stories should be told, as they have been by many historians, female and male. But Skocpol is doing sociology and politics, not hagiography.

Only the chapters on the failed male reform efforts of the Progressive Era have any plausible direct tie to the major features of the Social Security Act. Here Skocpol repeats her usual claim: the failure of the reformers at the national level in the Progressive Era forced them to work for new types of programs at the state level, one of which, Wisconsin, had an influence on the Social Security Act (1992:534). While I agree that experts from Wisconsin played a large staffing role in the creation of the Social Security Act, I think I showed in Chapter 5 that the Brandeis-Frankfurter network and members of the Rockefeller network had a far greater impact than the experts who are lionized in Wisconsin-influenced historical accounts. There just is not much left of any Wisconsin influence when all is said and done, except on making unemployment insurance decentralized, and less helpful. Skocpol's third case study does not have much more theoretical relevance than the other two.

## CONCLUSION

From my point of view, obviously, *Protecting Soldiers and Mothers* is not a very useful book. It is descriptively accurate on the topics it deals with, but its explanations for the events it recounts are inadequate. Although Skocpol writes about an alleged transformation of the parties, as if patronage did not remain a central issue (e.g., Tolchin and Tolchin 1971), she makes no effort to come to grips with the ability of the corporate community to shape both of the major political parties through campaign finance and other means, and to lobby Congress through access, expertise, and gifts. Nor is there even an allusion to the really serious state building accomplished in the Progressive Era by the corporate community, such as the Federal Reserve System, the Federal Trade Commission, and the Bureau of the Budget (e.g., Kolko 1963; Weinstein 1968).

Nonetheless, this book received prestigious awards from five learned societies, including the American Sociological Association and the American Political Science Association. Unless I can no longer recognize good books written from a different perspective, a hypothesis that is contradicted by my much higher regard for Finegold and Skocpol (1995), then something more than the quality of her analysis may be going on here. Perhaps her work has come to stand for something more general and symbolic in the minds of the social scientists who run organizations and sit on committees. I will explore this possibility in a brief final chapter, arguing that the transformation of state autonomy theory into historical institutionalism marks the end of an era in the American social sciences.

# The Return to Normalcy 8

## INTRODUCTION

Motivated by my long-standing disagreements with state autonomy theorists, I read *Protecting Soldiers and Mothers* several times the minute it was available from the publisher, breathed a sigh of relief because it was so easily refutable, and wrote a brief review on which the previous chapter is based (Domhoff 1992). Then I settled back to read the reviews I purposely had avoided until then, to see if I was out of sync, and if so, on what issues.

To my pleasant surprise, I was in the mainstream for a change, or at least the mainstream of reviewers. Alan Wolfe (1993), one of the structural Marxists of the 1970s, now a more conventional commentator, found little new or convincing in the book. Frances Piven (1993), coauthor of three seminal works cited in this book, was even less impressed; she doubted the conclusions drawn from the case studies, noted the "unexceptionable" nature of an emphasis on the importance of politics, and thought the theoretical "amalgam" seemed "a good deal like pluralism." Historians Alexander Keyssar (1993) and Michael Katz (1993) said some nice words like "ambitious" and "bold," but did not find her thesis convincing. Walter Korpi (1993:780), one of the theoreticians criticized in the book, notes that she gives a "partly misleading" account of his approach, not an unusual comment from those who have been critiqued by Skocpol, then proceeds to correct the record. Sociologist Jeff Manza (1993:96), while pointing out the merits of Skocpol's theory, notes that her critique of rival views is very inadequate.

Nor did the book fare any better with feminist scholars who are experts on the history of women, work, and welfare in the United States (e.g. Abramovitz 1993; Gordon 1993; Mink 1993; Scott 1993; Baker 1993). Although they used positive words such as "well-documented," "fascinating," "rich," and "tightly argued," and appreciated the fact there is now a full-length account of women's independent agency in reformist politics, they believed that male domination, class, race, and ethnicity were not given their proper weight. Among many additional criticisms, Linda Gordon (1993:146) further noted that it did not seem right to call the social insurance movement "paternalist" when it relied on formal criteria of eligibility and had no discretionary or caretaking dimensions. Ann Firor Scott

(1993:778) added that the programs were threatening to no one, and Mimi Abramovitz (1993:21) suggested that defining veteran's pensions as part of a "welfare state" means we should include the Merchant Seaman's Act of 1798, the Freedman's Bureau of 1865, and the National Health Board of 1879 as well. As we know from the previous chapter, Gwendolyn Mink (1993) believes the motivations of the reformist women were far more complex than Skocpol allows.

American historian Paula Baker, praised in Skocpol's book, and sharing her dislike for an emphasis on "simple patriarchal or business control over social policy," nonetheless casts doubt on Skocpol's maternalist story by saying that "her evidence consists of resolutions passed at annual meetings" (1993:460). Moreover, she points out that "almost half of the state federation of women's clubs failed to pass resolutions in favor of mother's pensions bills" and "most states passed this program without the benefit of resolutions from the State Congress of Mothers" (ibid.). "Where was the mighty influence?" she asks. Baker's review is devastating because it questions the book on its one original piece of archival data, and finds it wanting. Only an expert on the era who shares Skocpol's general theoretical framework could raise this point so effectively.

There were, however, two or three extremely positive reviews. Rosalind Rosenberg, a professor of American history who studies twentieth-century women, had nothing but kind words in her nine-paragraph review in the New York Times. True, she calls the prose "turgid," but she says the study is "monumental," a "welcome departure from abstract theorizing," and a "fundamentally optimistic work" (1993:16) Alan Brinkley, an expert on the New Deal, says the book is a "brilliant theoretical corrective to previous scholarship" (1994:43). He has his little criticisms here and there, but his positive review is the kind to be expected for a book destined to win prizes.

By and large, then, I thought I had done a fair job of judging the quality of Protecting Soldiers and Mothers. Then the awards started to appear from such varied sources as Phi Beta Kappa, the Social Science History Association, the Political Sociology Section of the American Sociological Association, and the Politics and History Section of the American Political Science Association. Most impressive of all, it won the political science association's Woodrow Wilson Foundation Award for the best book on politics, government, or international relations. The disjuncture between the negative commentary in most reviews by specialists and the many prizes awarded by general committees led to my curiosity about the reasons for this discrepancy. Is Skocpol (1993:157–58) right when she says that most reviewers, including Wolfe and Gordon, are too hidebound to recognize the "fresh questions" and "innovative answers" in her work, or is something else going on?

## THE NEW PLURALISM

To stimulate my thinking, I posed the paradox in casual conversations with several social scientists who knew of Skocpol and her work: how could an overly long rehash of secondary sources win so many awards? An auto-biographical article by Skocpol (1988/89) gave me further food for thought, and the statement accompanying the Woodrow Wilson prize delivered supportive evidence for my analysis.

Feminist colleagues provided my starting point. Their collective insight can be summarized as follows: Skocpol writes about women in a way acceptable to men while at the same time keeping feminist critics at bay by celebrating the successes of the women's movement in the Progressive Era. When I thought about this hypothesis, it did seem like the story she tells about these women has a little something for everybody. First, it is an "if only" story about how we almost had a maternalist welfare state with an emphasis on helping children and supporting women as mothers. This is a far less threatening scenario for men than the equal-rights feminism of the past thirty years. At the same time, Skocpol disarms feminist critics by stressing the "agency" of these women, who were able to plan and act successfully in the political arena even though they did not have the vote. This dimension was not lost on the Woodrow Wilson committee when it singled out the movement for mothers' pensions for comment: "The latter occurred, interestingly, at a time when women, the prime advocates, were unable to vote, but were able to build a political network to achieve their goal of mothers' pensions" (P.S. 1993:917).

There are also "positive lessons" for today that might resonate with a male audience (Skocpol 1992:538). Feminist discussions should be "considerably less elitist than those carried on today among middle-class American feminists." There should be more "solidarity" with "less privileged women," more honor for "values of caring and nurturance." Skocpol thinks "both individual and organized feminists may have to place a higher priority on policy goals that can bring Americans together across lines of ideology, class, race, and gender" (p. 539). Feminists should seek broader political alliances, and in doing so they "may well have to moderate priorities that are legitimate for upper-middle-class career women, but not so important (or even acceptable) to other Americans" (ibid.). Perhaps the three elderly males comprising the Woodrow Wilson Foundation award committee had these messages in mind when they wrote:

> The book is more than a history of these programs. It provides insights for those concerned to develop a broad political coalition to support universal social provisions. (P.S. 1993:917)

Given the high level of concern with gender issues in American society in recent decades, I believe a feminist interpretation of Skocpol's awards has considerable truth to it. To fully understand the success of *Protecting Soldiers and Mothers*, however, I think we need to see if these insights can be generalized, placed in an even larger context. Perhaps Skocpol writes about other issues besides women in a way that is acceptable to everyone for one reason or another. Perhaps she typifies the most ambitious and achievement-oriented members of her generation of social scientists. For information on this possibility, we turn to a short intellectual autobiography Skocpol wrote in the mid-1980s.

Skocpol tells her story by intertwining her career with the nature of her generation of college students. The purpose of the account is to explain how a small-town midwestern woman of middle-class origins (both grandfathers farmers, father a high school teacher, mother a homemaker and substitute teacher) could find "the breadth of imagination and the sheer ambitious daring" that she attributes to herself to do large-scale studies like her book on states and social revolution (1988/1989:628). She says it is because she is from the "uppity generation" of 1960s college students, graduating from "Moo U" (Michigan State) in 1968 and doing graduate work at Harvard from 1969 to 1975. She tells of measured steps of growing self confidence that might have been stifled if she had gone immediately to the Ivy League, where the incoming students supposedly start out very cosmopolitan and well-educated.

Skocpol then shows how gender came to matter at key turning points in her career, such as when some professors at Michigan State assumed that as a married woman she would not go to graduate school despite her excellent undergraduate work. Each time, though, gender receded into the background as various difficulties were overcome. In the 1980s, however, gender issues became more salient in her life due to the pressures of trying to "have it all" (pp. 639, 642). In this context her reading on the origins of the American welfare state led her to conclude that "women's movements and gender relations are, in fact, central to the formation of modern welfare states, and in particular critical to the social policies in the twentieth-century United States" (p. 641). Four sentences later she reports "The new insights I have gained in the process have given me more intellectual excitement than anything since discovering the core ideas for my first book." From that point on she became concerned with feminist issues.

Skocpol believes that her generation "revitalized the macroscopic and critical sides" of sociology based on its experiences in the 1960s (pp. 628, 630). It developed a critical attitude toward power relations, learned the effectiveness of protests and demonstrations, and would not take no for an answer. Although the turmoil generated in the social sciences by her generation "ended in the early 1980s," she argues that it changed sociology by its attention to conflict, domination, internationalism, and diversity (pp. 631–32).

Skocpol's congratulatory claims about a new generation changing a discipline may not be the whole story, however. They may not even be the most important part. Perhaps her role and accomplishments look very different to those from previous generations. What has this self-styled member of an "uppity generation" achieved from the point of view of those not part of it, or those within it who do not share her sense of activist accomplishment, for that matter? Is she really the thorn in the side of the old guard that she implies she is?

Take her book on the revolutions in France, Russia, and China, where she challenged Marxists by arguing that their theory of revolution is wrong and the state potentially autonomous. This is something most social scientists would be glad to hear, especially from someone in a generation with so many Marxists. Following her critique of Marxism, Skocpol turned her attention homeward in the 1980s, claiming that capitalists are not even a significant power group in the United States, music to the ears of pluralists everywhere, and of course class conflict is not a major issue either. Then in the 1990s she softened her image of the American state, although she vehemently denies it (Skocpol 1993:168), through her fascination with the well-educated, well-heeled women reformers of the Progressive Era, portraying them one dimensionally as valiant underdogs who selflessly exercised power through organizational skills, educational efforts, and ideological zeal (never money and connections), at the same time transcending class and ethnic divisions. By the end of the book there is also an element of boosterism. The victories were small and halting, and had some unintended consequences, but the maternalists are "apt" and "remarkable." There is no need to close her book on a "downbeat note" because "they left positive legacies, too," the ones about more caring, less elitism, and greater moderation (Skocpol 1992:536).

So what is Skocpol's allegedly uppity message? Coalitions and political parties have an impact. Capitalists are not powerful after all. The state is permeable. Most feminists are wrong about the women of the Progressive Era. Academic experts are important. Looking at this list, I conclude that Skocpol's main achievement in *Protecting Soldiers and Mothers* is to make pluralism respectable once again by overstating the altruism and success of maternalist women activists in the Progressive Era. Her focus on this movement has connected her work with feminism, which is the social movement from the 1960s with the most ongoing influence in the business world, the professions, and academia. She has created a synthesis of the new gender consciousness with the old pluralism while criticizing other feminists for allegedly overemphasizing patriarchy and class. Women's power in the Progressive Era made a pluralist out of Skocpol, and the mainstream is applauding. She is the prodigal daughter, safely returned to the eternal verities of a classless pluralism.

This analysis provides a possible explanation for the success of *Protecting Soldiers and Mothers* even though the book caricatures rival views and tells familiar tales on the basis of secondary sources: it reflects the return of political science and sociology to full normalcy when it comes to power and politics, completing a process of reintegration begun in the early 1980s. Its success marks the final step in the assimilation of the radicals in Skocpol's generation into the academic establishment as they approach their fifties, just in time to participate in the institutional governance given to that age group in American society.

Masking their empirical defeats of the previous fifteen years in their newly won acceptance by the mainstream, the state-centric theorists have declared victory and assimilated into the diverse ranks of the historical institutionalists, where they are likely to join the pluralist wing (e.g., Skocpol 1992:569; Orloff 1993:41–42; Finegold and Skocpol 1995:312, footnote 3). They insist they made a contribution by arguing that the state is not reducible to class logic, but they are no longer ready to talk about state autonomy in the American case, and for good reason, as the empirical material in this book demonstrates. Instead, they tell us that institutions matter, as do political parties and government officials.

But how much do parties and government officials matter in the United States when it comes to understanding the driving dynamics of the power structure? In a country that is best understood in terms of class-based economic power for well-known historical reasons, and in which any emphasis on class conflict is rejected by most social scientists, it does not seem to me that it is helpful to subordinate corporate power and class conflict into a more general—institutional—framework once again. State autonomy theory has been transformed and denatured only a few short years after its initial flowering, but the reluctance to develop a new class-based analysis of power in America is still very much with us.

# Notes

## Chapter 2: Defining and Testing the Class Dominance View

1.  The likelihood of very many new case studies is not great, however, because most social scientists accept Hugh Heclo's (1978) emphasis on experts in "issue networks" or Edward Laumann and David Knoke's (1987) focus on interest-group "domains." Although I do not discuss their work in this book, many of the arguments I make against state autonomy theorists apply to them as well.

2.  I will not count affiliates of university research institutes as corporate experts because they are employees of universities. However, to see how the Russian Research Institute at Harvard University was controlled by the Carnegie Corporation on key issues, see O'Connell (1989).

3.  Welfare is the conservative solution to unemployment, given begrudgingly only in times of disruption, always accompanied by stigmatization and victim-blaming in order to reinforce work norms (Piven and Cloward 1971). Liberals much preferred government employment to welfare during the New Deal, but lost to conservatives on the issue (Rose 1994:53–56, 77–80).

4.  From the corporate-conservative point of view, labor, liberals, and the Left are all collectivist, so the distinctions among them are minor. Since the corporate-conservatives' number one concern is unions, the failure to make distinctions between liberals and leftists makes sense.

5.  A donation of $1,000 almost equaled the average person's yearly salary in those days. In a poll taken in 1937, most people said a yearly income of $1,560 was enough for a family of four to live "decently" (Gallup and Robinson 1938:393).

6.  The favorite issue of the state autonomy theorists is something called *state building*, which turns out to be measured primarily by increases in budgets and employees, especially for new agencies. Calculated in terms of percentage increases and compared with other government agencies, these are, in effect, Who benefits? measures within the state/political network. Calculated in terms of the society as a whole, budgets and employees are an indicator of the importance of the state (Mann 1986), but such increases tell us nothing about who controls it.

## Chapter 3: New Deal Agricultural Policy

1.  Bulmer and Bulmer (1981:401–2), whose information on the Memorial is very helpful, do not see foundations as part of a corporate power structure, but as independent entities. They would not want to be associated with my overall analysis.

2.   The plan received further refinement in 1932 from Mordecai Ezekiel, a government agricultural economist who received his Ph.D. from the short-lived Brookings Institution graduate program. A friend of Wilson's, Ezekiel worked "to fuse the original Black-Ruml plan with Harriman's ideas. The new version called for direct payment to farmers willing to sign a contract to reduce production" (D. Hamilton 1991:188). Thus, government economists of the kind celebrated by Skocpol and Finegold must be given their due.

3.   Wheat farmers were exempt from worker pressures because they had mechanized in the face of leftist organizing in their migrant labor stream, displacing at least 150,000 of their 200,000 seasonal workers by 1933 (McWilliams 1942:91–102).

4.   This does not mean the program necessarily worked as expected. Overproduction remained a problem even with reduced acreage, and drought sometimes played a big role in reducing surpluses. In 1939 there were still large surpluses (e.g., Leuchtenberg 1963:255–56). The important point here is the power demonstrated by the ability to shape legislation. Nor did the program necessarily do anything positive for the economy as a whole. It may have shifted income from needy urban consumers who would spend it to higher income farmers and planters who would save it, buy more land and bid up land prices, or invest it in machinery that put farm workers on the relief roles. For a stinging critique of the economic rationale of the AAA by a former director of research for the National Recovery Administration, see Roos (1937:437–43).

## Chapter 5: How the Rockefeller Network
## Shaped Social Security

1.   Hereafter, as in Chapter 2, I will call the Laura Spelman Rockefeller Memorial simply the Memorial. In 1929 it was absorbed into the Rockefeller Foundation, but ten million dollars was left separate for what was renamed the Spelman Fund.

2.   Critchlow (1985:6–8) thinks the conservatism of the Brookings Institution on domestic economic policy contradicts my claims about the overall policy-planning network, but I noted its conservative turn many years ago (Domhoff 1970:184). I agree that the world of policy groups is complex within its corporate limits. There are principled disagreements on many issues, and foundations do not have direct control of most policy groups. In the case of Brookings, it was dominated by Moulton until his retirement in 1952, when he was replaced by the vice-president of the Rockefeller's General Education Board, who brought the organization back into the mainstream. Critchlow's findings are useful, but not his conclusions.

3.   Having described the Rockefeller network for the 1920s and 1930s, I should assure readers that I do not think this network remained a Rockefeller enterprise much past the 1950s. Once Rockefellers Senior and Junior passed from the scene, and their various aides retired or moved on to other opportunities, this legacy of people and endowments and institutions became part of the general infrastructure of the American ruling class and its policy-planning network, much like the Carnegie foundations.

4.   In a previous account of the Social Security Act, I wrongly said Richter worked for Metropolitan Life, for which I apologize (1990:57).

5.   Since Senator Robert Wagner of New York often worked with the Rockefeller network on legislative issues, it is a testimony to the independence and courage with which he is credited that he led the liberal experts and politicians in developing the National Labor Relations Act despite the clear Rockefeller opposition to it. The act is rightly called the Wagner Act.

## Chapter 6: Industrial Mobilization and the Military in World War II

1.   Nor does Hooks seem able to distinguish my conception of the power elite from that of Mills. In a paper in which he paints himself as an ecumenical compromiser who tries to find the best in all theories, he says I see a "nearly perfect" overlap between the "upper (capitalist-based) class and the economic, political, and military leaders of Mills' power elite" (Hooks 1993:38), thereby making it seem like I put military and political leaders in the upper class. What I said, of course, is that there is a nearly perfect overlap between Mills's concept of the power elite and the idea of a power elite as I redefined it, namely as a leadership group of the upper class that includes "active, working members of the upper class and high-level employees in private institutions controlled by members of the upper class" (Domhoff 1990:1).

2.   Although Hooks is solidly located in the state autonomy tradition, and sees his work as support for that theory, his book will not endear him to major American state autonomy theorists like Stephen Krasner (1978), Theda Skocpol (1980), and Stephen Skowronek (1982) because he is so critical of their work. He constantly chastises them for saying that the American state is weak when in fact the Pentagon makes it strong, or for overemphasizing the power of civilian agencies when in fact most "civilian state agencies are relatively weak" (e.g., Hooks 1991:225).

# References

Abramovitz, Mimi. 1993. "Women Who Fought Back." *Readings* December:18–23.

Abrecht, Stephen, and Michael Locker, eds. 1981. *CDE Stock Ownership Directory No. 5. Fortune 500*. New York: Corporate Data Exchange, Inc.

Adams, Gordon. 1982. *The Politics of Defense Contracting*. New Brunswick, NJ: Transaction Books.

Albertson, Dean. 1961. *Roosevelt's Farmer: Claude Wickard in the New Deal*. New York: Columbia University Press.

Alchon, Guy. 1985. *The Invisible Hand of Planning*. Princeton, NJ: Princeton University Press.

Alexander, Herbert. 1958. "The Role of the Volunteer Political Fund Raiser: A Case Study in New York in 1952." Ph.D. dissertation, Yale University, New Haven, CT.

Alexander, Herbert. 1971. *Financing the Election, 1968*. Lexington, MA: Heath Lexington.

Alexander, Herbert. 1976. *Financing Politics*. Washington, DC: Congressional Quarterly.

Alexander, Herbert. 1992. *Financing Politics*. Fourth edition. Washington, DC: Congressional Quarterly.

Allen, Michael P. 1978. "Economic Interest Groups and the Corporate Elite Structure." *Social Science Quarterly* 58:597–615.

Allen, Michael P. 1982. "The Identification of Interlock Groups in Large Corporate Networks: Convergent Validation Using Divergent Techniques." *Social Networks* 4:349–66.

Allen, Michael P. 1991. "Capitalist Response to State Intervention: Theories of the State and Political Finance in the New Deal." *American Sociological Review* 56:679–89.

Allen, Michael P. 1992. "Elite Social Movement Organizations and the State: The Rise of the Conservative Policy-Planning Network." *Research in Politics and Society* 4:87-109.

Alpert, Irvine, and Ann Markusen. 1980. "Think Tanks and Capitalist Policy." In *Power Structure Research*, edited by G. William Domhoff. Beverly Hills: Sage.

Alston, Lee, and Joseph Ferrie. 1985. "Resisting the Welfare State: Southern Opposition to the Farm Security Administration." In *The Emergence of the Modern Political Economy*, edited by Robert Higgs. Greenwich, CT: JAI.

Altmeyer, Arthur. 1966. *The Formative Years of Social Security*. Madison: University of Wisconsin Press.

Armstrong, Barbara N. 1932. *Insuring the Essentials: Minimum Wage, Plus Social Insurance—A Living Wage Problem*. New York: Macmillan.

Armstrong, Barbara N. 1965. "Oral History." Columbia University Library, New York.

Auerbach, Jerold S. 1966. *Labor and Liberty: The LaFollette Committee and the New Deal*. Indianapolis: Bobbs Merrill.

Bailey, Stephen. 1950. *Congress Makes a Law: The Story behind the Employment Act of 1964*. New York: Columbia University Press.

Baker, Leonard. 1984. *Brandeis and Frankfurter*. New York: Harper & Row.

Baker, Paula. 1993. "Featured Review." *American Historical Review* 98:458–60.

Baldwin, Sidney. 1968. *Poverty and Politics: The Rise and Decline of the Farm Security Administration*. Chapel Hill: University of North Carolina Press.

Baltzell, E. Digby. 1958. *Philadelphia Gentlemen: The Making of a National Upper Class*. New York: Free Press.

Baltzell, E. Digby. 1964. *The Protestant Establishment*. New York: Random House.

Baltzell, E. Digby. 1966. "Who's Who in America and the Social Register." In *Class, Status, and Power,* 2nd edition, edited by Reinhard Bendix and Seymour Martin Lipset. New York: Free Press.

Bellush, Bernard. 1975. *The Failure of the NRA*. New York: Norton.

Benedict, Murray. 1953. *Farm Policies in the United States, 1790–1950*. New York: Twentieth Century Fund.

Berkowitz, Edward, and Kim McQuaid. 1978. "Businessmen and Bureaucrats: The Evolution of the American Welfare System, 1900–1940." *Journal of Economic History* 38:120–41.

Bernstein, Barton. 1965. "The Removal of War Production Board Controls on Business, 1944–1946." *Business History Review* 39:243–60.

Bernstein, Barton. 1967. "The Debate on Industrial Reconversion: The Protection of Oligopoly and Military Control of the Economy." *American Journal of Economics and Sociology* 26:159–72.

Bernstein, Irving. 1950. *New Deal Collective Bargaining Policy*. Berkeley: University of California Press.

Bernstein, Irving. 1960. *The Lean Years*. Boston: Houghton Mifflin.

Bernstein, Irving. 1970. *The Turbulent Years*. Boston: Houghton Mifflin.

Bernstein, Michael. 1987. *The Great Depression*. New York: Cambridge University Press.

Black, John. 1929. Letter to Niels Olsen, April 1. Black Papers, Chronological Correspondence File, Wisconsin State Historical Society Archives.

Bloom, Jack. 1987. *Class, Race, and the Civil Rights Movement*. Bloomington: Indiana University Press.

Blum, Albert A. 1972. "Roosevelt, the M-Day Plans, and the Military-Industrial Complex." *Military Affairs* 34:44–46.

Blum, John. 1976. *V Was for Victory*. New York: Harcourt Brace Jovanovich.

Bonacich, Phillip, and G. William Domhoff. 1981. "Latent Classes and Group Membership." *Social Networks* 3:175–96.

Bowen, William. 1994. *Inside the Boardroom*. New York: Wiley.

Brand, Donald. 1988. *Corporatism and the Rule of Law*. Ithaca, NY: Cornell University Press.

Brandes, Stuart. 1976. *American Welfare Capitalism, 1880–1940*. Chicago: University of Chicago Press.

Breed, Warren. 1955. "Social Control in the Newsroom." *Social Forces* 33:326–36.

Breiger, Ronald. 1974. "The Duality of Persons and Groups." *Social Forces* 53:181–90.

Brigante, John. 1950. *The Feasibility Dispute*. Washington, DC: Committee on Public Administration Cases.

Brinkley, Alan. 1994. "For Their Own Good." *New York Review of Books* 41(May 26):40–43.

Brown, J. Douglas. 1927. Speech to New Jersey Federation of Labor, September 12. Brown Papers, Box 57, Speech File. Mudd Library, Princeton University, Princeton, NJ.

Brown, J. Douglas. 1935a. Letter to Edwin Witte, February 13. Brown Papers, Box 15, 1935 File. Mudd Library. Princeton University, Princeton, NJ.

Brown, J. Douglas. 1935b. Letter to Edwin Witte, February 23. Brown Papers, Box 15, 1935 File. Mudd Library, Princeton University, Princeton, NJ.

Brown, J. Douglas. 1935c. Letter to Murray Latimer, August 12. Latimer Papers, Box 1, Folder 2. George Washington University Library, Washington, DC.

Brown, J. Douglas. 1935d. Letter to Murray Latimer, Nov. 2. Latimer Papers, Box 1, Folder 2. George Washington University Library, Washington, DC.

Brown, J. Douglas. 1935e. Letter to Murray Latimer, July 12. Latimer Papers, Box 1, Folder 2. George Washington University, Washington, DC.

Brown, J. Douglas. 1965. "Oral History." Columbia University Library, New York.

Brown, J. Douglas. 1972. *An American Philosophy of Social Security*. Princeton, NJ: Princeton University Press.

Brownlow, Louis. 1958. *A Passion for Anonymity*. Chicago: University of Chicago Press.

Bulmer, Martin, and Joan Bulmer. 1981. "Philanthropy and Social Science in the 1920s: Beardsley Ruml and the Laura Spelman Rockefeller Memorial, 1922–29." *Minerva* 19:347–407.

Bunting, David. 1983. "Origins of the American Corporate Network." *Social Science History* 7:129–42.

Bunting, David. 1986. *The Rise of Large American Corporations, 1889–1919*. New York: Garland.

Burch, Philip. 1973. "The NAM as an Interest Group." *Politics and Society* 4:100–5.

Burch, Philip. 1981a. *Elites in American History. Vol. 2. From the Civil War To The New Deal*. New York: Holmes and Meier.

Burch, Philip. 1981b. *Elites in American History*. Vol. 3. New York: Holmes and Meier.

Burk, Robert. 1990. *The Corporate State and the Broken State*. Cambridge, MA: Harvard University Press.

Burns, Eveline. 1966. "Oral History." Columbia University Library, New York.

Burris, Val. 1987. "The Political Partisanship of American Business: A Study of Corporate Political Action Committees." *American Sociological Review* 52:732–44.

Burris, Val, and J. Salt. 1990. "The Politics of Capitalist Class Segments: A Test of Corporate Liberalism Theory." *Social Problems* 37:341–59.

Business Advisory Council. 1934. Memorandum on Unemployment Insurance: Comments by Members. General Correspondence, Department of Commerce. RG40, Box 784. National Archives II, College Park, MD.

Business Advisory Council. 1935. Views on the Wagner National Labor Relations Bill. General Correspondence, Department of Commerce. RG40, Box 784. National Archives II. College Park, MD.

Business Week. 1935a. "The Big Fight" (May 11):8–9.

Business Week. 1935b. "Advisers' Problems" (July 6):29.

Campbell, Christina. 1962. The Farm Bureau and the New Deal. Urbana: University of Illinois Press.

Campbell, Levin. 1946. The Industry-Ordnance Team. New York: Harcourt Brace.

Carosso, Vincent. 1970. Investment Banking in America. Cambridge, MA: Harvard University Press.

Carter, John. 1934. The New Dealers. New York: Literary Guild.

Castrovinci, J. 1976. "Prelude to Welfare Capitalism: The Role of Business in the Enactment of Workmen's Compensation Legislation in Illinois, 1905–12." Social Service Review 50:80–102.

Catton, Bruce. 1948. The War Lords of Washington. New York: Harcourt Brace.

Chambers, Clark. 1952. A Historical Study of the Grange, the Farm Bureau, and the Associated Farmers, 1929–1941. Berkeley: University of California Press.

Chambers, Clark. 1963. Seedtime of Reform. Minneapolis: University of Minnesota Press.

Chambers, William. 1964. The Democrats 1798–1964. Princeton, NJ: Van Nostrand.

Chernow, Ron. 1990. The House of Morgan. New York: Atlantic Monthly Press.

Claessen, Henri, and Peter Skalnik, eds. 1978. The Early State. The Hague: Mouton.

Clausen, Aage. 1973. How Congressmen Decide. New York: St. Martin's.

Clawson, Dan, Alan Neustadtl, and James Bearden. 1986. "The Logic of Business Unity: Corporate Contributions in the 1980s." Sociological Quarterly 51:797–811.

Clawson, Dan, Alan Neustadtl, and D. Scott. 1992. Money Talks. New York: Basic Books.

Cohen, Ronald, and Elman R. Service, eds. 1978. Origins of the State. Philadelphia: Institute for the Study of Human Issues.

Collins, Robert M. 1981. The Business Response to Keynes, 1929–1964. New York: Columbia University Press.

Colwell, Mary. 1980. "The Foundation Connection: Links among Foundations and Recipient Organizationas." In Philanthropy and Cultural Imperialism. Boston: Hall.

Colwell, Mary. 1993. Private Foundation and Public Policy. New York: Garland.

Conner, Valerie. 1983. The National War Labor Board. Chapel Hill: University of North Carolina Press.

Connery, Robert. 1951. The Navy and Industrial Mobilization in World War II. Princeton, NJ: Princeton University Press.

Conrad, David. 1965. Forgotten Farmers: The Story of Sharecroppers in the New Deal. Urbana: University of Illinois Press.

Costin, Lela. 1983. *Two Sisters for Social Justice*. Urbana: University of Illinois Press.

Cowdrick, Edward. 1928. *Pensions: A Problem of Management*. New York: American Management Association, Annual Convention Series, No. 75.

Critchlow, Donald. 1985. *The Brookings Institution, 1916–1952*. DeKalb: Northern Illinois University Press.

Dahl, Robert A. 1958. "A Critique of the Ruling Elite Model." *American Political Science Review* 52:463–69.

Dahl, Robert A. 1961. *Who Governs?* New Haven, CT: Yale University Press.

Dahl, Robert A. 1982. *Dilemmas of Pluralist Democracy*. New Haven, CT: Yale University Press.

Daniel, Cletus. 1981. *Bitter Harvest*. Ithaca, NY: Cornell University Press.

Daniel, Pete. 1984. "The New Deal, Southern Agriculture, and Economic Change." In *The New Deal and the South,* edited by James C. Cobb and Michael V. Namorato. Jackson: University of Mississippi Press.

Daniel, Pete. 1985. *Breaking the Land*. Urbana: University of Illinois Press.

Daniels, Arlene. 1988. *Invisible Careers*. Chicago: University of Chicago Press.

Davis, Allen. 1967. *Spearheads for Reform*. New York: Oxford University Press.

Davis, Allison, Burleigh Gardner, and Mary Gardner. 1941. *Deep South*. Chicago: University of Chicago Press.

Davis, Chester. 1929. Letter to John Black, March 22. Black Papers, Chronological Correspondence File. Wisconsin State Historical Society Archives.

Davis, Donald. 1982. "The Price of Conspicuous Production: The Detroit Elite and the Automobile Industry, 1900–1933." *Journal of Social History* 16:21–46.

Davis, Kenneth. 1986. *FDR: The New Deal Years, 1933–1937*. New York: Random House.

Davis, Kenneth. 1993. *FDR: Into the Storm*. New York: Random House.

Deakin, James. 1966. *The Lobbyists*. Washington, DC: Public Affairs Press.

Devine, Edward. 1939. *When Social Work Was Young*. New York: Macmillan.

Domhoff, G. William. 1967. *Who Rules America?* Englewood Cliffs, NJ: Prentice-Hall.

Domhoff, G. William. 1968. "The Power Elite and Its Critics." In *C. Wright Mills and the Power Elite,* edited by G. William Domhoff and Hoyt B. Ballard. Boston: Beacon.

Domhoff, G. William. 1970. *The Higher Circles*. New York: Random House.

Domhoff, G. William. 1972. *Fat Cats and Democrats*. Englewood Cliffs, NJ: Prentice-Hall.

Domhoff, G. William. 1974. *The Bohemian Grove and Other Retreats*. New York: Harper & Row.

Domhoff, G. William. 1978. *Who Really Rules? New Haven and Community Power Reexamined*. New Brunswick, NJ: Transaction.

Domhoff, G. William. 1979. *The Powers That Be*. New York: Random House.

Domhoff, G. William. 1983. *Who Rules America Now?* New York: Simon and Schuster.

Domhoff, G. William. 1987. "Where Do Government Experts Come From?" In *Power Elites and Organizations,* edited by G. William Domhoff and Thomas R. Dye. Beverly Hills: Sage.

Domhoff, G. William. 1990. *The Power Elite and the State: How Policy Is Made in America*. Hawthorne, NY: Aldine de Gruyter.

Domhoff, G. William. 1992. "The Death of State Autonomy Theory." *Critical Sociology* 19:103–16.

Domhoff, G. William. 1996. *Finding Meaning in Dreams: A Quantitative Approach*. New York: Plenum.

Domhoff, G. William, and Hoyt Ballard, eds. 1968. *C. Wright Mills and the Power Elite*. Boston: Beacon.

Dreier, Peter. 1981. "The Position of the Press in the American Power Structure." *Social Problems* 29:298–310.

Dunn, Marvin. 1980. "The Family Office: Coordinating Mechanism of the Ruling Class." In *Power Structure Research,* edited by G. William Domhoff. Beverly Hills: Sage.

Durr, Clifford. 1952. "The Defense Plant Corporation." In *Public Administration and Policy Development,* edited by Harold Stein. New York: Harcourt Brace.

Dye, Thomas R. 1976. *Who's Running America?* Englewood Cliffs, NJ: Prentice-Hall.

Eakins, David. 1966. "The Development of Corporate Liberal Policy Research in the United States, 1885–1965." Ph.D. dissertation, University of Wisconsin, Madison.

Eakins, David. 1969. "Business Planners and America's Postwar Expansion." In *Corporations and the Cold War,* edited by David Horowitz. New York: Monthly Review.

Emerson, Thomas. 1991. *Young Lawyer for the New Deal*. Savage, MD: Rowman & Littlefield.

Eitzen, Stanley, Maureen Jung, and Dean Purdy. 1982. "Organizational Linkages among the Inner Group of the Capitalist Class." *Sociological Focus* 15:179–89.

Eliot, Thomas. 1992. *Recollections of the New Deal*. Boston: Northeastern University Press.

Emerson, Thomas. 1991. *Young Lawyer for the New Deal*. Savage, MD: Rowman and Littlefield.

Eulau, Heinz, and John Sprague. 1964. *Lawyers in Politics*. Indianapolis, IN: Bobbs-Merrill.

Farnum, Richard. 1989. "The American Upper Class and Higher Education, 1880–1970." In Social Class and Democratic Leadership, edited by Harold Bershady. Philadelphia: University of Pennsylvania Press.

Feagin, Joe, and Kelly Riddell. 1990. "The State, Capitalism, and World War II: The U. S. Case." *Armed Forces & Society* 17:53–79.

Feigenbaum, Harvey. 1985. *The Politics of Public Enterprise: Oil and the French State.*y Princeton, NJ: Princeton University Press.

Finegold, Kenneth. 1981. "From Agrarianism to Adjustment: The Political Origins of New Deal Agricultural Policy." *Politics and Society* 11:1–27.

Finegold, Kenneth, and Theda Skocpol. 1984. "State, Party, and Industry: From Business Recovery to the Wagner Act in America's New Deal." In *Statemaking and Social Movements,* edited by Charles Bright and Susan Harding. Ann Arbor: University of Michigan Press.

Finegold, Kenneth, and Theda Skocpol. 1995. *State and Party in America's New Deal*. Madison: University of Wisconsin Press.

Fisher, Donald. 1993. *Fundamental Development of the Social Sciences*. Ann Arbor: University of Michigan Press.

Fite, Gilbert. 1954. *George N. Peek and the Fight for Farm Parity*. Norman: University of Oklahoma Press.

Flacks, Richard. 1988. *Making History*. New York: Columbia University Press.

Folsom, Marion. 1970. "Oral History." Columbia University Library, New York.

Fosdick, Raymond. 1933. Letter to John D. Rockefeller, Jr. Rockefeller Family Archives, Record Group 2 (OMR), Economic Reform Interests, Box 16, Folder 127. Rockefeller Archive Center.

Fosdick, Raymond. 1934. Letter to John D. Rockefeller, Jr., March 22. Rockefeller Family Archives, Record Group 2, Economic Reform Interests, Box 16, Folder 127. Rockefeller Archive Center.

Fosdick, Raymond. 1952. *The Story of the Rockefeller Foundation*. New York: Harper & Brothers.

Fosdick, Raymond. 1956. *John D. Rockefeller, Jr: A Portrait*. New York: Harper & Brothers.

Freudenthal, Elsbeth. 1940. "The Aviation Business in the 1930s." Reprinted in *The History of the American Aircraft Industry*, edited by G. R. Simonson. Cambridge, MA: MIT Press, 1968.

Galbraith, John. 1992. *The Culture of Contentment*. Boston: Houghton Mifflin.

Gallup, George, and Claude Robinson. 1938. "American Institute of Public Opinion—Surveys, 1935–38." *Public Opinion Quarterly* 2:373–98.

Gans, Herbert. 1979. *Deciding What's News*. New York: Pantheon.

Gaus, John, and Leon Wolcott. 1940. *Public Administration and the United States Department of Agriculture*. Chicago: Public Administration Service.

General Education Board. 1930. *The General Education Board: An Account of Its Activities, 1902–1914*. New York: General Education Board.

Gilbert, Jess, and Carolyn Howe. 1991. "Beyond 'State vs. Society': Theories of the State and New Deal Agricultural Policies." *American Sociological Review* 56:204–20.

Gillam, Richard. 1975. "C. Wright Mills and the Politics of Truth: The Power Elite Revisited." *American Quarterly* 28:461–79.

Gitelman, H. M. 1984. "Being of Two Minds: American Employers Confront the Labor Problem, 1915–1919." *Labor History* 25:189–216.

Gitelman, H. M. 1988. *Legacy of the Ludlow Massacre*. Philadelphia: University of Pennsylvania Press.

Goertzel, Ted. 1985. "Militarism as a Sociological Problem." *Research in Political Sociology* 1:119–39.

Goldfield, M. 1987. *The Decline of Organized Labor in the United States*. Chicago: University of Chicago Press.

Goldthorpe, John. 1991. "The Uses of History in Sociology: Reflections on Some Recent Tendencies." *British Journal of Sociology* 42:211–30.

Gordon, Linda. 1993. "Gender, State, and Society: A Debate with Theda Skocpol." *Contention* 2:139–56.

Gordon, Linda. 1994. *Pitied But Not Entitled*. New York: Free Press.

Graebner, William. 1980. *A History of Retirement*. New Haven, CT: Yale University Press.

Graebner, William. 1982. "From Pensions to Social Security: Social Insurance and the Rise of Dependency." In *The Quest for Security,* edited by John N. Schact. Iowa City: Center for the Study of the Recent History of the United States.

Green, Marguerite. 1956. *The National Civic Federation and the American Federation of Labor, 1900–1925.* Washington, DC: Catholic University of America Press.

Gross, Bertram. 1966. "Social Systems Account." In *Social Indicators,* edited by Raymond Bauer. Cambridge, MA: MIT Press.

Gross, James. 1974. *The Making of the National Labor Relations Board.* Albany: State University of New York Press.

Gross, James. 1981. *The Reshaping of the National Labor Relations Board.* Albany: State University of New York Press.

Gross, Neal. 1943. "A Post Mortem on County Planning." *Journal of Farm Ecoinonmics* 25:644–61.

Grubb, Donald. 1971. *Cry from the Cotton.* Chapel Hill: University of North Carolina Press.

Hall, Donald. 1969. *Cooperative Lobbying.* Tucson: University of Arizona Press.

Hamilton, David. 1991. *From New Day to New Deal.* Chapel Hill: University of North Carolina Press.

Hamilton, Richard. 1972. *Class and Politics in the United States.* New York: Wiley.

Hamilton, Richard. 1975. *Restraining Myths.* New York: Wiley.

Hamilton, Richard. 1991. *The Bourgeois Epoch.* Chapel Hill: University of North Carolina Press.

Hammond, Paul. 1961. *Organizing for Defense.* Princeton, NJ: Princeton University Press.

Hansen, Alvin, Merrill Murray, Russell Stevenson, and Bryce Stewart. 1934. *A Program for Unemployment Insurance and Relief in the United States.* Minneapolis: University of Minnesota Press.

Hardin, Charles. 1946. "The Bureau of Agricultural Economics under Fire." *Journal of Farm Economics* 28:635–68.

Harvey, Charles. 1982. "John D. Rockefeller, Jr., and the Social Sciences." *Journal of the History of Sociology* 4:1–31.

Hawley, Ellis. 1966. *The New Deal and the Problem of Monopoly.* Princeton, NJ: Princeton University Press.

Hayes, Erving. 1936. *Activities of the President's Emergency Committee for Employment.* Concord, NH: Rumford.

Heard, Alexander. 1962. *The Costs of Democracy.* New York: Doubleday.

Heclo, Hugh. 1978. "Issue Networks and the Executive Establishment." In *The New American Political System,* edited by Anthony King. Washington, DC: American Enterprise Institute.

Hicks, Clarence. 1930. Letter to John D. Rockefeller, Jr., October 2. Rockefeller Family Archives, Educational Interests, Box 80, Folder 573. Rockefeller Archive Center.

Hicks, Clarence. 1941. *My Life in Industrial Relations.* New York: Harper & Brothers.

Higley, John, and Gwen Moore. 1981. "Elite Integration in the U.S. and Australia." *American Political Science Review* 75:581–97.

Himmelberg, Robert. 1976. *The Origins of the National Recovery Administration*. New York: Fordham University Press.

Hoey, Jane. 1966. "Oral History." Columbia University Library, New York.

Hooks, Gregory. 1985. "The Battle of the Potomac: United States Economic Mobilization for World War II." Ph.D. dissertation, University of Wisconsin, Madison.

Hooks, Gregory. 1990. "From an Autonomous to a Captured State Agency: The Decline of the New Deal in Agriculture." *American Sociological Review* 55:29–43.

Hooks, Gregory. 1991. *Forging the Military-Industrial Complex: World War II's Battle of the Potomac*. Urbana: University of Illinois Press.

Hooks, Gregory. 1993. "The Weakness of Strong Theories; The U.S. State's Dominance of the World War II Investment Process." *American Sociological Review* 58:37–53.

Hunter, Floyd. 1953. *Community Power Structure*. Chapel Hill: University of North Carolina Press.

Hunter, Floyd. 1959. *Top Leadership, USA*. Chapel Hill: University of North Carolina Press.

Huntington, Samuel. 1961. *The Common Defense*. New York: Columbia University Press.

Huntington, Samuel. 1969. "The Defense Establishment: Vested Interests and the Public Interest." In *The Military-Industrial Complex and United States Foreign Policy*, edited by Omer Carey. Pullman: Washington State University Press.

Industrial Relations Counselors, Inc. 1936. Report on Finances. Rockefeller Family Archives, Record Group 2. Economic Reform Interests, Box 16, Folder 127. Rockefeller Archive Center.

Ingham, John. 1978. *The Iron Barons*. Westport, CT: Greenwood.

Irons, Peter. 1982. *The New Deal Lawyers*. Princeton, NJ: Princeton University Press.

Jacoby, Sanford. 1993. "Employers and the Welfare State: The Role of Marion B. Folsom." *The Journal of American History* 47:525–56.

Jamieson, Stuart M. 1945. *Labor Unionism in American Agriculture*. Washington, DC: U.S. Government Printing Office.

Janeway, Eliot. 1951. *The Struggle for Survival*. New Haven, CT: Yale University Press.

Janowitz, Morris. 1960. *The Professional Soldier*. New York: Free Press.

Jenkins, J. Craig, and Barbara Brents. 1989. "Social Protest, Hegemonic Competition, and Social Reform." *American Sociological Review* 54:891–909.

Jenkins, J. Craig, and Teri Shumate. 1985. "Cowboy Capitalists and the Rise of the 'New Right': An Analysis of Contributors to Conservative Policy Formation Organizations." *Social Problems* 33:130–45.

Jennings, M. Kent. 1964. *Community Influentials: The Elites of Atlanta*. New York: Free Press.

Jensen, Gordon. 1956. "The National Civic Federation: American Business in the Age of Social Change and Social Reform, 1900–1910." Ph.D. dissertation, Princeton University, Princeton, NJ.

Johnson, Stephen. 1976. "How the West Was Won: Last Shootout for the Yankee-Cowboy Theory." *Insurgent Sociologist* 6:61–93.

Kadushin, Charles. 1974. *The American Intellectual Elite*. Boston: Little, Brown.

Kahl, Joseph. 1959. *The American Class Structure*. New York: Rinehart.

Kaplan, A. D. H. 1944. *Liquidation of War Production*. New York: McGraw-Hill.

Karl, Barry. 1963. *Executive Reorganization and Reform in the New Deal*. Cambridge, MA: Harvard University Press.

Karl, Barry. 1974. *Charles E. Merriam and the Study of Politics*. Chicago: University of Chicago Press.

Katz, Irving. 1968. *August Belmont: A Political Biography*. New York: Columbia University Press.

Katz, Michael. 1993. "Roads Not Taken." *Contemporary Sociology* 22:775–77.

Kessler-Harris, Alice. 1982. *Out to Work*. New York: Oxford University Press.

Key, V. O., Jr. 1949. *Southern Politics in State and Nation*. New York: Knopf.

Keyssar, Alexander. 1993. "The Long and Winding Road." *Nation* 256:566–70.

Kirkendall, Richard. 1964. "Social Science in the Central Valley of California: An Episode." *California Historical Society Quarterly* 43:195–218.

Kirkendall, Richard. 1966. *Social Scientists and Farm Politics in the Age of Roosevelt*. Columbia: University of Missouri Press.

Kirkendall, Richard. 1990. "The Second Secretary Wallace." *Agricultural History* 64:199–206.

Klass, Bernard. 1969. "John D. Black, Farm Economist and Political Advisor, 1920–1942." Ph.D. dissertation, University of California, Los Angeles.

Klehr, Harvey. 1984. *The Heyday of American Communism*. New York: Basic Books.

Kofsky, Frank. 1993. *Harry S. Truman and The War Scare of 1948*. New York: St. Martin's.

Koistinen, Paul. 1973. "Mobilizing the World War II Economy: Labor and the Industrial-Military Alliance." *Pacific Historical Review* 42:443–78.

Kolko, Gabriel. 1963. *The Triumph of Conservatism*. New York: Free Press.

Korpi, Walter. 1993. "American Exceptionalism in Social Policy Development." *Contemporary Sociology* 22:779–81.

Krasner, Stephen. 1978. *Defending the National Interest*. Princeton, NJ: Princeton University Press.

Lampman, Robert. 1962. *The Share of Top Wealth-Holders in National Wealth*. Princeton, NJ: Princeton University Press.

Latham, Earl. 1959. *The Politics of Railroad Coordination, 1933–1936*. Cambridge, MA: Harvard University Press.

Latimer, Murray. 1933. Memorandum on Work for Federal Government. Rockefeller Foundation, Record Group 1.1, Series 200, Box 348, Folder 4143. Rockefeller Archive Center.

Latimer, Murray. 1934. Correspondence with Industrial Relations Counselors, Inc., on Salary and Taxes. Latimer Papers, Box 9, Folder 12. George Washington University Library, Washington, DC.

Latimer, Murray. 1935. Letter to Robert Gooch, March 20. Latimer Papers, Box 1, Folder 2, George Washington University Library, Washington, DC.

Latimer, Murray. 1936. Memorandum to Members of the Social Security Board

(March 23). Altmeyer Papers, Box 2, Folder on Clark Amendment. Wisconsin State Historical Archives, Madison.

Latimer, Murray, and S. Hawkins. 1938. "Railroad Retirement System in the United States." Unpublished manuscript. Special Collections Division, George Washington University Library, Washington, DC.

Laumann, Edward, and David Knoke. 1987. *The Organizational State*. Madison: University of Wisconsin Press.

Laumann, Edward, Tony Tam, John Heinz, Robert Nelson, and Robert Salisbury. 1992. "The Social Organization of the Washington Establishment during the First Reagan Administration." *Research in Politics and Society* 4:161–88.

Leffler, Melvyn. 1992. *A Preponderance of Power*. Stanford: Stanford University Press.

Leotta, Louis. 1975. "Abraham Epstein and the Movement for Old Age Security." *Labor History* 16:359–78.

Leuchtenburg, William. 1963. *Franklin D. Roosevelt and the New Deal*. New York: Harper & Row.

Levine, Edward. 1973. "Methodological Problems in Research on the Military-Industrial Complex." In *Testing the Theory of the Military-Industrial Complex*, edited by Steven Rosen. Lexington, MA: Lexington Books.

Lieberson, Stanley. 1971. "An Empirical Study of Military-Industrial Linkages." *American Journal of Sociology* 76:562–84.

Linn, James. 1935. *Jane Addams: A Biography*. New York: Appleton Century.

Lipset, Seymour. 1960. *Political Man*. New York: Doubleday.

Lipset, Seymour. 1982. "The Academic Mind at the Top." *Public Opinion Quarterly* 46:143–68.

Logan, John, and Harvey Molotch. 1987. *Urban Fortunes*. Berkeley: University of California Press.

Lorsch, Jay, and Elizabeth MacIver. 1989. *Pawns or Potentates?* Cambridge, MA: Harvard Business School.

Lubove, Roy C. 1968. *The Struggle for Social Security, 1900–1935*. Cambridge, MA: Harvard University Press.

Lundberg, F. 1937. *America's Sixty Families*. New York: Vanguard.

Lynch, David. 1946. *The Concentration of Economic Power*. New York: Columbia University Press.

Mace, Myles. 1971. *Directors: Myth and Reality*. Cambridge, MA: Harvard University Press.

Majka, Linda, and Theo Majka. 1982. *Farm Workers, Agribusiness and the State*. Philadelphia: Temple University Press.

Manley, John F. 1973. "The Conservative Coalition in Congress." *American Behavioral Scientist* 17:223–47.

Mann, Michael. 1986. *The Sources of Social Power*. Vol. 1. New York: Cambridge University Press.

Mann, Michael. 1993. *The Sources of Social Power*. Vol. 2. New York: Cambridge University Press.

Manza, Jeff. 1993. "The Elusive Polity." *Contention* 3:87–101.

Mariolis, Peter. 1975. "Interlocking Directorates and Control of Corporations." *Social Sciences Quarterly* 56:425–39.

Mastick, Seabury. 1929. Letter to Beardsley Ruml, Oct 5. Spelman Fund, Series 4, Box 18, Folder 358. Rockefeller Archive Center.

Matthews, Donald. 1954. *The Social Background of Political Decision-Makers*. New York: Doubleday.

May, Stacy. 1933. Interoffice Correspondence, Oct. 7. Rockefeller Foundation, Record Group 1.1, Series 200, Box 394, Folder 4666. Rockefeller Archive Center.

McCammon, Holly. 1995. "The Politics of Protection: State Minimum Wage and Maximum Hours Laws for Women in the United States, 1870–1930." *Sociological Quarterly* 36:217–49.

McConnell, Grant. 1953. *The Decline of Agrarian Democracy*. Berkeley: University of California Press.

McConnell, Grant. 1966. *Private Power and American Democracy*. New York: Knopf.

McCune, Wesley. 1943. *The Farm Bloc*. New York: Doubleday, Doran.

McCune, Wesley. 1956. *Who's Behind Our Farm Policy?* New York: Praeger.

McLeod, M. 1988. "Quiet Power: Women Volunteer Leaders." Ph.D. dissertation, Yale University, New Haven, CT.

McQuaid, Kim. 1979. "The Frustration of Corporate Revival in the Early New Deal." *Historian* 41:682–704.

McQuaid, Kim. 1982. *Big Business and Presidential Power from FDR to Reagan*. New York: Morrow.

McWilliams, Carey. 1939. *Factories in The Field*. Boston: Little, Brown.

McWilliams, Carey. 1942. *Ill Fares the Land*. Boston: Little Brown.

Melone, Albert. 1977. *Lawyers, Public Policy and Interest Group Politics*. Washington, DC: University Press of America.

Mertz, Paul. 1978. *New Deal Policy and Southern Rural Poverty*. Baton Rouge: Louisiana State University Press.

Millett, John. 1954. *Army Service Forces: The Organization and Role of the Army Service Forces*. Washington, DC: Department of the Army.

Mills, C. Wright. 1956. *The Power Elite*. New York: Oxford University Press.

Mingos, Howard. 1930. "Birth of An Industry." Reprinted in *The History of the American Aircraft Industry*, edited by G. R. Simonson. Cambridge, MA: MIT Press, 1968.

Mink, Gwendolyn. 1986. *Old Labor and New Immigrants in American Political Development, 1870–1925*. Ithaca, NY: Cornell University Press.

Mink, Gwendolyn. 1993. "Welfare Mothers." *Women's Review of Books* (Jan. 10):16–17.

Mink, Gwendolyn. 1995. *The Wages of Motherhood*. Ithaca, NY: Cornell University Press.

Mintz, Beth. 1975. "The President's Cabinet, 1897–1972." *Insurgent Sociologist* 5:131–48.

Mintz, Beth, and Michael Schwartz. 1983. "Financial Interest Groups and Interlocking Directorates." *Social Science History* 7:183–204.

Mintz, Beth, and Michael Schwartz. 1985. *The Power Structure of American Business*. Chicago: University of Chicago Press.

Mizruchi, Mark. 1982. *The Structure of the American Corporate Network, 1904–1974*. Beverly Hills, CA: Sage.

Mizruchi, Mark. 1983. "Relations among Large American Corporations, 1904–1974." *Social Science History* 7:165–82.

Moffett, Guy. 1933. Memorandum of Interview with Arthur Young and Bryce Stewart. Spelman Fund, Series 5, Box 5, Folder 276. Rockefeller Archive Center.

Molotch, Harvey. 1976. "The City as a Growth Machine." *American Journal of Sociology* 82:309–30.

Molotch, Harvey. 1979. "Capital and Neighborhood in the United States." *Urban Affairs Quarterly* 14:289–312.

Moore, Gwen. 1979. "The Structure of a National Elite Network." *American Sociological Review* 44:673–92.

Moskos, Charles. 1974. "The Concept of the Military-Industrial Complex: Radical Critique or Liberal Bogey?" *Social Problems* 21:498–512.

Mulherin, James P. 1979. "The Sociology of Work and Organizations: Historical Context and Pattern of Development." Ph.D. Dissertation, University of California, Berkeley.

Murphy, Bruce. 1982. *The Brandeis/Frankfurter Connection*. New York: Oxford University Press.

Myers, Gustavus. 1917. *The History of Tammany Hall*. New York: Boni and Liveright.

Nathanson, Charles. 1969. "The Militarization of the American Economy." In *Corporations and the Cold War*, edited by David Horowitz. New York: Monthly Review.

Nelson, Daniel. 1969. *Unemployment Insurance: The American Experience, 1915–1935*. Madison: University of Wisconsin Press.

Neustadtl, Alan, and Dan Clawson. 1988. "Corporate Political Groupings: Does Ideology Unify Business Political Behavior?" *American Sociological Review* 53:172–90.

Neustadtl, Alan, Denise Scott, and Dan Clawson. 1991. "Class Struggle in Campaign Finance? Political Action Committee Contributions in the 1984 Elections." *Sociological Forum* 6:219–38.

*New York Times*. 1935a. "Business Advisers Uphold President," May 3.

*New York Times*. 1935b. "Council to Issue Reports," May 9.

*New York Times*. 1935c. "Urges Two Changes in Work Insurance," May 17.

*New York Times*. 1935d. "W. Aldrich Quits Business Council," August 8.

Nossiter, Bernard. 1990. *Fat Years and Lean*. New York: Harper and Row.

O'Connell, Charles. 1989. "Social Structure and Science: Soviet Studies at Harvard." Ph.D. dissertation, University of California, Los Angeles.

Odendahl, Theresa. 1990. *Charity Begins at Home*. New York: Basic Books.

Ohl, John. 1985. *Hugh S. Johnson and the New Deal*. DeKalb: Northern Illinois University Press.

Ohl, John. 1994. *Supplying the Troops: General Somervell and American Logistics in World War II*. DeKalb: Northern Illinois University Press.

Orloff, Ann. 1993. *The Politics of Pensions*. Madison: University of Wisconsin Press.

Orloff, Ann, and Eric Parker. 1990. "Business and Social Policy in Canada and the United States, 1920-1940." *Comparative Social Research* 12:295-339.

Orloff, Ann, and Theda Skocpol. 1984. "Why Not Equal Protection? Explaining the Politics of Public Social Spending in Britain, 1900-1911, and the United States, 1880-1920." *American Sociological Review* 49:726-50.

Ostrander, Susan. 1984. *Women of the Upper Class*. Philadelphia: Temple University Press.

Ostrander, Susan. 1987. "Elite Domination in Private Social Agencies: How It Happens and How It Is Challenged." Pp. 85–102 in *Power Elites and Organizations*, edited by G. W. Domhoff and T. Dye. Beverly Hills, CA: Sage.

Overacker, Louise. 1932. *Money in Elections*. New York: Macmillan.

Overacker, Louise. 1933. "Campaign Funds in a Depression Year." *American Political Science Review* 27:769–83.

Overacker, Louise. 1937. "Campaign Funds in the Presidential Election of 1936." *American Political Science Review* 31:473–98.

Overacker, Louise. 1941. "Campaign Finance in the Presidential Election of 1940." *American Political Science Review* 35:701–27.

Overacker, Louise. 1945. "Presidential Campaign Funds, 1944." *American Political Science Review* 39:899–925.

*P.S.* 1993. "Awards Page" *P.S.* 26:91.

Paletz, David, and Robert Entman. 1981. *Media Power Politics*. New York: Free Press.

Parrish, Michael. 1970. *Securities Regulation and the New Deal*. New Haven, CT: Yale University Press.

Patterson, James T. 1967. *Congressional Conservatism and the New Deal*. Lexington: University of Kentucky Press.

Payne, Elizabeth. 1988. *Reform, Labor, and Feminism*. Urbana: University of Illinois Press.

Peltason, Jack. 1952. "The Reconversion Controversy." In *Public Administration and Policy Development, edited by Harold Stein*. New York: Harcourt Brace.

Perkins, Frances. 1930. Letter to Beardsley Ruml, Nov 5. Spelman Fund, Series 4, Box 9, Folder 275. Rockefeller Archive Center.

Perkins, Frances. 1946. *The Roosevelt I Knew*. New York: Harper & Row.

Perkins, Van. 1969. *Crisis in Agriculture: The Agricultural Adjustment Act and the New Deal, 1933*. Berkeley: University of California Press.

Peschek, Joseph. 1987. *Policy-Planning Organizations*. Philadelphia: Temple University Press.

Pichardo, Nelson. 1990. "The Case for Elite Social Movement Organizations: The Associated Farmers of California, Inc." Paper presented to the 85th Annual Meeting of the American Sociological Association, August 11–15, Washington, D.C.

Pilisuk, Marc, and Thomas Hayden. 1965. "Is There a Military-Industrial Complex Which Prevents Peace?" *Journal of Social Issues* 21:67–117.

Piven, Frances. 1993. "Book Review." *American Political Science Review* 87:790–91.

Piven, Frances, and Richard Cloward. 1971. *Regulating the Poor*. New York: Pantheon.

Piven, Frances, and Richard Cloward. 1977. *Poor People's Movements*. New York: Random House.

Piven, Frances, and Richard Cloward. 1982/1985. *The New Class War.* New York: Random House.

Platt, Anthony. 1969. *The Child Savers.* Chicago: University of Chicago Press.

Polenberg, Richard. 1972. *War and Society: The United States, 1941–1945.* Philadelphia: Lippincott.

Polsby, Nelson. 1963 [1980]. *Community Power and Political Theory.* New Haven, CT: Yale University Press.

Potter, David. 1972. *The South and the Concurrent Majority.* Baton Rouge: Louisiana State University Press.

Powell, Thomas. 1934. Letters to Barbara Armstrong and Thomas Eliot. Latimer Papers, Box 19, Folder 4. George Washington University Library, Washington, DC.

Powell, Thomas. 1969. *Race, Religion, and the Promotion of the American Executive.* Columbus: Ohio State University.

Quadagno, Jill S. 1988. *The Transformation of Old Age Security.* Chicago: University of Chicago Press.

Rae, John. 1968. *Climb to Greatness.* Cambridge, MA: MIT Press.

Reagan, Patrick. 1982. "The Architects of Modern National Planning." Ph.D. dissertation, Ohio State University, Columbus.

Reich, Michael. 1973. "Military Spending and the U.S. Economy." In *Testing the Theory of the Military-Industrial Complex,* edited by Steven Rosen. Lexington: Lexington Books.

Reisler, Mark. 1976. *By the Sweat of Their Brow: Mexican Immigrant Labor in the United States, 1900–1940.* Westport, CT: Greenwood.

Robbins, Rainard. 1936. "Status of Industrial Pension Plans As Affected by Old Age Benefits Section of the Social Security Act." New York: Social Science Research Council.

Robertson, David. 1994. *Sly and Able.* New York: Norton.

Rochester, Anna. 1936. *Rulers of America.* New York: International Publishers.

Rockefeller, John 3d. 1930. Letter to Father, March 14. Rockefeller Family Archives, Educational Interests, Box 80, Folder 573. Rockefeller Archive Center.

Roos, Charles. 1937. *NRA Economic Planning.* Bloomington, IN: Principia.

Roose, Diana. 1975. "Top Dogs and Top Brass." *Insurgent Sociologist* 5:53-63.

Rose, Nancy. 1994. *Put to Work: Relief Programs in the Great Depression.* New York: Monthly Review.

Rosen, Elliott. 1977. *Hoover, Roosevelt and the Brain Trust.* New York: Columbia University Press.

Rosenberg, Rosalind. 1993. "How the Safety Net Got Torn." *New York Times Book Review* (January 31):16.

Ross, Robert L. 1967. "Dimensions and Patterns of Relating among Interest Groups at the Congressional Level of Government." Ph.D. dissertation, Michigan State University, East Lansing.

Rowley, William. 1970. *M. L. Wilson and the Campaign for the Domestic Allotment.* Lincoln: University of Nebraska Press.

Roy, William. 1983. "Interlocking Directorates and the Corporate Revolution." *Social Science History* 7:143-64.

Ruml, Beardsley. 1928. Memo to Arthur Woods, November 30. Laura Spelman

Rockefeller Memorial Collection, Box 48, Folder 495 ("Agricultural Survey—Black 1928–30"). Rockefeller Archive Center.

Ruml, Beardsley. 1929. Letter to John Black, March 6. Black Papers, Chronological Correspondence File. Wisconsin State Historical Society Archives.

Russell, Bertrand. 1938. *Power: A New Social Analysis.* London: Allen and Unwin.

Salmond, John. 1990. *The Conscience of a Lawyer.* Tuscaloosa: University of Alabama Press.

Saloutos, Theodore. 1960. *Farmer Movements in the South.* Berkeley: University of California Press.

Saloutos, Theodore. 1982. *The American Farmer and the New Deal.* Ames: Iowa State University Press.

Salzman, Harold, and G. William Domhoff. 1980. "The Corporate Community and Government: Do They Interlock?" In *Power Structure Research*, edited by G. William Domhhoff. Beverly Hills: Sage.

Salzman, Harold, and G. William Domhoff. 1983. "Nonprofit Organizations and the Corporate Community." *Social Science History* 7:205–16.

Samuelson, Franz. 1985. "Organizing for the Kingdom of Behavior." *Journal of the History of the Behavioral Sciences* 21:33–47.

Saunders, Charles. 1966. *The Brookings Institution: A Fifty-Year History.* Washington: Brookings Institution.

Schlabach, Theron. 1969. *Edwin E. Witte: Cautious Reformer.* Madison: State Historical Society of Wisconsin.

Schlesinger, Arthur. 1957. *The Decline of the Old Order.* Boston: Houghton Mifflin.

Schlesinger, Arthur. 1959. *The Coming of the New Deal.* Boston: Houghton Mifflin.

Schlesinger, Arthur. 1960. *The Politics of Upheaval.* Boston: Houghton Mifflin.

Schneiderman, Howard. 1992. "Out of the Golden Ghetto." *Society* 29:78–83.

Schriftgiesser, Karl. 1960. *Business Comes of Age.* New York: Harper and Row.

Schriftgiesser, Karl. 1967. *Business and Public Policy.* Englewood Cliffs, NJ: Prentice-Hall.

Schuby, T. D. 1975. "Class Power, Kinship and Social Cohesion: A Case Study of a Local Elite." *Sociological Focus* 8:243–55.

Schulman, Bruce. 1991. *From Cotton Belt to Sunbelt.* New York: Oxford University Press.

Schwartz, Charles, and G. William Domhoff. 1974. "Probing the Rockefeller Fortune." Nomination of Nelson A. Rockefeller to Be Vice-President of the United States. Committee on the Judiciary, 93d Congress. Washington, DC: U. S. Government Printing Office.

Schwartz, Michael. 1976. *Radical Protest and Social Structure.* New York: Academic Press.

Schwarz, Jordan. 1981. *The Speculator: Bernard M. Baruch in Washington, 1917–1965.* Chapel Hill: University of North Carolina Press.

Scott, Ann. 1993. "Discovering Women." *Contemporary Sociology* 22:777–79.

Seider, Maynard. 1977. "Corporate Ownership, Control, and Ideology: Support for Behavioral Similarity." *Sociology and Social Research* 62:113–28.

Selznick, Philip. 1947. *TVA and the Grass Roots.* Berkeley: University of California Press.

Shelley, Mack C., II. 1983. *The Permanent Majority.* Tuscaloosa: University of Alabama Press.

Shoup, Laurence, and William Minter. 1977. *Imperial Brain Trust.* New York: Monthly Review.

Sinclair, Barbara. 1982. *Congressional Realignment, 1925–1978.* Austin: University of Texas Press.

Sinclair, Barbara. 1985. "Agenda, Policy, and Alignment Change from Coolidge to Reagan." In *Congress Reconsidered,* edited by Lawrence Dodd and Bruce Oppenheimer. Washington, DC: Congressional Quarterly.

Sitterson, J. Carlyle. 1946. *Development of the Reconversion Policies of the War Production Board, April 1943 to January 1945.* Special Study No. 15. Washington: U. S. Civilian Production Administration.

Sklar, Holly, and Robert Lawrence. 1981. *Who's Who in the Reagan Administration.* Boston: South End.

Skocpol, Theda. 1979. *States and Social Revolution.* New York: Cambridge University Press.

Skocpol, Theda. 1980. "Political Response to Capitalist Crisis: Neo-Marxist Theories of the State and the Case of the New Deal." *Politics and Society* 10:155–202.

Skocpol, Theda. 1984. "Emerging Agendas and Recurrent Strategies in Historical Sociology." In *Vision and Method in Historical Sociology,* edited by Theda Skocpol. New York: Cambridge University Press.

Skocpol, Theda. 1986/1987. "A Brief Reply." *Politics and Society* 3:331–32.

Skocpol, Theda. 1988. "The Limits of the New Deal System and the Roots of Contemporary Welfare Dilemmas." In *The Politics of Social Security in the United States,* edited by Margaret Weir, Ann Orloff, and Theda Skocpol. Princeton, NJ: Princeton University Press.

Skocpol, Theda. 1988/1989. "An 'Uppity Generation' and the Revitalization of Macroscopic Sociology: Reflections at Mid-Career by a Woman from the Sixties." *Theory and Society* 17:627–43.

Skocpol, Theda. 1992. *Protecting Soldiers and Mothers.* Cambridge, MA: Harvard University Press.

Skocpol, Theda. 1993. "Gendered Identities in Early U.S. Social Policy." *Contention* 2:157–82.

Skocpol, Theda, and Edwin Amenta. 1985. "Did the Capitalists Shape Social Security?" *American Sociological Review* 50:572–75.

Skocpol, Theda, and Kenneth Finegold. 1982. "State Capacity and Economic Intervention in the Early New Deal." *Political Science Quarterly* 97:255–78.

Skocpol, Theda, and John Ikenberry. 1982. "The Political Formation of the American Welfare State in Historical and Comparative Perspective." Paper presented at the meeting of the American Sociological Association, San Francisco.

Skocpol, Theda, and John Ikenberry. 1983. "The Political Formation of the American Welfare State in Historical and Comparative Perspective." In *Comparative Social Research,* edited by Richard F. Tomasson. Greenwich, CT: JAI.

Skowronek, Stephen. 1982. *Building a New American State.* Cambridge: Cambridge University Press.

Slater, Jerome, and Terry Nardin. 1973. "The Concept of a Military-Industrial Complex." In *Testing the Theory of the Military-Industrial Complex,* edited by Steven Rosen. Lexington, MA: Lexington Books.

Smith, James, and Stephen Franklin. 1974. "The Concentration of Personal Wealth, 1922–1969." *American Economic Review, Papers and Proceedings* 64:162–67.

Smith, Jean. 1990. *Lucius D. Clay.* New York: Henry Holt.

Smith, R. Elbertson. 1959. *The Army and Economic Mobilization.* Washington: Department of the Army.

Social Science Research Council. 1934. *Decennial Report 1923–1933.* New York: Author.

Social Science Research Council. 1937. *Annual Report 1936–1937.* New York: Author.

Somers, Herman Miles. 1950. *Presidential Agency: The Office of the War Mobilization and Reconversion.* Cambridge, MA: Harvard University Press.

Sonquist, John, and Thomas Koenig. 1975. "Interlocking Directorates in the Top U.S. Corporations." *Insurgent Sociologist* 5:196–229.

Soref, Michael. 1980. "The Finance Capitalists." In Maurice Zeitlin, ed., *Class, Conflict, and the State.* Cambridge: Winthrop.

Stepan-Norris, Judith, and Maurice Zeitlin. 1989. " 'Who Gets the Bird?' or, How the Communists Won Power and Trust in America's Unions: The Relative Autonomy of Intraclass Struggles." *American Sociological Review* 54:503-524.

Stepan-Norris, Judith, and Maurice Zeitlin. 1991. " 'Red Unions' and 'Bourgeois' Contracts?" *American Journal of Sociology* 96:1151-1200.

Stewart, Bryce. 1930. *Unemployment Benefits in the United States.* New York: Industrial Relations Counselors, Inc.

Stewart, Bryce. 1933. "Memorandum: Government Work of Bryce M. Stewart." Rockefeller Foundation, Record Group 1.1, Series 200S, Folder 4143, Rockefeller Archive Center.

Stewart, Bryce, and Meredith Givens. 1934. "Planned Protection Against Unemployment and Dependency: Report on a Tentative Plan for a Proposed Investigation." Prepared for SSRC. Rockefeller Foundation, Record Group 1.1, Series 200, Box 398, Folder 4723, Rockefeller Archive Center.

Stone, Clarence. 1989. *Regime Politics.* Lawrence: University of Kansas Press.

Stone, I. F. 1942. *Business As Usual.* New York: Modern Age Books.

Su, Tie-Ting, Alan Neustadtl, and Dan Clawson. 1992. "The Coalescence of Corporate Conservation, 1976 to 1980: The Roots of the Reagan Revolution." *Research in Politics and Society* 4:135–60.

Sutton, Francis, Seymour Harris, Carl Kaysen, and James Tobin. 1956. *The American Business Creed.* Cambridge, MA: Harvard University Press.

Sweezy, Paul. 1953. "The American Ruling Class." In Paul Sweezy, ed., *The Present As History.* New York: Monthly Review Press.

Swope, Gerard. 1934. Letter to Daniel Roper, January 9. General Correspondence, Department of Commerce. RG 40, Box 784. National Archives II, College Park, MD.

Taylor, Paul. 1983. *On the Ground in the Thirties*. Salt Lake City: Peregrine Smith Books.

Thometz, Carol. 1963. *The Decision Makers: The Power Structure of Dallas*. Dallas: Southern Methodist University Press.

Tolchin, Martin, and Susan Tolchin. 1971. *To the Victor . . . Political Patronage from the Clubhouse to the White House*. New York: Random House.

Tugwell, Rexford. 1933. *The Industrial Discipline and the Governmental Arts*. New York: Columbia University Press.

Turner, Jonathan, and Charles Starnes. 1976. *Inequality: Privilege and Poverty in America*. Los Angeles: Goodyear Publishing.

U.S. Bureau of the Budget. 1946. *The United States at War*. Washington: USBOB.

U.S. Civilian Production Administration. 1947. *Industrial Mobilization for War: History of the War Production Board and Predecessor Agencies, 1940–1945*. Washington: USCPA.

U.S. Government. 1938. *The Budget of the United States Government for the Fiscal Year Ending June 30, 1939*. Washington: United States Government Printing Office.

U.S. Senate, 76th Congress. 1939. *Violations of Free Speech and Rights of Labor, Part 45, The Special Conference Committee*. Washington, DC:USGPO.

Useem, Michael. 1978. "The Inner Group of the American Capitalist Class." *Social Problems* 25:225–40.

Useem, Michael. 1979. "The Social Organization of the American Business Elite and the Participation of Corporate Directors in the Governance of American Institutions." *American Sociological Review* 44:553–71.

Useem, Michael. 1980. "Which Business Leaders Help Govern?" In *Power Structure Research*, edited by G. William Domhoff. Beverly Hills: Sage.

Useem, Michael. 1982. "Class in the Rationality in the Politics of Managers and Directors of Large Corporations in the United States and Great Britain." *Administrative Science Quarterly* 27:199–226.

Useem, Michael. 1984. *The Inner Circle*. New York: Oxford University Press.

Valdes, Dennis. 1991. *Al Norte: Agricultural Workers in the Great Lakes Region, 1917–1970*. Austin: University of Texas Press.

Van den Berg, Axel. 1988. *The Immanent Utopia*. Princeton, NJ: Princeton University Press.

Vittoz, Stanley. 1987. *New Deal Labor Policy and the American Industrial Economy*. Chapel Hill: University of North Carolina Press.

Voss, Kim. 1993. *The Making of American Exceptionalism*. Ithaca, NY: Cornell University Press.

Wala, Michael. 1994. *The Council on Foreign Relations and American Foreign Policy in the Early Cold War*. Providence, RI: Berghahn.

Wall, Bennett, and George Gibb. 1974, *Teagle of Jersey Standard*. New Orleans: Tulane University Press.

Webber, Michael. 1990. "The Material Bases of the Democratic Party: Class and Campaign Finance in the 1930s." Ph.D. dissertation, University of California, Santa Cruz.

Webber, Michael. 1991a. "Business, the Democratic Party, and the New Deal." *Sociological Perspectives* 34:473–92.

Webber, Michael. 1991b. "Campaign Finance and the New Deal." *Journal of Political and Military Sociology* 19:253–70.

Webber, Michael, and G. William Domhoff. 1996. "Myth and Reality in Business Support for Democrats and Republicans in the 1936 Presidential Election." Unpublished paper, Department of Sociology, University of San Francisco.

Weiner, Merle. 1978. "Cheap Labor and the Repression of Farm Workers." *Insurgent Sociologist* 8:181–90.

Weinstein, James. 1968. *The Corporate Ideal in the Liberal State*. Boston: Beacon.

Weinstein, James. 1975. *Ambiguous Legacy: The Left in American Politics*. New York: Franklin Watts.

Whatley, Warren. 1983. "Labor for the Picking: The New Deal in the South." *Journal of Economic History* 43:905–29.

White, Gerald. 1980. *Billions for Defense*. University: University of Alabama Press.

White, Shelby. 1978. "Cradle to Grave: Family Offices Manage Money for the Very Rich." *Barron's* (March 20):9–11.

White, William. 1905. "Folk, The Story of a Little Leaven in a Great Commonwealth." *McClure's Magazine* (December):118–20.

Wiebe, Robert. 1962. *Businessmen and Reform*. Cambridge, MA: Harvard University Press.

Williams, Beryl. 1948. *Lillian Wald*. New York: Julian Mennen.

Witte, Edwin E. 1963. *The Development of the Social Security Act*. Madison: University of Wisconsin Press.

Wittman, Donald. 1973. "Parties as Utility Maximizers." *American Political Science Review* 67:490–498.

Wolf, Charles. 1972. "Military-Industrial Simplicities, Complexities, and Realities." In *The Military-Industrial Complex*, edited by Sam Sakesian. Beverly Hills: Sage.

Wolfe, Alan. 1993. "The Mothers of Invention." *New Republic* 208(Jan. 4/11):28–35.

Wolff, Edward. 1995. *Top Heavy: A Study of the Increasing Inequality of Wealth in America*. New York: Twentieth Century Fund.

Wolfinger, Raymond. 1960. "Reputation and Reality in the Study of Community Power." *American Sociological Review* 25:636–44.

Wright, Gavin. 1986. *Old South, New South*. New York: Basic Books.

Wrong, Dennis. 1979. *Power: Its Forms, Bases and Uses*. New York: Harper and Row.

Young, Arthur. 1933. "Grant from Rockefeller Foundation to Cover Expense of Cooperation with Government Agencies." Rockefeller Foundation Collection, Record Group 1.1, Series 2005, Box 348, Folder 4143. Rockefeller Archive Center.

Zeitlin, Maurice. 1974. "Corporate Ownership and Control: The Large Corporations and the Capitalist Class." *American Journal of Sociology* 79:1071–1119.

Zeitlin, Maurice, Lynda Ewen, and Richard Ratcliff. 1974. "New Princes for Old? The Large Corporation and the Capitalist Class in Chile." *American Journal of Sociology* 80:87–123.

Zink, Harold. 1930. *City Bosses in the United States*. Durham: Duke University Press.

Zweigenhaft, Richard. 1975. "Who Represents America?" *Insurgent Sociologist* 5:119–30.

Zweigenhaft, Richard, and G. William Domhoff. 1982. *Jews in the Protestant Establishment*. New York: Praeger.

Zweigenhaft, Richard, and G. William Domhoff. 1991. *Blacks in the White Establishment? A Study of Race and Class in America*. New Haven, CT: Yale University Press.

# Index

# SOCIAL INSTITUTIONS AND SOCIAL CHANGE

*An Aldine de Gruyter Series of Texts and Monographs*

EDITED BY

## James D. Wright